GW00362567

Introduction

Ask a young couple what kind of garden they would most like to own and the chances are you will get an answer such as, 'Oh, something pretty . . . with a nice patio . . . and a lawn . . . a rockery, perhaps . . . and, oh yes, somewhere to grow our own vegetables.' Invite them to put their requirements in the form of a plan and the result is likely to be a muddle bordering on chaos.

But show the same couple a selection of plans or sketches incorporating the desired features and they'll quickly pick one out and say, 'That's it! That's just what we want.'

There you have the idea behind this book: not to try to inform you *how* to design your garden (this, after all, requires a mixture of artistry, skill and knowledge which takes a landscape architect years to acquire) but to offer a choice of garden plans professionally designed to meet the needs of a wide spectrum of home owners.

It's almost too much to expect your particular site to match exactly one of the shapes and sizes shown, or your own list of needs and preferences, but you will find that most of the plans can be adapted to your individual requirements without difficulty. And providing your plot is not *smaller* than the minimum size given, the plan can be usually suited to it.

OUR GARDEN DESIGNS

We have chosen the 20 sets of circumstances most likely to include your own, and there is a design for each. Four of them relate to ASPECT, for this has a telling effect on perhaps the most used feature of the small garden — the patio or sitting-out place. If the aspect at the back of the house is southerly, the patio can then obviously be sited in the best place — as an extension of the home. If the aspect is northerly, there will be no sun unless the leisure area is removed from the immediate vicinity of the house — and the warmth of sunshine is highly desirable, at least in temperate zones like the British Isles. Easterly and westerly aspects need skilful treatment if the most is to be made of them, not only in relation to the sitting-out place, but to the siting of the main planting areas. Designs 1 to 4 deal with this.

A site with a pronounced SLOPE presents problems not easily solved by the amateur. The difficulty is most acute when the incline is directly downwards or directly upwards from the back of the house. Designs 5 and 6 offer attractive solutions.

Few plots can be accepted as ideal. But some have the fortune to overlook a pleasant VIEW — a bonus which, properly harnessed, will enhance the potential of the garden. Clearly it must be preserved in the best possible way, so that garden and prospect become a single enchanting picture. The other side of the coin is an unsightly or unwanted view — an ugly building, a row of chimney pots and TV aerials, an electricity pylon — which it is desirable to conceal or at least camouflage. Designs 7 and 8 show ways in which the professional's skill can make the best of either circumstance — the good view and the bad.

Another difficulty that often presents itself is the plot of awkward SHAPE — not necessarily erratically so, but one too narrow, too square, too wedge-shaped to make an agreeable garden simple to design. But it can be done, even to the extent of turning the irregular shape to advantage (see Designs 9 to 13).

The latter part of the 20 plans is devoted to the special needs of the individual family. The young couple with a NEW HOUSE are faced with the task of making a garden out of the rough, bare, or weed-ridden plot surrounding it — often, these days, a plot that is rather small. This couple, above all, need help, for they can hardly be expected to have any experience of design, gardening or growing plants. Design 14 should help to set them on their way.

But when a FAMILY arrives, the couple's needs are altered. Space must be found for play — a climbing frame, a swing or see-saw and, of course, room for ball games on however small a scale. And that favourite of all toddlers, a sand pit (preferably within sight of Mother in the kitchen) which can be converted later, when it is safe to do so, into an ornamental pool. Planting may be affected, too, with the accent being put on shrubs and grass rather than vulnerable border and bedding plants. Design 15 shows how to overcome the problems while preserving an attractive garden.

The business couple with no children who will have little time for gardening outside week-ends (when other leisure pursuits may often take preference) need a garden without frills that makes limited demands. For them we have designed a FORMAL GARDEN, Design 16).

By contrast, the RETIRED COUPLE have a lot more time but, perhaps, less energy. Such couples need a garden in which they can enjoy their leisure, entertain their friends, and also work happily without becoming overtired (Design 17).

Inevitably, there are people who delight in the beauty and tranquillity of a garden but look upon its maintenance as a necessary chore rather than a pleasure. For them — but also for those who would like to spend more time gardening but don't have it to spare — the LOW MAINTENANCE garden, Design 18, is included.

WATER has enormous fascination in a garden. At rest, it reflects light and mirrors both surrounding planting and the ever changing sky while providing unending interest with the fish, wildlife, and plants that inhabit or frequent it. In motion, it offers sparkle and music — the perfect accompaniment to the peace of a garden. In more practical terms, water is a real labour-saver — a feature which, once established, needs little or no maintenance. Design 19 shows how a delightful garden can be based on the intelligent use of water.

Lastly — even though you may not yet have a SWIMMING POOL — Design 20 suggests how a pool can be accommodated without dominating the appearance of the modestly-sized garden to an undesirable degree.

Planning a Garden

If you, or your needs, are not directly accommodated by one of the designs in this book, it is likely that sections or features of one or more will attract you, and you may well be able to compose a design to your liking using them as component parts.

But there will always be some people, with strong creative instincts, who will wish — whether guided or not by our designs — to plan their own garden. And why not? As the work of construction develops and, later, the planting begins to mature, the amateur designer can gain tremendous pleasure — if the plan turns out to be a success. On the other hand, he or she may have to confess to disappointment, if not to complete failure. That's a risk the amateur has to take. For 15 years the Daily Express (of which co-author Donald Farthing has been gardening editor since 1950) ran an annual garden design competition for its readers, excluding professional landscape architects. But the winning design that looked good on paper did not always come up to expectations when laid out as a garden at the Chelsea Show. In that time only a single gold medal was won. When, however, the planning of the Daily Express Chelsea garden was put into the hands of a professional (co-author Guy Farthing) he achieved eight gold medals in ten years, with next-to-top awards in the other two.

Whether you feel capable of designing your own garden or are content to copy or adapt a professional plan, it's still worth learning the basic principles of garden design — if only to give you a better understanding of the thinking behind the various plans in this book.

WHAT KIND OF GARDEN?

Just as an architect needs a brief from the client who wants a house built, so the landscape architect or garden designer should begin by knowing what kind of garden is required, including a list of choices and preferences. If you are planning your own garden, you must still have these important facts clear in your mind. What these might be are largely covered by the designs in this book — the needs of newly-weds, business folk, the elderly or those who wish for an easily-run garden; the desire to solve the problem of a difficult shape or aspect.

STUDY THE PLOT

The next step is to study the plot — not just for a few minutes, but carefully over a few days. Decide what is worth preserving — a beautiful tree, a stone outcrop, a natural bank, a pleasing view — and what should go. Desirable as most trees are, one must be practical, If a tree is darkening living rooms or depriving an important part of the plot of light, there's no room for sentiment: have it felled. If you have a conscience — and indeed we all should — plant a replacement in a more suitable position: a place where it can be seen and admired at a little distance, or provide shade on a hot summer's day.

Privacy must always be a major consideration. But before you decide to spend a great deal of money on fencing or hedging plants to enclose the whole plot, ask yourself, 'Is it all really necessary?' Do you, for instance, need privacy in the front garden? Would it not be better (not to mention cheaper) to leave the garden open for passers-by to enjoy, to offer a welcome to the approaching visitor?

And is there any real need to fence or hedge in that part of the garden not close to the house? Any sort of screen inevitably causes shade and loss of light to some plants. More than that, it denies the opportunity of vistas or glimpses of the neighbours' gardens, having the effect of extending the boundaries of your own garden. An effective compromise is to plant groups of shrubs, perhaps with an ornamental tree or two, along the boundaries in place of the traditional fence or hedge. A much more natural look is achieved, and the rigid outlines of the plot are no longer obvious. (An example of 'twinned' gardens will be found in Design 10.)

If the need to exclude animals — or, in some cases, roving children — makes a screen desirable, it's worth remembering that a living one (a hedge) is cheaper than timber, brick or concrete, and more attractive. Suitable subjects include beech, hornbeam, quickthorn or holly. Many conifers, especially *Cupressocyparis Leylandii*, make a splendid, fast-growing screen, but do not always deter animals.

LIST THE FEATURES

The next step is to make a list of the features you wish your garden to embrace, heading it with the essential ones. It's a mistake to try to include too many; it is far better to start with a simple canvas and leave the more intricate embroidery till later. Most gardens are designed round a lawn — and this is not surprising, for nothing sets off plants and flowers better, or is more soothing; no surface is more pleasant to sit or lie on. But, in the smallest gardens, a lawn can be difficult to maintain in good condition, and paving stones, gravel, or stone chippings may be a better choice.

Before deciding where to site the patio and the main planting areas, including the vegetables, take into account aspect — the position of the sun at various times of the day. (Designs 1 to 4 demonstrate the importance of aspect, and offer ways to make the best use of it.)

A garden is only as good as its soil, and the garden planner should be guided by its type. Clay retains moisture — sometimes to the extent of making drainage necessary. Chalk and sand drain rapidly, and dry out quickly. The best soil a gardener can wish for is a deep, easily worked loam. But if he is not blessed with it, he need not despair: with the right treatment — the addition of bulky organic matter in quantity — even the poorest soil can be made fertile and the heaviest soil lightened.

Another key consideration is the degree of alkalinity or acidity of the soil, measured by the pH factor. A figure of seven is referred to as neutral — anything below is acid, anything above, alkaline, which means the soil contains lime. Most soils range between pH5 and 8, and you can easily make a check with an inexpensive soil testing outfit (take samples from various parts of the plot). Some plants have strong objections to lime, which locks up the iron they need: in this bracket are rhododendrons, azaleas, camellias, and summer-flowering heathers, plus a range of other attractive shrubs. Clematises, the carnation family, the brassicas (cabbages, sprouts, etc.), peas and beans flourish best in limey soil.

Acid soils can be brought nearer neutrality by the addition of lime or ground chalk: limey alkaline ones less with the frequent use of sulphate of ammonia and sulphate of iron. But, on the whole, it will be found better to accept the natural character of the soil and plant accordingly. Be guided by what grows well in the district, both in the wild and in neighbouring gardens.

PLANNING YOUR GARDEN

But before anything can be planted, the garden must be planned — without hurry and with care, for it's going to be there a long time. Alterations can be both difficult and costly.

First list the features you have decided upon — patio, lawn, paths, trees, shrubs, flower borders or beds, vegetable plot, play areas and so on. Next take some sheets of plain paper and make some trial sketches — simply plotting in the desired features as blocks or shapes, without any detail. When you achieve an arrangement that appeals to you — keeping in mind the governing factors of size, aspect, surroundings, and existing features — try to give it the professional touch. There are tricks which can make an otherwise ordinary, dull garden both attractive and intriguing. It should, for example, have an axis governing the placement of the component areas of the garden.

If, as is more often the case than not, the plot is rectangular, it is an advantage to angle the axis, and so negate the rigid shape. Ideally, there should be a focal point — which may well locate itself naturally at the far end of the axis — towards which the eye is led.

Unless a formal garden is planned, in which straight lines and geometrical shapes are acceptable and even desirable, the amateur will usually do best with curves — not fussy ones, but long, flowing, gentle curves.

The setting-out plans show the radial points where pegs should be sited to describe arcs for the curves.

If the plot is flat, don't accept the fact. Introduce one or more changes of level and you at once achieve an interest and charm that would otherwise be lacking. This need not involve any great amount of earth moving: one has only to remove 22 cm (9 in.) of soil from one area, and mound it in another, to create a 44–cm (18–in.) change of level. Often — as when linking two lawns — 15 cm (6 in.) is enough to bring about the desired effect. The excavation of a pool provides ample soil to create a sizeable rock garden, with interesting slopes, or a bank at the far end of the garden — a feature which, if there is open ground beyond, can create the illusion that the garden has no intervening boundary.

Paths, especially in the small garden, can occupy a significant proportion of the available space — space that could otherwise be usefully employed. So keep them to a minimum, and keep them functional. A path designed purely for access should be as direct as possible; no-one wants a corkscrew route from gate to front door, or a winding one from house to garden shed. But where the path is planned simply for pleasure — as when flanking a flower border, or passing through an area of shrubs — gentle curves are perfectly acceptable. Grass paths, if wide enough, are always attractive. But avoid the common practice of making a stepping stone path across grass. Although you can set the stones low enough to permit the mower to pass over them, the edges call for frequent trimming — a lengthy and tedious job.

THE FINAL PLAN

Once you have all the details as well as the main points settled you can produce your final plan. Use a sheet of squared graph paper and decide on the appropriate scale. Draw in the boundaries, then the major features — including existing ones, such as trees — and finally the minor features and details.

MARKING OUT THE GARDEN

Then take your plan on to the plot and mark in the key points with pegs, and outline the lawn, beds and borders with strong twine and pegs. A length of garden hose is useful in delineating curves. Now check the proportions and balance of your plan from a good vantage point — an upstairs window is recommended. And finally, check the positioning of trees, paths and structures (such as greenhouse, screens or pergola) from both living room windows and patio — the places from which the garden will be most often viewed. When — and only when — you are completely satisfied that nothing can be improved, you can set about building your garden.

HOW TALL DOES YOUR GARDEN GROW?

In each garden you will see a key to the type of plants distributed in the garden plan. Three main groups apply; shrubs over 1.8 m (6 ft), shrubs 1–2 m (3–6 ft) and ground cover. Here are the key symbols which have been used throughout and an illustration of their height in relation to a 1.8 m (6 ft) man.

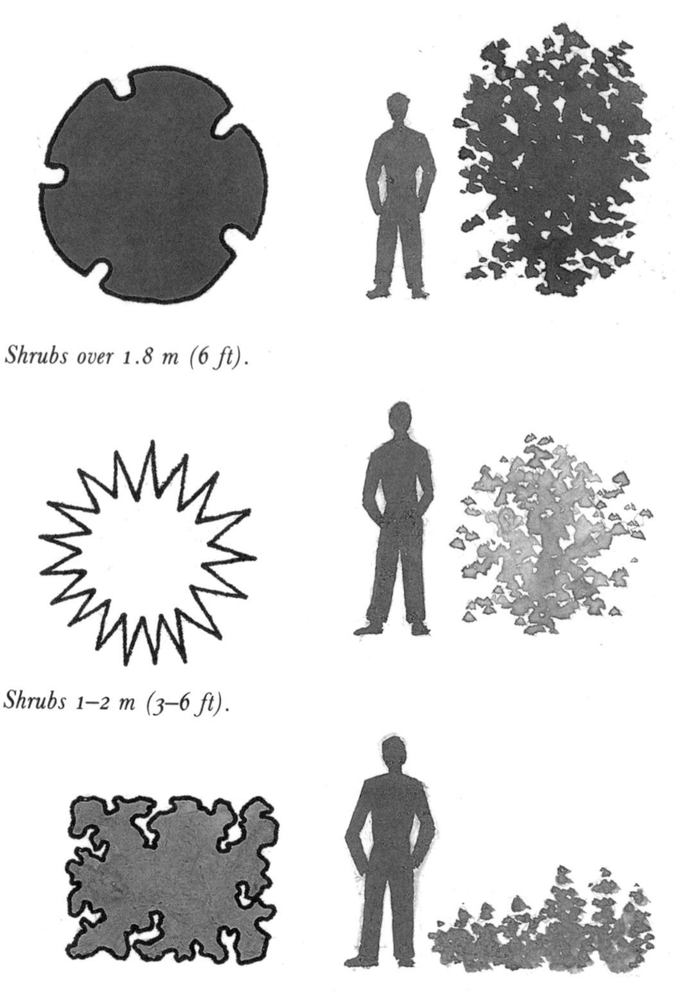

Shrubs over 1.8 m (6 ft).

Shrubs 1–2 m (3–6 ft).

Ground cover or herbaceous plants.

1 Garden Facing South

A south-facing plot is, of course, the sunniest of all, and the owner should make the most of his good fortune. A successful example (shown here) is a Daily Express garden which won a gold medal at Chelsea. The design makes fullest use of the southerly aspect, while the skilful use of curves and subtle changes of level produce a result that is restful yet stimulating.

The generous patio — an extension of the domestic living space — looks out over a large pool (so cooling on a hot day) to a lawn which sweeps up the garden to an arresting feature, a timber arbour shaded by climbing plants. This is one of three places from which the garden can be viewed and enjoyed in comfort, the others being the patio with its attendant roses and flower-filled urns, and the wooden bench opposite the pool. This is sheltered by ornamental trees and shrubs which have another important function — to conceal the greenhouse and the kitchen garden, an easily accessible, slightly raised, plot which lends itself to intensive cultivation.

We mentioned changes of level . . . the lawn is slightly dished along the greater length of its spine, and falls away into the longer grass bordering the pool. The path leading to the greenhouse area rises up shallow steps, causing the island shrub bed to incline upwards to the general slightly elevated level of the rear of the garden.

This design shares its sunny warmth with a cool sophistication that meets the needs of the house owner with a modern outlook.

This garden is a clear example of the way in which the severe lines of the average suburban garden can be effectively disguised — a skill which, as can be proved all too often, is lacking in almost every garden laid out by its owner.

The perspective view illustrated overleaf — seen as if from a window of the house — reveals the graceful, curving lines of this sun-filled garden. Yet there is coolness, too — provided by the water of the pool, reflecting the planting beyond and the passing clouds, and by the background trees, giving shade for the summerhouse.

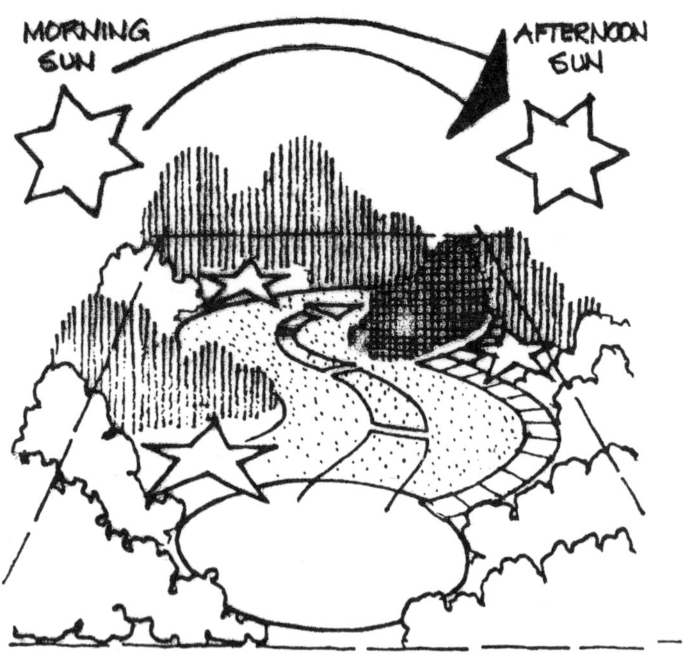

How the sun moves across the garden, always favouring the house and patio. Stars show the balanced focal points whilst the undulating arrow shows the main path of vision.

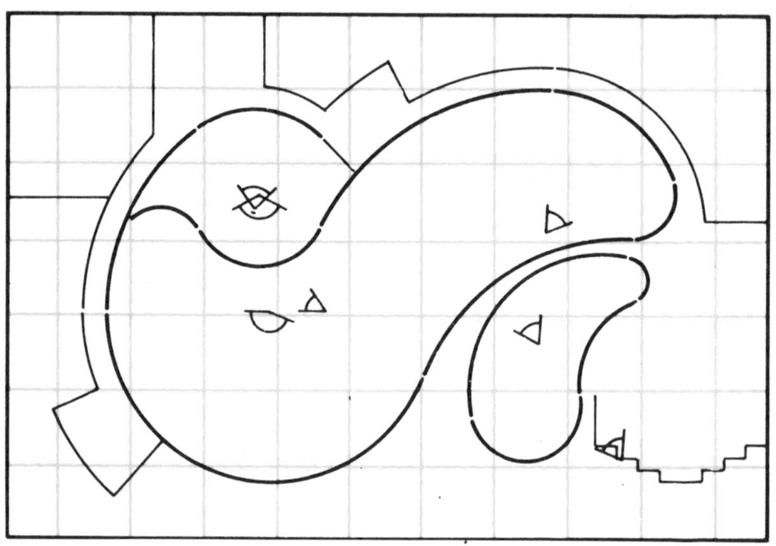

Setting out plan showing radial points. Each square represents 2 × 2 m.

POOL EDGE

Where a soft edge between water and lawn is required.

Excavate the pool area to a depth of 45–60 cm (18–24 in.) Lay a butyl liner on 25–50 mm (1–2 in.) of sand, tucking the edges over as shown in the sketch.

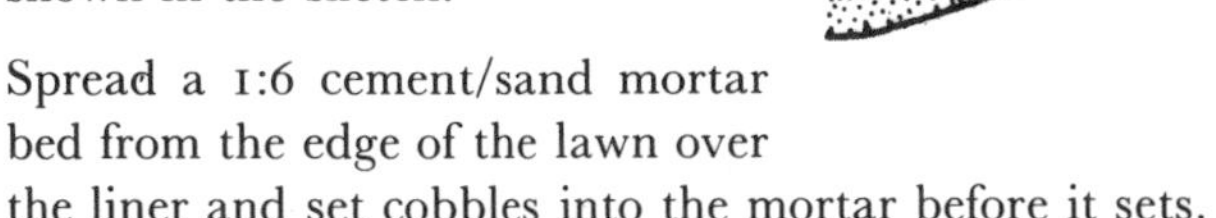

Spread a 1:6 cement/sand mortar bed from the edge of the lawn over the liner and set cobbles into the mortar before it sets.

Use Silglaze to neutralise any lime and to bring out the colour of the cobbles.

Size of liner required, regardless of the shape or depth of the pool, is worked out like this:

Length of liner — Overall length of the pool plus twice the maximum depth, plus 20.5 cm (8 in.) for overlap.

Width of liner — Overall width of the pool plus twice the maximum depth, plus 20.5 cm (8 in.) for overlap.

For pool edge against paving see page 21.

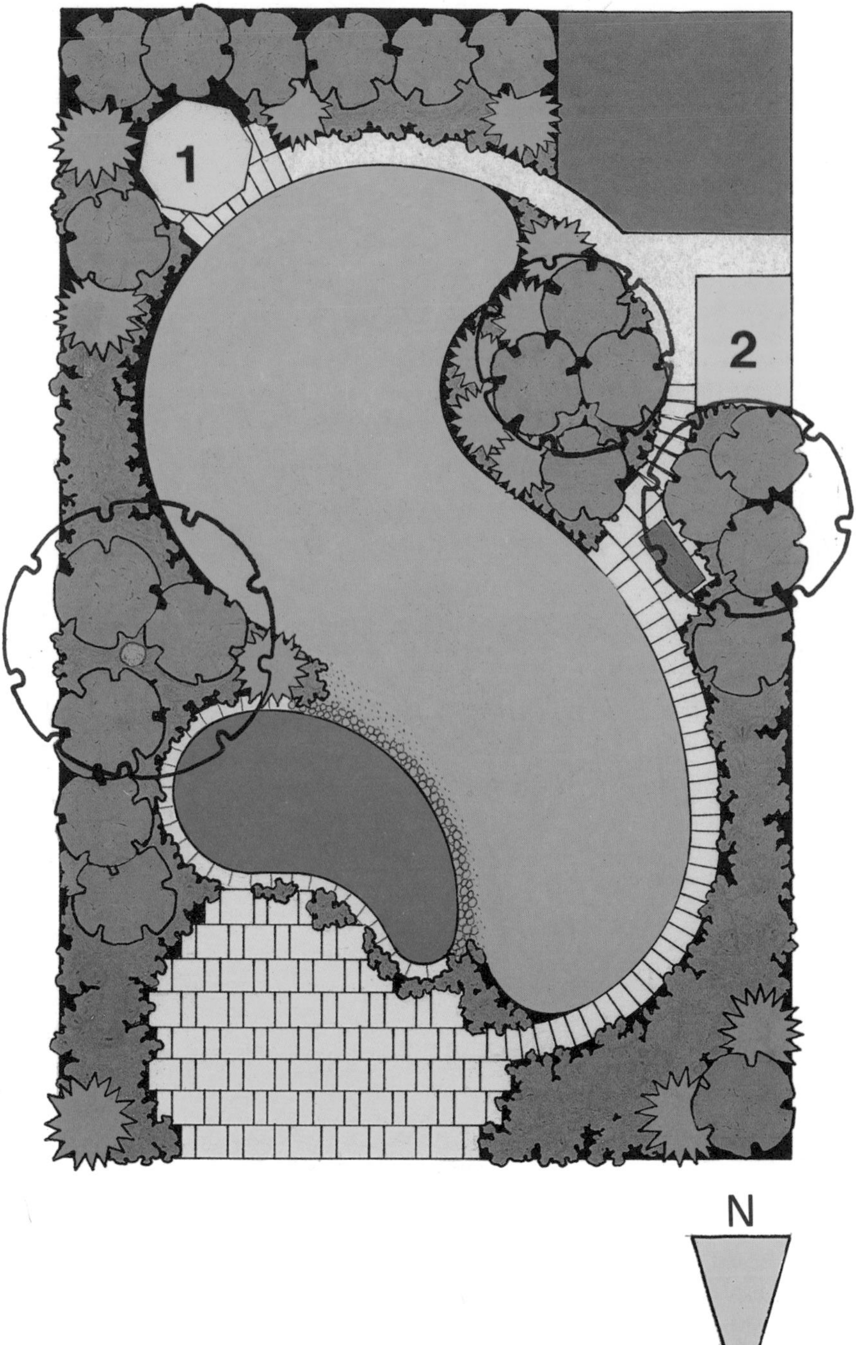

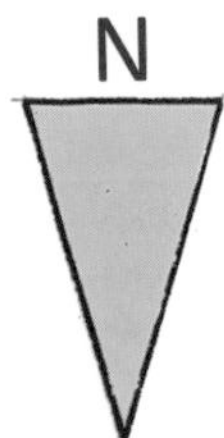
N

The plan shows how the chosen features have been carefully balanced around the S-shaped lawn, and how the regular lines of the plot have been concealed.

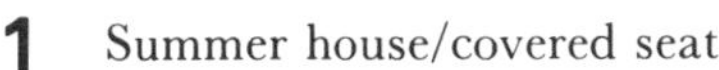

1 Summer house/covered seat

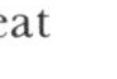

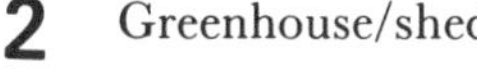

2 Greenhouse/shed

3 Seat

Lawn

Pool

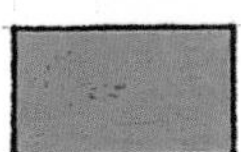

Vegetables

Gravel

Shrubs over 1.8 m (6 ft)

Shrubs 1–2 m (3–6 ft)

Ground cover or
Herbaceous plants

2 Garden Facing West

If a southerly aspect is the most desirable for a garden, with maximum sunshine benefiting both house occupants and plants, a westerly one has much in its favour. The heat of the noonday sun does not fall directly on the house, yet plenty is available at that part of the day — afternoon and evening —when leisure hours are most usually available.

The patio sited in the right-hand corner of our west-facing garden in fact receives sun from mid-day, or even earlier, till sunset or close to it — and at any time of the year. A pool overlooked by a small tree at the far end lends coolness to this sun-trap.

A feature of the garden is that all is not unfolded at a glance. Sit on the patio and the curving path draws the eye through some solid shrub planting . . . hiding what? (It happens to be the greenhouse and vegetable areas.) Let the gaze wander further up the garden and it is interrupted by the shrubs forming the backcloth to the pool. A walk up the path reveals the upper lawn and its surrounding planting — the top half of the figure eight which forms the basis of the design. In the far corner is another ornamental tree — the focal point terminating the line of vision from the kitchen (from which, as the housewife well knows, the garden is most frequently seen by her). Curves soften the rectangular outlines of the plot, and the best visual use is made of its length by siting the vegetable plot to the side, rather than at the end of the garden. To give additional interest, the far lawn could be elevated by 15 cm (6 in.), in which case the path should be gradually raised to this level as it approaches the junction of the two lawns.

The vista from the house windows at once poses the question: 'Just how big is this garden — where does it end?' The illusion of infinite depth is fostered by the introduction of a second lawn, form-

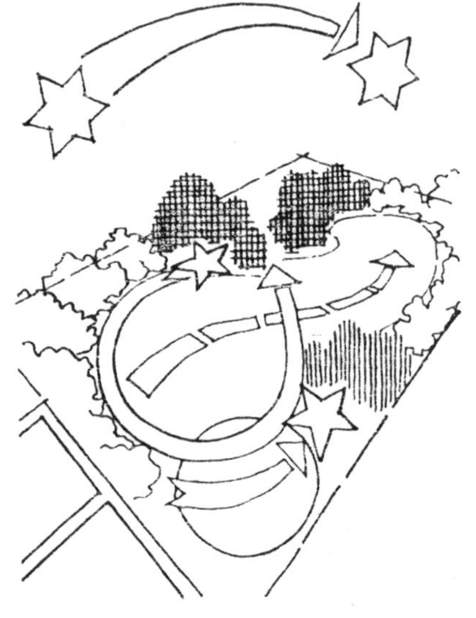

How the sun moves, always favouring the patio. Stars show the opposing focal points; arrows show the main paths of vision.

ing a narrow waistline, cinched in by tall, dense planting. The ornamental tree and shrubs on the right are mirrored by the small pool, while those on the left embrace the statue or bird bath as a focal point.

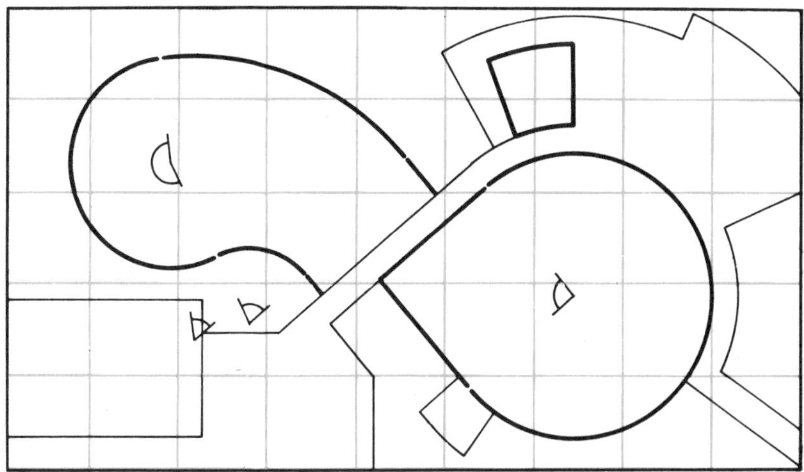

Setting-out plan showing radial points. Each square represents 2 × 2 m.

POOL EDGE

Where pool borders path or patio.

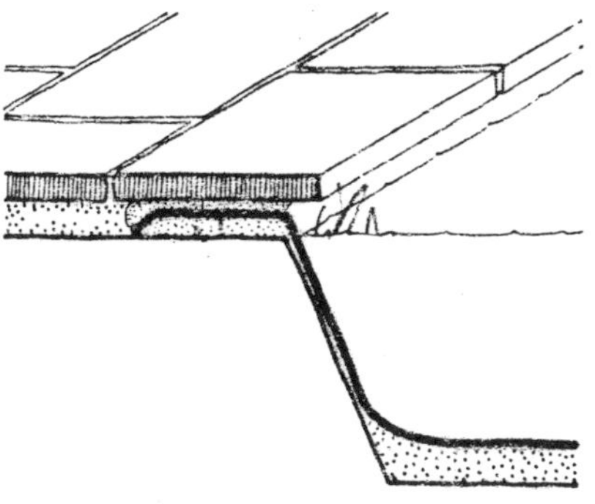

Excavate the pool area, lay a butyl liner on sand, and bed the overlap in a 1:6 cement/sand mortar mix.

Bed the paving slabs immediately surrounding the pool on 1:8 cement/sand mortar, allowing an overhang of approximately 5 cm (2 in.). Ensure that the whole of the edging is level, using a spirit level on a length of straight board.

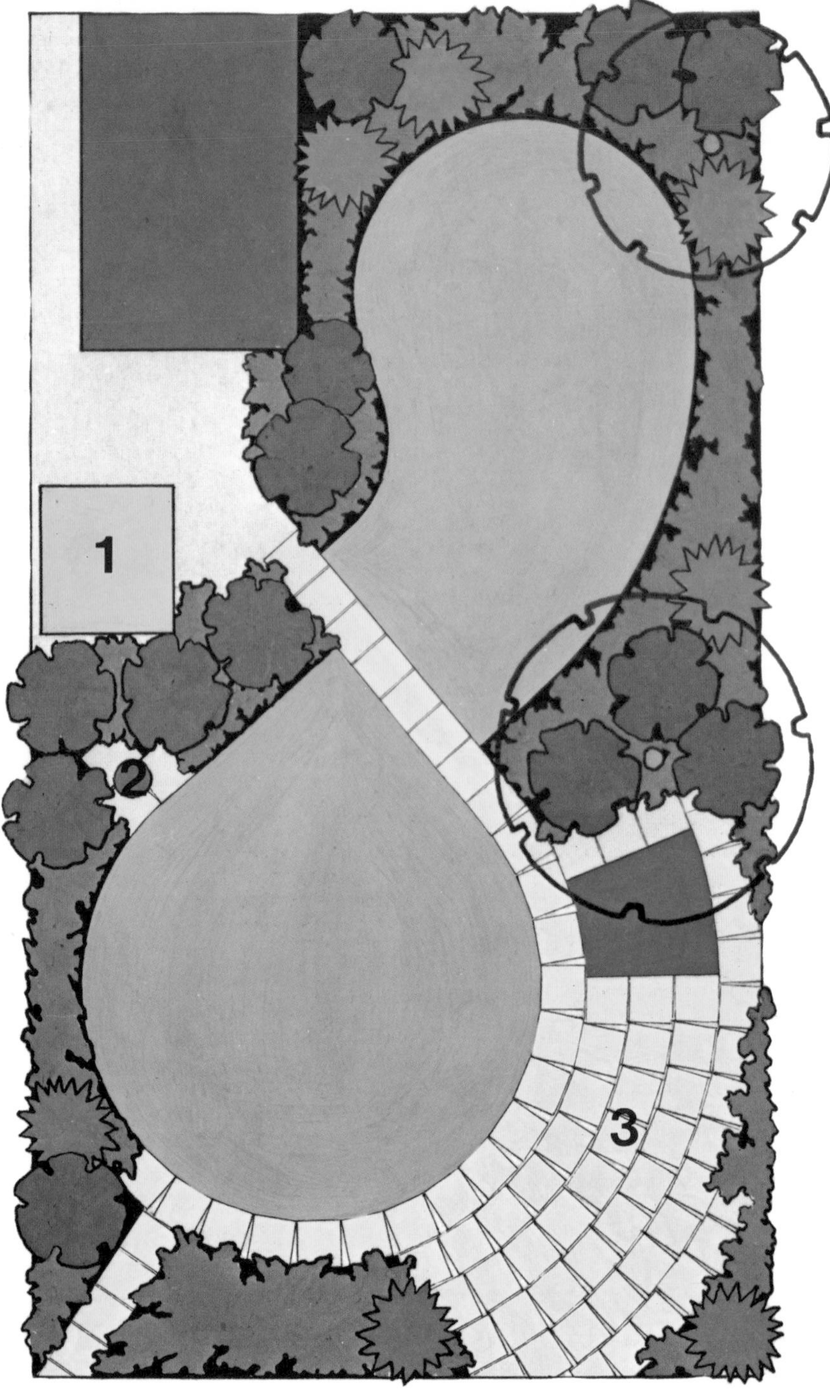
1
2
3

The plan shows the twin axes — the first, from the supposed kitchen window (bottom left), takes the eye the length of the garden; the second, originating from the patio outside the lounge (bottom right) where most sun can be enjoyed, gives a view across the lawn to a stone ornament.

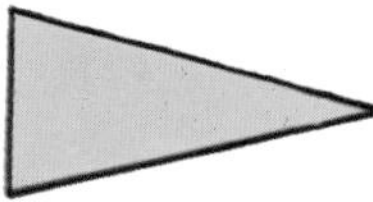

1 Greenhouse

2 Statue/ birdbath

3 Patio

 Lawn

 Vegetables

 Pool

 Gravel

 Shrubs over 1.8 m (6 ft)

 Shrubs 1–2 m (3–6 ft)

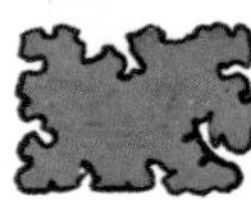 Ground cover or Herbaceous plants

3 Garden Facing East

It may be pleasant to walk out on to a patio bathed in morning sunshine, but few of us have time to spend on leisure at the beginning of the day. What we need is a sitting-out place favoured with sun from, say, noon till evening. And, in the east-facing garden, that means siting the patio on the north (south-facing) side so that it collects maximum sun. In our design, this is reached either from the living room (on right) or kitchen (on left). A small ornamental tree on the far side of the patio gives shade in the summer months at the hottest time of the day, while attendant low-growing shrubs or flower-filled tubs are sufficient to break the prevailing south-west wind. This sitting-out place is far enough away from the house to catch the evening sun.

The basis of the design is a simple, kidney-shaped lawn giving both space and interest. It is partly encircled by a path of square paving stones that 'grows' out of the patio and finally arrives at the focal point — a statue or a stone seat.

The utility area is at the rear of the garden, well concealed by a screen of shrubs. Those on the north side, plus the tree, hide the shed. The greenhouse is optional; the owner may prefer to devote the space to extra vegetables or soft fruit.

The planting relies mainly on well-chosen shrubs, with colourful herbaceous subjects in the middle of the garden, directly facing the patio. It is important to include a substantial number of evergreens, not only for winter interest but for their foliage. Climbers — roses, clematises, or a wisteria — should back the patio. The small planting area beneath the kitchen windows could be filled with roses or scented herbs.

The garden is ideally suited to a medium sized plot of about 18 metres by 11 metres (60 by 35 feet).

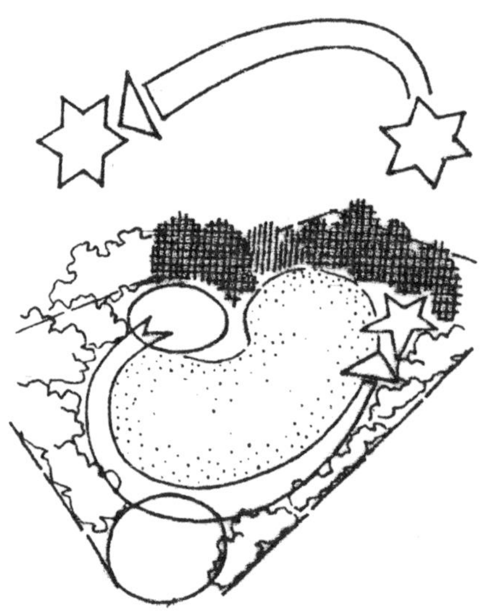

The patio is sited to gather the sun in the latter part of the day. From here the path sweeps round to a focal point.

Any extra length can be utilised for vegetables or even a small orchard.

The patio has the advantage of not only receiving the afternoon and evening sun, but of giving shelter from cold east or north winds. The significance of the small statue as a focal point (when viewed from the house) is clearly seen. And yet again, the curving lawn, disappearing round a mid-distance prominence, leaves the visitor intrigued by what — and how much — lies beyond.

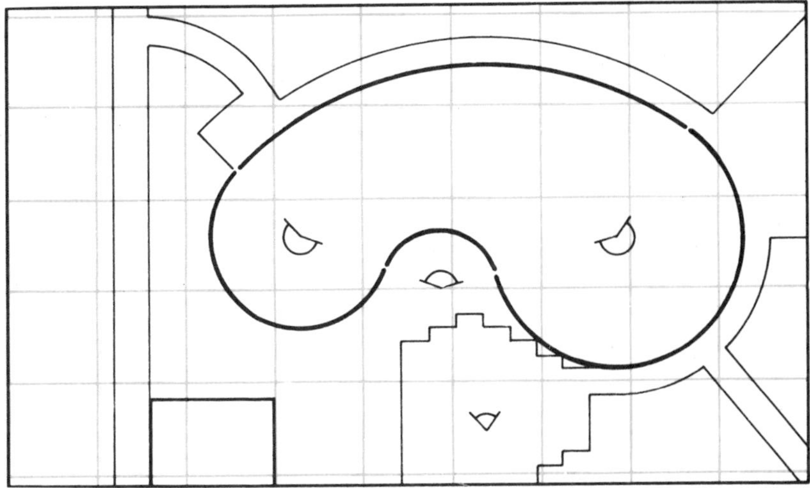

Setting out plan showing radial points. Each square represents 2 × 2 in.

PAVING

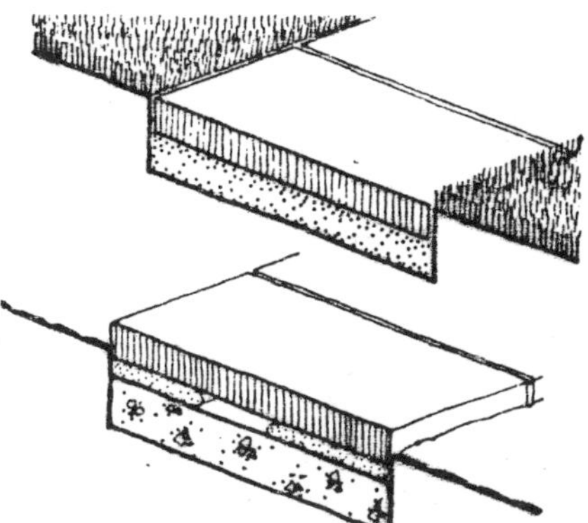

Where a path has turf on both sides.

Lay the paving slabs on a 5 cm (2 in.) bed of sand with four dabs of mortar. Using a spirit level, tap level with a wooden mallet. The joints should be mortared in to ensure that the sand bed is protected. The surface of the slabs should be below the level of the turf to facilitate mowing.

Where a path has a bed or border on one or both sides, or where the ground has been built up or is unstable.

Lay a bed of 7.5–10 cm (3–4 in.) of concrete (1 part cement, 2 parts sand, 4 parts aggregate). Bed the paving slabs on 1:6 mortar. The joints need not be mortared.

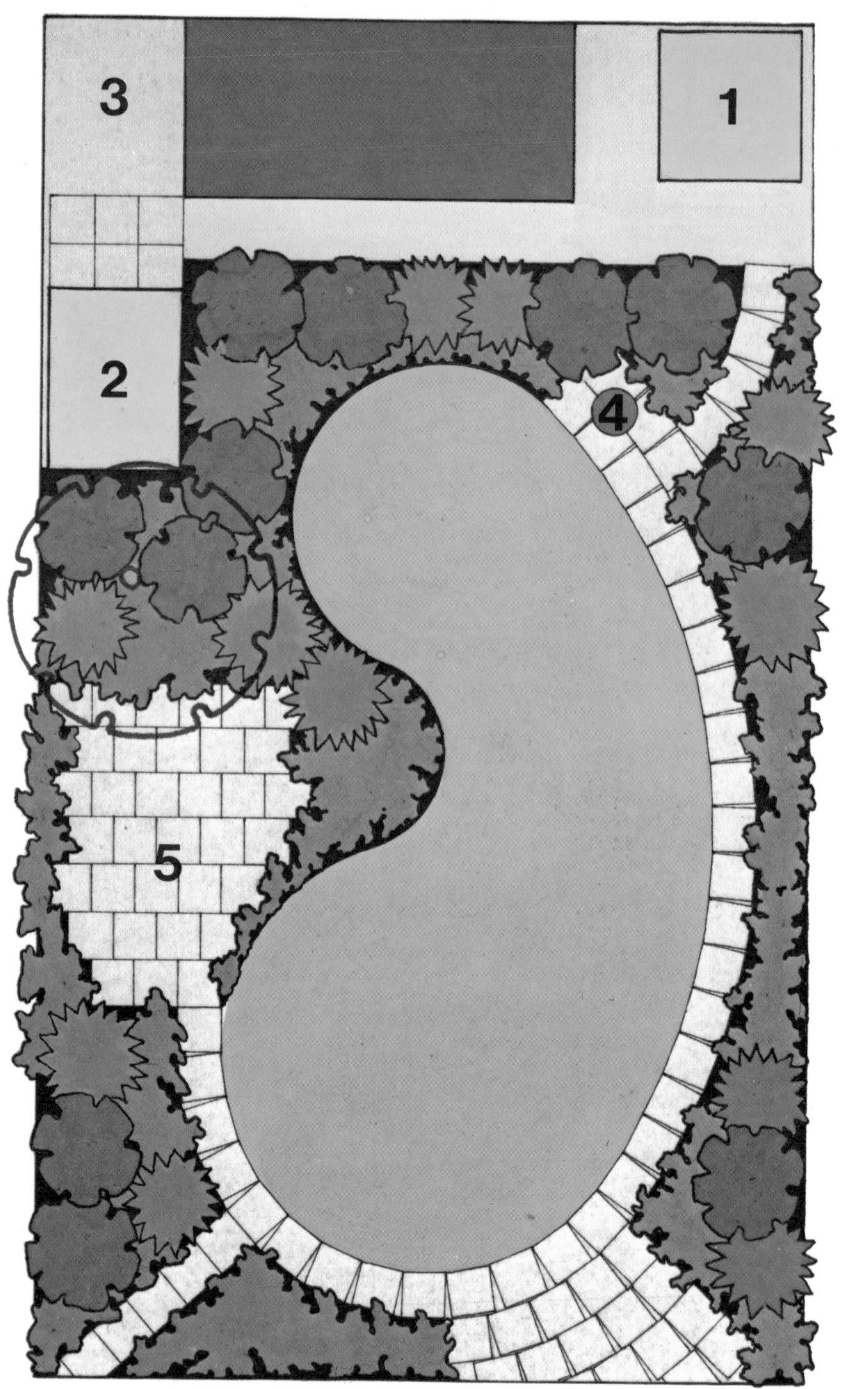

3
1
2
4
5

This is a simple garden to lay out. Fix the outline of the lawn and the rest — path, paved areas, shrub and herbaceous borders — falls into place. The well-screened rear (productive) area can be organised as desired.

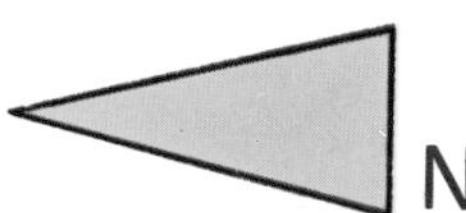

1 Shed

2 Greenhouse

3 Compost/refuse

4 Statue

5 Patio

Lawn

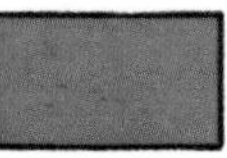
Vegetables

Gravel

Shrubs over 1.8 m (6 ft)

Shrubs 1–2 m (3–6 ft)

Ground cover or Herbaceous plants

4 Garden Facing North

For every house that happily faces south at the back, there's one that faces north. But that need cause the owner no heartache. It simply means that the leisure area is moved out into the sun. In our suggested design, it is sited to the right, so that one can bask in the sunshine (when available!) all day long and receive the last lingering rays when the sun sinks, in the west.

This garden shows that straight lines and rectangular shapes are no hindrance to a pleasing design if carefully used. The paving (all square slabs, easily laid) is nicely balanced by the two L-shaped lawns and their attendant borders of shrubs, roses, herbaceous plants and — if you wish — bedding plants or annuals. The first lawn spreads itself like a carpet before the living room and, with its shade and nearby pool, provides a cool place to enjoy in the warmest days of summer.

A pair of offset plant barriers — for that is what they are — conceal enough of the upper part of the garden to make it interesting (note the steps up from the patio — creating a slight, but important, change of level). Room has been found for a built-in barbecue — almost an essential piece of outdoor-living equipment these days.

Hidden from both the patio and lower lawn is an area that can be used as the owner wishes — for vegetables, for fruit (the shape is convenient for a netted cage) or, if there are children, for play equipment.

The elevation demonstrates the rewarding effects of a simple change of level. The raised upper lawn, approached by two steps, automatically 'dishes' the lower one and creates slightly banked flower borders.

Although perhaps too formal for a rural setting, this simple design is ideally suited to the small suburban or town site.

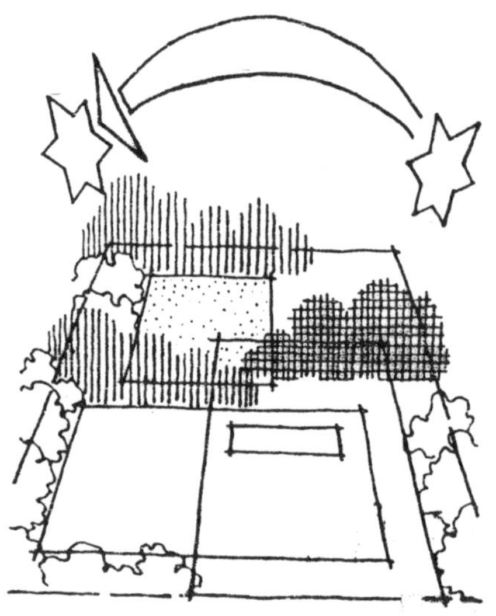

No sun reaches the back of the house, so the leisure area is moved out, but is still easily accessible.

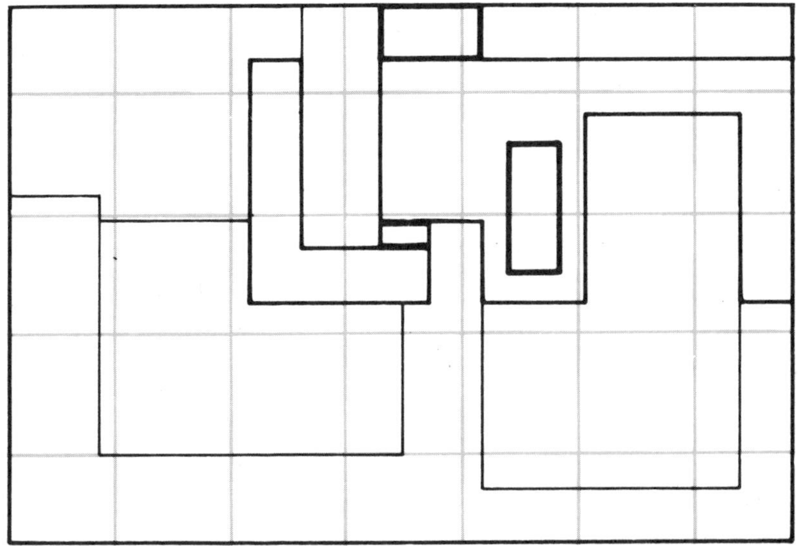

Setting out plan. Each square represents 2 × 2 m.

BARBECUE

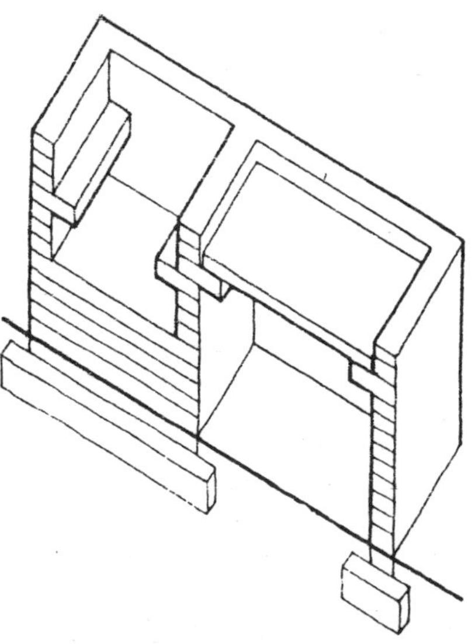

With store for logs and charcoal.

Use a well-baked stock brick (your local builder's merchant will advise). Overall size:
60 × 194 × 90 cm
(2 ft × 6 ft 4 in. × 3 ft).

Foundations: Dig trenches 30 cm (1 ft) wide and 25 cm (10 in.) deep, and fill with concrete to within 7.5 cm (3 in.) below ground level.

Build up the bricks as indicated, using a mortar mix of 2 parts cement, 1 part hydrated lime, 10 parts sand.

The drawing shows a paving slab 90 × 45 cm (3 ft × 1 ft 6 in.) supported by bricks built into the wall. Similar supports are shown for the grille which can be made by a local blacksmith or ironworker.

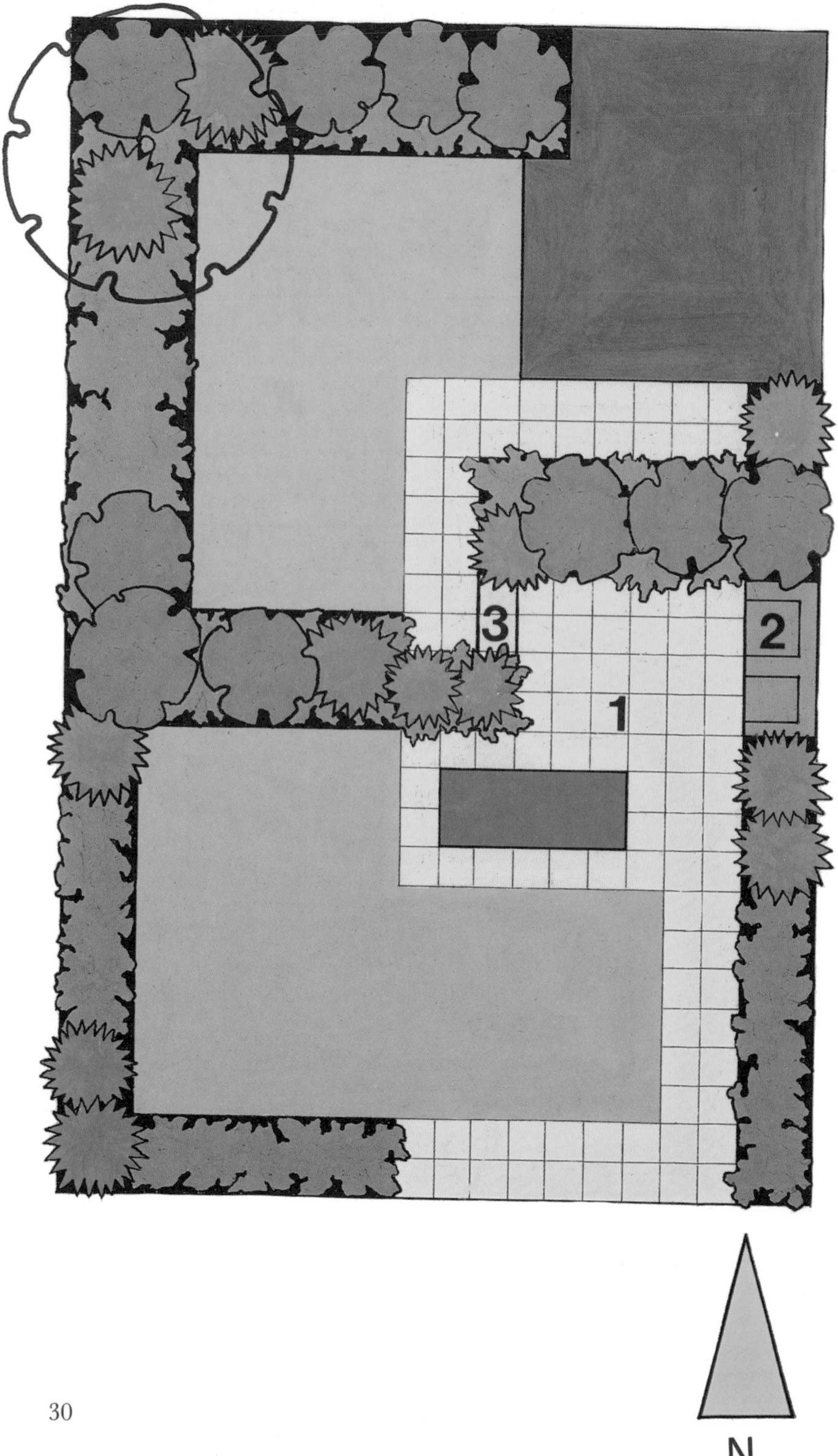

3

2

1

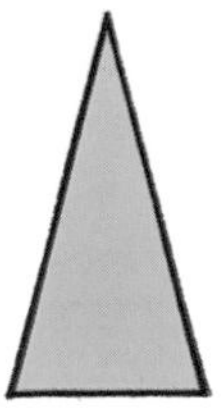

The plan shows that a garden can be made interesting without the use of curves. The juxtaposition of rectangular spaces provides seclusion and shelter, transforming a potentially cold site into a warm and cosy one.

1 Patio

2 Barbecue

3 Step

Lawn

Vegetables

Pond

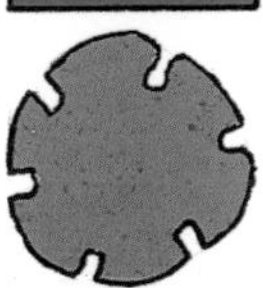

Shrubs over 1.8 m (6 ft)

Shrubs 1–2 m (3–6 ft)

Ground cover or Herbaceous plants

5 Garden Sloping Away from the House

A house with a garden that slopes away from it is a house with a view, distant or limited. This gives the opportunity to design the garden as an integral part of that view. As with the garden that rises away from the house, the slope should be put to work to produce compelling and intriguing effects.

In our plan for this situation, the fall of the site is harnessed to allow water to tumble from an upper pool into a second and then a third pool, all three of which are overlooked by the patio, and intersected by a winding staircase that leads down to and around a level, curved lawn. Further steps approach an area of longer grass in which fruit trees are planted; while on the right a ramp gives access to shed and vegetable plot, well guarded by closely planted shrubs.

This is a garden of pleasantly informal character. The upper (nearer) part simulates an alpine scene, with rocks buttressing the patio area and bordering the pools. Full use is made of alpine plants and conifers, particularly those of a conical or fastigiate nature. Rocks in the less steep gradients are interspersed with small areas of scree (gravel or stone chippings), with procumbent and trailing plants. Think, if you like, of a miniature mountainside flowing down to a more fertile lower region, where growth is more luxurious — and there you have the key to the planting backing the lawn, and providing the link with that view beyond.

The illustration shows how the garden is designed to make use of the descending slope, affording an unhindered view — just as one might enjoy it from a hilltop. From the patio the path runs down through the pools and among irregular rocks to what might be an alpine lawn. Beyond, only the

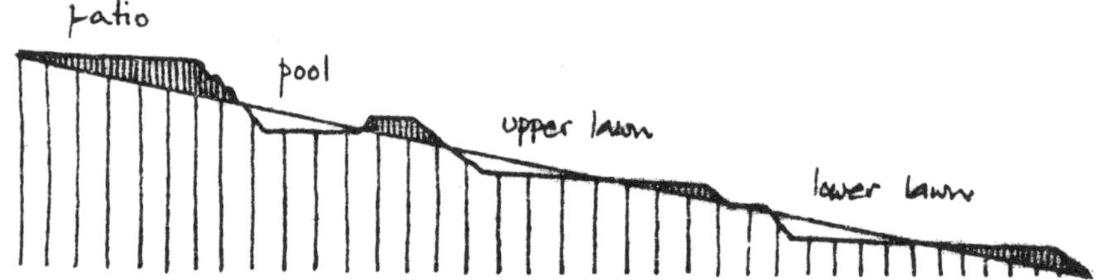

The sectional drawing shows how the steep gradient is transformed into four distinct, level areas — each with a character of its own. The opportunities for creating attractive rock slopes are obvious.

upper parts of the trees and shrubs are seen, once again creating that sense of mystery that it so important in a garden, whatever its type.

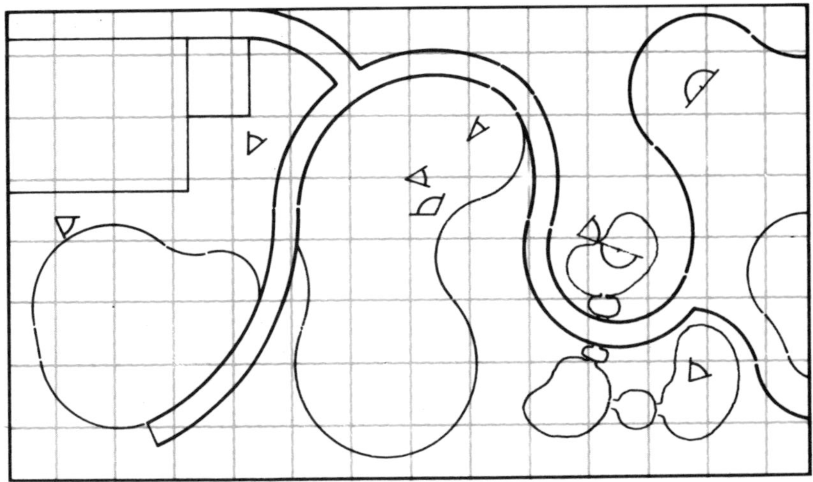

Setting-out plan showing radial points. Each square represents 2 × 2 m.

ROCK GARDEN

It is important to lay the rocks as rows of steps, not haphazardly, to simulate natural strata or outcrops.

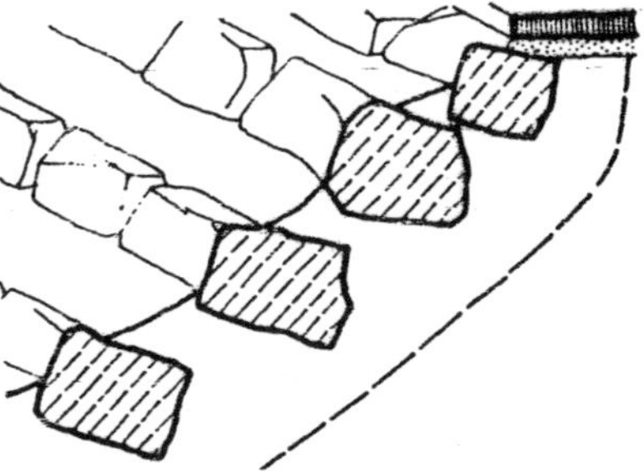

Individual rocks should be placed so that the top surface slopes back slightly into the hill or mound, to collect rainwater and also to prevent erosion of top soil.

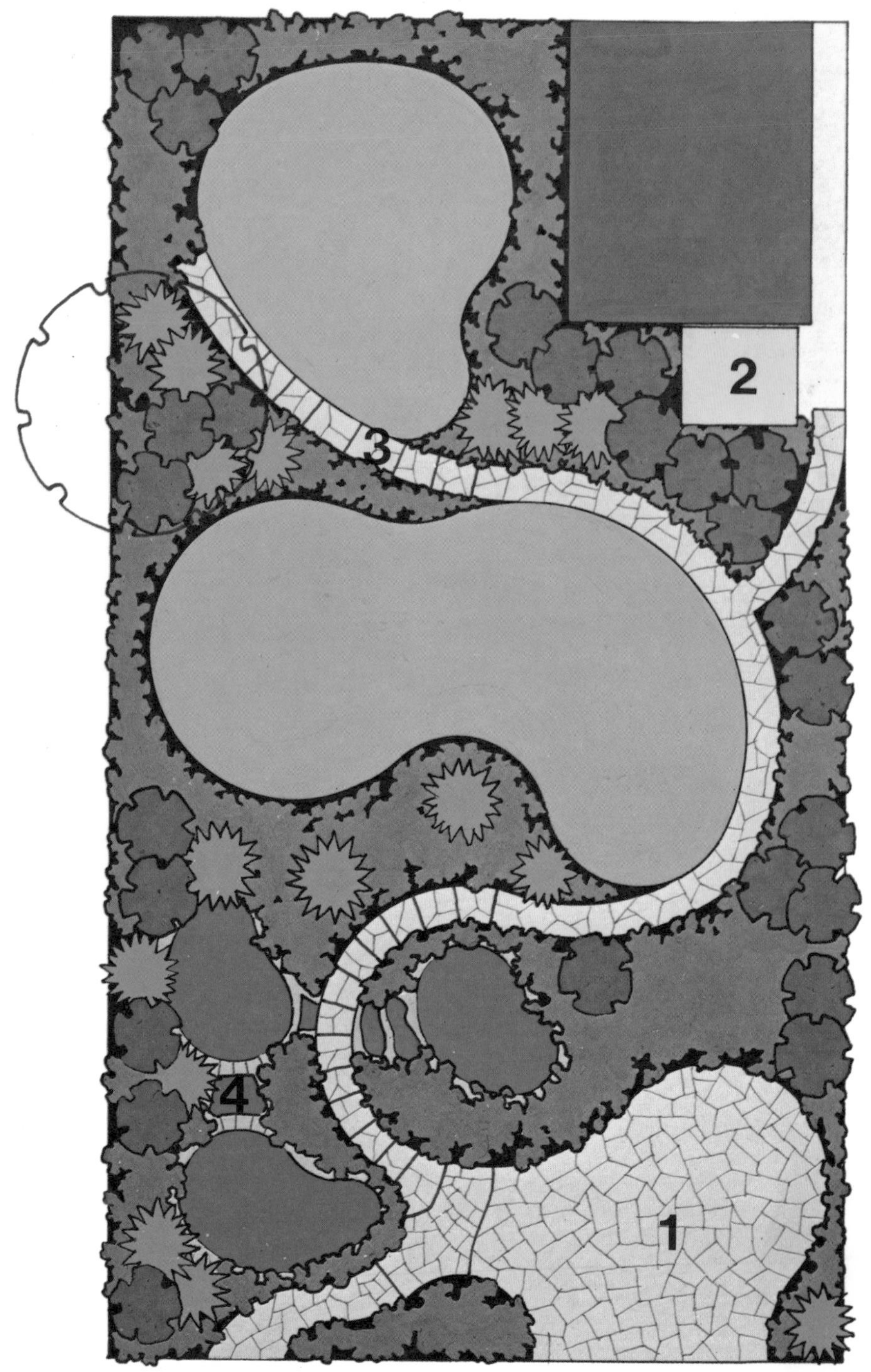
2
3
4
1

A plan (vertical view) is necessary for the laying-out of any garden, so that the various features can be accurately defined. But, in this case, the plan gives an impression very different from that of the elevation view on the next page. Here you can see only the curved shapes — the snaking path, the trio of pools, the curved lawns.

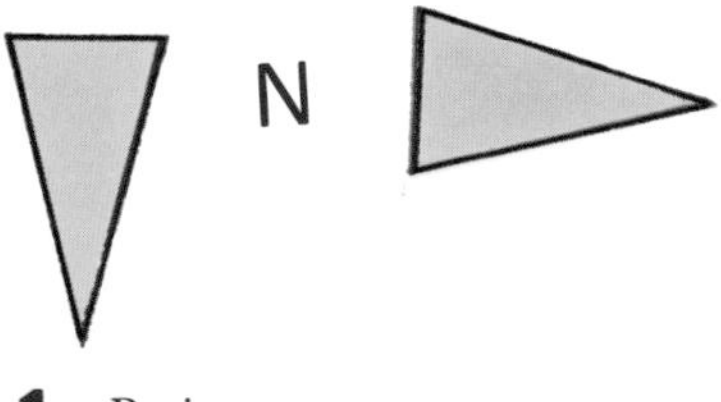

N

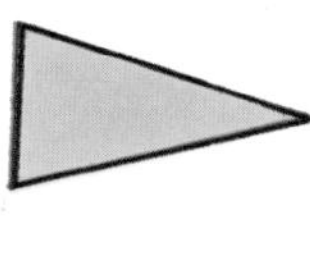

1 Patio

2 Shed

3 Steps

4 Waterfall

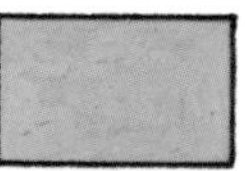

Lawn

Vegetables

Pond

Shrubs over 1.8 m (6 ft)

Shrubs 1–2 m (3–6 ft)

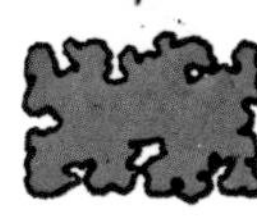

Ground cover or Herbaceous plants

6 Garden Sloping Towards the House

A site rising away from the back of the house is always regarded as 'difficult'. But with thought and careful planning the apparent disadvantages can become of value. The slope, for example, allows water to cascade from the upper pool into the lower ones, making a delightful feature for the two-level patio area. The wall retaining the lowest pool, and the steps, provide useful seating for guests at a summer party. The lawn above the upper pool is approached by further steps and, with its surrounding planting, supplies a pleasant area for relaxation. A diagonal ramp invites exploration of what lies beyond. This turns out to be the productive part of the garden — vegetables and fruit — with an attendant shed, well hidden behind a bold group of shrubs. The mower, as well as other tools, will need to be kept in this shed because it affords easiest access to the lawn (hence the ramp, and not steps).

The planting of a sloping site has to be done with care. Besides the visual considerations, the possibility of soil washing away must always be kept in mind, and if any gradient is at all steep, some minor terracing — perhaps with a few large stones or logs — may be necessary. Ground cover is invaluable as a stabilising agent and should be used extensively.

In our design, two trees, supported by shrubs, form the basis of the planting. The borders on each side of the garden can be planted as the owner wishes — with shrubs, roses, or herbaceous subjects or, perhaps most happily, with a mixture of all three. The beds attending the pools offer opportunities for introducing aquatic and trailing plants, with alpines in the drier areas.

Paving — almost an essential adjunct of formal ornamental pools — plays an important part in this garden. The frequent changing of levels and the attendant planting combine to give it additional attraction.

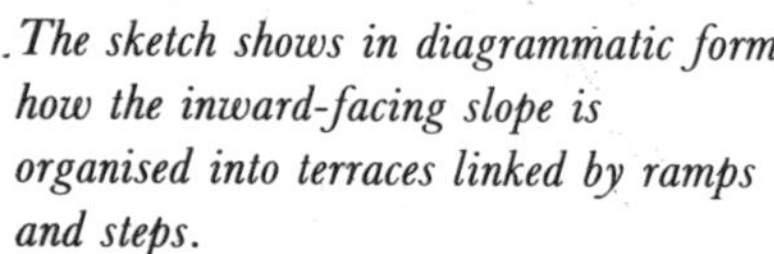

The sketch shows in diagrammatic form how the inward-facing slope is organised into terraces linked by ramps and steps.

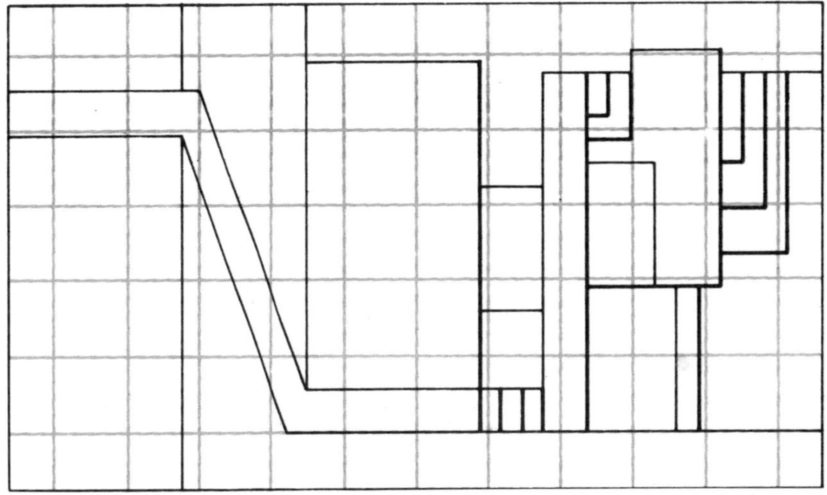

Setting-out plan. Each square represents 2 × 2 m.

STEPS

Form a concrete base for the steps with 15 cm (6 in.) risers and with treads the width of the paving slab minus 5 cm (2 in.).

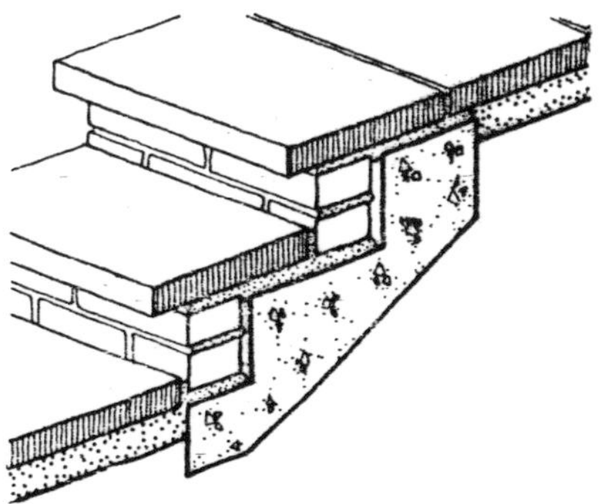

Lay two courses of bricks and bed the paving slab on a cement/sand mortar bed allowing 4 cm ($1\frac{1}{2}$ in.) overhang.

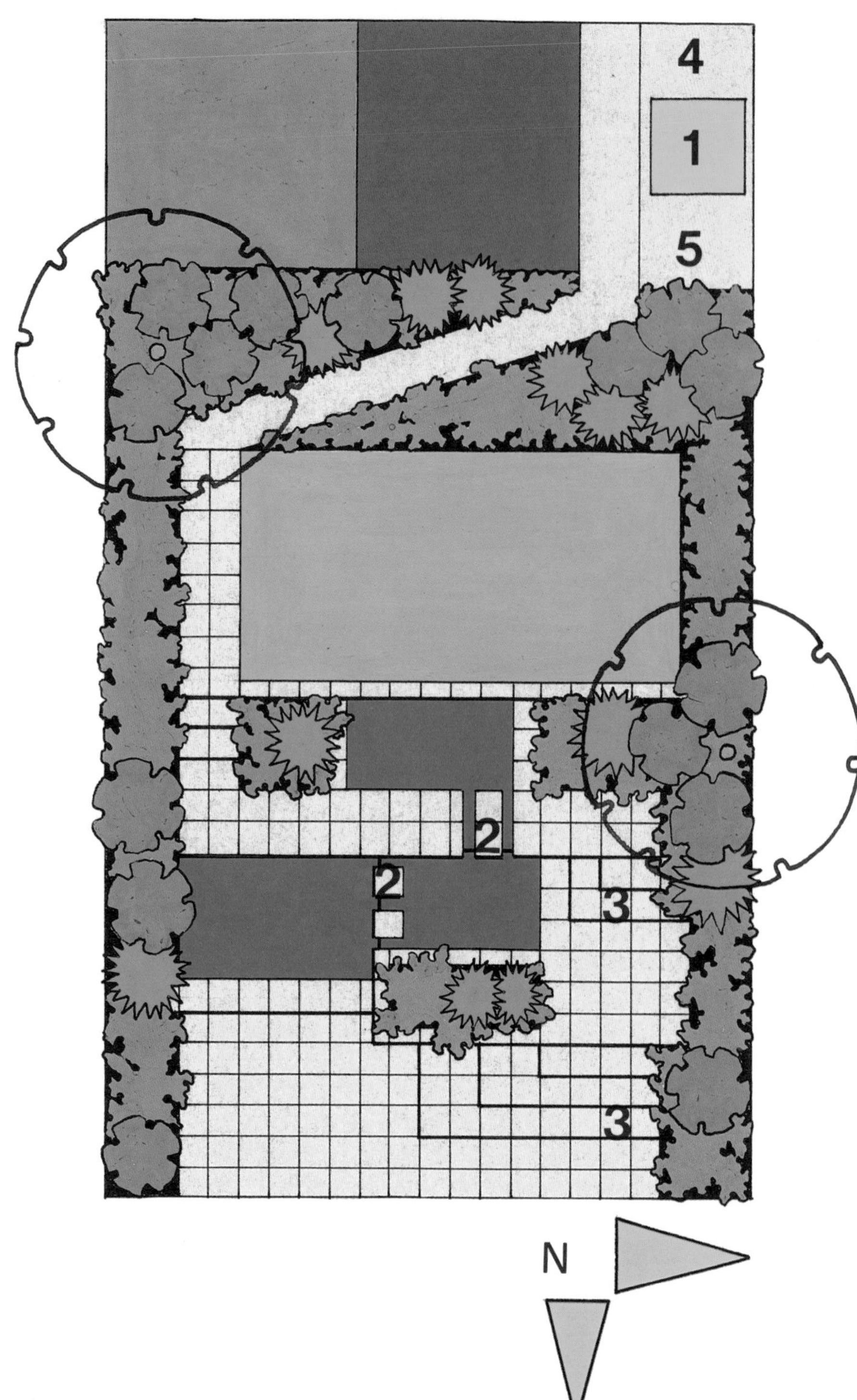
4
1
5
2
2
3
3
N

The difficulties of the site do not prevent the inclusion of all the features one would expect to find in a normal plot on level ground.

1 Shed
2 Waterfall
3 Steps
4 Compost
5 Potting area

Lawn

Pool

Vegetables

Fruit

Shrubs over 1.8 m (6 ft)

Shrubs 1–2 m (3–6 ft)

Ground cover or Herbaceous plants

7 Garden to Screen an Eyesore

Unless you live in the country, there's always the chance of an eyesore, or at least an unwelcome view, obtruding on the garden. Or maybe you don't want to be overlooked from the windows of a house on an opposing plot. A screen of trees is the obvious long-term solution, but trees need time to grow and something more immediate is required from the garden design. The one we show tackles the problem boldly with a 2.7 metre (8–ft) wall (it could well be less: the actual height needed can be determined by trial and error, using a long cane, or perhaps a ladder). The wall itself is in no way an eyesore — as it might be if it stood on its own, since it forms the back of a pergola-covered patio area and is softened by climbing plants (also used along the boundary wall or fence). A pool, conforming with the rectangular pattern of the garden, completes an interesting leisure area, which faces a neat lawn backed by shrubs. A sundial, or statue, gives character to the far end of the garden, mainly occupied by a second lawn, useful as a play area for children (alternatively the ground could be used for vegetables or fruit). At the very back is the long-term screen — most quickly achieved by the conifer *Cupressocyparis Leylandii*, which can put on a metre (three feet) a year once it is established.

Use is made of the screening wall to hide the lean-to shed or greenhouse (if greenhouse, the two large bushes on the far side would be omitted, to allow maximum light).

The paving chosen is a warm brick — specially hard paving bricks must be used.

The perspective view gives conclusive proof of the efficacy of the screening operation. As soon as the wall-backed pergola is built, the

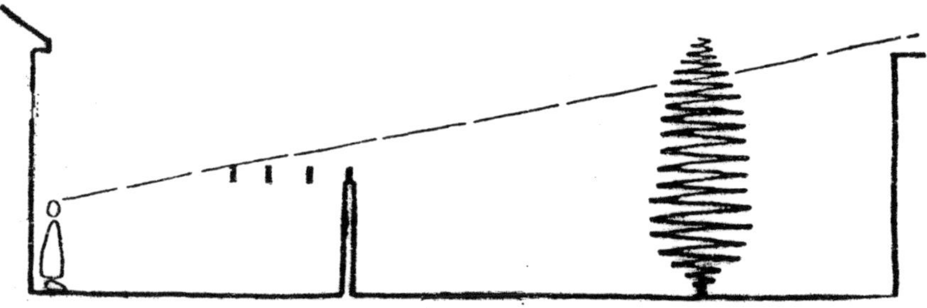

The wall, backing the pergola, does the main job of screening the eyesore — immediately. In later years, conifers at the rear of the garden will round off the strategy.

owners have a secluded leisure area in which to relax and forget the offending eyesore.

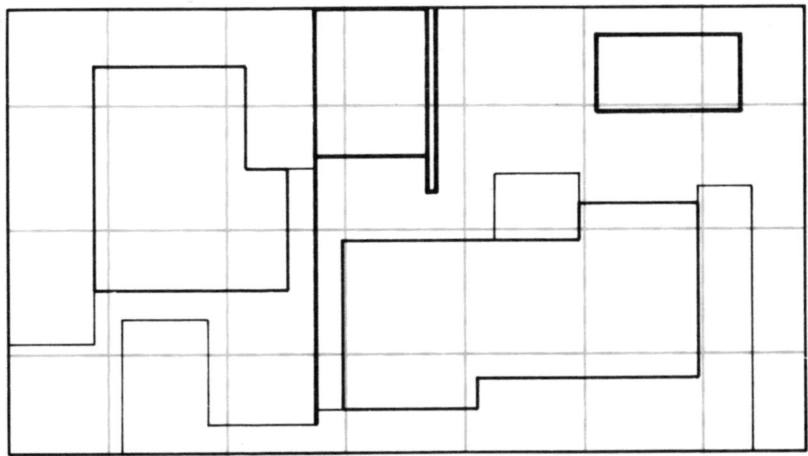

Setting out plan. Each square represents 2 × 2 m.

PERGOLA

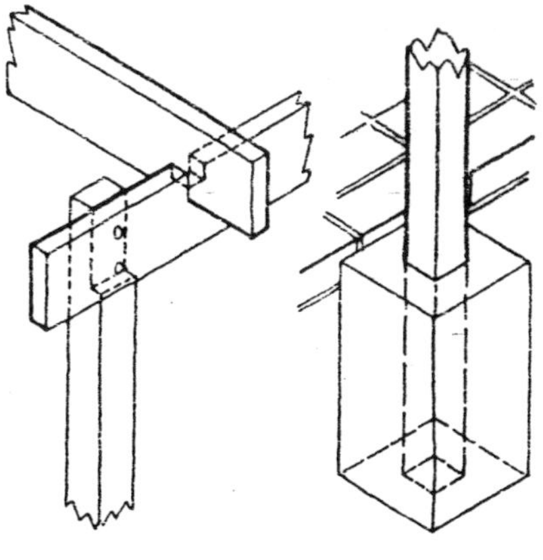

Columns: Dig holes 22 × 22 × 50 cm (9 × 9 × 20 in.) deep. Place a 7.5 cm (3 in.) square timber post in each hole, backfilling with concrete. Cut 2.5 cm (1 in.) notches in the tops of the columns to take the horizontal members.

Horizontal members: Screw three 15 × 5 cm (6 × 2 in.) joists to the top of the columns. Cut notches 2.5 × 4 cm (1 × $1\frac{1}{2}$ in.) wide in the tops of the joists and in the bottom of the cross members at the points of intersection. Fix the six 15 × 4 cm (6 × $1\frac{1}{2}$ in.) cross members to the joists. Apply two coats of preservative stain to all timbers.

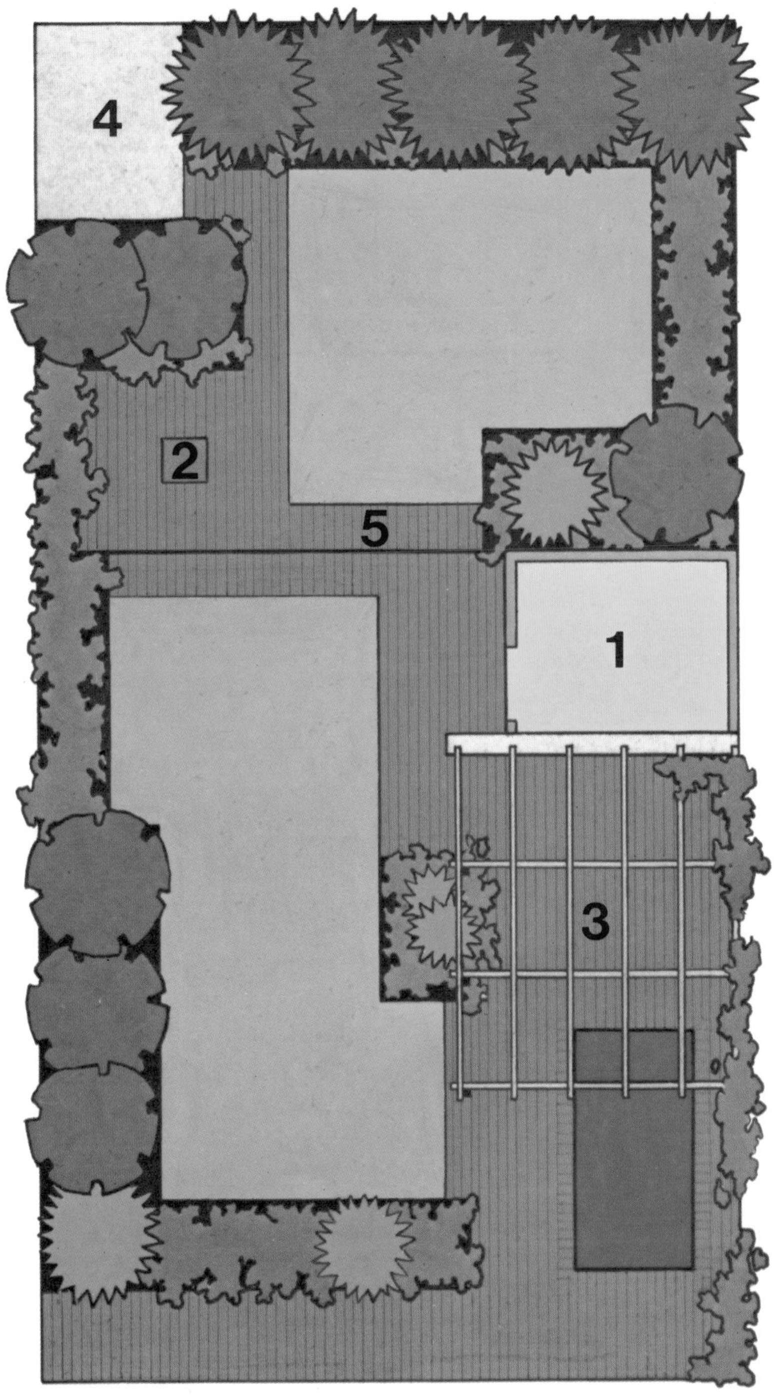
4
2
5
1
3

Balance is a necessary part of garden design — and it is not lacking here. The major feature of the high wall is counter-weighted by the long lawn on the left and the paved area with its focal point of a stone sundial or statue.

1 Greenhouse/shed

2 Statue

3 Pergola

4 Refuse/compost

5 Step

Lawn

Brick paving

Pool

Conifers

Shrubs over 1.8 m (6 ft)

Shrubs 1–2 m (3–6 ft)

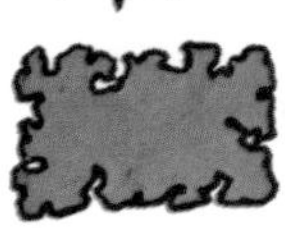

Ground cover or Herbaceous plants

8 Garden With a View

. . . by which we mean, of course, a desirable view. If you are lucky enough to have this valuable asset to your property, everything possible must be done not only to perserve it, but to create a gracious setting for it — just as one would seek to find the perfect frame for a work of art. It is patently necessary to leave the end of the garden open. But equally, because the view will most commonly be enjoyed from the rear windows of the house and its adjoining patio, the planting must be planned with care, with thought for the eventual spread of ornamental trees and shrubs. The ideal arrangement is to confine tall-growing subjects to the side boundaries, with medium and short-growers sloping towards the centre — as our central group on the right and the opposing group towards the rear demonstrate.

The major part of this uncluttered, easily run garden is, not surprisingly, taken up with the two interestingly shaped lawns, whose smooth green swards make the perfect foreground for the distant view. The effect of this is enhanced by the raising of the terrace.

The long path, originating from the patio, invites a stroll towards the view and, by its winding nature, seems to unite the garden with it. A pleasing prospect merits more than one viewpoint, and the secluded, sheltered seat offers a delightful vista.

Crazy paving, less popular these days, has been chosen for this garden because its informality suits the flowing lines. It must be laid well and smoothly, using warm, subdued colours.

Where does this garden end? That's the question the designer — and, in due course, the owner — wants the visitor to ask. It was the same question Capability Brown loved to pose, and one of the tricks that he used to persuade guests in the big house that the host's estate extended far into

The sketch shows how the view from the raised terrace is framed by the planting each side of the garden. The foreshortening that would result from an unbroken lawn is avoided by creating two lawns of different size and shape, dividing them with a winding path, and leading the eye to the view by a slower, less direct route.

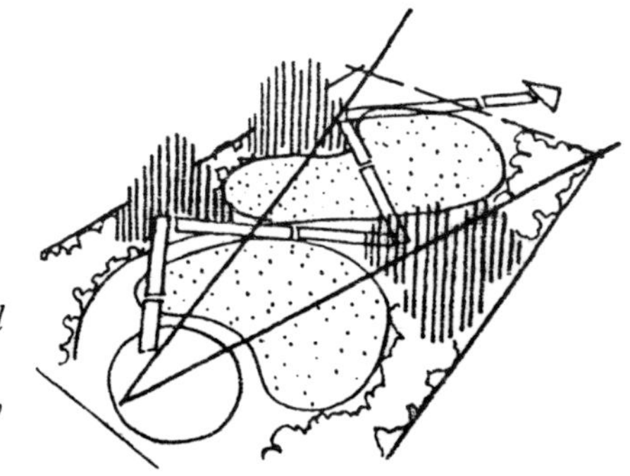

the distance was the ha-ha, a deep hidden ditch separating the garden from the fields — and cattle — beyond. An invisible boundary is still desirable in the modern garden with a view — and the deep, wide ditch may yet be a useful way of deterring unwanted visitors, while preserving the uninterrupted view. As an alternative, we suggest the small-mesh material sold for garden windbreaks which is almost invisible at a distance.

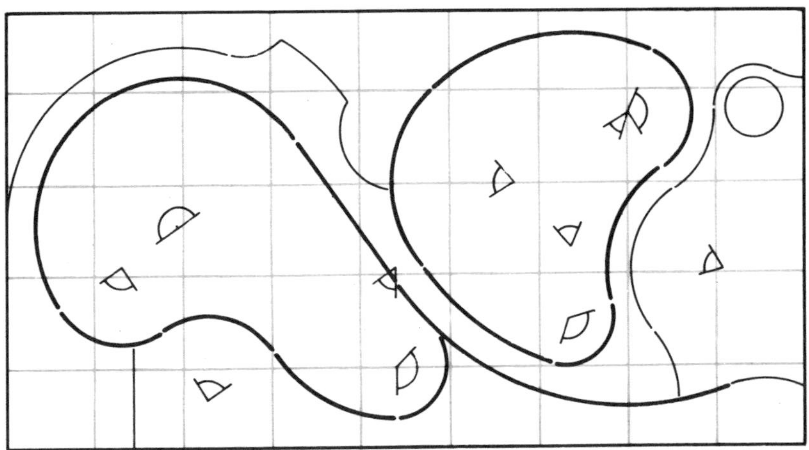

Setting-out plan showing radial points. Each square represents 2 × 2 m.

GARDEN BENCH

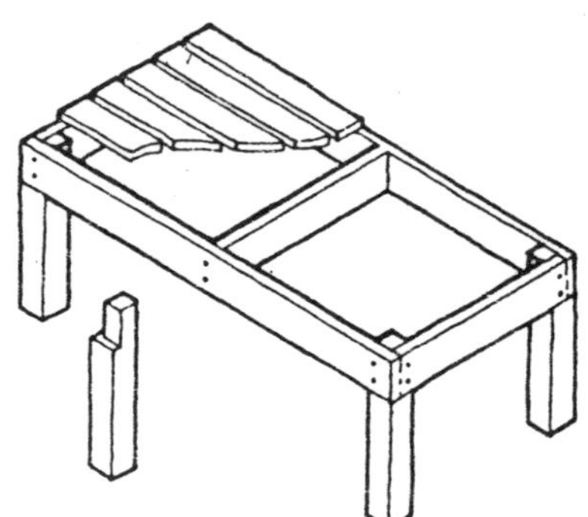

Height 120 × 60 × 45 cm (4 ft × 2 ft × 18 in.) high.

Legs: 7.5 × 7.5 cm (3 × 3 in.) by 45 cm (18 in.). Cut out 2 × 8.5 cm ($\frac{3}{4}$ × 3 $\frac{1}{2}$ in.) pieces on two sides.

Seat frame: Two 10 × 2.5 × 120 cm (4 in. × 1 in × 4 ft) members. Three 10 × 2.5 × 55 cm (4 in. × 1 in. × 1 ft 10 in.) members.

Slats: Six 7.5 × 2 × 120 cm (3 in. × $\frac{3}{4}$ in. × 4 ft) slats.

Before assembly, apply two coats of preservative stain, which can be obtained from any timber supplier, to all timber. Ask for 'planed soft wood'.

Use 5 cm (2 in.) long brass or non-ferrous screws to assemble legs and frame, and 4 cm (1$\frac{1}{2}$ in.) screws for the slats.

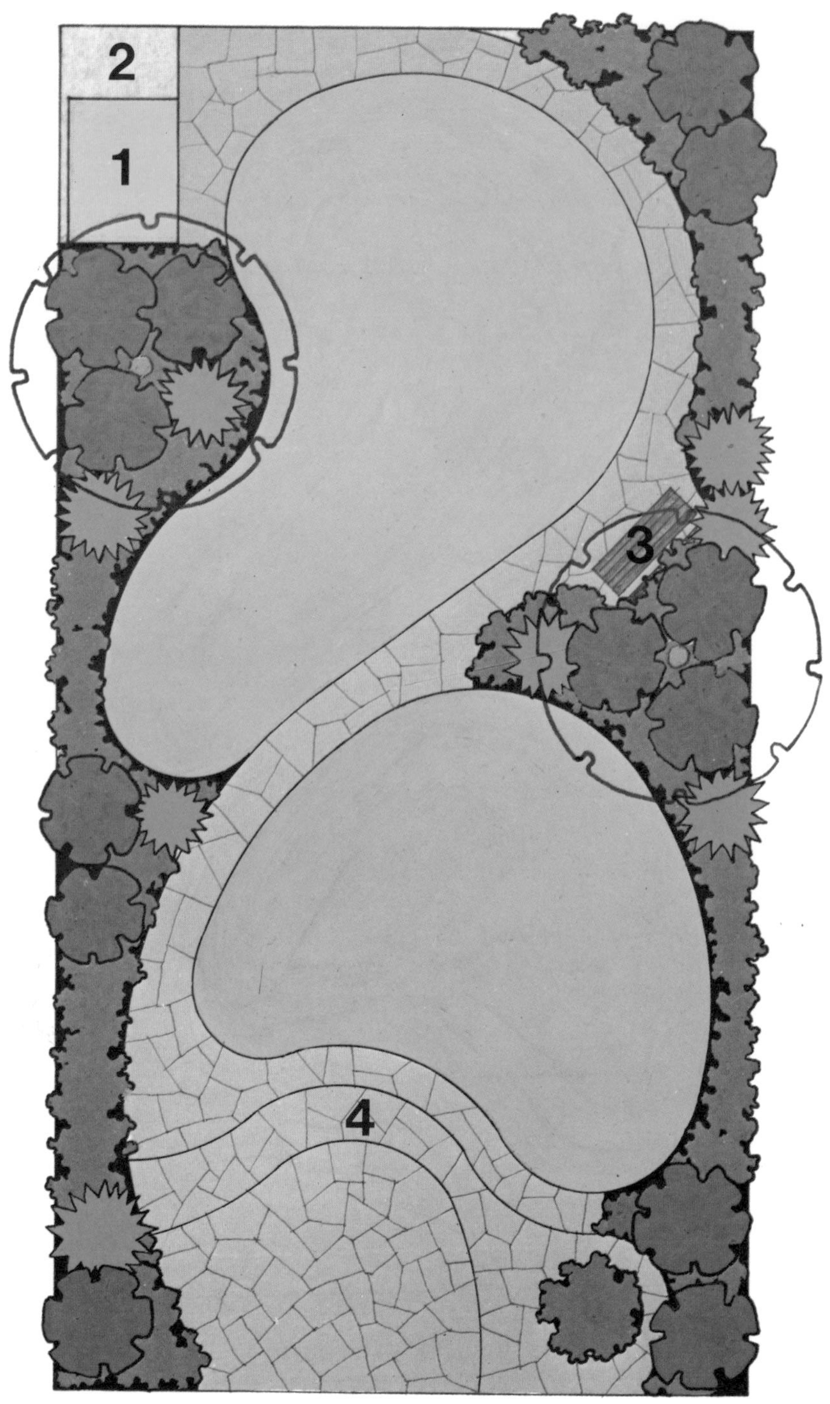
2
1
3
4

The two opposing trees are not sited solely to help frame the view. The one on the right provides shade for a seat facing across the further lawn; the tree on the left conceals the shed or greenhouse beyond it.

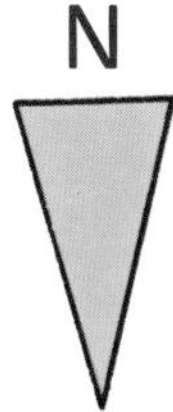

1 Shed

2 Compost

3 Bench

4 Step

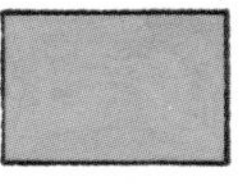
Lawn

Random paving

Shrubs over 1.8 m (6 ft)

Shrubs 1–2 m (3–6 ft)

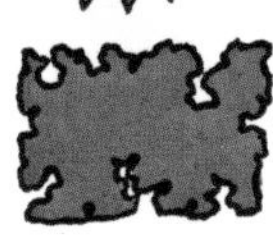
Ground cover or Herbaceous plants

9 Long, Narrow Garden

Before the 1939–45 war, houses were commonly built on long, narrow plots, and it is rare to find such a garden well designed. The first essential is to break up the plot into sections to reduce its length to the eye. The next is to defeat the constriction of the closely parallel boundaries by off-setting the axis. A glance at the plan shows how this can be achieved.

The square-paved patio is separated from the garden beyond by two rectangular pools. Cross these to begin the interesting walk past the twin lawns and the neighbouring triangular borders. The perspective view shows how these cunningly conceal what lies beyond at each stage, the final barrier guarding what turns out to be the real end of the garden — the tool shed and vegetable plots.

It will, of course, take several years for the trees and shrubs to reach the stage of maturity that makes the ultimate effect possible. But the garden can be made very attractive in the intervening years by planting herbaceous plants and annuals, including taller growing kinds like mallows and sweet peas (in clumps) between the young shrubs.

Although the garden is shown in a rural setting, it can be equally effective in suburb or town.

Looking at the completed garden from the patio, it is hard to realise that it is confined by a long, narrow plot. Compare it with the dreary, unimaginative gardens one so often sees — long, thin lawn, bounded by a thin, straight path and strap-like borders following the line of the fences.

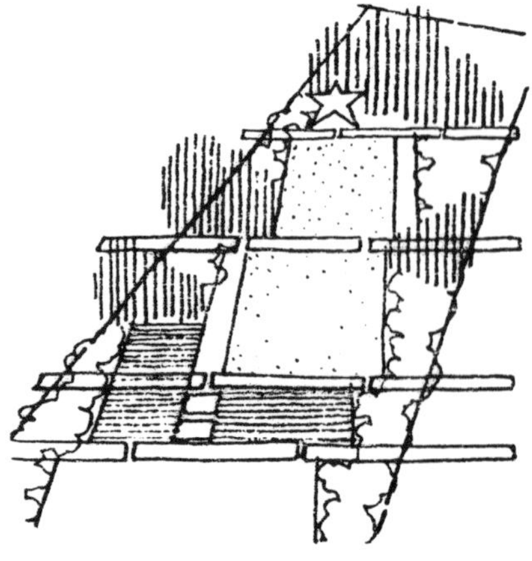

The sketch demonstrates how the long plot is broken up into interlinking sections — each one a stepping-stone to the next, and culminating in a focal point at the end of the off-set axis.

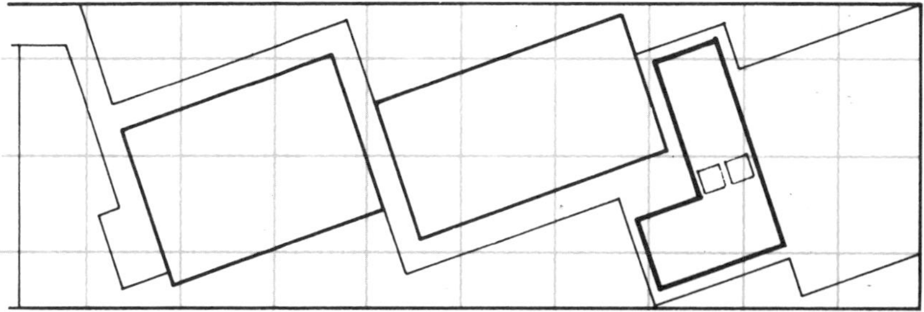

Setting-out plan. Each square represents 2 × 2 m.

GRAVEL PATH

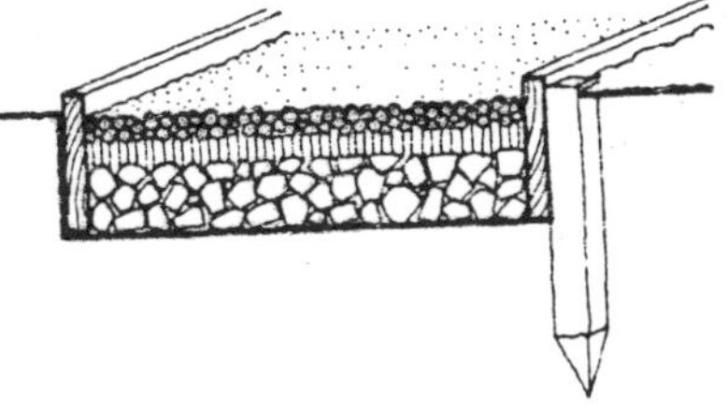

Dig out the topsoil to a depth of 12.5 cm (5 in.). Treat 15 × 2.5 cm (6 × 1 in.) edging boards with preservative and fix them to 4 × 4 × 38 cm ($1\frac{1}{2}$ × $1\frac{1}{2}$ × 15 in.) long pegs driven into the ground.

Lay 7.5 cm (3 in.) of hardcore (broken stones, brickbats, etc.) and consolidate.

Lay and roll approximately 3 cm (1 in.) of hoggin (small pebbles bound with clay). Roll into the hoggin about 2.5 cm (1 in.) of 6 mm ($\frac{1}{4}$ in.) gravel.

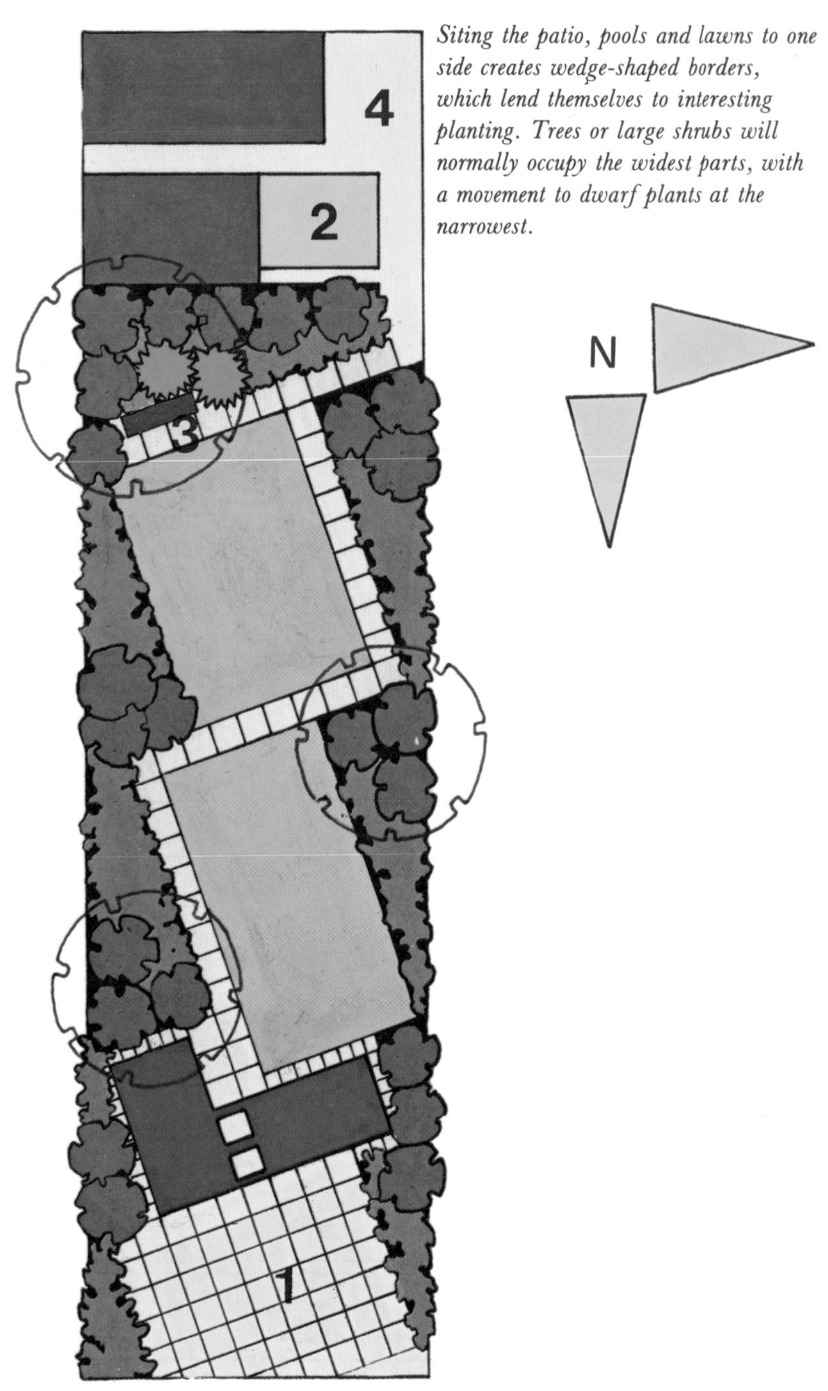

Siting the patio, pools and lawns to one side creates wedge-shaped borders, which lend themselves to interesting planting. Trees or large shrubs will normally occupy the widest parts, with a movement to dwarf plants at the narrowest.

1 Terrace

2 Shed/greenhouse

3 Bench

4 Compost

Lawn

Pool

Vegetables

Gravel

Shrubs over 1.8 m (6 ft)

Shrubs 1–2 m (3–6 ft)

Ground cover or Herbaceous plants

10 The 'Twinned' Garden

Small plots are today the rule rather than the exception when new dwellings are built — so small, in fact, that owners used to more space may feel claustrophobic and shut in. There is a simple solution, if a pair of neighbours can agree: the 'twinning' of their gardens. Each will want to preserve some privacy, but this need not involve a barrier down the length of their common boundary; a wall or fence a third of the way down, to ensure that the patio area is not overlooked, is usually sufficient — as is shown in our design (in this, a brick wall is employed). Beyond that, the boundary is delineated only by an area of rough grass between the gardens' lawns — an area enlivened in spring by daffodils and other bulbs. The planting is deliberately kept low to allow the eye to travel on into the neighbouring garden, giving the impression that each of the gardens extends much farther than in fact it does.

The left-hand garden has an interesting sequence of slightly raised beds abutting the wall, the last one rounding the end of the wall to form a link with the adjoining garden. The patio of the right-hand garden is dominated by a pool of generous size, crossed by a bridge. Both patios have crazy paving which is carried on into the paths bounding the lawns. The surrounding planting is similar — mainly shrubs, roses and herbaceous subjects, some of which serve to screen the vegetable plots at the rear.

Climbers decorate the wall, whose expanse can additionally be relieved by two or more 'windows' with grilles.

The perspective drawing is the view from the patio of the left-hand garden, as one would gaze around the end of the dividing wall. Imagine how different the vista would be were the wall (or fence, or hedge) continued the whole length of the plot! But by using the artifice of 'twinning', the garden takes on an air of almost infinite space.

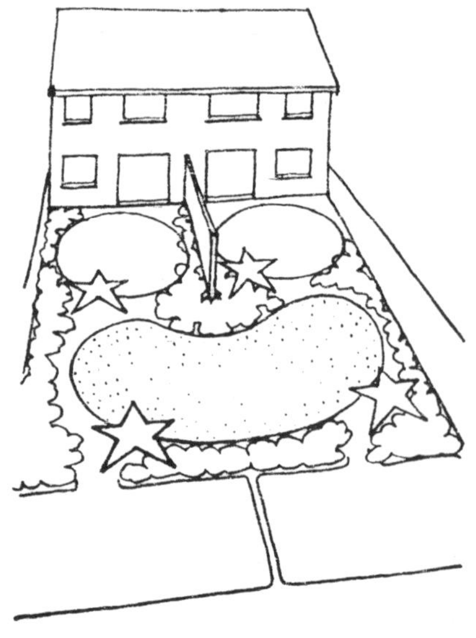

Two semi-detached houses, each with its garden and its privacy — but with TWICE the normal view, DOUBLE the feeling of space.

‘Twinning’ is not, admittedly, for the family with small children or pets that need to be confined. But there must be hundreds of thousands of homes that would be enriched by the linking of neighbouring gardens.

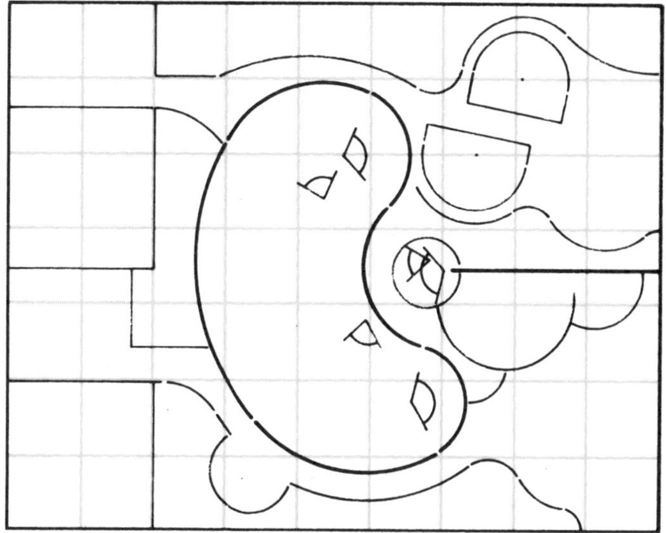

Setting-out plan showing radial points. Each square represents 2 × 2 m.

FREE-STANDING WALL

Before building a boundary wall, check with the local authority and your house deeds for any height restriction. Also get approval from the local Technical Service Department — and your neighbour.

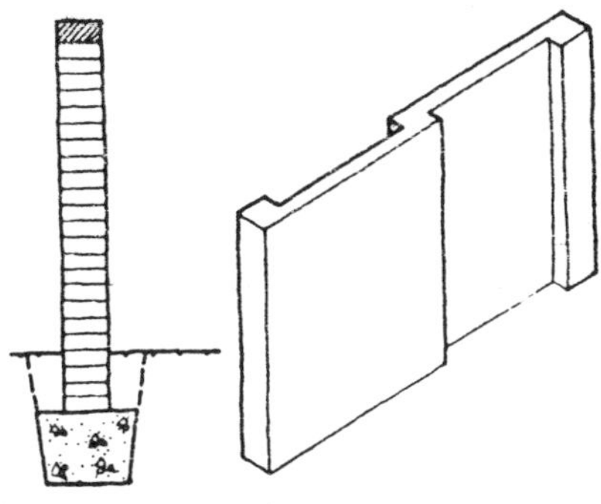

The wall shown is 150 cm (5 ft) high and 300 cm (10 ft) long. Dig a trench 60 cm (2 ft) deep and 45 cm (1 ft 6 in.) wide and half fill it with concrete (1 part cement, 2 parts sand, 4 parts coarse aggregate).

It is advisable to use a good brick that will stand up to frost and continual weathering. Lay with mortar consisting of 1 part cement, 1 part lime, 6 parts builder's sand. The wall, 11 cm ($4\frac{1}{2}$ in.) thick, should have 22 cm (9 in.) square piers at each end and in the middle. It is sometimes necessary, if a cheaper brick has been used, to finish the top of the wall with a course of engineering bricks as a coping.

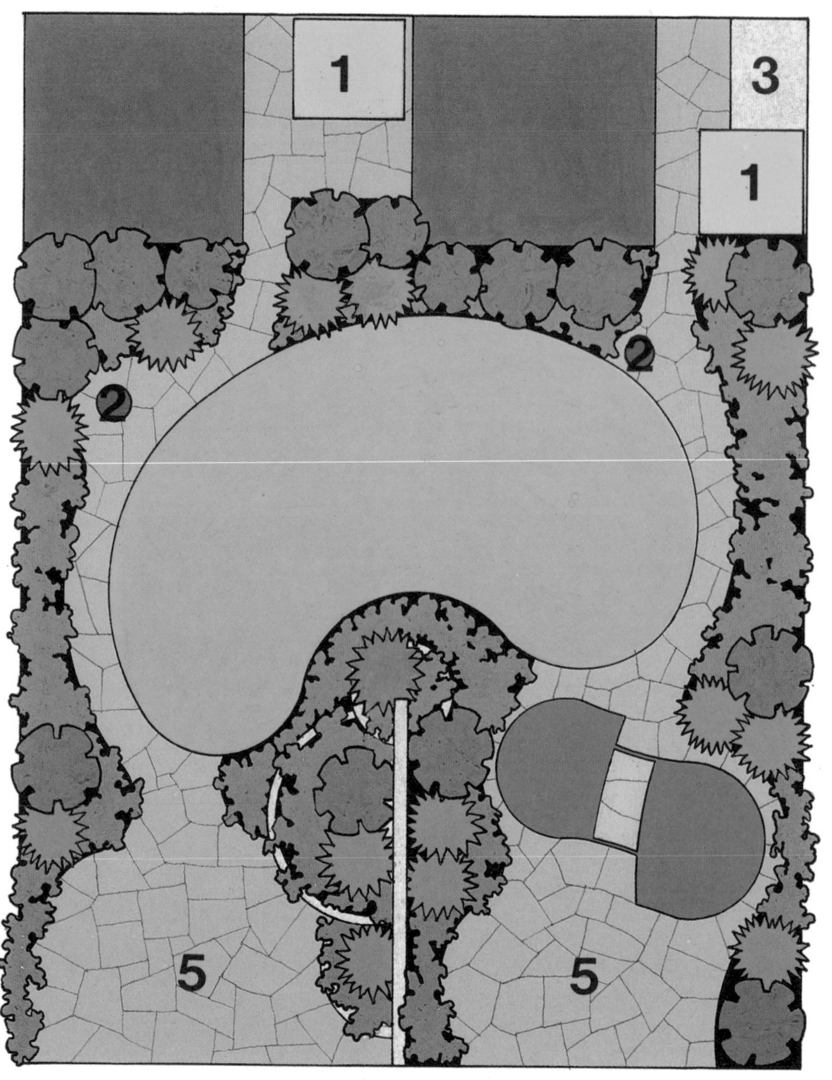
1
3
1
2
2
5
5

Twinning may not be for everyone, but it is a wonderful way to create the illusion of extra space and mystery.

1 Shed
2 Statue/birdbath
3 Compost/potting area
4 Raised bed
5 Patio

Lawn

Vegetables

Pool

Shrubs over 1.8 m (6 ft)

Shrubs 1–2 m (3–6 ft)

Ground cover or Herbaceous plants

11 Small Town Garden

Because of the limited length of plots on new housing estates, gardens as broad as they are long (or almost so) are becoming increasingly common. The size is often no more than eight metres (25 feet) square, and this involves careful planning — not only in the design, but in the planting.

In the plan we show, spaces are created for various purposes, and maximum use of them is made. Curves defeat the square outline of the plot. Tiny lawns, especially in urban areas, are rarely successful, and gravel has been substituted. Spaces not used for permanent planting are paved with warm-coloured brick. This allows the introduction of a variety of containers, both for ornamental plants, and for the growing of fruit and vegetables (e.g., tomato tubs, strawberry and potato barrels). These can be arranged to suit both the aspect and the wishes of the owner.

A single tree — more would overcrowd the plot — provides a focal point and shade for the seat beneath it. A pool, complementary in shape to that of the gravel area, provides extra interest and, if a small fountain were incorporated, movement and sound.

Care must be taken not to plant shrubs that would, in time, tend to 'take over' and prove an embarrassment. At the same time, the more solid the planting at the rear of the garden (providing there is no view to be preserved) the better, since the boundary fence or wall can thus be hidden, and the impression given that more might lie beyond.

Although small, this is a garden that can provide a great deal of interest to the plant enthusiast, as well as a peaceful retreat from the noise and bustle of town life.

Containers with seasonal planting provide extra colour to complement the background of shrubs, chosen for their all-year-round interest. The pool is sited close to the

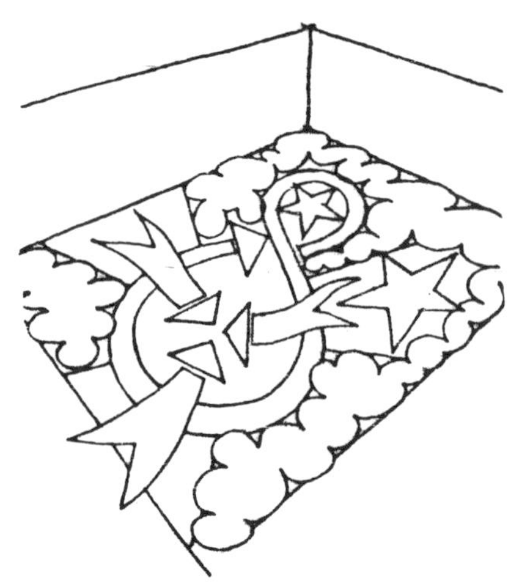

The main features of this small, squarish garden — the approach steps, the space for containers on the left, the ornamental pool, the shade seat — are set around the central meeting place, gravelled for all-weather use.

seat so that all the activity that water attracts can be in view. Maintenance is at a very low level — a fact that the busy town-dweller will appreciate.

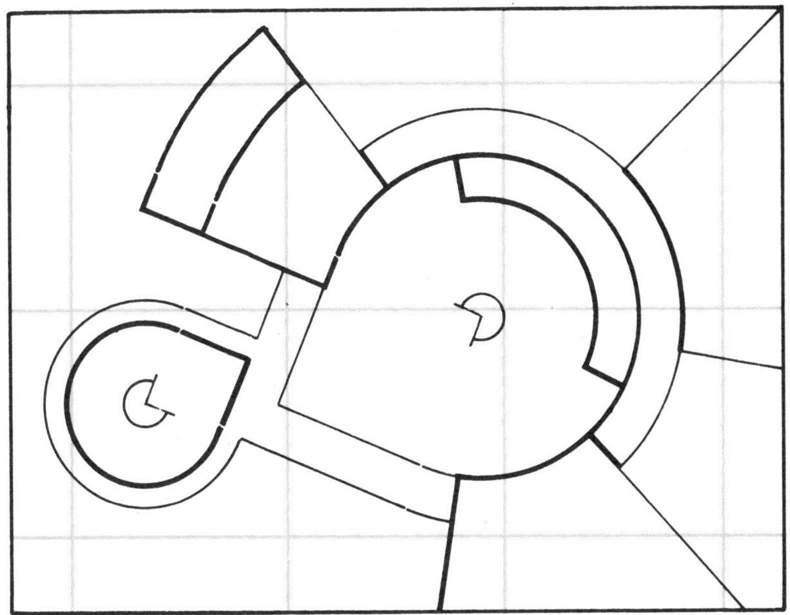

Setting-out plan showing radial points. Each square represents 2 × 2 m.

BRICK STEPS

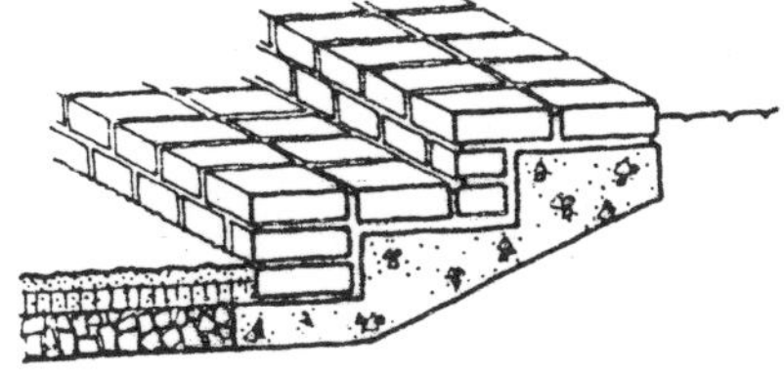

The 'tread' or 'going' of steps should be far broader than those inside a building. They not only look better but are easier to walk up.

Form a concrete base with 32 cm (13 in.) treads and 15 cm (6 in.) risers. Bed the bricks (frost-resistant type) with mortar (1 part cement, 4 parts sand).

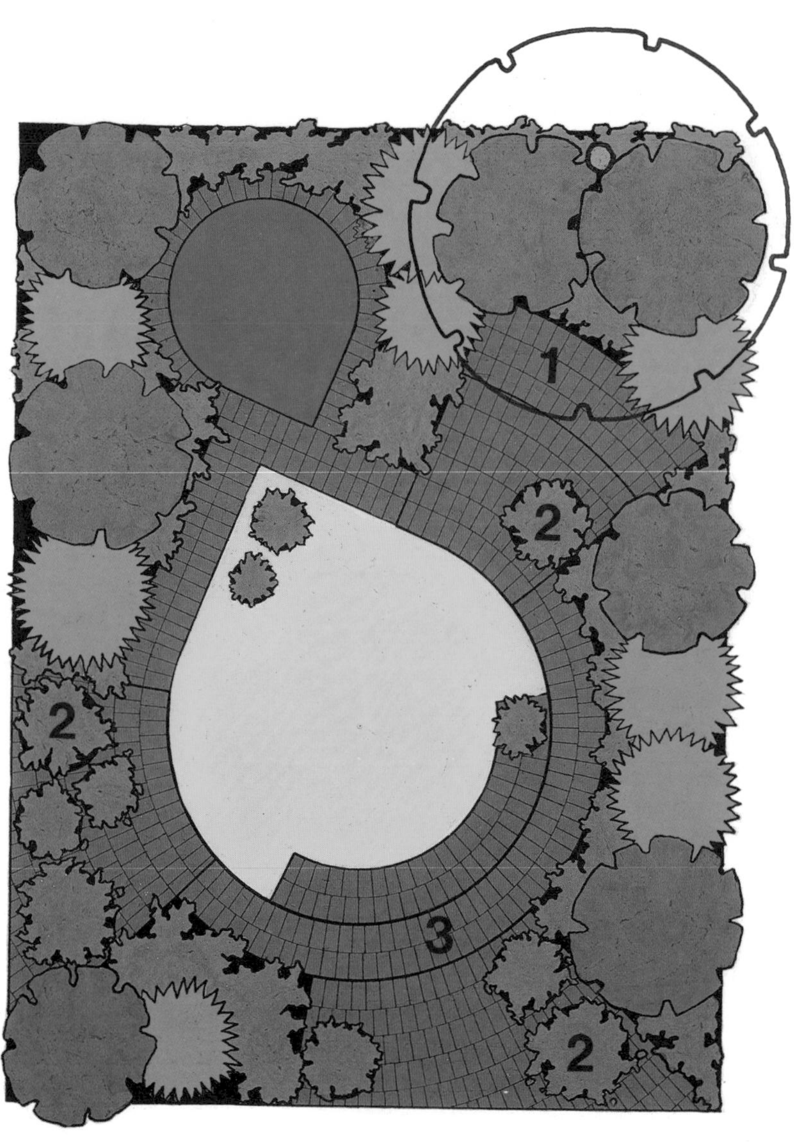
1
2
2
3
2
2

This design was translated into fact at the 1980 Chelsea Show and won a top award. The use of warm-coloured brickwork and the sympathetic planting created the feeling of tranquil seclusion desirable in a town (or indeed, any) garden.

1 Brick bench

2 Tubs/pots

3 Steps

 Brick

 Gravel

 Pool

 Shrubs over 1.8 m (6 ft)

 Shrubs 1–2 m (3–6 ft)

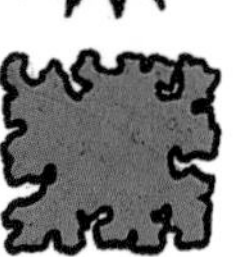 Ground cover or Herbaceous plants

12 Garden for a Widening Plot

By no means all plots are of regular, rectangular shape. And that may not be a bad thing, especially if the plot widens out generously: for then the designer has the opportunity to use the extra space to create the illusion that the garden is much bigger than it really is. Study our design and imagine that you are looking at the view from the patio. The immediate prospect is a semi-circular lawn and a pool of the same shape — the lower half of the 'S' theme — with a rich, solid backing of conifers and shrubs behind the curving path. You might think this screen marks the rear boundary of the plot . . . were it not for the glimpse of a further curving lawn with more trees beyond. And what is the significance of the pergola — is it guarding the entrance to an unseen part of the garden? How far does the lawn sweep round, what lies at the end of it? Is there, hidden away, a kitchen garden, a greenhouse?

All these questions compel you to set off to explore the garden — to satisfy your curiosity. And that means the design has succeeded in one of its major intentions. With the advantage of a plan view, you can see all the answers — that the pergola does indeed provide the threshold to the utility section, so well concealed; that the lawn does, of course, end in an intimate shrub-lined corner.

Although conifers, ornamental trees and shrubs must form the basis of the planting, the owner of this garden has plenty of scope for introducing roses or herbaceous plants, while that extra space in the widening plot will grow a lot of food.

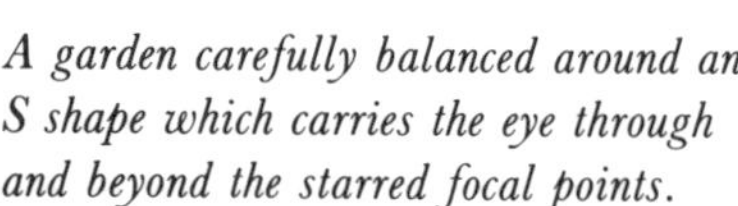

A garden carefully balanced around an S shape which carries the eye through and beyond the starred focal points.

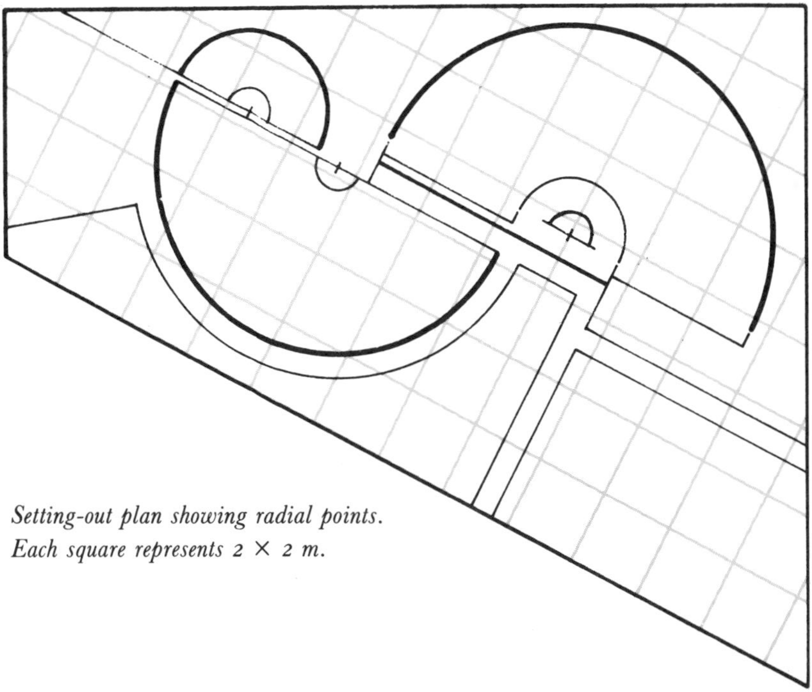

Setting-out plan showing radial points. Each square represents 2 × 2 m.

PERGOLA

Use planed softwood as follows.

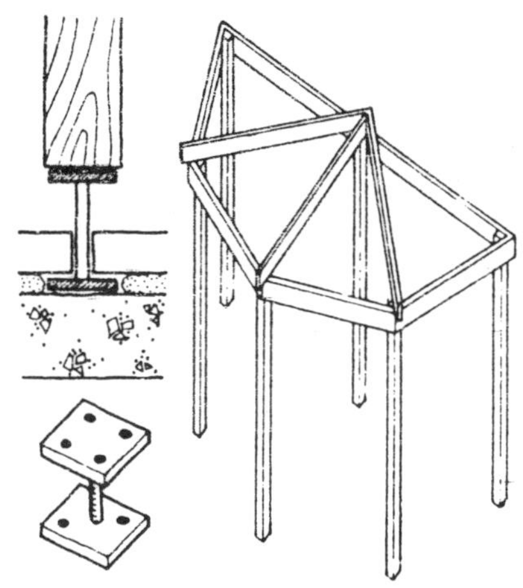

Six 7.5 × 7.5 × 220 cm (3 in. × 3 in. × 7 ft) posts;
Four 15 × 2.5 × 120 cm (6 in. × 1 in. × 4 ft) perimeter members;
One 15 × 2.5 × 300 cm (6 in. × 1 in. × 10 ft) member;
Three 15 × 2.5 × 150 cm (6 in. × 1 in. × 5 ft) members.

To prevent rotting of timber posts at ground level, mild steel 'shoes' can be screwed to the bottom of the posts and bolted into the concrete base: or use Metposts, steel sockets let into the ground.

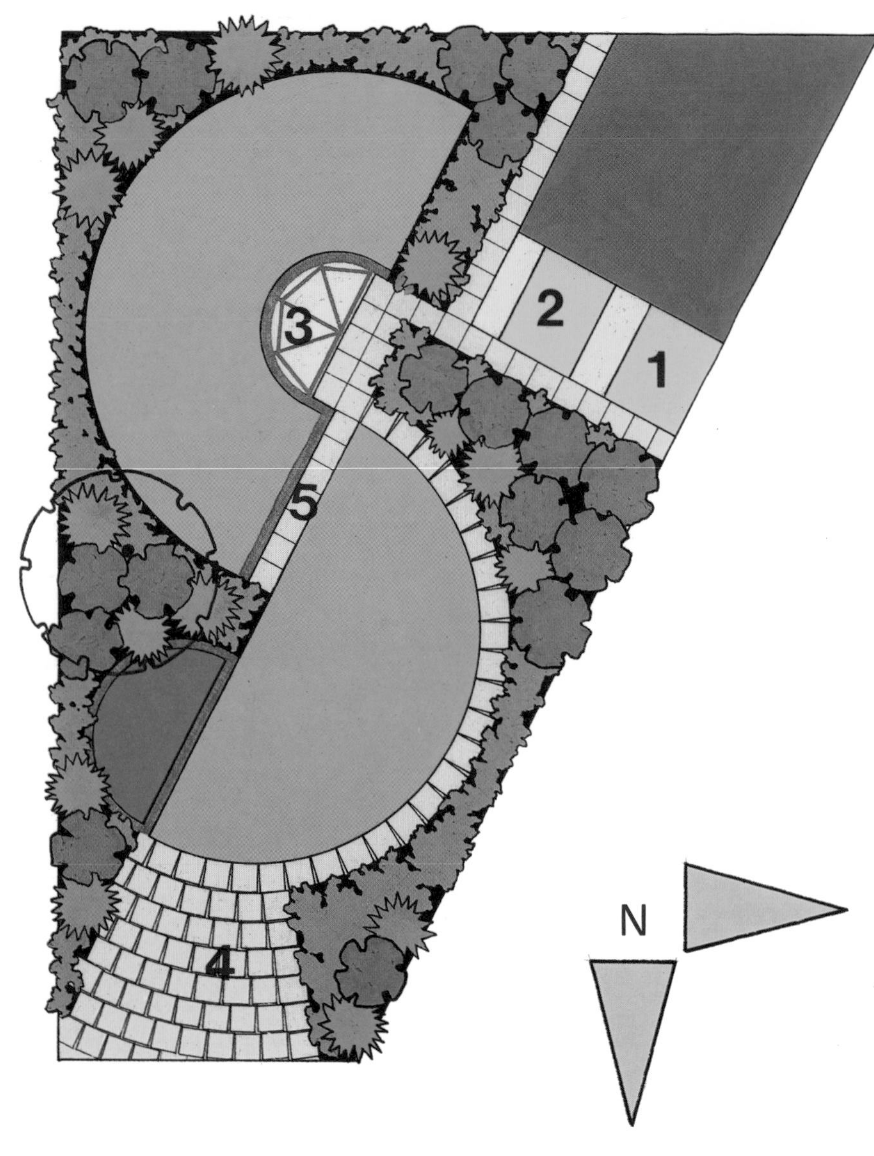

The plan and picture tell their own story — of a beautiful garden that asks to be explored. It offers the promise that the stroll will be fully rewarded.

1 Shed
2 Greenhouse
3 Pergola
4 Patio
5 Step

Lawn

Vegetables

Pool

Shrubs over 1.8 m (6 ft)

Shrubs 1–2 m (3–6 ft)

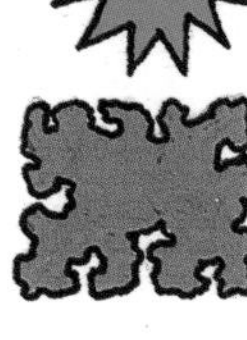
Ground cover or
Herbaceous plants

13 Garden for a Narrowing Plot

The plot that narrows is by no means uncommon — you'll find one or more on every housing estate. And the owner usually wishes he hadn't got it, fearing the difficulty of making an attractive garden within its limiting boundaries. Our design shows one way in which the problems can be solved. First note that, contrary to what you might expect, a geometrical theme has been chosen for the geometrical type of plot. This concentrates the eye on the shapes within the garden rather than on the triangular nature of its boundaries. So we have lawns of octagonal shape, attended by an octagonal pool — the whole served by square paving stones. Next observe that, from the house windows or the patio, the eye is drawn to the summer house and the long border that embraces it rather than to the narrow part of the garden. But it is by no means obvious that the plot is all that narrow at the end — or that it ends at all at the convergence of the two boundaries. The path disappearing between the closely planted trees and shrubs is designed to deceive the eye into recognising that much more might lie beyond. In fact there are only the vegetable plot and the compost heap — important though they are.

The positioning of the summer house is no accident. It provides a pleasing prospect — the pool with its central fountain or statue, the lawns, the shrubs or roses on the far side — and the eye is taken away from the narrower area. The plot that seemed so unpromising has yielded a garden full of promise!

The drawing of the garden as seen from the house windows (overleaf) emphasises the importance of the summerhouse in the design. The angle at which it is approached by the path dividing the twin lawns distracts the mind from any thoughts of the garden's increasing narrowness.

This apart, the summerhouse offers a very pleasant reverse view across the wider part of the garden.

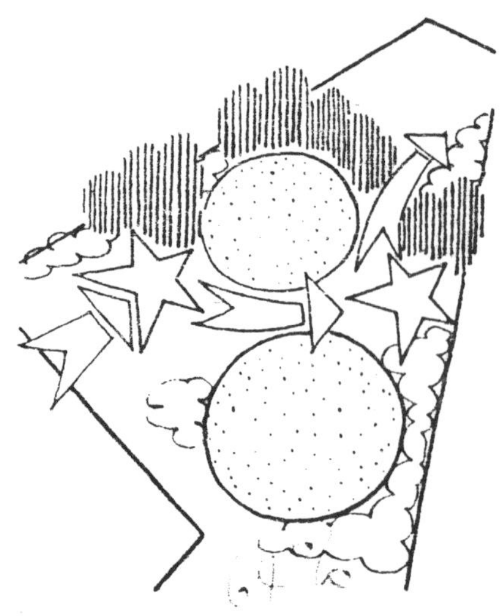

The arrows clearly show how the eye will move through this garden whilst registering the starred focal points.

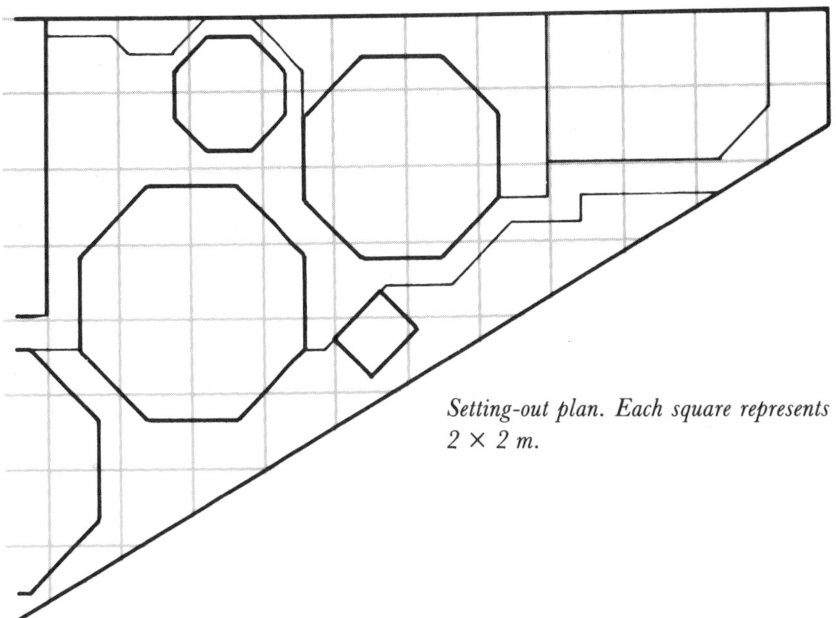

Setting-out plan. Each square represents 2 × 2 m.

FORMAL POOL

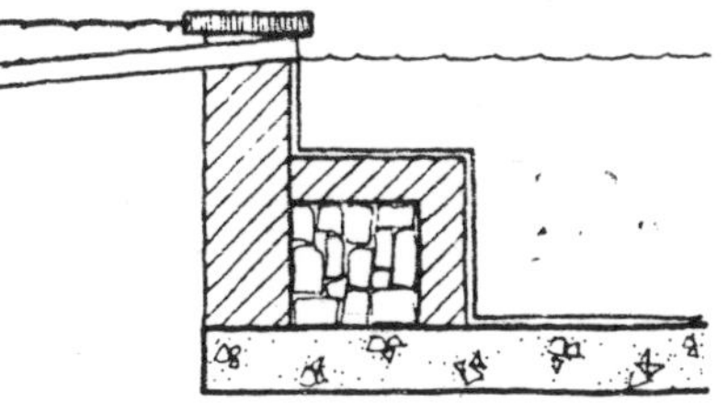

Procedure if a concrete pool is preferred to one using a flexible liner.

Form a 15 cm (6 in.) thick concrete base (1:2:4 cement:sand:aggregate). Lay 20 cm (8 in.) dense concrete block or brick sides with hardcore infill.

Overflow: 5 cm (2 in.) diameter PVC pipe is set at the required water level and takes excess water underground to a soakaway (a deep hole filled with hardcore).

Line the interior of the pool with a sand/cement render mixed with a proprietary waterproofing agent.

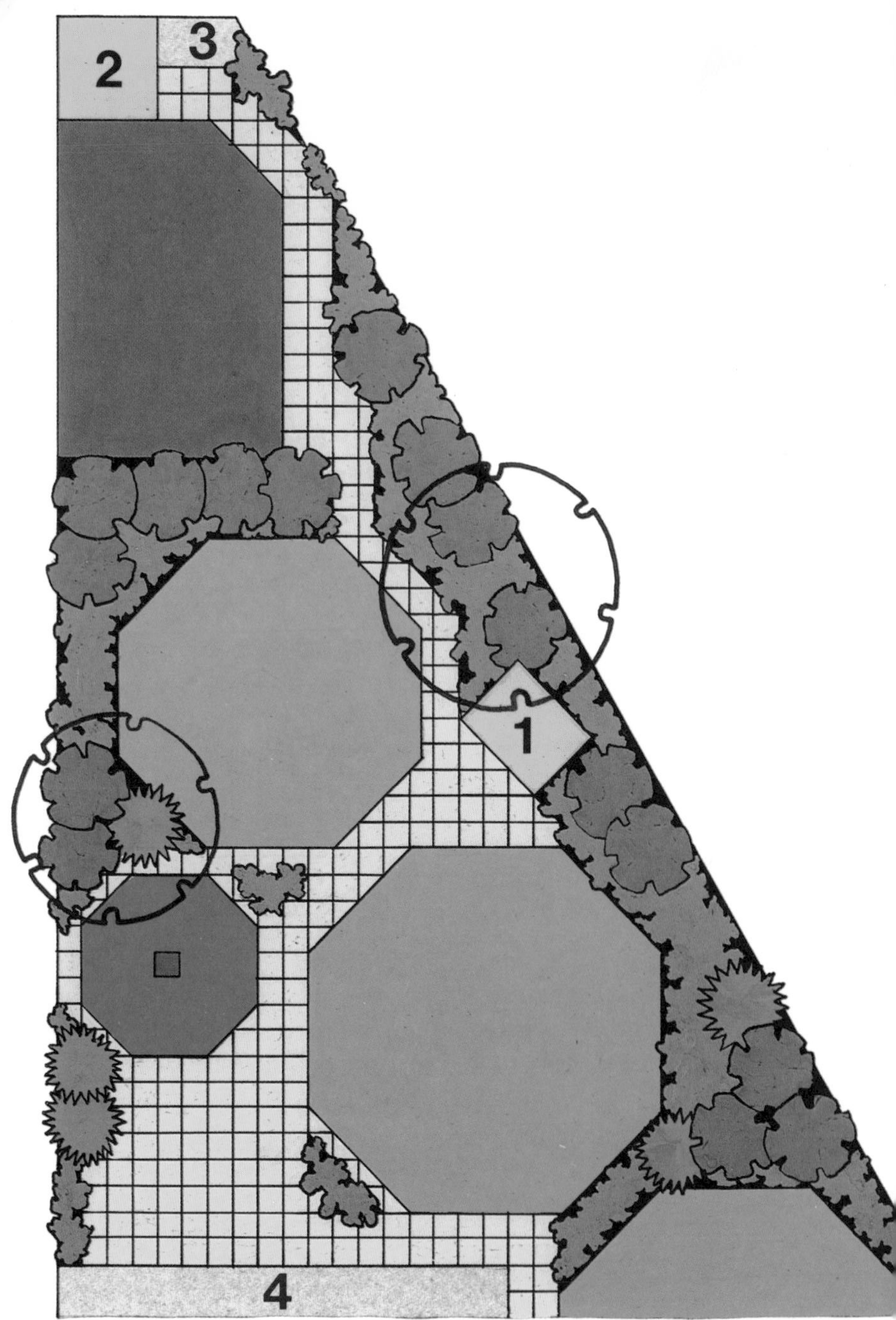
3
2
1
4

Once again, the need is to disguise the awkward shape of the plot. So the eye is led first to the pool, then across to the summerhouse, then up a path . . . which vanishes. Can anyone honestly say that the garden narrows to an insignificant point — without pre-knowledge of the designer's secret?

1 Summerhouse

2 Greenhouse

3 Compost

4 House

 Lawn

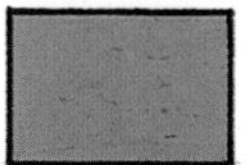 Vegetables

 Pool

 Shrubs over 1.8 m (6 ft)

 Shrubs 1–2 m (3–6 ft)

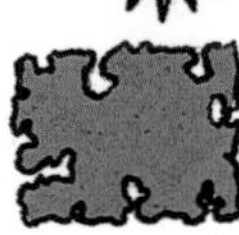 Ground cover or Herbaceous plants

14 Garden for a Young Couple

Marriage brings its problems — not least of which is the planning and laying out of the plot on which the new home is built. It's all the more difficult because, in almost every case, neither partner has had any experience of gardening and plants, let alone design. So, if they are to be helped, it must be with a simple plan and straightforward planting, offering easy upkeep. But they will also want an attractive garden, with a spacious leisure area where they can relax, have summer meals and entertain their friends.

The design we show meets all these needs — in a plot that can be as small as 12 by 8 metres (40 by 27 feet), a not uncommon size these days. The patio is cleanly paved, with an L-shaped pool to cool it and give interest. (If preferred, this could be omitted and replaced with tubs or other containers for seasonal flowers.) Screening the area, on the left, is a fence with climbers, while a wall of openwork blocks, pierced by an arch that gives an intriguing glimpse of the garden beyond. This is approached by stepping stones across the pool. The open side gives on to a level lawn which sweeps round behind the screen wall, inviting inspection of the hidden part of the garden.

The planting is simple, requiring little upkeep and relying, in the main, on two ornamental trees, shrubs, and — along the border on the right — roses. Ground cover is used where possible although, with so little maintenance needed, the newly-weds may well be willing to tackle any weeding as a form of relaxation.

Most young couples have to start off with a small house. And there's no better way of increasing the available space than by creating an outdoor living room. That is exactly what this design succeeds in

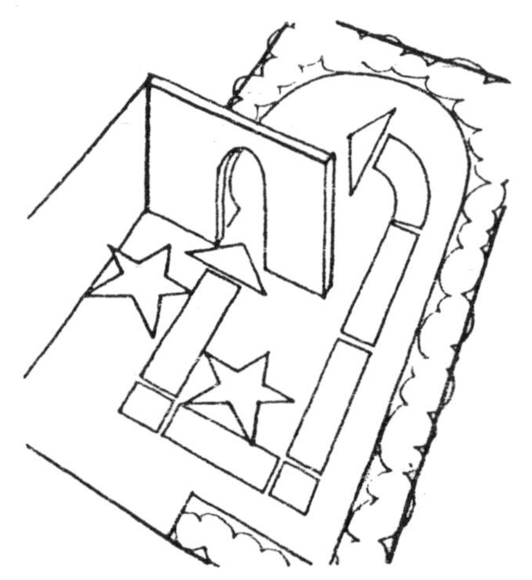

The wall may seem something of a luxury, but it serves many purposes. It cosily contains the paved area, where meals can be taken and friends entertained; the archway offers inviting glimpses of the garden beyond; and the wall can host attractive climbing plants.

doing. Sunshine is trapped, cold winds are warded off, paving allows use after rain, pools and grass bring coolness in hot weather. Here is a place where life can be lived in comfort for many weeks of the year and where informal parties can be held — in much the same way as the Romans passed their leisure hours in their open courtyards.

So there it is — an easily run garden, a pleasing garden, a garden in which the young couple will soon take pride.

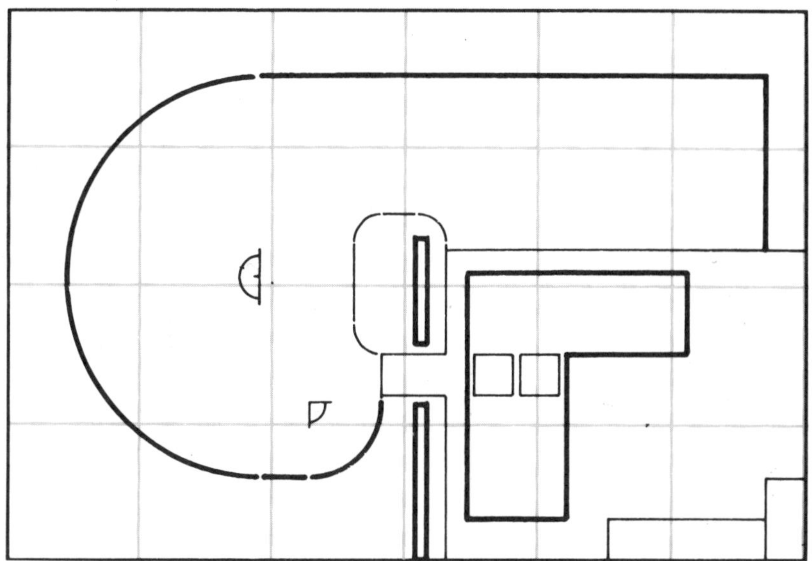

Setting-out plan showing radial points. Each square represents 2 × 2 m.

BRICK SCREEN AND ARCHWAY

Build brick piers to each side of the archway and at each end of the screen, 23 × 23 cm (9 × 9 in.) building up the walling with 11.5 cm ($4\frac{1}{2}$ in.) .'honeycomb' brickwork.

Build the arch with two courses of 23 cm (9 in.) bricks. A temporary timber semi-circular frame should be used to support the brickwork while it sets, and ensure that a true arch is constructed. Notice the 'key bricks in the centre of the arch.

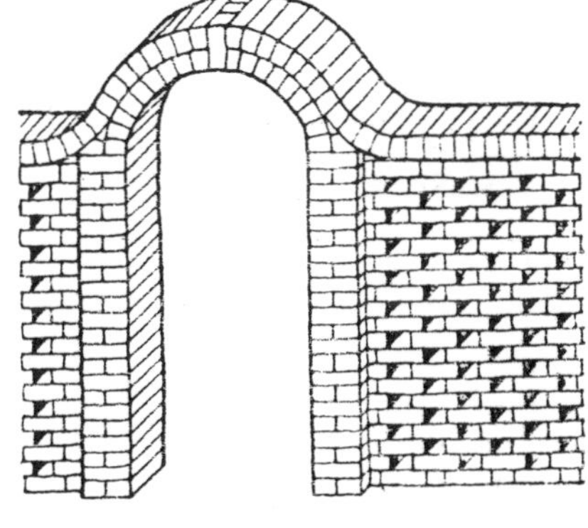

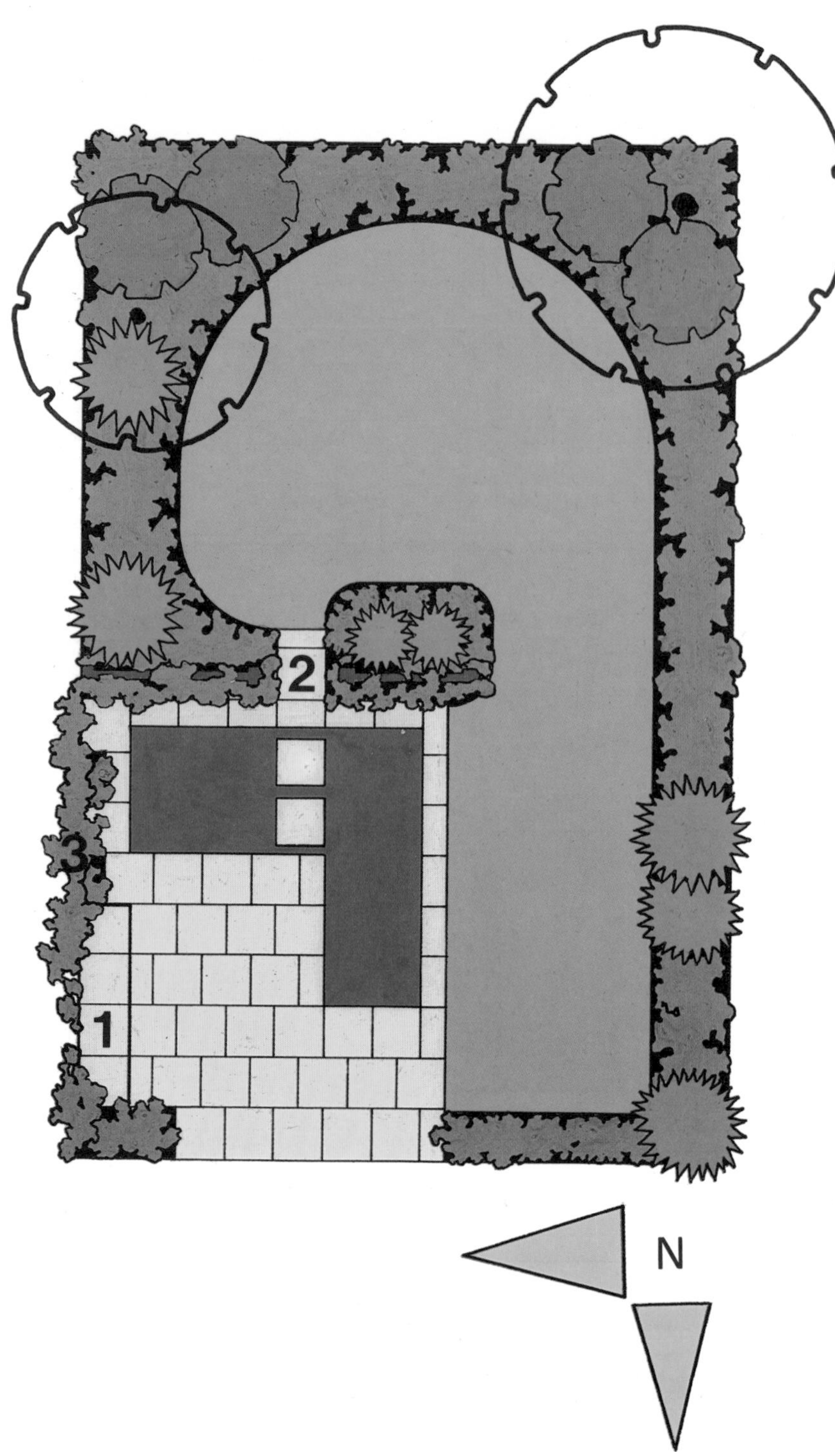
2
3
1
N

The plan shows that this is a garden simple to lay out and straightforward to plant. The young couple will enjoy the limited amount of work necessary and find a speedy reward for their labours.

Lawn

Pool

Shrubs over 1.8 m (6 ft)

Shrubs 1–2 m (3–6 ft)

Ground cover or
Herbaceous plants

1 Seat

2 Arch in wall

3 Climbers

15 Garden for a Growing Family

Keen gardeners with a young family have problems to face over a number of years — problems that are ever changing. The garden must provide facilities for play from an early age — and different kinds of play. At the same time the parents, if they value their garden, will not want to sacrifice all its beauty and the pleasure they derive from gardening.

The design we show tackles them in two ways: the provision of areas for play, and planting that is not too vulnerable — both of which are capable of being easily changed — all within the framework of an attractive lay-out. Two very shallow steps (rounded with no sharp corners) lead on to a smooth paved terrace in an arm of which is sited a sandpit, simply converted into a paddling pool later, and finally into an ornamental one. The lawn, at first, is a plain, kidney-shaped one on which games can be played. Later, it is suggested that a shrub peninsula be built out into it, to give better concealment of the greenhouse and shed, and to give an air of mystery. Beyond the lawn and to the right is a Wendy house which can be replaced by a summerhouse later. The rear area has many possibilities. Until the toddler stage is passed, the whole might well be devoted to food-growing. Later it could become a play area, perhaps with a swing or slide, or even a brick wall against which a ball can be bounced or small cricket played (don't forget to protect the greenhouse!). Or again, the space might be shared between play and vegetables. When, finally, the children grow up, the whole area becomes available for food.

For some years, the planting emphasis should be on small trees and shrubs, with only thornless roses and low-growing perennials. As the children learn to respect plants, choicer subjects can increasingly be used.

All families grow up — and so do gardens. By the time the trees and shrubs have matured, the children will have lost interest in either sandpit or paddling pool, and the Wendy house. So an ornamental

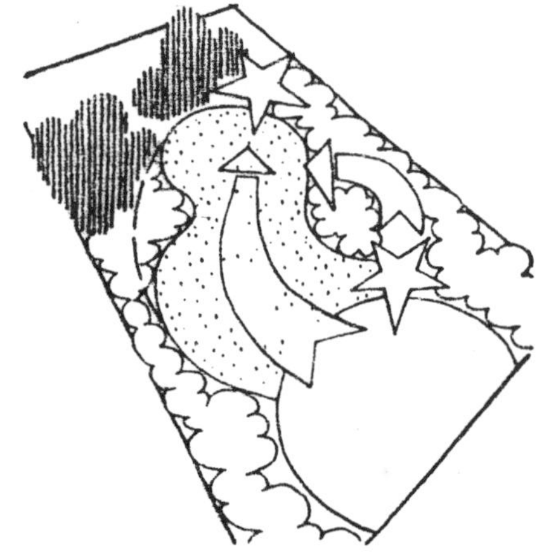

The sandpit/pool and Wendy house/summerhouse are the focal features.

pool and a summerhouse can take their places.

It may be that the lawn — used so long for hectic ball games — will need reseeding with a fine-grass mixture.

In the end, it becomes a pleasant and enjoyable garden for retirement — with only the grandchildren to worry about . . .

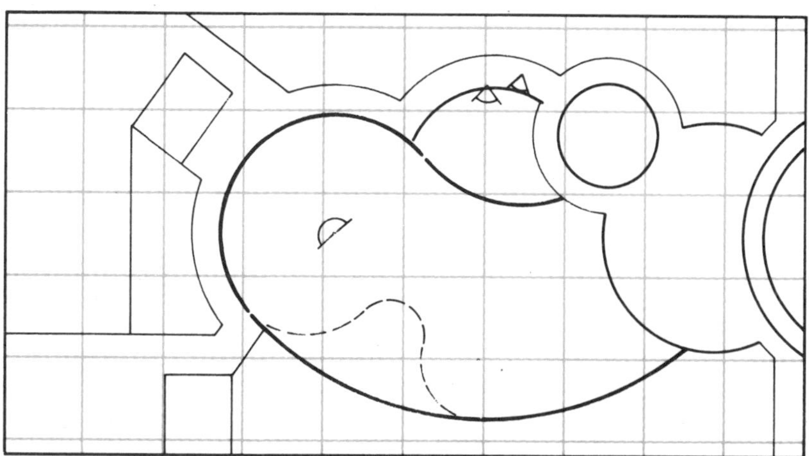

Setting-out plan showing radial points. Each square represents 2 × 2 m.

SANDPIT/POOL

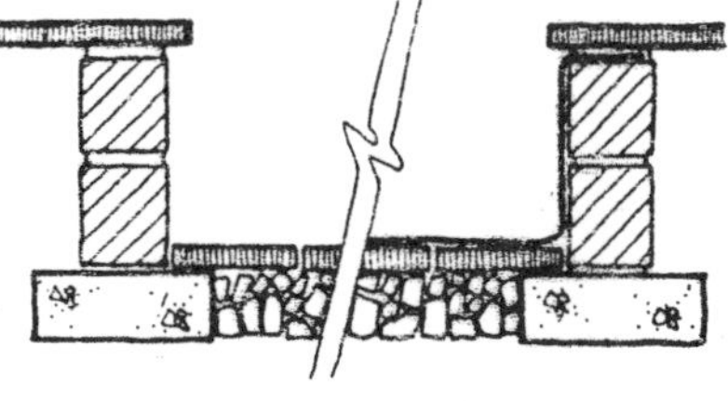

A well-drained sandpit surrounded by paving is easily constructed, and can readily be adapted to make a formal pool in later years.

Excavate a circle 70 cm (2 ft 4 in.) deep. Place concrete 15 cm (6 in.) deep and 40 cm (16 in.) wide around the edge to form the foundation for the low wall. Lay clean rubble or broken bricks in the bottom of the excavation to the level of the foundation.

Using 20 cm (80 in.) thick concrete blocks or bricks, build up the retaining walls to 7 cm (3 in.) below ground level. Place 4 cm ($1\frac{1}{2}$ in.) precast paving slabs in the bottom leaving 1 cm ($\frac{1}{2}$ in.) gaps for good drainage. Bed the surrounding paving on mortar. Fill the pit with clean coarse sand as desired.

To convert to a pool, lift the surrounding paving, spread 5 cm (2 in.) of sand over the floor and lay a butyl liner, re-laying the paving stones to overlap the edge.

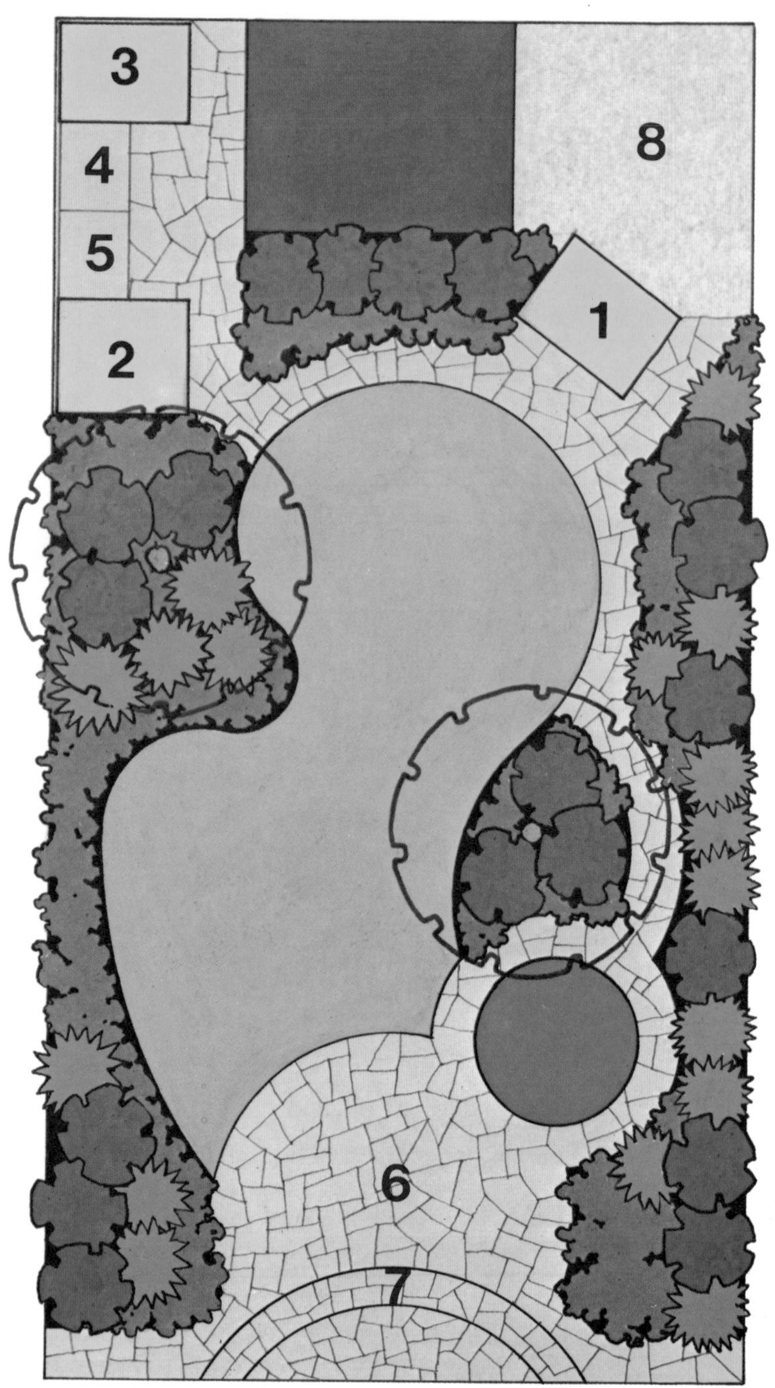
3
4
5
2
8
1
6
7

A garden for the family should appeal to and interest all its members — from the youngest to the oldest. Here there is space and opportunity for children's games and amusement, room for Mother to relax (while keeping an eye on the toddlers), and space for Father to grow flowers and vegetables.

1 Summerhouse
2 Greenhouse
3 Shed
4 Refuse
5 Compost
6 Patio
7 Steps
8 Play area

Lawn

Vegetables

Pool

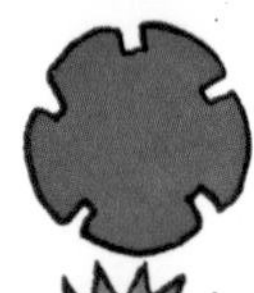
Shrubs over 1.8 m (6 ft)

Shrubs 1–2 m (3–6 ft)

Ground cover or Herbaceous plants

16 Formal Garden

One has only to travel by train through any suburban district to notice how dull and unimaginative are the rows of back gardens. Nearly all are, of course, rectangular plots — some short, some long — but in almost every case the lawn follows the lines of the fence on each side, and is bounded by narrow, straight borders. It's almost as if the owners are hypnotised by the strict rectangularity of their piece of land. But why not, if formality appeals, base the design on other geometrical shapes — the circle, for instance, as in our suggested plan? Here two circular lawns are linked in simple but intriguing fashion by a path that leads from the brick-paved patio around one side of the first lawn and then divides to encompass an architectural feature (statue, sundial or bird bath) before resuming its passage around the further lawn, and thence to the sheltered, three-sided bench — a pleasant spot in which to rest and gaze back down the garden. The twin circles within the rectangular plot create interesting shapes for the planting of trees — one on each side — shrubs, roses and herbaceous subjects. The central feature simply begs to be surrounded with massed geraniums or petunias in summer and daffodils, hyacinths or tulips in spring.

Amenities include, on one side of the patio, a small pool and on the other, a permanent barbecue. Instead of a vegetable plot, an area is provided — alongside the bench — for containers in which tomatoes, potatoes and other crops can be grown.

Seen from the house or patio, as in the illustration overleaf, the effect is that of a green-carpeted stage, with colourful, graceful scenery and interesting props — the quiet pool on the left, the brick barbecue opposite, the central statue, sundial or bird bath, the seat dominating the backcloth. It is

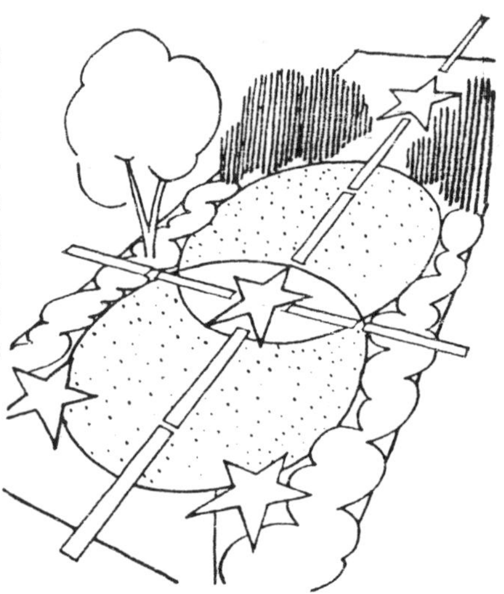

Formality appeals to many gardeners, and the main features in this garden are carefully disposed around and on the central axis, culminating in the sheltered bench at the far end.

not difficult to imagine the players — family, friends — who will bring the stage to life with pleasant informality.

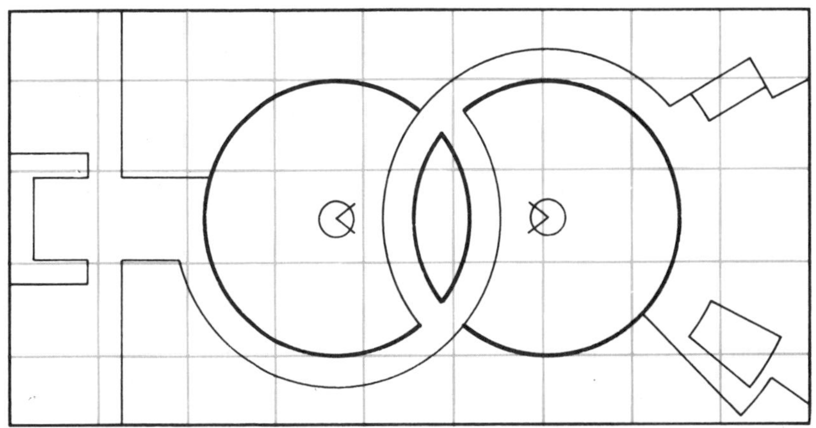

Setting-out plan showing radial points. Each square represents 2 × 2 m.

ARBOUR

Overall dimensions: 300 cm (10 ft) long, 198 cm (6 ft 6 in.) deep, 260 cm (8 ft 6 in.) high.

Materials: Two panels of standard fencing 183 × 183 cm (6 × 6 ft); three 183 × 60 cm (6 × 2 ft) standard trellis panels; three 90 × 60 cm (3 × 2 ft) trellis panels; six 7.5 × 7.5 × 245 cm (3 in. × 3 in. × 8 ft) high posts; four 15 × 2.5 × 198 cm (6 in. × 1 in. × 6 ft 6 in.) lengths of planed soft wood to form the top of the frame.

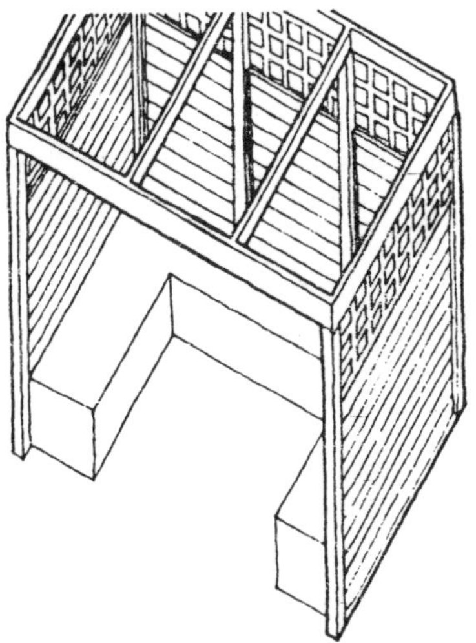

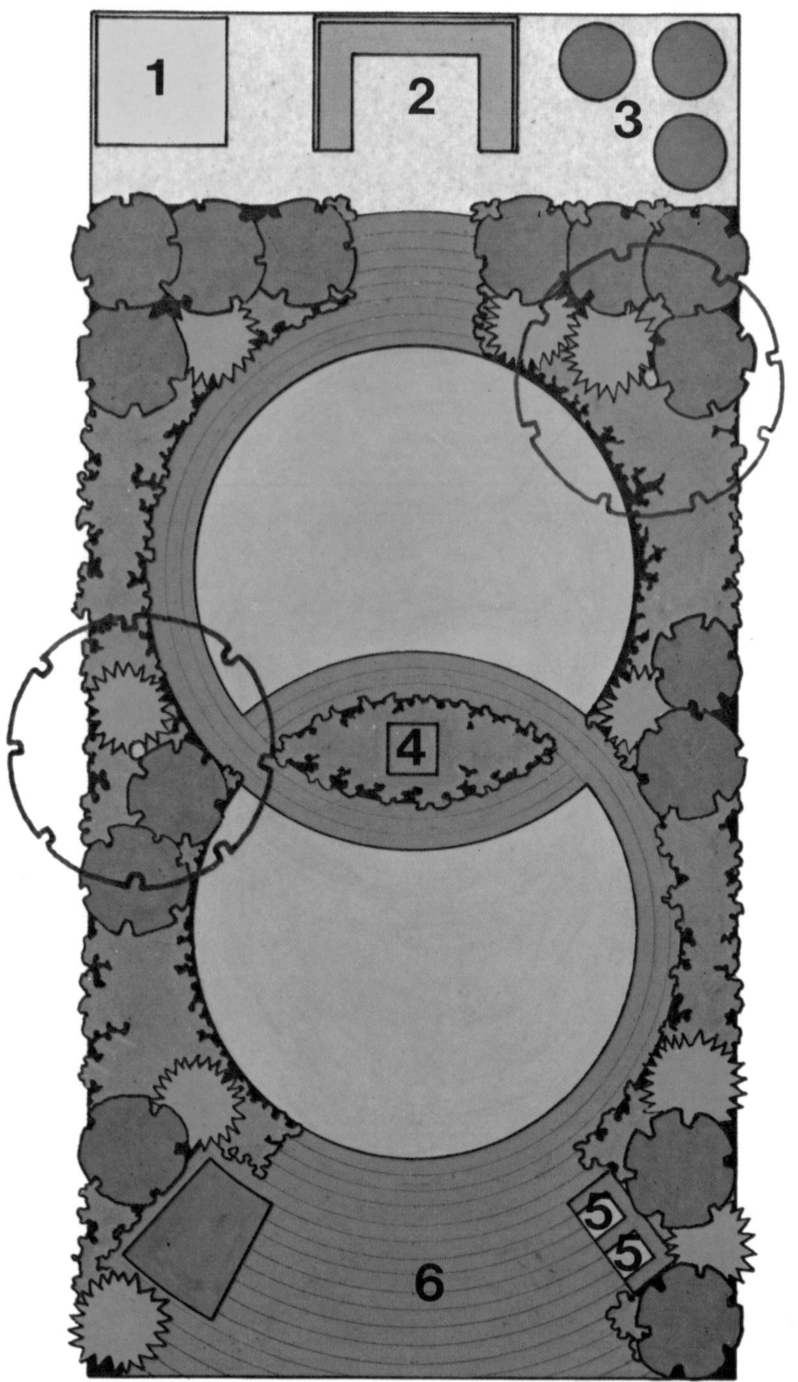
1
2
3
4
5
5
6

Although symmetry is the keynote of the formal garden, a perfectly symmetrical arrangement of the component parts would run the risk of being uninteresting, even boring. So, except for the twin lawns, which are identical and exactly opposed on each side of the central stone ornament, good balance is preferred — the pool with the barbeque; the tree on the left with that, further back, on the right; the path skirting the lower lawn on the right with that linking with it on the left.

1 Shed

2 Arbour

3 Strawberry tub

Potato tub

Refuse tub

4 Statue/birdbath

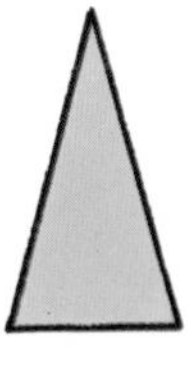

N

5 Barbecue

6 Brick patio

Lawn

Pool

Gravel/concrete

Shrubs over 1.8 m (6 ft)

Shrubs 1–2 m (3–6 ft)

Ground cover or
Herbaceous plants

17 Garden for a Retired Couple

There comes a time when, however willing the spirit, the flesh is not up to putting in the number of hours in the garden it did. In other words, it is a time when leisure is all-important. So the need for the retired (or ageing) couple is a garden that is tranquil, restful and easily run.

A major part of the design with these aims in mind is taken up with a stone-and-brick patio (pergola-covered to provide shelter, dappled shade, and space for entertaining), a semi-circular pool, and a long, curving lawn — all capable of easy maintenance. The same can be said of the planting — trees, shrubs, some perennials, all thickly mulched to deter weeds.

Retired people often enjoy growing a few vegetables, and pottering in a greenhouse. Provision is made for both — though, with digging in mind, the area of the kitchen garden is kept small, but still large enough to give supplies of vegetables and fruit for many months of the year. And that is important for people old enough and with time enough, to appreciate the freshness and flavour of home-grown food.

Yet the accent, in this garden, is on freedom: freedom to do only as much or little work as the happy couple feel like, freedom — and space — to laze, to sleep, to dream.

Our retired couple, relaxing on the patio, command a view of the garden in all directions. All is linked by the curving lawn. Bold, close planting hides and protects the productive plot and the greenhouse or shed.

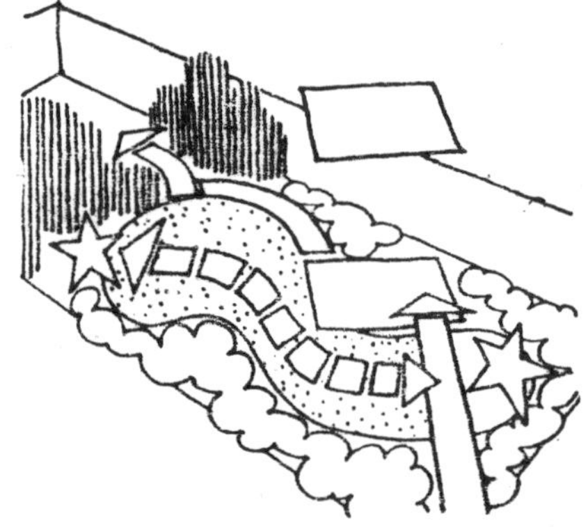

This design, suited to a narrow plot, attracts the eye along the arrows to the starred focal points. It would fit the plots on which so many semi-detached houses are built. The limitations of the plot are disguised by the disposition of the spaces, the starred features, the outlines and the angles at which they are set.

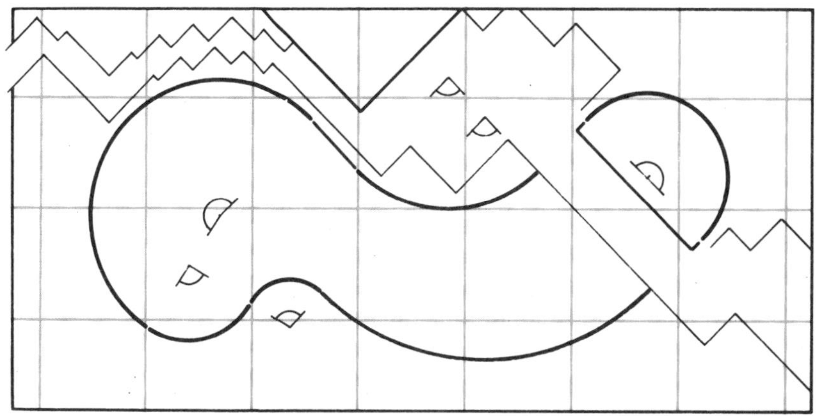

Setting-out plan showing radial points. Each square represents 2 × 2 m.

RAISED PLANTER/ BOUNDARY WALL

The construction is similar to that in Garden 10 except that the walling containing the soil should be 22 cm (9 in.) thick.

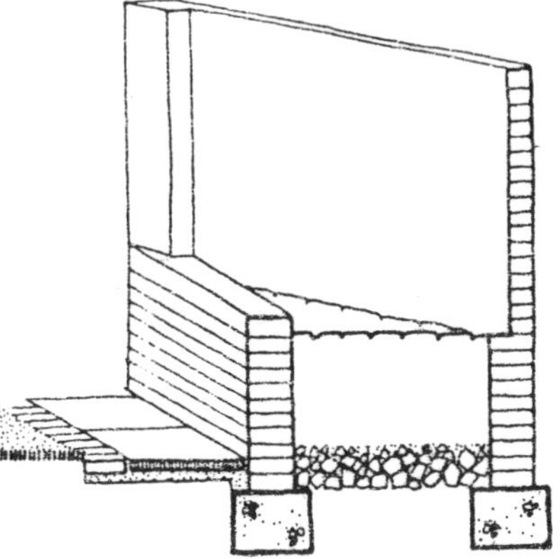

Before placing topsoil in the planter, fill the bottom with 10 cm (4 in.) of stones or rubble, covered with a layer of gravel and then sand. This will assist drainage, which will be further helped if a few vertical joints are left open just above ground level.

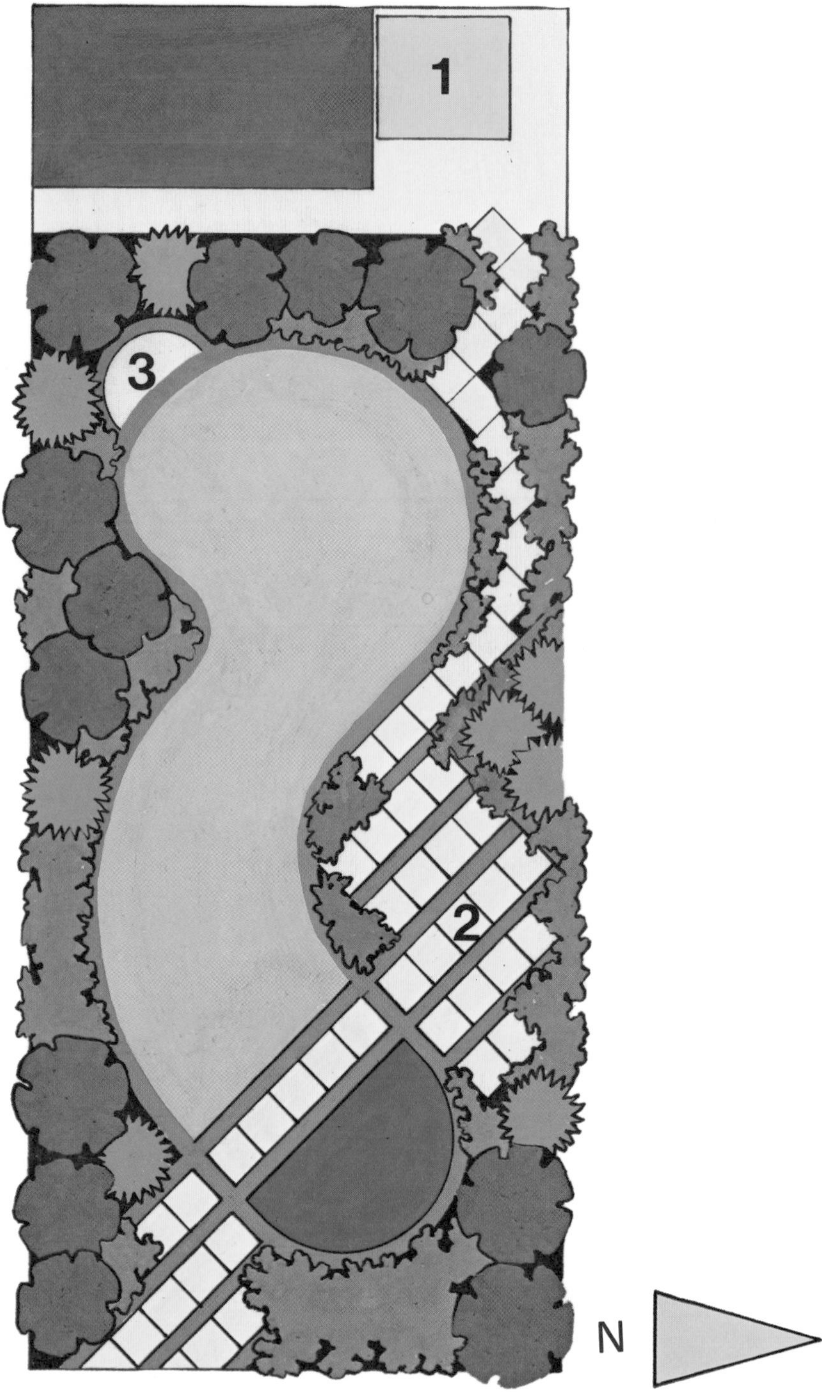

1

3

2

N

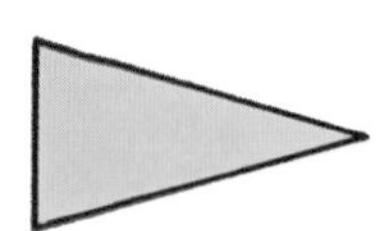

The patio is the central feature of this design, the climber-clad pergola offering the quiet, sheltered retreat which a retired couple can enjoy to the full. It commands a view of the garden in all directions, from the pool to the focal point of the statue or birdbath. All is linked by the curving lawn. Bold, close planting hides and protects the productive plot and the greenhouse or shed.

1 Greenhouse

2 Patio with pergola

3 Seat or statue

 Lawn

 Vegetables

 Pool

 Gravel/concrete

 Shrubs over 1.8 m (6 ft)

 Shrubs 1–2 m (3–6 ft)

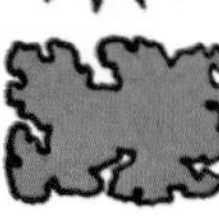 Ground cover or Herbaceous plants

18 Low Maintenance Garden

One way to create a garden needing little maintenance is to let Nature take a prominent part. And that is the way chosen for our design for a plot of modest size. It is dominated by a mature tree (if this does not figure in your site, it is worth knowing that trees up to 6 metres (20 feet) tall can be ordered from, and planted by, specialist firms). Grass is, of course, the most natural cover for the major area of the garden — but grass needs frequent mowing. Choose it if you don't mind this quite pleasant exercise — an air cushion (hover) machine would be the most suitable kind. But gravel, which we have shown, needs no attention except an occasional raking and treatment once a year with a simazine weedkiller to keep it clean. Circular log cuts make an unusual and attractive pathway: unlike paving stones they need little or no sweeping, and preserve the natural appearance of the garden.

The bole of the tree is surrounded by a timber seat. Immediately behind is a raised bed of shrubs, retained by logs driven upright into the ground. Opposing the tree is a group of foliage shrubs, with climbers — which can be wisteria or clematis, firethorn or variegated ivy — although purists, wishing to conform with the natural theme, may prefer such hedgerow climbers as honeysuckle and sweet briar. The garden is approached by three gently angled steps, retained with stout logs and attended by groups of wooden tubs for shrubs, bulbs, crops, or seasonal flowers. The rear areas are occupied by a summerhouse (or shed) and, protected by a screen of bamboo, a space for compost heap or bonfire.

The Low Maintenance Garden could perhaps be called the Organised Wild Garden — for there's little doubt it will appeal to the lover of countryside plants, birds, and wildlife generally. It could, if you like, be planted entirely with species that are to be found growing in the woods, fields and hedgerows.

This is not only the most natural-looking garden in our collection but the simplest design. Descend the broad steps and stroll down past the tree — the only major feature — till you come to the summerhouse. But there's more to it than that . . .

Remember that it is illegal to dig up and remove any wild plant without the permission of the owner of the land. Fortunately many of the more common kinds are easily raised from seed, which several seed firms can supply.

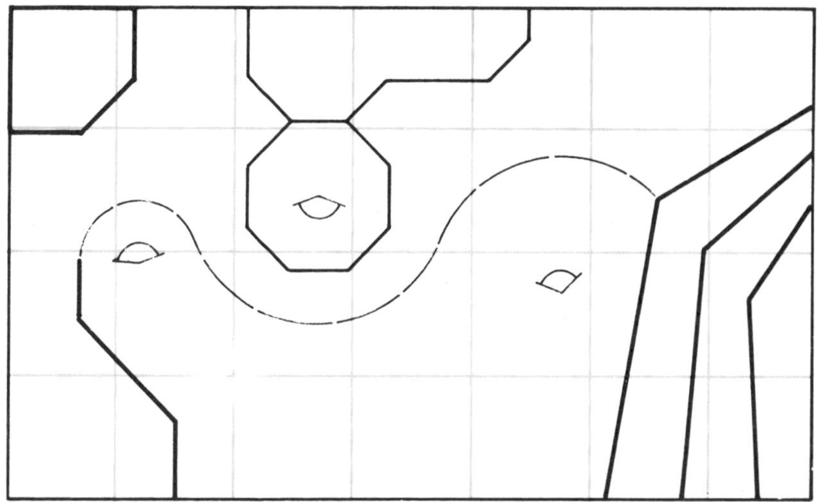

Setting-out plan showing radial points. Each square represents 2 × 2 m.

LOG PAVING AND STEPS

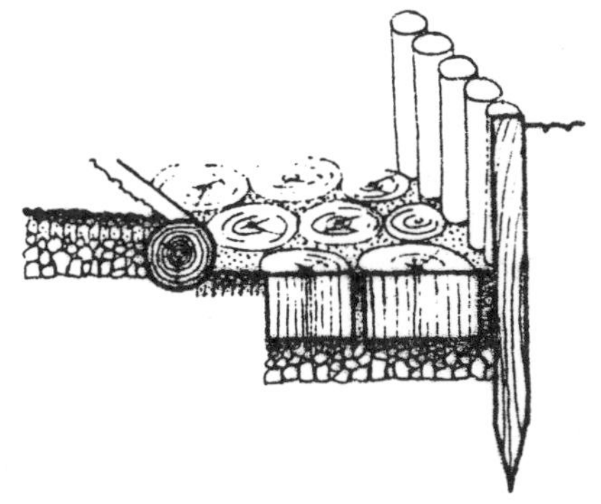

Log paving: Cut, or order, 15 cm (6 in.) sections of suitable tree trunks. Excavate 22 cm (9 in.) of soil. Lay 7 cm (3 in.) of crushed stone or gravel over the area to be paved to ensure good drainage. Lay the sections as close as possible and infill the gaps with gravel or stone chippings.

Log step: Set 15 cm (6 in.) diameter logs in place. Hammer in 5 × 5 × 30 cm (2 × 2 × 12 in.) stakes behind the ends of the logs and secure with strong nails. Backfill behind each log to form a step with 10 cm (4 in.) of hardcore, 2.5 cm (1 in.) of hoggin and 2.5 cm (1 in.) of gravel.

Raised bed: Hammer a row of 90 cm (36 in.) long and 50–70 cm (2–3 in.) diameter larch poles into the ground, and saw off level 45 cm (18 in.) above ground level. Infill with soil.

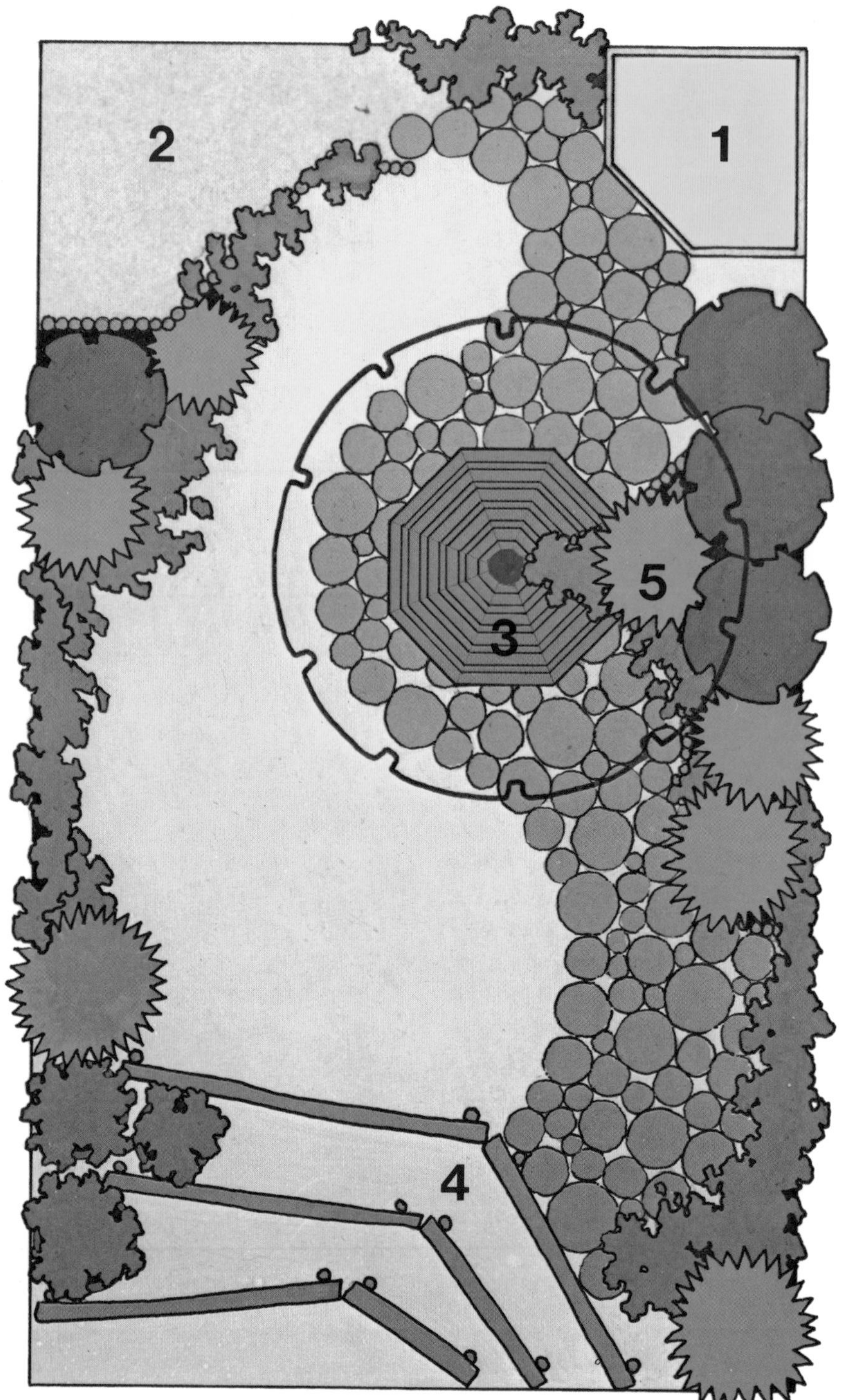
1
2
3
4
5

The plan shows the interesting use made of tree trunk off-cuts — a timber yard is the best source — which, carefully laid, provide an all-weather walk-way to the seating around the tree and the summerhouse beyond.

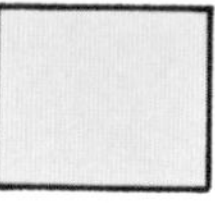
Gravel

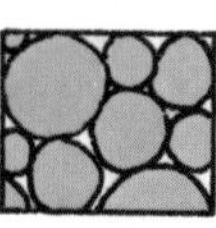
Logs

Shrubs over 1.8 m (6 ft)

Shrubs 1–2 m (3–6 ft)

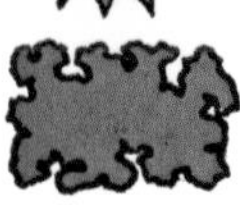
Ground cover or Herbaceous plants

1 Summerhouse

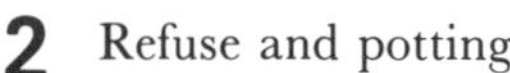
2 Refuse and potting

3 Bench under tree

4 Steps

5 Raised planter

19 Garden with the Accent on Water

There's a magic about water that cannot be denied. It offers reflections, movement, music — and tranquillity. So it is not surprising that, to many, it is a highly desirable feature of the modern garden. The garden we show will be recognised by visitors to the 1979 Chelsea Flower Show as the one designed for the Daily Express by Guy Farthing, and which won for them a gold medal for the third year running.

There are three linked pools, all hexagonal in shape and conforming with the geometrical theme on which the design is based. The upper, right-hand, pool has a bubbling fountain which sends the water cascading into the middle pool and thence — stilled by the stepping-stone bridge — to the third pool from which it is invisibly pumped back to the first pool.

Inevitably there is a great deal of paving, for it is no good having a sophisticated arrangement of pools without plenty of space surrounding it — space for relaxing and listening to the splashing of the water, for eating meals in its presence, for watching the darting movement of fish, dragon flies and other wildlife that water always attracts.

Yet the water feature is but a component part — though an important one — of a garden whose twin lawns, trees, shrubs and roses, flower-filled containers and productive area combine to create a garden that is both beautiful and exciting.

There are two focal points in this garden. If you sit on the elevated right-hand part of the patio, your gaze will be focused on the sheltered seat overlooking the left-hand pool. But take the two steps down to the lower area and you find yourself looking over the stepping-stone bridge and across the twin lawns to the statuary in the distant right-hand corner.

It is conceded that this is not a cheap garden to lay out, mainly because of the large number of paving stones needed. But, as was proved at the Chelsea Show, it has great character and charm, and the years of enjoyment it will provide

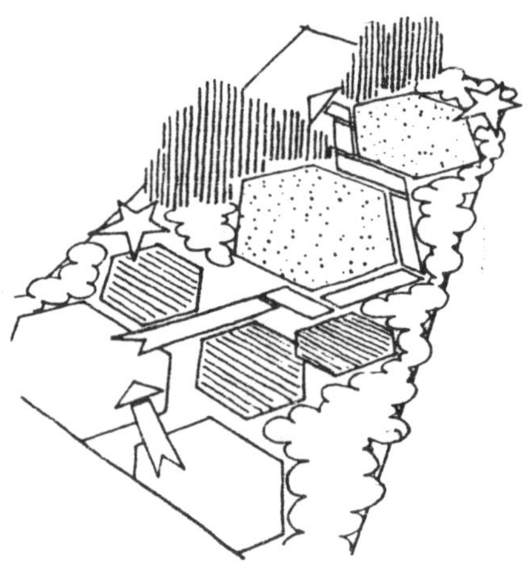

The arrows show the eye's movement and the stars, the two focal points.

may be thought to justify the initial cost.

The spacious, split-level patio offers full scope for outdoor leisure pursuits, and the entertainment of friends in gracious style. Not every garden can provide the music of water in such a setting as accompaniment to a summer's evening barbecue!

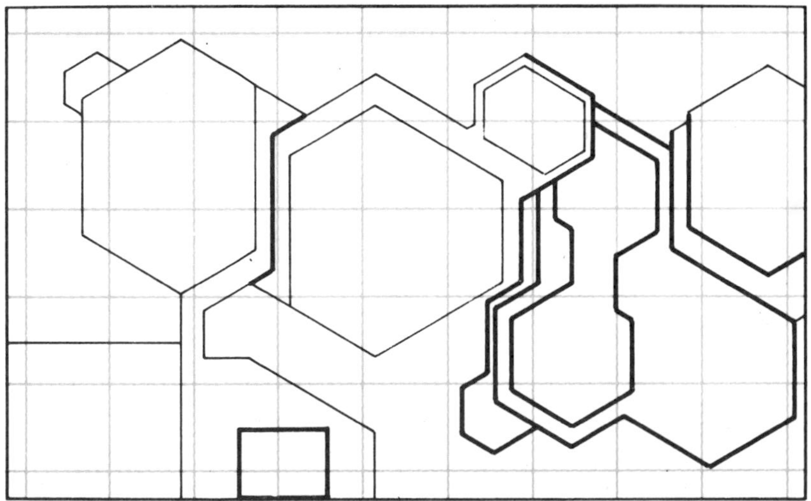

Setting-out plan. Each square represents 2 × 2 m.

WATERFALL

Build pools on two levels, lining them with either butyl or waterproof render.

It is important to provide sufficient lip or overhang, say 5 cm (2 in.), in order to throw the water into the lower pool. The wider the waterfall, the more powerful must be the pump (submersible) to recirculate the water and to throw it over the fall.

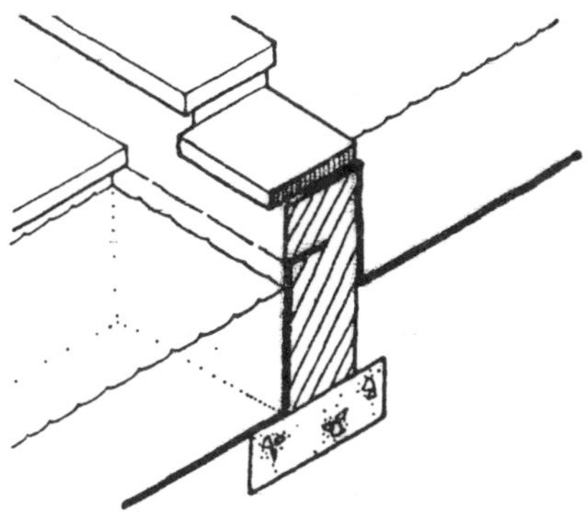

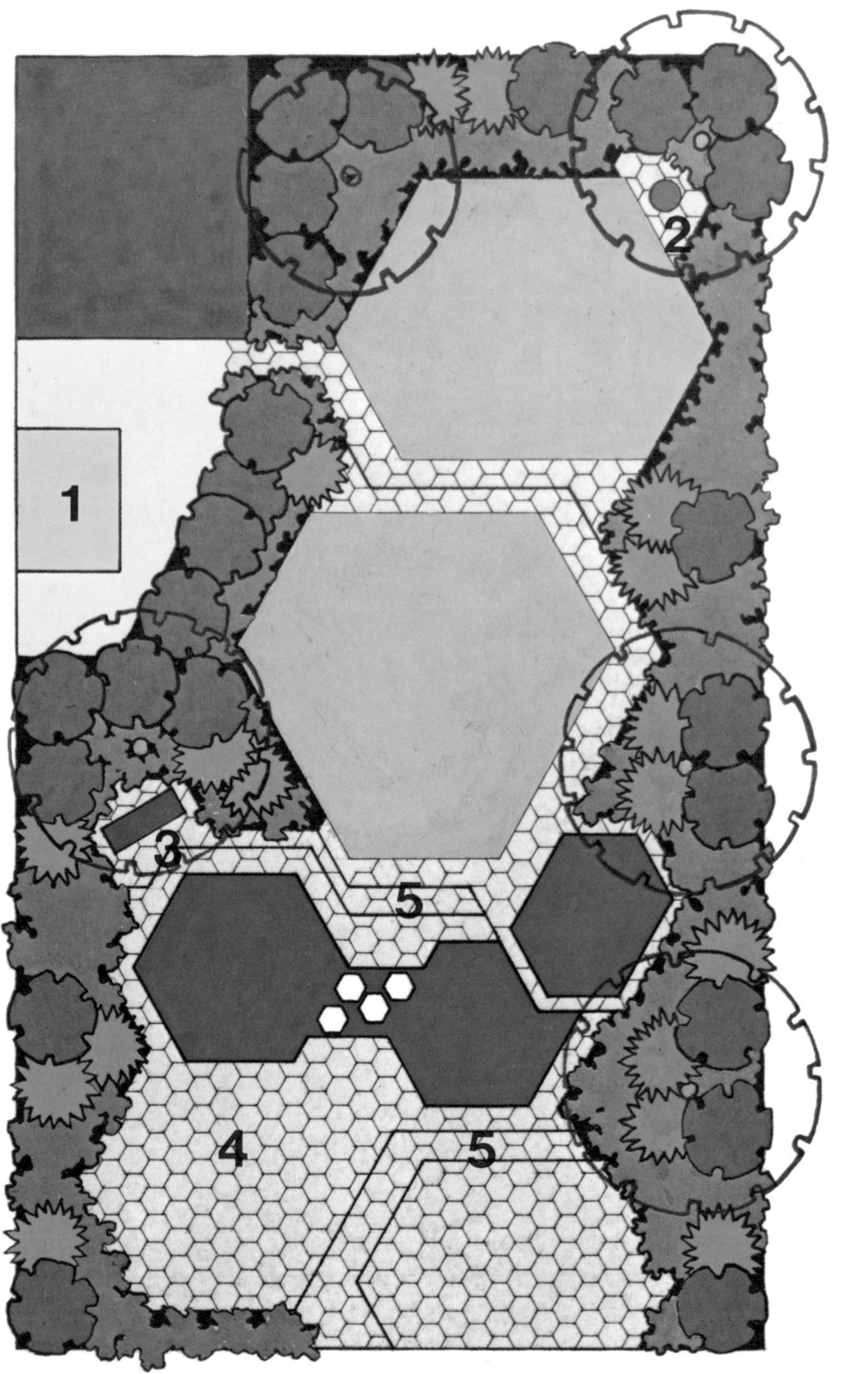
1
2
3
5
4
5

The plan view reveals how the garden is based on the concept of the hexagon. But it is not so geometrically exact that the hexagons are all perfect shapes; the fact cannot be detected at eye level and is in any case unnecessary.

1 Greenhouse

2 Statue

3 Bench

4 Patio

5 Steps

 Lawn

 Vegetables

 Pool

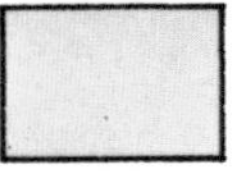 Gravel or concrete

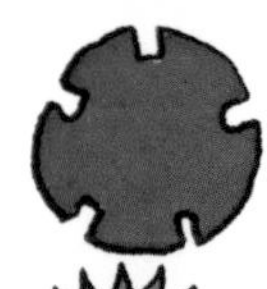 Shrubs over 1.8 m (6 ft)

 Shrubs 1–2 m (3–6 ft)

 Ground cover or Herbaceous plants

20 Garden with a Swimming Pool

Can a swimming pool be accommodated in a garden of modest size without spoiling its appearance? No problem — if it is tackled in a sensible way. In the garden we have designed, the whole of the swimming pool area has been accommodated in the rear half of the plot, leaving the front half intact as a garden. But this does not prevent the pool being sited in pleasant surroundings.

Assuming that the average depth of the pool is two metres (6 feet) — it will probably be one metre (three feet) at the shallow end and two and a half or three metres (eight or nine feet) at the deep end — it follows that if the pool is excavated to an average depth of one metre (four feet), that volume of soil is available to be spread around the site to raise the surrounding level by 60 cm (2 ft), leaving the pool at the desired depth. It is therefore approached from the garden by four 15–cm (6–in.) steps.

A swimming pool needs filtering and probably (in a temperate climate) heating as well, so provision is made for a shed to house the equipment. A changing room is also desirable and this is placed in the far corner. Between these two sheds a series of solar heating panels has been sited. These are at their most efficient in summer, and can greatly reduce heating costs. On two sides the pool is sheltered by a variety of flowering shrubs — an extension, in fact, of the border bounding the path and lawn of the garden below. On the opposing side another border culminates in thickly planted shrubs, dominated by an ornamental tree to conceal the utility part of the pool area.

The siting of the pool in the back half of the garden, its elevated position, and its partial concealment by planting on each side of the steps all combine to mould it unobtrusively into the garden scene.

This section sketch indicates why it is unnecessary to expend time, labour and perhaps money in excavating to the full depth of the intended pool. A large amount — up to half — of the removed soil can be used to build up the surrounding ground to give the full depth required. This technique also solves the problem of disposing of the excavated soil.

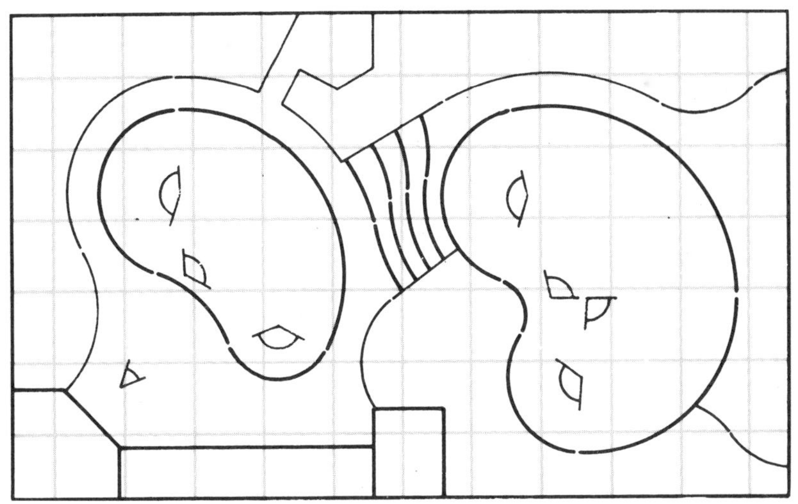

Setting-out plan showing radial points. Each square represents 2 × 2 m.

SWIMMING POOL

Diagram right shows only the principle of the mechanical plant required. The construction of the pool and the installation of the plant should be left to a reputable swimming pool contractor.

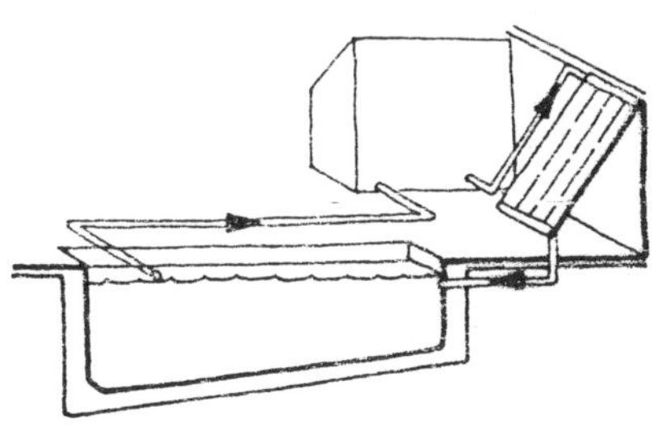

To ensure a high standard of hygiene, the water in the pool must be regularly filtered by pumping the water out of the pool and through a filter housed in a suitable shed, and returning it to the pool via underground pipes.

A gas or oil boiler can also be installed and connected to the system to heat the pool water, but solar panels have been proved to be most effective in warming pool water in the summer, and save the cost of gas or oil fuel.

The panels must face within 5 degrees of due south for maximum efficiency. Their area should be about half the surface area of the pool, but take advice from the manufacturers. The series of panels can easily be connected to the filter system and require no pump or pipework.

It is essential to cover the pool at night with an insulating floating blanket in all but the warmest weather to keep the heat in. Room should be made in the shed for chemicals, nets and vacuuming equipment for cleaning the pool walls and floor.

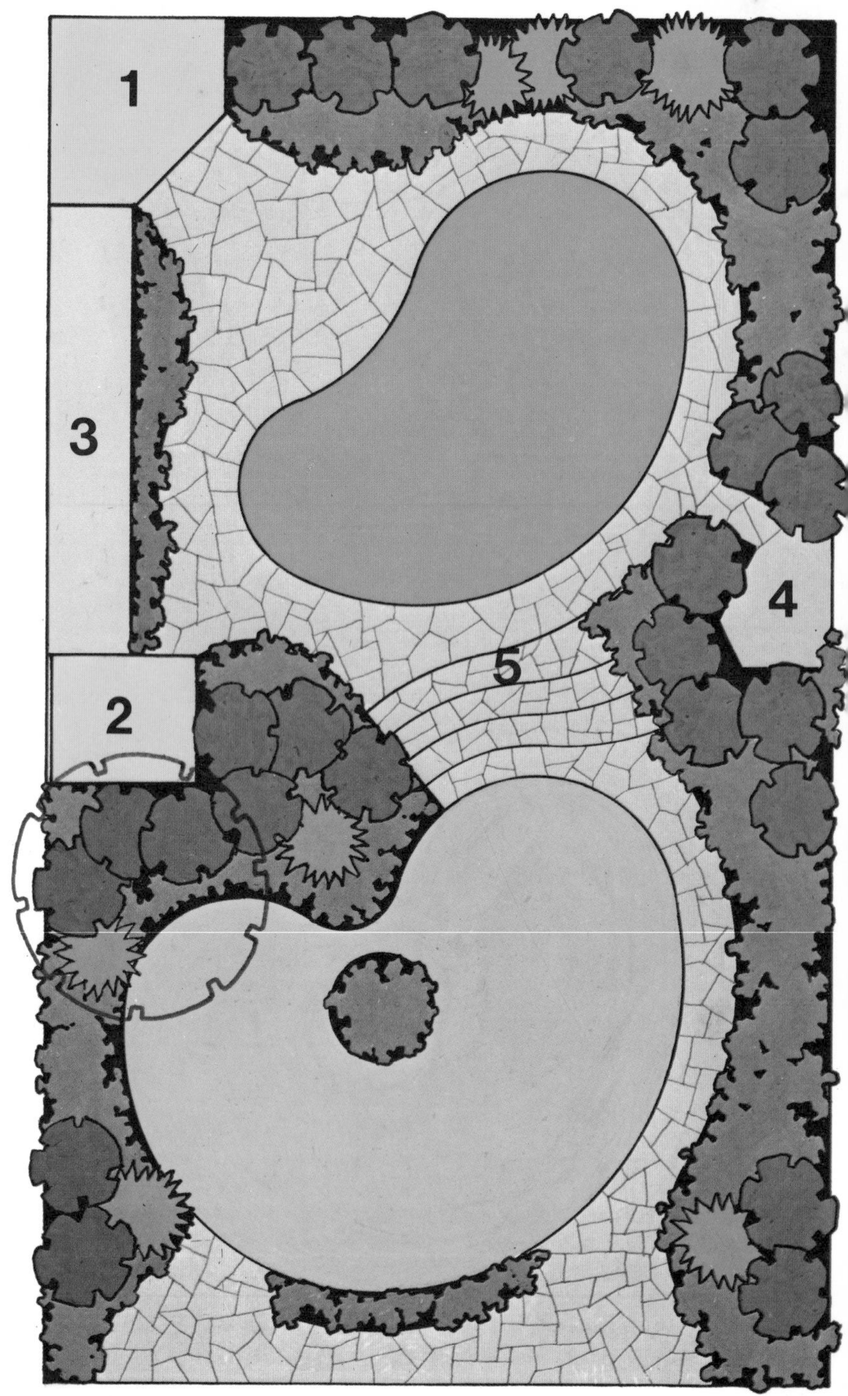
1
3
2
4
5

The curving shape of the pool is echoed by that of the lawn, which affords a pleasant, well-sheltered place for sunbathing after the swim.

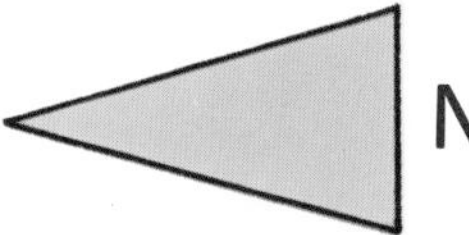

1 Changing room/summerhouse

2 Plant/filter room

3 Solar heating panels

4 Refuse

5 Steps

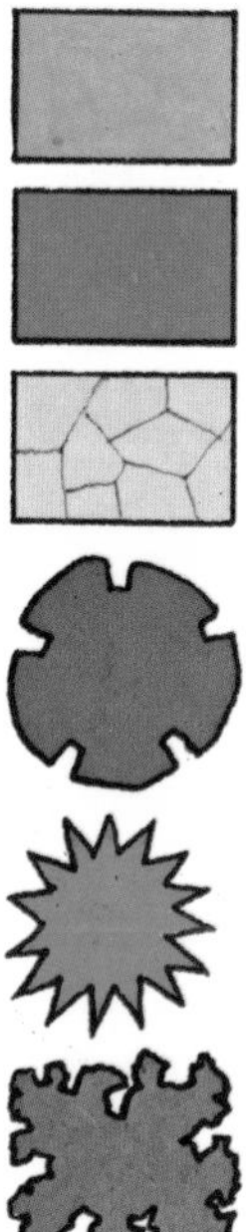

Lawn

Pool

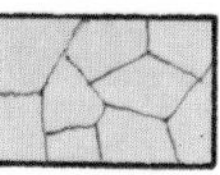

Paving

Shrubs over 1.8 m (6 ft)

Shrubs 1–2 m (3–6 ft)

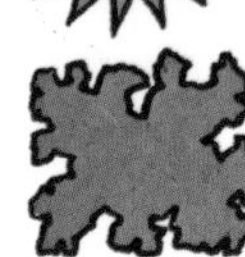

Ground cover or Herbaceous plants

Garden Plant Choice

D = Deciduous E = Evergreen SE = Semi-Evergreen

ORNAMENTAL TREES

Plant name Species or variety	*Ultimate height*	*Flowering period*	*Characteristics*
Acer (D) griseum (paperbark maple)	5 m + (16 ft +)	—	Orange-brown, peeling bark, attractive in winter
negundo 'variegatum' (ash-leafed maple)	8 m + (26 ft +)	—	Leaves conspicuously bordered silvery-white
pseudoplatanus 'Brilliantissimum'	5 m + (16 ft +)	—	Young foliage glowing shrimp-pink in spring
Arbutus (E) unedo (strawberry tree)	5 m (16 ft)	Sep–Nov	Small, bell-shaped white flowers; red fruit
Betula (D) pendula (silver birch)	20 m (66 ft)	—	A graceful tree with white bark; autumn tints
p. Youngii	6 m (20 ft)	—	This is a more weeping form of silver birch
Catalpa (D) bignonioides (Indian bean tree)	6 m + (20 ft +)	July–Aug	Large, heart-shaped leaves; white flowers
Cercis (D) siliquastrum (Judas tree)	8 m (26 ft +)	April–May	Rosy-lilac flowers are produced on bare branches
Cotoneaster (SE) hybridus pendulus	5 m + (16 ft +)	May–June	Cascades of red berries in autumn and winter
Crataegus (D) oxyacantha (syn. coccinea plena) 'Paul's Scarlet'	5 m (16 ft)	May	A double, scarlet form of the May or Hawthorn
Gleditsia (D) triacanthos 'Sunburst'	6 m (20 ft)	—	A striking tree with bright yellow young foliage
Ilex (E) (holly) aquifolium	10 m + (33 ft +)	—	Common holly; berries only on female trees

Plant name *Species or variety*	*Ultimate height*	*Flowering period*	*Characteristics*
a. 'Golden King'	4 m + (13 ft +)	—	Bold yellow margins; produces attractive berries
a. 'J. C. van Tol'	4 m + (13 ft +)	—	An almost spineless form; good for berries
a. pyramidalis	4 m + (13 ft +)	—	Pyramidal in outline, and free-fruiting
Laburnum (D) alpinum (Scotch laburnum)	8 m + (26 ft +)	May–June	Lovely yellow tassels of bright yellow flowers
'Vossii''	6 m + (20 ft +)	May–June	This is a beautiful form and very free-flowering
Liquidambar (D) styraciflua (sweet gum)	6 m + (20 ft +)	—	Grown for its spectacular crimson autumn colour
Magnolia (D) soulangiana	6 m (20 ft)	April	Huge white flowers, stained petunia at base
stellata	4 m (13 ft)	March–April	Star-like white flowers, very freely produced
Malus (D) (crab apple) floribunda	6 m (20 ft)	April	Red in bud opening to pink-flushed white blossom
'Golden Hornet'	6 m (20 ft)	April–May	Clusters of small yellow fruit that lasts well
'John Downie'	10 m (33 ft)	April–May	Very attractive orange and red edible fruit
'Profusion'	6 m (20 ft)	April–May	Red blossom freely produced; young leaves purple
sargentii	3 m (10 ft)	April	White blossom followed by small red fruit
Parrotia (D) persica	5 m (16 ft)	Jan–March	Grown mainly for its rich autumn colour
Prunus (D) dulcis (common almond)	8 m (26 ft)	March	Early and very reliable; clear pink flowers
cerasifera 'Pissardii'	7 m (23 ft)	April	Plum-coloured foliage; pinkish-white blossom
persica 'Prince Charming' (peach)	5 m (16 ft)	April	Double, rose-red flowers borne on naked stems
'Pink Perfection' (cherry)	6 m (20 ft)	April–May	Bright pink buds open to paler, double blossom

Plant name Species or variety	*Ultimate height*	*Flowering period*	*Characteristics*
'Shirotae' (cherry)	6 m (20 ft)	April–May	Large, semi-double, snow-white, fragrant flowers
subhirtella autumnalis	6 m (20 ft)	Nov–March	Pale pink, semi-double blossom on bare stems
Pyrus (D) salicifolia pendula (willow-leafed pear)	5 m (16 ft)	April	Silver-grey, willow-like leaves; white flowers
Rhus (D) typhina (star's horn sumach)	5 m (16 ft)	—	Large, divided leaves turn orange-red in autumn
Robinia (D) pseudoacacia 'Frisia'	6 m (20 ft)	—	Bright yellow, pinnate leaves spring to autumn
Salix (D) purpurea pendula	5 m (16 ft)	—	Small weeping tree with long, pendulous branches
Sorbus (D) aria lutescens (whitebeam)	10 m (33 ft)	—	Leaves open with a white felt, later grey-green
aucuparia (mountain ash)	12 m (39 ft)	May–June	Creamy-white flowers and orange-red berries

CONIFERS

Plant name Species or variety	*Ultimate height*	*Hedging*	*Characteristics*
Cedrus (E) atlantica glauca (blue cedar)	30 m + (98 ft +)	No	A magnificent conifer with grey-blue foliage
deodara aurea (golden Deodar)	20 m (66 ft)	No	Golden-yellow in spring, becoming greenish
Chamaecyparis (E) lawsoniana (Lawson's cypress)	30 m + (98 ft +)	Yes	Dark green, fan-like sprays of foliage; good screen
l. columnaris	9 m (30 ft)	No	A narrow form with attractive blue-grey foliage

Plant name *Species or variety*	*Ultimate height*	*Best aspect*	*Flowering period*	*Characteristics*
I. 'Fletcheri'	7 m (23 ft)	Yes		Grey-green, feathery foliage
I. 'Green Hedger'	20 m (66 ft)	Yes		Makes a dense hedge of rich green foliage
I. lanei	15 m (49 ft)	Yes		Feathery sprays of rich gold; cone-shaped
I. lutea	12 m (39 ft)	Yes		Large, flattened sprays of yellow foliage
Cryptomeria (E) japonica 'Elegans'	8 m (26 ft)	No		Feathery; deep rose tints in autumn and winter
x Cupressocyparis (E) leylandii (Leyland cypress)	30 m (98 ft)	Yes		The fastest-growing conifer; makes a tall hedge
Ginkgo (D) biloba (maidenhair tree)	20 m + (66 ft +)	No		Distinctive, five-lobed leaves; yellow in autumn
Juniperus (E) chinensis aurea (Chinese juniper)	8 m (26 ft)	No		Dainty yellow foliage; forms a slender column
communis hibernica (Irish juniper)	5 m (16 ft)	No		Forms a slender but dense column; rich green
horizontalis glauca	1.5 m (5 ft)	No		This is a very useful ground-hugging juniper
Picea (E) abies (Christmas tree)	30 m + (98 ft +)	No		The popular Christmas tree needs no description
breweriana (Brewer's weeping spruce)	20 m (66 ft)	No		Forms a green fountain of long, drooping branches
pungens 'Koster'	10 m (33 ft)	No		A conical tree with silver-blue foliage
Taxus (E) baccata (yew)	15 m + (49 ft +)	Yes		Dark green foliage; makes a superb hedge
Thuja (E) occidentalis 'Holmstrupii'	4 m (13 ft)	No		A narrowly conical, slow-growing tree; rich green
o. lutescens	5 m (16 ft)	No		Pale, yellowish-green flattened sprays; conical

SHRUBS

There is a vast range of shrubs from which to choose, and selection must inevitably be based partly on personal taste and partly on the special requirements of the plants (especially soil). The following list embraces what we consider to be the more desirable shrubs for the gardens in this book. You will find those requiring a lime-free soil, and those that can be regarded as 'below-eye-level' (low-growing) shrubs, listed in separate tables.

Plant name *Species or variety*	*Ultimate height*	*Flowering period*	*Characteristics*
Aralia (D) elata (Japanese angelica tree)	4 m (13 ft)	Aug–Sep	Huge, pinnate leaves; sprays of white flowers
Arundinaria (E) japonica (bamboo)	4 m (13 ft)	—	Willow-like foliage on bamboo canes; dense growth
Berberis (E) darwinii	2 m ($6\frac{1}{2}$ ft)	April–May	Massess of small golden flowers; blue berries
stenophylla	3 m (10 ft)	April–May	Arching branches studded with yellow flowers
Buddleia (D) alternifolia	4 m (13 ft)	June–July	Produces a cascade of arching branches; mauve
davidii 'Royal Red'	4 m (13 ft)	July–Aug	Red-purple spikes of flowers on arching stems
Choisya (E) ternata (Mexican orange blossom)	3 m (10 ft)	May	Fragrant white flowers set against glossy leaves
Cornus (D) mas (Cornelian cherry)	5 m (16 ft)	Feb.	Masses of small yellow flowers on bare stems
Cortaderia (E) selloana (syn. argentea) (pampas grass)	3 m (10 ft)	Sep–Nov	Tall, silvery plumes above large spiky leaves
Corylus (D) avellana contorta (corkscrew hazel)	5 m (16 ft)	Feb–March	Quaintly twisted branches and yellow catkins
Cotoneaster (SE) franchetii sternianus	4 m (13 ft)	May–June	Small pink flowers followed by orange-red berries
Cytisus (D) battandieri	5 m (16 ft)	June	Cone-shaped clusters of fragrant, yellow flowers
Elaeagnus (E) pungens maculata	4 m (13 ft)	—	Leaves are boldly splashed with bright yellow

Plant name *Species or variety*	*Ultimate height*	*Flowering period*	*Characteristics*
Escallonia (E) 'Donard Brilliance'	2 m ($6\frac{1}{2}$ ft)	June–July	Arching branches of crimson flowers; glossy leaves
Fatsia (E) japonica	3 m (10 ft)	Oct–Nov	Bold, hand-shaped leaves; milky-white flowers
Forsythia (D) 'Lynwood' (golden bell bush)	3 m (10 ft)	March–April	A mass of rich yellow flowers on erect branches
Hamamelis (D) mollis (Chinese witch hazel)	5 m (16 ft)	Dec–March	Sweetly fragrant, yellow flowers on naked branches
Hibiscus (D) syriacus 'Blue Bird' (tree hollyhock)	2 m ($6\frac{1}{2}$ ft)	Aug–Sep	Large violet-blue flowers with dark eyes; striking
s. 'Woodbridge'	2 m ($6\frac{1}{2}$ ft)	Aug–Sep	A variety with handsome rose-pink flowers
Hypericum (SE) 'Hidcote'	2 m ($6\frac{1}{2}$ ft)	July–Aug	Large, golden yellow, saucer-shaped flowers
Kolkwitzia (D) amabilis 'Pink Cloud' (beauty bush)	2 m ($6\frac{1}{2}$ ft)	May–June	Bell-like, soft pink flowers on feathery branches
Lonicera (E) nitida 'Baggesen's Gold' (Chinese honeysuckle)	4 m (13 ft)	—	Small, golden leaves becoming greenish in autumn
Mahonia (E) 'Charity'	3 m (10 ft)	Jan–Feb	Terminal clusters of fragrant, yellow flowers
japonica	2 m ($6\frac{1}{2}$ ft)	Feb–March	Fragrant, yellow flowers; attractive leaves
Osmanthus (E) delavayi	3 m (10 ft)	April	Small, white flowers; fragrant; spreading habit
Philadelphus (D) (mock orange) 'Enchantment'	4 m (13 ft)	June–July	Arching ropes of fragrant white flowers
Phormium (E) tenax (New Zealand flax)	3 m (10 ft)	—	Sword-shaped leaves, producing a striking effect
Ribes (D) sanguineum 'Pulborough Scarlet' (flowering currant)	3 m (10 ft)	March–April	Racemes of rich red flowers; a fast grower
Sambucus (D) nigra aurea (golden elder)	5 m (16 ft)	—	Golden yellow leaves, tending to deepen with age

Plant name *Species or variety*	*Height*	*Flowering period*	*Characteristics*
Spartium (D) junceum (Spanish broom)	3 m (10 ft)	June–Aug	Yellow flowers shaped like those of the pea
Spiraea (D) x arguta (bridal wreath)	3 m (10 ft)	April	Tall, arching sprays of small, white flowers
x bumalda 'Anthony Waterer'	2 m ($6\frac{1}{2}$ ft)	July–Sep	Broad, flattened heads of tiny carmine flowers
x b. 'Goldflame'	2 m ($6\frac{1}{2}$ ft)	July–Aug	Young growth gold, turning more green later
Symphoricarpos (D) albus (snowberry)	3 m (10 ft)	July	Small rosy flowers are followed by white berries
Syringa (D) vulgaris 'Madame Lemoine' (lilac)	6 m (20 ft)	May	Creamy-white buds open to pure white; double
v. 'Michael Buchner'	6 m (20 ft)	May	A double lilac with pale, rose-lilac flowers
v. 'Mrs Edward Harding'	6 m (20 ft)	May	A semi-double variety with claret-red flowers
v. 'Souvenir de Louis Spaeth'	6 m (20 ft)	May	Single, wine-red blooms; a reliable variety
Tamarix (D) pentandra (tamarisk)	5 m (16 ft)	Aug	The bush becomes a foaming mass of pink flowers
Viburnum (D) fragrans	4 m (13 ft)	Nov–Feb	Fragrant, white flowers tinged with pink
x juddii	2 m ($6\frac{1}{2}$ ft)	April–May	Clusters of sweetly scented pale pink flowers
opulus sterile (snowball bush)	5 m (16 ft)	May–June	White flowers held in ball-shaped heads
tinus (E) (laurustinus)	4 m (13 ft)	Dec–April	White flowers, pink in bud; blooms winter

LOW-GROWING SHRUBS (below-eye-level shrubs)

Plant name Species or variety	*Ultimate height*	*Flowering period*	*Characteristics*
Berberis (D) thunbergii atropurpurea	1.5 m (5 ft)	May	Reddish-purple foliage, colours more in autumn
Cornus (D) alba sibirica (Westonbirt dogwood)	1.5 m (5 ft)	June	Sealing-wax red stems in winter; autumn colour
Cotoneaster (D) horizontalis	1.8 m (6 ft)	June	Wall or ground cover; abundant red berries
Cytisus (D) x praecox	1.8 m (6 ft)	April–May	A spectacular, tumbling mass of cream
Daphne (D) mezereum	1.5 m (5 ft)	Feb–March	Small mauve flowers; an exquisite fragrance
Fuchsia (D) 'Madame Cornelissen'	1.8 m (6 ft)	July–Oct	Large-flowered, red and white; may need shelter
'Mrs Popple'	1.5 m (5 ft)	July–Oct	A hardy variety; scarlet sepals, violet petals
Hydrangea (D) macrophylla Hortensia type	1.8 m (6 ft)	July–Sep	These are the well-known 'mophead' hydrangeas
Lacecap type	1.8 m (6 ft)	July–Sep	The coloured ray florets form a ring round edge
Hypericum (E) calycinum	30 cm (1 ft)	July–Aug	Large golden flowers; a fine ground cover
Lavandula (E) (lavender) 'Munstead'	75 cm ($2\frac{1}{2}$ ft)	July	Compact plant; lavender-blue flowers; aromatic
'Twickel Purple'	75 cm ($2\frac{1}{2}$ ft)	July	Grey-green aromatic lavender-blue flowers
Mahonia (E) aquifolium	1.8 m (6 ft)	March–April	Clusters of yellow flowers; decorative leaves
Philadelphus (D) 'Manteau d'Hermine'	1.5 m (5 ft)	June	Dainty, double, white flowers; good fragrance
Potentilla (D) 'Elizabeth'	1.5 m (5 ft)	June–Oct	Forms a dome-shaped bush; primrose yellow flowers
'Katherine Dykes'	1.5 m (5 ft)	June–Oct	Covered with canary yellow flowers all summer
'Princess'	75 cm ($2\frac{1}{2}$ ft)	June–Oct	Pink flowers borne all summer

Plant name Species or variety	*Height*	*Flowering period*	*Characteristics*
Prunus (E) laurocerasus 'Otto Luyken'	1.5m (5 ft)	April	White, candle-like flower spikes; shiny leaves
Santolina (E) chamaecyparissus nana (cotton lavender)	75 cm ($2\frac{1}{2}$ ft)	June–July	Silver-grey, woolly foliage; yellow flowers
Senecio (E) laxifolius	90 cm (3 ft)	June–July	Silver-grey, woolly leaves; yellow daisy flowers
Weigela (D) florida variegata	1.5 m (5 ft)	June	Cream-edged leaves; clear, pale pink flowers
'Bristol Ruby'	1.8 m (6 ft)	June	A very free-flowering variety with red flowers
Yucca (E) filamentosa	1.8 m (6 ft)	July–Aug	Sword-like leaves; impressive creamy flower spike
flaccida 'Ivory'	1.8 m (6 ft)	July–Aug	Spiky leaves with curly white threads; striking

SHRUBS FOR A LIME-FREE SOIL

These shrubs can still be grown where lime exists, in beds of acid, lime-free soil built up at least 30 cm (1 ft) above ground level. Alternatively they can be planted in containers filled with similar soil. If the lime content of the soil is only slightly excessive, the plants can be treated annually with sequestered iron.

Low-growing shrubs (below eye level) are indicated by an asterisk*

Plant name Species or variety	*Ultimate height*	*Flowering period*	*Characteristics*
***Azalea** (D) luteum	1.5 m (5 ft)	May–June	Orange-yellow, funnel-shaped flowers; strongly fragrant
Knaphill, Exbury hybrids	1.8 m (6 ft)	May	Wide colour range and good autumn colour
Kurume and other hybrids (E)	90 cm (3 ft)	April–May	Most form a mass of small flowers; need shade
mollis hybrids	1.5 m (5 ft)	May	Trusses of large flowers in various colours

Plant name *Species or variety*	*Height*	*Flowering period*	*Characteristics*
Camellia (E) japonica 'Adolphe Audusson'	3 m (10 ft)	March–April	Semi-double, blood red with conspicuous stamens
j. 'Lady Vansittart'	3 m (10 ft)	March–April	Semi-double flowers, white striped with pink
x williamsii 'Donation'	3 m (10 ft)	April	Large, semi-double deep pink flowers; erect
x w. 'Francis Hanger'	3 m (10 ft)	March–April	A striking single white; erect growth habit
x w. 'J. C. Williams'	3 m (10 ft)	March–April	A beautiful camellia; large, single pink blooms
***Kalmia** (E) latifolia (calico bush)	1.8 m (6 ft)	June	Rose-coloured flowers set against glossy leaves
***Pernettya** (E) mucronata	90 cm (3 ft)	April	Pink, red or white berries on female; needs male
Pieris (E) 'Forest Flame'	2 m ($6\frac{1}{2}$ ft)	April	Brilliant red young leaves; creamy flowers
formosa forrestii 'Wakehurst'	3 m (10 ft)	April	Young foliage resembles bright red flowers
***Rhododendron** (E) (species) impeditum	45 cm ($1\frac{1}{2}$ ft)	April	Blue flowers carried over small, oval leaves
praecox	1.5 m (5 ft)	Feb–March	Actually a hybrid; translucent rosy-purple
williamsianum	45 cm ($1\frac{1}{2}$ ft)	April–May	Coin-shaped leaves; pink, bell-shaped flowers
yakushimanum	1.2 m (4 ft)	May	Pink buds, opening to white; leathery leaves
Rhododendron (E) (large-flowered hybrids) 'Betty Wormald'	1.5 m + (5 ft +)	April–June	Immense trusses of large, pink, frilled flowers
'Britannia'	1.5 m + (5 ft +)	April–June	Gloxinia-shaped glowing crimson trusses
'Cynthia'	1.5 m + (5 ft +)	April–June	Widely funnel-shaped deep rose flowers
'Kluis Sensation'	1.5 m + (5 ft +)	April–June	Bright scarlet flowers with darker spots
'Mrs John Millais'	1.5 m + (5 ft +)	April–June	Pink buds open to reveal lovely white blooms
'Purple Splendour'	1.5 m + (5 ft +)	April–June	Funnel-shaped, purple-blue with black markings

Plant name *Species or variety*	*Ultimate height*	*Flowering period*	*Characteristics*
***Rhododendron** (E) (dwarf hybrids) 'Blue Tit'	90 cm (3 ft)	April–May	Soft blue, open bells, intensifying with age
'Carmen'	45 cm (1½ ft)	May	Waxy, blood red, bell-shaped flowers
'Elizabeth'	1.5 m (5 ft)	April–May	Orange-red, trumpet-shaped flowers

SHRUB ROSES

Plant name *Species or variety*	*Ultimate height*	*Colour*	*Characteristics*
Rosa x alba (white rose of York)	3 m (10 ft)	White	Richly scented, semi-double, about 7.5 cm (3 in)
R. 'Canary Bird'	2 m (6½ ft)	Butter yellow	Saucer-shaped blooms on arching stems, in May
R. centifolia (cabbage rose)	2 m (6½ ft)	Pink	Large, double, richly scented; fragrant leaves
R. gallica officinalis (red rose of Lancaster)	1.5 m (5 ft)	Crimson	Semi-double, richly fragrant; prominent anthers
Hybrid musk 'Cornelia'	3 m (10 ft)	Rose pink	Makes a wide, sturdy bush with good foliage
Hybrid musk 'Elmshorn'	3 m (10 ft)	Crimson	Large trusses of cup-shaped blooms; brilliant
Hybrid musk 'Penelope'	3 m (10 ft)	Shell pink	Clusters of semi-double blooms; red hips
R. 'Nevada'	3 m (10 ft)	Creamy white	Arching stems with large, single flowers
R. rugosa 'Frau Dagmar Hastrop'	1.8 m (6 ft)	Pale pink	Heavy crop of crimson hips; makes a good hedge
R. rugosa 'Roseraie de l'Hay'	1.8 m (6 ft)	Reddish purple	Double flowers about 10 cm (4 in) across
R. rugosa 'Sarah van Fleet'	2 m (6½ ft)	Soft pink	Flowers continuously from June to Sept.

CLIMBERS AND WALL SHRUBS

Plant name *Species or variety*	*Ultimate height*	*Best aspect*	*Flowering period*	*Characteristics*
Campsis (D) (trumpet vine) grandiflora	6 m (20 ft)	S–W	Aug–Sep	Trumpet-shaped, orange-red flowers
radicans	6 m (20 ft)	S–W	Aug–Sep	Clusters of orange and scarlet flowers
Ceanothus (E) (Californian lilac) 'Burkwoodii'	3 m (10 ft)	S–W	July–Sep	Rich, dark blue flowers on a rounded bush
'Delight'	3 m (10 ft)	S–W	May	Long, strong blue panicles; a hardy variety
Chaenomeles (D) (flowering quince) x superba 'Crimson and Gold'	2 m ($6\frac{1}{2}$ ft)	Any	March–April	Deep crimson with contrasting golden anthers
x s. 'Knap Hill Scarlet'	2 m ($6\frac{1}{2}$ ft)	Any	March–April	Profusion of bright orange-scarlet flowers
Clematis (D) flammula (Virgin's Bower)	8 m + (26ft +)	Any	Aug–Oct	White, sweetly-scented flowers; silky seed heads
x jackmanii	5 m + (16 ft +)	E–S–W	July–Oct	Large, violet-purple flowers borne freely
montana	8 m + (26 ft +)	Any	April–May	Profusion of white flowers 5 cm (2 in) across
m. rubens	8 m + (26 ft +)	Any	April–May	A pink form with bronze-purple young shoots
patens	5 m + (16 ft +)	E–S–W	May–June	Creamy-white flowers, 10–15 cm (4–6 in) across
viticella	5 m + (16 ft +)	E–S–W	July–Oct	Violet, blue, or reddish-purple flowers

Plant name *Species or variety*	*Ultimate height*	*Best aspect*	*Flowering period*	*Characteristics*
Garrya (E) elliptica	3 m (10 ft)	N–E	Jan–Feb	Silky, grey-green catkins, best on male plants
Hedera (E) (ivy) canariensis	8 m + (26 ft +)	Any	—	Large, bright, glossy leaves, strong-growing
colchica dentata variegata	8 m + (26 ft +)	Any	—	Large leaves shaded green, cream, grey, yellow
helix 'Buttercup'	8 m + (26 ft +)	Any	—	New leaves golden yellow, greener with age
Hydrangea (D) petiolaris	8 m + (26 ft +)	N–E–W	June–July	Heads of white flowers like lacecap hydrangeas
Jasminum (D) nudiflorum (winter jasmine)	4 m (13 ft)	Any	Nov–March	Butter-yellow flowers set against green stems
officinale (sweet jasmine)	8 m + (26 ft +)	Any	June–Aug	Twining climber with fragrant white flowers
Lonicera (D) (honeysuckle) x americana	3 m + (10 ft +)	E–S–W	June–Sep	Profusion of rose-apricot, fragrant flowers
japonica 'Halliana' (E)	6 m + (20 ft +)	E–S–W	June–Oct	Creamy biscuit coloured, and ve y fragrant
periclymenum 'Serotina' (late Dutch honeysuckle)	3 m + (10 ft +)	E–S–W	July–Sep	Re dish purple ana yellow; heavy fragrance
Parthenocissus (D) henryana	9 m (30 ft)	N–W	—	Dark green leaves with silvery variagation
quinquefolia (Virginia creeper)	9 m (30 ft)	Any	—	Brilliant scarlet autumn colour, self-clinging
Polygonum (D) baldschuanicum (Russian vine)	7.5 cm + (25 ft +)	Any	July–Oct	Foaming mass of small white flowers; vigorous

Plant name *Species or variety*	*Ultimate* *height*	*Hedging*	*Characteristics*	
Rosa (D) various climbers and ramblers	3 m + (10 ft +)	S–W	May–Oct	'Perpetual flowering' type are best; use ramblers for pillars and pergolas
Vitis (D) (vine) coignetiae	9 m + (30 ft +)	S–W	June–July	Really huge leaves, with rich autumn colours
vinifera 'Brandt'	9 m + (30 ft +)	S–W	June–July	Purple grapes; good leaf colour; edible
Wisteria (D) sinensis	9 m + (30 ft +)	S–W	May–June	Long racemes of fragrant, pale lilac flowers

GROUND COVER

Plant name *Species or variety*	*Height*	*Flowering* *period*	*Characteristics*
Ajuga (bugle) reptans atropurpurea	10 cm (4 in)	May–June	Forms a reddish-purple carpet; blue flowers
r. variegata	15 cm (6 in)	May–June	White and grey variegation; blue flowers
Alchemilla mollis (lady's mantle)	45 cm ($1\frac{1}{2}$ ft)	June–July	Soft sprays of yellow-green flowers; round leaves
Artemisia (wormwood) 'Lambrook Silver'	90 cm (3 ft)	—	A robust plant with silvery-grey foliage
'Silver Queen'	60 cm (2 ft)	—	Attractive, silvery, divided leaves; bushy
Aubrieta various varieties; colours include blues, purples, reds, and pinks	15 cm (6 in)	April–May	Forms a dense cushion; cut back after flowering
Bergenia (elephant ears) 'Ballawley'	30 cm (1 ft)	April–May	Large, thick leaves; red stems; rose-red flowers
cordifolia	30 cm (1 ft)	March–April	Large, heart-shaped leaves; deep pink flowers

Plant name Species or variety	*Ultimate height*	*Flowering period*	*Characteristics*
Brunnera macrophylla (perennial forget-me-not)	45 cm ($1\frac{1}{2}$ ft)	April–June	Heart-shaped leaves and sprays of blue flowers
Campanula portenschlagiana	10 cm (4 in)	June–Sep	Masses of deep blue flowers on training stems
Dianthus (pink) allwoodii 'Ian'	30 cm (1 ft)	June–Aug	Glowing crimson flowers against greyish leaves
deltoides	10 cm (4 in)	June–Aug	Brilliant scarlet blooms over green foliage
'Doris'	30 cm (1 ft)	June–Sep	Succession of warm pink flowers with deeper centre
Geranium endressii 'Wargrave Pink'	45 cm ($1\frac{1}{2}$ ft)	May–Sep	Clear, silvery-pink flowers in profusion
'Johnson's Blue'	45 cm ($1\frac{1}{2}$ ft)	May–Sep	Masses of cup-shaped, bright blue flowers
sanguineum lancastrense 'Splendens'	25 cm (10 in)	June–Sep	Rose-pink flowers on plant of spreading habit
Helianthemum (rock rose) Many varieties; mostly pinks or yellows	10–15 cm (4–6 in)	June–Aug	Evergreen, usually greyish, foliage; best in sun
Helleborus niger (Christmas rose)	30 cm (1 ft)	Jan–Feb	White, open flowers with golden stamens
orientalis (Lenten rose)	45 cm ($1\frac{1}{2}$ ft)	Feb–April	White, plum, or maroon flowers; fingered foliage
Hosta (Plantain lily) fortunei	60 cm (2 ft)	July–Aug	Large, handsome leaves; lilac flower spikes
f. albo marginata	75 cm ($2\frac{1}{2}$ ft)	July–Aug	Leaves prettily edged with cream variegation
f. aurea marginata	75 cm ($2\frac{1}{2}$ ft)	July–Aug	Leaves edged light yellow; mauve flower spikes
sieboldiana	60 cm (2 ft)	July–Aug	Large, blue-green leaves; lilac-mauve flowers
Hypericum calycinum (see low-growing-shrubs list) coris	15 cm (6 in)	June–Sep	Golden yellow flowers 12 mm ($\frac{1}{2}$ in) across

Buying a property
PORTUGAL

CADOGANguides

Contents

About the authors

Harvey Holtom has lived in Madrid for 20 years, where has worked as a teacher, translator, photographer and writer. He is currently the correspondent for the *Time Out* website. He is married to Spain but confesses to a long-standing affair with Portugal and has visited the country on many occasions.

John Howell established John Howell & Co in Sheffield in 1979 and by 1997 it had become one of the largest and most respected law firms in the north of England, employing over 100 lawyers. On moving to London in 1995, John Howell has gone on to specialize in providing legal advice to clients buying property abroad.

Acknowledgements

Harvey Holtom would like to thank: Alison Roberts, Lisbon, for putting up with pestering questions; Len Port, Lagoa, for answering questions and providing valuable insights; Ed Owen, Madrid, for some useful contacts; Siobahn and Aidon McMahon, Malveira da Serra, Lisbon, for some useful insights; Mick Nijjar, for some useful answers; the sales staff at Vista Ibérica Publicações Lda.; Peter Salt of Avenida Properties, Lagos; Emma Hollen of Hamptons International; Peter Kaleta for the loan of materials; Maggi Riach, for putting up with me; Anne Parish of Algarve Rentals; the Portuguese Tourism Office, Madrid; Jose Flores Porto, Madrid.

Navigator Guides would like to thank Harvey Holtom, John Howell for his legal expertise, Jane Belford for her invaluable help as editor, Sarah Rianhard-Gardner for design and Yvette Douglas for DTP.

Conceived and produced for Cadogan Guides by **Navigator Guides Ltd**, The Old Post Office, Swanton Novers, Melton Constable, Norfolk NR24 2AJ
www.navigatorguides.com
info@navigatorguides.com

Cadogan Guides
165 The Broadway, Wimbledon, London SW19 1NE
info.cadogan@virgin.net
www.cadoganguides.com

The Globe Pequot Press
246 Goose Lane, PO Box 480, Guilford, Connecticut 06437–0480

Cover and photo essay design by Sarah Rianhard-Gardner
Cover/photo essay photographs © John Miller
Maps © Cadogan Guides, drawn by Map Creation Ltd
Editor: Jane Belford
Proofreading: Susannah Wight
Indexing: Isobel McLean

Printed in Italy by Legoprint
A catalogue record for this book is available from the British Library
ISBN 1-86011-108-4

Please help us to keep this guide up to date. We have done our best to ensure that the information in this guide is correct at the time of going to press. But places and facilities are constantly changing, and standards and prices in hotels and restaurants fluctuate. We would be delighted to receive any comments concerning existing entries or omissions. Authors of the best letters will receive a copy of the Cadogan Guide of their choice.

Introduction

Good things, they say, come in small packages. If the expression may be applied to countries, then Portugal is certainly a package that is filled almost to bursting point.

Formerly a great imperial power and major player on the world stage during the Age of Discoveries in the 15th and early 16th centuries, in later days the country slowly became a backwater within Europe, a condition that was if anything made more profound during Salazar's long dictatorship. Portugal has only recently begun to emerge from this state of lethargy. With the political freedoms won as a result of the 1974 Revolution and the prosperity that came with membership of the EU from 1986, Portugal has advanced tremendously. The economic view at the moment does not look too good, as the country is in the midst of a recession, but what cannot be denied is the new-found confidence of Portugal and its people.

For the would-be homebuyer, Portugal has much to offer. It is no longer the property bargain basement it perhaps was a decade or two ago, but at the same time there is still a flourishing market, with apartments, townhouses, villas and country houses to suit all pockets if you look hard enough. Although it was never previously considered an investors' market, there are signs that this has begun to change, and quality properties for letting or later resale are beginning to look like a smart move.

According to some estimates, almost 90 per cent of properties bought by foreigners are in the Algarve region. For many, the equation is simple: the Algarve *is* Portugal. The much-bandied-about figure of approximately 3,000 hours of sunshine a year, a winter that you barely notice, numerous golf courses, marinas and other sports facilities as well as a ready-made ex-pat community to slip into are undeniably powerful arguments in favour of the area. But there is so much more to this little country that by focusing solely on the Algarve you may miss out on all sorts of other charms. Portugal has gorgeous green mountains and valleys in the north; superb beaches and picture postcard fishing villages the whole length of its coastline; gentle landscapes in the central area; and the mystical, magical southern planes of the Alentejo. Then there is the quirky but unfailingly appealing and increasingly cosmopolitan capital, Lisbon, and its rival and second city, the industrious, prosperous Oporto (Porto to the Portuguese). 'Culture vultures' can indulge themselves looking at the cities' superb ecclesiastical and civil architecture and nosing around in any number of museums that range from the quaint and old-fashioned to hands-on and modern. The active can enjoy hill-walking, deep sea fishing, surfing and windsurfing, scuba-diving, whale-watching, horse-riding and golf, too. And Portugal is just a couple of hours or so by air from most of northern Europe – so the dream is not impossible.

Bemvindo!

First Steps and Reasons for Buying

02

There could be any number of reasons why you would choose Portugal as a destination for regular holidays, lengthy stays or as somewhere to buy property. The climate is clearly one factor, as is the country's undoubted beauty and the variety of different landscapes. So too is the cost of living. Portugal is still relatively cheap when compared with countries in northern Europe, though prices are creeping up. The cost of properties varies hugely from one region to another and between different types and standards of property, but there is probably something there for anyone who can just about afford to buy. Portuguese people are, on the whole, friendly, welcoming and exquisitely well mannered.

In a recent survey, published by *The News* (Portugal's leading English-language newspaper), people were asked why they would want to go and live in Portugal. Not surprisingly, the weather won most votes (27 per cent) but, interestingly, it was 'the Portuguese people' who came a close second (with 25 per cent). Clearly living in a country where you can get on easily with the local people is an important factor in choosing to buy there. In fact only 5 per cent felt that the availability of golf and other sporting activities was a reason, while beaches and the cost and availability of property were, respectively, the reasons given by 15 per cent of potential settlers. A further 10 per cent cited the ease of getting to Portugal on budget flights as the chief reason for wanting to buy there.

Why Portugal?

Except for a few (important) procedural differences, buying a property in Portugal is not unlike buying property anywhere else. It comes down to figuring out realistically how much you can afford to pay, finding an area where a property within your budget is available, searching for one that you like and then going through a series of legal and financial procedures which are not simple but not as complicated as they might seem either.

When you start to think seriously about buying in Portugal, though, there are several questions that need serious consideration before you start making any moves. The answers to those questions may well dictate where and what you end up buying. This chapter gives you a brief overview of the issues involved. In Chapter 3, **Where in Portugal**, the country is divided up and examined region by region, with sample property prices included. Chapter 4, **Selecting a Property**, looks in depth at issues such as travelling to and from Portugal, how to search, the variety of properties available and the different types of professional help that you should seek. Solicitor and international lawyer John Howell takes you step-by-step through the nitty-gritty of making the purchase in Chapter 5, **Making the Purchase**, and deals with other related issues, including important tax issues, in Chapter 6, **Financial Implications**. Chapter 7, **Settling In**, deals with many aspects of moving to Portugal and living there, and Chapter 8, **Letting Your Property**, covers the issues involved for those who plan to use their home only some of the time and to make rental income from it. There is an extensive reference section with detailed information, addresses, websites, a Portuguese glossary and other useful information.

City Life

Deciding to live in a big city in Portugal means choosing between Lisbon and Oporto, as no other city really qualifies as 'big'. Both have much that is attractive, but neither really compares in terms of stress levels to life in a big northern European city. Living here means access to entertainment and cultural activities, shopping, spectator sports, nightlife, varied dining and proximity to schools, hospitals and services of all types. There are also likely to be better job prospects and possibilities of running a business. As well as this, Lisbon, particularly, is becoming quite cosmopolitan, so you can find a more mixed crowd of acquaintances.

Neither city is particularly large, which means that if you decide not to live in the centre, then suburban life is an option that still allows you to enjoy all the good things that the city has to offer. Even so, Lisbon and Oporto do have their share of traffic problems, noise and urban blight, which may be precisely what you are hoping to avoid by choosing Portugal in the first place. Lisbon is also quite expensive these days, especially when it comes to accommodation, either rented or purchased, and Oporto is not far behind. If you live in these cities you may have to make do with an apartment as opposed to a house with a garden, although you may be able to find this in the suburbs.

Provincial Capitals and Small Towns

Provincial capitals in the Portuguese context are cities where the number of inhabitants may vary between 50,000 and slightly more than 100,000. Only 15 towns or cities in the country exceed the 50,000 mark and many are much smaller. As a rule smaller Portuguese cities offer a better quality of life than the bigger cities, and a certain tranquillity that city-dwellers may find enviable. Living in such places implies proximity to just about everything, including shopping, entertainment and services, all of which may even be within walking distance from your home. And cheaper house prices too.

In some places the range of entertainment may be more limited, as may available job opportunities. Small-town living can also sometimes feel quite parochial and, with a less cosmopolitan population, your range of possible acquaintances is necessarily more reduced. Learning the language becomes much more important if you are to integrate successfully – not that this a problem provided you are prepared to take up the challenge!

Villages and Rural Isolation

For those who can adapt to it, living in a small village or even in the middle of nowhere is ideal. Offering peace and quiet, a million miles from the madding crowds, traffic, pollution and stress, the rural life has much to recommend it.

For those who want a property that is unique, villages and rural areas may offer cheaper, older properties for renovation and allow buyers to indulge themselves, lovingly restoring and rebuilding the house to their own taste. There are many cases of former farmhouses and virtual ruins that have been converted into splendid residences or even country hotels, with unique and original décor. Then again, doing this can work out far more expensive than originally budgeted, since many older country properties do not have proper foundations, rarely have damp coursing, and as a result a conversion job can easily turn into a complete rebuilding project. Remember, too, that the cost of installing basic utilities such as water and electricity can be extremely high.

It may also be difficult to sell on a rural property, however beautifully restored it is, since what may be an ideal retreat for the original purchaser simply may not appeal to other buyers. In rural areas, the lack of facilities, shops and services can be a problem, which may only be solved by car-dependency. This is particularly true where children are involved: how far is it to the nearest school – and what if the nearest school is not to your liking? Are there any other children for them to play with nearby? The lack of services and isolation can also become a serious problem for elderly people as they get older and frailer. Plunging headlong into the rural adventure is not to be done lightly; it requires serious thought beforehand.

Purpose-built *Urbanizações* and Villas

Mainly though not exclusively an Algarve phenomenon, purpose-built *urbanizações* (housing estates or resort developments) are where many foreigners choose to buy their second or holiday home. *Urbanizações* are relatively new developments that have sprung up over the last 30 years or so. Some are exclusive, with luxury villas blending into the carefully landscaped (and inevitable) golf course, restaurants, shopping and entertainment facilities all within the estate boundaries. Very often they look directly on to the beach; if not, then it is rarely far away. There is usually a site manager and a team of backup staff for maintenance, security and problem-solving. Other *urbanizações* are less exclusive but still offer a fairly comprehensive range of on-site facilities. Most offer a good selection of properties too, running the whole gamut from apartments of different sizes through to 'townhouses' (semis) to luxury villas. Buying a property in an *urbanização* is quite different from buying anywhere else. Developers usually present a range of properties to suit different budgets so choosing one is not unlike buying a suit off the peg, with price variations determined by the label and the quality of the cloth. The purchasing process can be quite simple. *Urbanizações* are often built with the foreign buyer in mind, so sales staff speak English and purchase contracts are standardized. The properties themselves are usually in good condition, often with plenty of 'mod-cons' and without the problems usually found in older houses. Life on an *urbanização* is generally trouble-free and does not make many demands on residents who appreciate having everything to hand.

The downside is that properties on *urbanizações* have a certain sameness about them – one apartment is much like another, which can give the feeling of being on a housing estate. Choosing to buy on an *urbanização* also implies acceptance of a certain lifestyle, one that other ex-pats have bought into, since the majority of homeowners in such places are foreign. Because many properties are used by their owners for rental purposes, those who live there permanently may find the constantly changing stream of holidaymakers who come for a week or two and then disappear bothersome, especially if they are rowdy. If you are thinking of buying on an *urbanização* with a view to living there permanently, bear this in mind. Consider too what life is like over the full 12-month cycle. It may well be that, after the animated, lively holiday months, you find that you have only a few year-round neighbours (and what if you do not get on with them?) and that the *urbanização* may become overly quiet during the low season.

Pitfalls and Things to Remember

Between making the decision to buy a Portuguese property and sitting down in it for the first time there are many stages. You have to make sure every step of the way that you are not walking in the wrong direction, or treading on a landmine. At the moment the Portuguese property market is booming and there is a lot of property for sale at a range of prices. True bargains, though, are few and far between, and, while it is never wise to make a hasty decision on a property, it is equally not smart to delay for too long – or someone else might jump in before you. Do research as much as possible so that you have a full and clear idea of what is available, where and at what price. After that you can start narrowing down your research to properties of a specific type, within your price range and in an area that you like. That way, when you find the place that you just 'know' is right you will not be buying on a whim but on the basis of sound, comparative judgement.

Remember too that, while procedures have been simplified and many of the 'cowboys' have been kicked out of the market, buying a property is never an absolutely straightforward process; there is a lot of bureaucracy involved and there are still some rip-off merchants around. You are, after all, on foreign territory and therefore much more likely to make a wrong move or get duped than you would be buying at home. There are fewer horror stories these days than there were some years ago. But there are still innocent souls who walk into traps with their eyes wide open and end up with property or land that cannot be resold or capitalized on from rentals, because they were ill-informed and for example did not know about plans to build a road through the back garden, failed to order a structural survey or even failed to check whether their plot of land could ever actually be built on.

Until recently, many people saved on taxes by putting the property in the name of an offshore company. While for some the system worked well for a time, the Portuguese government has recently clamped down hard on this, meaning that a considerable number of people have run into trouble with the tax authorities. Similarly, for years many people have knowingly under-declared the value of their property to save on SISA (property transfer tax). The days of this ruse are numbered and anyone found under-declaring is looking at a heavy fine or worse. In both cases the situation is complex and in a state of flux as new laws come on to the statute books. You can therefore only expect to get correct information and reliable advice from a qualified tax expert.

For more detailed information, *see* **Making the Purchase**.

No guidebook can ever substitute for sound, professional and above all independent advice. You could use a UK or Portugal-based lawyer; it does not matter which, provided they are professional and know what they are talking about. They could save you a lot of money in the long run.

Boa sorte!

Why Buy?

With air travel cheaper than ever before, it has become easier and easier to own and make use of a second home in Portugal. Many do, in fact, have a property there which they zip off to several times a year whenever they can for short stays or full-blown holidays. Depending on the use you hope to make of the property, you need to do a lot of thinking regarding its location and type, as well as considering many other issues.

If you want a property to spend a few days in now and again and possibly a longer holiday once a year, then an apartment at the cheaper end of the market will probably serve the purpose. This is especially the case if you plan to use it only to sleep and eat in. As will be seen in **Where in Portugal**, the absolute cheapest property you will find in the western Algarve costs around €65,000 (though there could be the odd urgent sale going for a bargain price) and closer to Faro airport, in the central Algarve, you could spend at least €10–15,000 more. Expect to pay similar prices in the coastal area close to Lisbon. Prices go up quite steeply from there. Other areas may be cheaper but much further away from airports. This could be a drawback, since there is little point in buying a property for occasional use when getting to it means spending several hours driving or sitting on a bus. That weekend break might not yield much in terms of relaxation if the apartment is not readily accessible. On the other hand, if you plan to invite friends or family members along with you on your trips then a small apartment may not fit the bill.

A Second Home

If, as many people do, you intend to buy a second home with the idea of moving there permanently later in life, a resort apartment is not what you really need. It is one thing to visit a place occasionally, but quite another living there permanently. Look at the property and its location carefully. Can you really see yourself there all year round? If not, then you will have to consider offloading the holiday home at some point and looking for something more suitable for future permanent residence. If you are a frequent visitor, though, you are in a very good position to do this calmly, over a period of time, and are much more likely to gain a good idea of what you might eventually want, and where to look for it.

You should also think about what happens while you are not there. Unoccupied properties can be a sitting target for burglars or vandals and if not watched over regularly may suffer damage from the elements. It is in your interests to organize some form of supervision by a reliable neighbour who is easily contacted, keeps a set of keys and is authorized to call in plumbers, electricians, glaziers or painters. In the same way, bills for taxes and utilities must be paid on time and can easily get forgotten when the owner is away for long periods. The consequences of unpaid bills could be serious so it is advisable to leave a float of money in a local bank account, to be topped up every so often, and give instructions for bills to be paid by standing order. If you buy on an *urbanização*, it is likely that the services included will cover some of these aspects, certainly those related to maintenance and repair. Property maintenance is, in fact, a thriving business that is a spin-off of the property boom in the main tourist areas. Some estate agents offer maintenance services as part of their post-sales service and there are a good many companies that specialize in providing these services. A fee may get you a better service than that provided by the friendly neighbour, and without any obligations to return any favours.

Finally, an unoccupied property that is only used occasionally does not generate any income, only costs. If you have sufficient money to buy and have only this in mind, then there is no problem, especially as it is unlikely that the property will actually lose value should you eventually want to sell. If, however, buying the property stretches your financial means to the limit, you may consider recouping some of the outlay or defraying costs by letting it out to holidaymakers at times when you do not plan to be there.

See further **Letting Your Property**.

A First Home

If you have reached the point where you plan to buy a property, move there and live in it permanently, then you are making a much greater commitment than the second homebuyer and consequently a whole host of other issues come into play. Depending on the state of your finances, you may be able to buy a Portuguese property without first selling up back home, which is a very lucky situation to be in. You may then decide to earn some income from letting your house back home or wait for the right moment to sell it and then invest the money from the sale elsewhere. And if you are well-off enough to do neither then you still have somewhere to stay when you take a trip home. On the other hand, if you have fewer resources you may have to sell first in order to be able to finance the property in Portugal. If this is the case you have to be absolutely sure that what you make on the sale at home will be enough to cover the type of property you want to buy. There may also be a time overlap, since there is no guarantee that you will find your dream property in Portugal the day after you have finalized the sale back home – and you have to live somewhere in the meantime. Renting is the obvious answer for this interim period and is dealt with in **Selecting a Property**. Alternatively, if you can arrange a second mortgage to buy the Portuguese property then there is less pressure to sell your UK property so quickly.

Whatever your financial situation, buying as a first home means giving it all up, leaving behind family, friends, a way of life that may be all you have known until now. This point should not be exaggerated, of course. Portugal is a lot closer than Australia or South Africa so your loved ones are not on the other side of the earth. Moving permanently does mean therefore that the choice of property and location is even more important than when buying a second home, if only for the simple fact that it is a long-term commitment. The wrong choice could be a cause of much disappointment after the initial thrill of moving to a new country has worn off.

Investment

Until fairly recently, buying in Portugal was not seen as much of an investment. This was because property prices there had not traditionally risen by much more than inflation – meaning quick returns were most unlikely and any profit could be wiped out by capital gains tax. The idea of buying a home in Portugal was traditionally seen as investing in peace and quiet and happiness. There is now plenty of evidence that the situation is changing, however, especially for those buying quality properties in the more fashionable areas. Property is fast becoming a very smart investment. Only a couple of decades ago Algarve villas would change hands for just a few thousand pounds. If you bought a villa then for, say, £10,000 (which works out at just over €14,000 at the current exchange rate), this same sum will now buy you nothing – anywhere. A villa, even a small one, in the cheapest part of the Algarve will cost at least 10 times (and probably more) that amount now. In recent years properties in the area have been rising by between 20 and 25 per cent annually. As availability becomes scarcer – and with strict building restrictions in place – there is no reason to expect this trend not to continue, at least for the foreseeable future. As well as watching a property go up in value, rental of well-located properties can give good returns, too, often more than 10 per cent of the total value annually. This may not, of course, apply to all areas of the country, and buying with expectations of making a profit is very much influenced by location. It is hard to see a small stone farmhouse in Trás-os-Montes, however lovingly restored and however gorgeous the surroundings, ever being much of a money-earner. But quality properties in popular beach locations are certainly places to think about if you aim to make some money from your purchase.

Living in Portugal

As with anywhere else, life in Portugal has its positive points and of course its downside, although it has to be said that the pros almost certainly outweigh the cons, otherwise the huge number of foreigners currently resident there would choose to go elsewhere. The main points for, and against, living there may be summed up as follows:

The Upside...

• **The weather**. The climate, especially in the southern half of the country, is mild year-round. In the Algarve, particularly, winter is a word that is almost meaningless to British people used to British cold and rain, and Madeira offers good weather practically all year.

• **Portugal is generally considered to be a country of warm, hospitable and polite people**. The long-held historical links between Portugal and Britain also count, and the British are generally well received.

• **Crime rates are relatively low, though rising**. Violent crime is not common; pick-pocketing, car theft and burglary are the crimes most suffered by foreign residents.

• **The existence of a large ex-pat community** (if that is what you want) means you will be able to find others with backgrounds and interests similar to your own.

• The fact that so many foreigners have been buying properties has meant that **purchasing procedures have become less complex**. A large number of English-speaking property agents and solicitors are now on hand locally to facilitate the process.

• **The most popular areas, generally those with a lot of tourist development, have improved their infrastructure** in recent years, a process that is ongoing.

• **EU membership** has enabled Portugal to advance and develop much over the past 20 years, yet it still retains a great deal of its enchanting, old-fashioned ways and is far less spoilt by development than other countries where you might consider buying.

• **Development has increased the number of opportunities for finding work or establishing a business**, although you shouldn't automatically assume it will be easy to do this.

• **Property prices** remain tempting for purchasers from more expensive northern European countries, while the cost of living is still lower – despite recent (substantial) rises in both sectors.

• **Indications are that for those thinking of buying as an investment, a property may yield significantly greater returns** than previously, especially in the more sought-after areas. This applies both to rental income and resale.

• **Budget flights** between the UK and Ireland and Portuguese destinations have become more frequent.

• **Excellent food**, especially from the sea, and a wealth of unsung, often little-known but nevertheless high-quality wines.

• **Good golf courses**, often in stunning locations, and other well-built and maintained sports facilities, especially for watersports.

• **Exciting nightlife and entertainment** in the larger towns and cities. Lisbon is now thought by those in the know to be replacing Barcelona as the 'partying capital' of the Iberian peninsula.

• **A generally relaxing, stress-free lifestyle**, especially for those who are not so interested in 'partying'.

• **EU membership** and the system of mutual rights and obligations that is essentially the same for citizens of all member states.

• **Portugal is to host the Euro 2004 football tournament**, which may prove a definite plus if you are a football fan, and which will bring money in to the country and help the economy even if you are not.

... and the downside

• **Jobs remain hard to find** for foreigners outside certain, well-defined sectors (*see* pp.19–23, and 'Working and Employment', pp.198–209).

• **Salaries, even if you do find a job, are amongst the lowest in the EU.**

• **The economy is currently suffering from a deep recession**, which by the end of the first quarter 2003 was reckoned to be its worst ever (as confirmed by the Bank of Portugal's April report).

• **Much of the development over the past 20 years has been fuelled by EU grants to underdeveloped regions**. With enlargement of the EU eastwards, much of the aid previously destined for Portugal, Spain and Greece will (from May 2004 onwards) be channelled to former Eastern Bloc countries.

• **Despite attempts at streamlining and rationalization, bureaucracy remains a persistent problem**. One homeowner said: 'It can take a long time for the bureaucracy to grind through for final exchange of contracts – from the initial signing of the promissory contract to the final exchange took me eight months on a newly built property.'

• **Away from the more developed tourist areas, infrastructure may be woefully lacking.**

• **Tourist areas, despite the advantages of infrastructure, can become unbearably busy during the peak season**. Instead of getting away from the madding crowd, you may find yourself at the centre of it.

• **Costs associated with buying a property can add considerably to the overall price** especially if the purchaser has not thoroughly researched such questions as unpaid back taxes or the costs of refurbishing a property.

• **Despite budget airlines, frequent travellers will find that costs mount up**. If financial resources are limited, a property nearer to home might start looking like a more attractive prospect.

• **Properties standing empty for long periods may be easy prey for burglars.**

• **Old-fashioned charm may wear off after a while**, and your enjoyment of the laid-back way of life could turn to boredom.

• **Unless you speak reasonable Portuguese it may be quite hard to penetrate into local communities**, which you might find reserved and a little inward-looking.

Festa de Futebol

On 12 June 2004 in the Dragão Stadium, Oporto, the referee will blow his whistle and start the UEFA Euro 2004 tournament. Sixteen national sides will take part, 15 of them by virtue of having qualified, plus Portugal which, as host nation, bypassed the qualifying stage. This competition, leading to the Henri Delaunay Trophy, is the biggest sporting event ever held in Portugal and the benefits, it is hoped, will be an improvement in sporting facilities (much needed in Portugal), the knock-on effect on tourism, the increase in national self-esteem and the message to the rest of the world that Portugal is capable of organizing great events as it did with the EXPO '98 in Lisbon. The organizers claimed recently that there will be an economic boost of up to €1.15 billion. The previous tournament, held in 2000, was attended by more than a million spectators and the final stages captured a worldwide cumulative audience of over seven billion viewers, making it the third most-watched sporting event in the world. Portugal hopes to improve on these figures. To this end, massive amounts of money have been spent on new state-of-the-art stadia and the redevelopment of existing ones. Games will be held in Aveiro, Braga, Coimbra, Faro/Loulé, Guimarães, Leiria, Lisbon and Oporto. Both Lisbon and Oporto, cities with more than one major club, are providing two stadia each. The majority will have a capacity of around 30,000, with the exception of F.C. Porto's Dragão Stadium, with room for 50,000, Sporting's new José Alvalade, also holding 50,000; Benfica's new Estadio da Luz, where the final will be held on 4 July, will have a capacity of 65,000. If England qualifies and gets drawn in the same group as Portugal next November 30th, then the team will have to play two of their games in the new Estadio do Algarve, between Faro and Loulé, which may be a reason to buy a property there for rental purposes. Or not!

More information is available at www.euro2004.com.

- **Though lower than in most parts of Europe, the cost of living is nevertheless rising** – a factor to bear in mind if you plan to live on a pension. The current UK pensions 'crisis' is reported to be hitting would-be purchasers.

- **The housing market is not infinite and genuine bargains are getting fewer**. In the more sought-after locations, prices can in fact be prohibitive unless your budget is limitless.

- **Driving** can, at times, be a hair-raising experience and **traffic** in larger towns and cities as well as tourist areas can be unpleasant.

- **Portugal is to host the Euro 2004 football tournament**, which may ruin your summer if you are not a football fan.

EU Membership

Another factor that makes Portugal attractive is its EU membership and the inherent advantages that this implies – something that people in the UK are only slowly becoming aware of. It is useful to know that a system of mutual rights and obligations between member states guarantees all EU citizens four fundamental rights:

- **The right to move freely and remain in the territory of member states.**
- **The right to vote and to stand as a candidate in local and European Parliament elections in the member state of residence.**
- **Entitlement to protection in a non-EU country in which a citizen's own member state is not represented, by the diplomatic or consular authorities of any other member state.**
- **The right to petition the European parliament and to apply to the European ombudsman.**

More specifically, provided you are not considered to be a danger to public health or order, as a British or Irish citizen resident in Portugal you can become a resident and enjoy practically the same rights as nationals of that country. Residency brings with it the following benefits:

- **The right to take up any kind of paid employment, register as a jobseeker, and claim unemployment benefits, if you are entitled to them. This also means the same rights over working conditions, pay, sick leave, holidays, redundancy, trade union membership and access to vocational training. There are exceptions: the armed forces or police and certain public posts are excluded.**
- **You can enrol your children in Portuguese state schools and, provided you fulfil the entry requirements, you can also study at a Portuguese university.**
- **There is no restriction on the right to open a bank account, move money in and out of the country as nationals do, or apply for mortgages.**

Rights, of course, imply obligations. Residents, like nationals, are subject to the law of the land and must pay their taxes. Many residents seem conveniently to forget this, but penalties for tax evasion are getting heavier in Portugal, *see* **Financial Implications**.

Working in Portugal

EU Citizens

All EU citizens technically belong to the same huge, continent-wide labour market. An electrician from Lisbon can rewire a house in Liverpool just as a Liverpudlian plumber can fix pipes in Lisbon – provided they can find the work, that is. EU directives are very clear on this issue. As jobseekers in any EU country, citizens of any member state enjoy the following rights:

- **Equal treatment with nationals. Any EU worker has the right to enter employment in any member state under the same conditions as nationals.**
- **This also means that for access to employment nationals cannot be favoured solely on the grounds of their nationality.**
- **Where incentive measures for recruiting national workers exist, all EU workers must be counted as national workers in the application of such measures.**

Access to employment may depend on the possession of certain qualifications, diplomas, experience or linguistic skills – for instance, a knowledge of the national language sufficient for the job.

In terms of the type of work to which you have access rights, EU guidelines are also very clear:

- **You may apply for any job for which you feel you are qualified, except for certain public service posts. Member states may reserve certain posts for their nationals if the jobs involve the exercise of powers conferred by public law and the safeguarding of the general interests of the state or local authorities (e.g. diplomatic service, police, judiciary, armed forces).**
- **Most public sector jobs in the areas of health, education, the provision of commercial services and research for civil purposes are open to all EU nationals and are not subject to any restrictions on the grounds of nationality. Since access to public jobs varies from one country to another, you should always ask the national authorities for specific information – see the fact sheet 'Right of access to employment'.**
- **You may also apply for vocational and professional training anywhere in the European Union; ask for the fact sheet 'National education systems'. As well as this you may conduct research anywhere in the European Union. See the fact sheet 'Training and mobility of researchers'.**

All these fact sheets may be obtained by calling **t** 0800 581 591 (in the UK).

Of course, simply having the right to work in no way means you will find a job easily. Some areas of work are still much more available in theory than in practice. Overall, though, the bureaucratic procedures required of British and other EU citizens who wish to work in Portugal are fairly straightforward, and as painless as they can be given the tendency for bureaucracy.

Europe-wide, the unemployment situation varies from country to country. This means that anyone's real chances of finding work in their chosen field depend not so much on the system of rights in place as the practical realities of the labour market at any time. In the case of Portugal, the reality may be tougher than you expect. Unemployment, while low throughout the second half of the 1990s until 2002, is slowly rising again, and Portugal has suffered a serious recession throughout the first half of 2003. Officially the recession is now over (if the authorities are to be believed) and Portugal currently sits in the middle of the EU unemployment league table, with a figure of 7.3 per cent. Inevitably, this must affect your chances of finding work.

Non-EU Citizens

Conversely, since Portugal became an EU member the situation has become much more restrictive for anyone from outside the EU. Big 'door-openers' are: if you are proposing to set up a business; if you can demonstrate you have ample funds to live on; or (if you do have an offer of work) a statement from a company certifying that you are an essential employee. Depending on your country of origin, requirements vary but essentially you need a visa before travelling to Portugal. Technically you cannot come to seek work. This is not to say that you cannot look for a job while on a holiday visit, but if you are made an offer of employment the authorities can refuse you a work permit if there is a suitably qualified Portuguese (or EU) person registered at the employment office in the same area.

Even with a job offer, you are obliged to get a visa from the Portuguese consulate nearest to your home residence, which can mean a return trip home before taking up the job – if indeed the visa is granted. There are many non-EU citizens now working in Portugal, including those from Eastern Europe in the construction business, Brazilians in all types of jobs and Africans (principally from the former colonies of Angola and Mozambique). Not all of them work legally and there are suggestions that in future even those with work permits may have problems renewing them.

Issues to Consider

Whether or not you are an EU passport holder, there are some issues that affect everybody who plans to work in Portugal. So take a long, hard, objective look at your skills, qualifications and experience. Do you know if there is a demand for someone with your profile in the part of Portugal where you plan to live, or any other part for that matter? Can you get your qualifications recognized? If the answer to either or both of these questions is 'no', are you prepared to lower your expectations and work in a different field? Can you compete with locals who may have similar qualifications and are native speakers of the language? Is your Portuguese good enough? Are you willing to overcome the language barrier by learning Portuguese to a high standard? Remember that Portuguese salaries are amongst the lowest in Europe. Are you prepared to live on a salary that barely allows for much more than just survival?

English-speakers do in fact have a certain advantage over other foreigners and native Portuguese – their language. Traditionally a nation of overseas traders and now with an important tourist industry to look after, the Portuguese have always been aware of the advantages that come with speaking languages – many are very talented natural linguists. Since many are eager to learn English or improve on what they already know, there is always demand for TEFL teachers. Qualified schoolteachers can also find work in private or international schools where the language of instruction is English.

Many people work in the tourist industry. Seasonal work is usually available in resorts, especially in bars, pubs, restaurants and clubs. The large ex-pat community also creates employment opportunities for people with skills to offer, as many residents feel more comfortable dealing with English-speakers. A glance at the English-language press throws up some surprises. Among some of the situations vacant in a recent edition of *The News* were: a physiotherapist's assistant, a maid, cooks, waiters, telemarketers, receptionists, a hairdresser, an electrician, a tiler and a gardener. Of those, only the receptionist's job specifically required a bilingual person. Nobody should be fooled into thinking that jobs are abundant but it is clear that English speakers with skills can find openings serving the needs of the anglophone community. There is, of course, the property business. At the bottom end there may be work trying to 'tout' timeshares to tourists, but there are also 'proper' jobs within the industry. Here a background in law or economics, with some marketing experience, may well prove an advantage.

There are also high-powered jobs at the other end of the market, though you have to have special and highly prized skills to find a niche there. Large foreign firms, for example, employ international staff, especially at management levels. Those holding MBAs and with language skills are well placed to find jobs within the world of banking, import–export, IT and construction (though nowadays, at the level of engineer, the labour is mostly done by Africans and Ukrainians).

As an EU citizen, you no longer require a work permit to work in Portugal, but must apply for a **residency card** (*cartão de residência*) if staying in the country for more than 183 days. If you take up a temporary job of fewer than 183 days' duration, typically in the tourist industry, you need not apply for a residency permit. For temporary jobs whose duration is greater than three months but less than a year, you must apply for a temporary residency permit. Even if you are not planning to work, you still need to apply for residency if you plan to stay in the country permanently. For details of application procedures *see* 'Bureaucracy', pp.194–6, and for more on all aspects of working and teaching in Portugal *see* **Settling In**.

Self-employment and Starting a Business

If you are a professional with skills to offer you may decide to go it alone, take the risks and operate as a freelancer (*trabalhador por conta própria*) or a sole trader (*empresário em nome individual*). Language teachers, translators, interpreters, journalists, photographers, graphic artists, craftsmen and others often choose this option. Depending on the work you intend to do or the business you aim to establish, you may be required to prove that you are suitably qualified to be allowed to start working. This is not the case for freelance English teachers or translators, but naturally is required of doctors, dentists, veterinary surgeons and lawyers. The processes involved in getting foreign qualifications recognized is one of the areas that has proved most resistant to EU 'harmonization' plans, and can be long and tortuous (*see* **Settling In**). Self-employed workers have unlimited liabilities, and all possessions could be confiscated and auctioned off if large debts are accumulated. Working in this way does, however, mean certain tax breaks. Business owners who run limited companies are only liable for the capital invested in it.

Setting up a business requires an inspired idea, serious market research, a detailed business plan, sufficient capital and a lot of hard work. Operating from premises also means unbelievable amounts of bureaucracy, affording no short-cuts and requiring tremendous patience. This is despite recent attempts by government to cut back on red tape and streamline procedures. An example of these attempts is the *Loja do Cidadão*, the 'Citizen's Shop', a one-stop centre with branches in Lisbon, Oporto and several other provincial capitals. Practically every branch of the administration is represented there under one roof. So, if the procedures themselves are still complex, at least you do not have to go to a dozen different offices in various parts of town. The road to business success is a bit like Portuguese highways, there is a lot of wreckage lying by the wayside. Many have tried and failed but this need not be the case. It all depends on how you approach it.

To register as a self-employed person, all non-Portuguese workers must first have a **residency card**, which as explained is obtained easily by EU citizens. In the case of non-EU citizens, a **work permit** is also required. This is a 'Catch-22' situation, since you cannot have a work permit without a job. And having a job implies contracted work (working *a conta de outrém*) and not self-employment (*trabalhador por conta própria*). The only real way around this is to get a work permit allowing you to work for a company, and then become self-employed later – once you have your foot in the door.

Learning Portuguese

Around 200 million people in the world greet others with a *Bom dia*. Portuguese ranks eighth among the most spoken languages in the world (third among the western languages, after English and Castilian). It is the official language of seven countries and since 1986 has been one of the official languages of the European Union. Anyone who aims to spend long periods in Portugal, especially those intending to buy a property and take up residence there, should seriously consider learning Portuguese. This is not only a matter of common courtesy to your hosts, but vital if you are to make the best of your time there, if only as a survival tool. While in the tourist areas and larger cities it is not difficult to find English-speaking Portuguese property agents, lawyers, doctors and other professionals, you cannot always assume this will be the case. Further afield you are even less likely to find people who can help you in your own language. Even if your life and dealings are mainly within the ex-pat community, there will be times when understanding and making yourself understood in Portuguese will be necessary. Dealing with officialdom, bank clerks, plumbers, cleaning staff, waiters, shopkeepers and policemen will inevitably mean having to communicate in Portuguese, while in emergency situations explaining yourself could be a matter of life or death.

A word of warning: while Portuguese belongs to the same family of languages (all derived from Latin) as Spanish, French and Italian, and on paper looks remarkably like its neighbour, Castilian Spanish, it is nevertheless a language all of its own with certain characteristics that can make it difficult to learn, at least in the initial stages. Pronunciation, for a start, is considerably more complex than that of Castilian or Italian and the abundance of closed vowels and 'shushing' consonants make it sound, to the unfamiliar ear, like an eastern European language. This means comprehension of spoken Portuguese can be difficult at first. While it is often possible to make an inspired guess as to the meaning of written Portuguese – you do not have to be a genius to work out what *modere a sua velocidade* means on the highway – it might not be so obvious if someone says this to you at machine-gun speed. Any attempts you make at speaking Portuguese, however clumsy, will be appreciated and people will usually listen patiently, speak back to you slowly and generally try to help you.

The Portuguese language and how to set about learning it will be looked at in greater depth in 'Learning and Speaking Portuguese', pp.257–9. *See* also 'Portuguese for Survival', pp.292–8, for a Portuguese-English glossary.

Educating and Raising Children

If you have children, or are planning to, there are a whole set of issues that are vitally important. By moving to Portugal, you will be allowing your children to participate in all the good things that you expect to find there, especially the generally slower pace and healthier lifestyle. Like many other EU countries, Portugal has watched its birth-rate decline as its macroeconomic and development statistics have gone up. In Portugal, however, unlike child-hostile societies such as Britain, babies are cooed over, and children generally are both 'seen and heard'. The climate and the lifestyle may well mean your children can play outdoors, out of sight, in places where you would not dream of letting them go to at home. Children may, in fact, provide a passport into local society, as they will probably pick up the language and make friends more quickly than you do. Your first and most lasting Portuguese friends could well be the parents of the children that your own make friends with.

You do, however, need to look seriously at the question of education and make your child's interests a top priority. The availability, or lack, of good schools is certainly a factor that should influence your decision when it comes to choosing the area that you settle in. It comes down to three choices, two of which may not be an option unless you have sufficient financial resources. You may choose either to send your children to a local state school, which is free, with instruction in Portuguese, or put them into one of the many private schools that provide education in English (or another European language such as French or German), or send them off to boarding school in Britain or another country. The second and third options are only open to you if you can afford private education, which is universally expensive. Despite this, it seems the majority of foreign residents do choose to send their children to fee-paying private English-language schools, of which there are many in the areas with greater concentrations of ex-pats. If you cannot afford the second or third options, and are not convinced that putting your children through the state system is the answer either, then perhaps you should think again about moving to Portugal.

Whatever you decide to do, remember that education in Portugal is now compulsory from ages six to 15, and pre-school (from ages three to five), though optional, is now widely available. During the Salazar years, education was considered a privilege – available only for the middle and upper classes. Education for the masses was thought of as dangerous. It was not until after the 1974 revolution that it became enshrined as a right of every individual. The result is that illiteracy levels are still around 10 per cent of people over the age of 15, much higher than in Greece or Spain. Many illiterate people are elderly women in rural areas and school drop-outs. Overall, Portuguese education has improved greatly as a result of reforms that took place in the late 1980s, but it still has a long way to go. In recent years, the government has channelled considerable sums of money into the state system but the results have been patchy to say the least. In fact, on a par with the health system, education is one area where achievements have fallen disappointingly short of the expectations that such investment would warrant. Clearly, just throwing money at the problem has not been the answer and there is much debate going on about educational reforms. In fairness, the system is not all bad – many of Portugal's leading figures, politicians, writers and intellectuals are products of the state system.

See further 'Education', pp.227–9.

State Education

More than 85 per cent of Portuguese children attend publicly funded educational institutions. State education is free, apart from the cost of books and school lunches. Education policy is determined by the Ministry of Education. On mainland Portugal a ministerial department manages and administers each educational level and five regional bodies implement policies and provide guidelines, support and coordination to all non-higher educational institutions. Municipal-level local education centres also have a role in co-ordinating and assisting non-higher education. Universities and other higher education institutions are autonomous. In the autonomous (offshore) regions of Madeira and the Azores, education administration is the responsibility of regional governments through education secretariats.

Education at pre-primary level is optional, though recommended. It is provided both by state-run and private nurseries (*jardims de infância*) which are free and fee-paying respectively. Even if you plan to send your child to a private school later, a state-run *jardim de infância* is a good option to start, since your child will quickly learn Portuguese there. Compulsory primary education (*ensino básico*) starts at six, is free and consists of three phases (6–9, 10–11 and 12–15 years of age).

Between 15 and 18, young people who have successfully completed the first nine years of primary education then go on to either *ensino secundário* (general upper secondary education) or to an *escola profissional* (vocational school). Within the general system they may opt to take *cursos gerais* (general courses, which are more for academically inclined students wishing to go to university) or more specialized *cursos tecnológicos* (technology courses). The vocational courses equip young people with a trade and are aimed more at helping students get their bearings in the job market after the age of 18. Parallel to this system, and open to young people between 14 and 24, are apprenticeship schemes and initial training schemes in various employment sectors.

Higher education in Portugal includes university and polytechnic education and may be provided by public, private or co-operative higher education institutions. In order to gain access to higher education, students must have successfully passed the 12th year of schooling or passed an equivalent, national examination. Universities and polytechnics award the degrees of *bacharelato*, a first degree, after three years of study, and *licenciatura*, a full degree, after between four and six years. Masters and doctors degrees may only be awarded by universities. The system is currently over-subscribed, with far more applicants than there are places available. Those who can do so opt to study abroad or in private universities.

Private Schools

Sending children to a private school where instruction is in English, or in some other European language, is favoured by the majority of foreign residents. In ex-pat areas there are many schools that offer either British or American syllabuses or the International Baccalaureate. Most take children from pre-school until the end of secondary education. The emphasis, in general, is on providing a broad, well-rounded education. As well as academic achievement, the arts and sports are considered an important part of education and the aim is usually to help children realize their personal as well as their academic potential. These schools are often to be found in suburban locations with spacious grounds and excellent facilities both inside and outside the classroom. The pupils often have a mix of different nationalities, helping to give children a more international outlook on life and a wealth of contacts in other countries, which can prove useful in their future careers. A very high percentage of young people who graduate from international schools go on to universities in the USA and Europe. If you can afford it, you may well prefer this option. Not all such institutions, though, come up to scratch and you should beware of cut-price establishments whose standards may be low. Talk to parents, teachers and former pupils of as many schools as possible before settling on any one.

Health Services

The Portuguese public health system is one of those areas which, despite tangible improvements in recent years, is still not performing as well as it should and standards of healthcare are lower than those in northern Europe. As with education, health spending has increased – in 2000 it was 7.8 per cent of GDP – but there are many deficiencies in the system. There are also plenty of horror stories and reports are common of long waiting lists for hospital admission, 'Dantesque' scenes in emergency wards, gross understaffing (Portugal aims to incorporate 10,000 Spanish-trained nurses into its system by 2004) and chaotic (mis)management that turns even brand new hospitals into disaster areas.

The coalition government that came to office in 2002 plans to overhaul and modernize health services. One innovation will be new regulations that allow the private sector to take part in the management and funding of hospital units and hospital services will increasingly be contracted out to the private sector. The basic aims are to reduce waiting lists, reform prescription procedures, cut spending on drugs and introduce genetic research and gene therapy. It remains to be seen how much impact these reforms will have on the system but the fact that the government is taking the issue seriously is encouraging.

As it stands at present, the Portuguese public health system, run by the Health Ministry (*Ministério de Saúde*), provides free or low-cost healthcare to all who contribute to social security (*segurança social*) as well as their family members. Retired people, including EU pensioners, are also entitled to these services. Portugal has reciprocal agreements with most European countries. In the case of UK citizens, free in-patient treatment in general wards of official hospitals is provided on production of a UK passport (other EU nationals must present form E111). Secondary examinations, X-rays and laboratory tests may have to be paid for. A nominal charge will be made for medical treatment at local health centres (*centros de saúde*), which are generally open 8am–8pm. Some non-essential prescribed medicines may be charged for and dental treatment is not free. This agreement is also effective in Madeira and the Azores (although in Madeira a fee must be paid for GP consultation, which can then be refunded by an appointed bank). Those wishing to take advantage of it should inform the doctor prior to treatment that they wish to be treated under EU social security arrangements. Private treatment must be paid for in full. Medical fees paid whilst in Portugal cannot be reimbursed by the British NHS.

Given the deficiencies of the current system, many foreigners, both visitors and residents, understandably opt to take out private health insurance. The public and private systems have existed parallel to one another for some time and there are plenty of private practitioners, clinics and hospitals throughout Portugal, especially where foreign residents need them, in popular tourist and resident areas. *See* further 'Health and Emergencies', pp. 229–31.

Retirement

Not surprisingly, Portugal is many people's idea of the ideal place to retire. Those who already own a second home and spend their holidays there imagine living out their twilight years in a relaxed fashion, enjoying glorious weather and an outdoor lifestyle most of the year around. There are many retirees already living in Portugal – 4,700 British people to according UK government figures, mainly in the Algarve, and to a lesser extent in Madeira and other parts of the country. Those in receipt of a state pension find that it stretches a little further than it would at home. A recent Eurostat report showed a basket of basic supermarket goods to be more expensive there than in Spain, France or Italy, the three other most popular retirement destinations. A pension from any EU country may be transferred to a bank account in any other member state. This means that if you live in Portugal, on opening a bank account you can receive your pension there once you have established your residency. If you have worked in Portugal prior to retirement, you may be eligible for a Portuguese state pension (generally not very much) or one for which contributions paid in at home, or in another member state, are taken into account when calculating the amount payable.

Pensioners who are planning to head off to the sun should only make their decision after seeking expert advice. You need to know exactly how far your pension and savings will stretch and you have to be aware of future currency fluctuations, especially since Britain now seems unlikely to join the Euro in the immediate future. Another issue – one that is becoming increasingly more important – is the current UK pensions crisis. In the last five years, one in three UK pension schemes has been scrapped – over 700 schemes in 2002 alone.

Pensioners, like everybody else, must choose their location carefully, possibly even more so than younger people. Proximity of amenities and services, especially health services, becomes increasingly important the older you get. Distance from your children and other family members should also be considered. While you are still fit and active this may not be a problem, but what about if you start getting frail? This is one reason why living in a country cottage or a house on a mountain, pretty and appealing as they may be, is not necessarily the answer for retirees.

See further **Financial Implications**, and 'Retirement', pp. 196–8.

Visas and Permits

There are certain documents that anybody intending to reside in Portugal, whether from an EU country or outside, must obtain. The most essential ones are the tax or fiscal card and the residency card.

Tax/Fiscal Card

The tax or fiscal card, (*cartão de contribuinte*) is obligatory for residents and non-residents who have financial dealings in Portugal. Even if you plan to buy a holiday home and only visit infrequently you must still obtain the card before purchasing, as you will be liable for taxes on your property and must therefore have a fiscal number (*número de identificação fiscal/NIF*). The card is very easy to obtain. Simply go to your local tax office (the Portuguese Inland Revenue is the *Ministerio de Finanças*, generally just known as *finanças*), taking your passport and a photocopy of the identification pages.

The card you are issued, together with the number, will be quoted in all dealings and is necessary to open a bank account and to register your property.

Residency Card

A residency card (*cartão de residência*) must be applied for by all those European Union, European Economic Area and Swiss citizens who are paid workers (*trabalhador por conta de outrém*), who wish to act as a sole trader (*empresário em nome individual*) or become self-employed (*trabalhador por conta própria*). Similarly, those who wish to live off their own means (*vivendo de outros rendimentos*), students (*estudantes*) or family members of any of the above (*familiares*) must also apply for the residency card.

The paperwork involved is not too horrendous and you must make your application at the Foreigners' Department (*Serviço de Estrangeiros e Fronteiras/SEF*) closest to your place of residence.

Employed Workers

Documents to be presented:

- **Application forms. There are two; one is 'Modelo 700', the other is 'Modelo 703' (yellow, specific for EU citizens). Both are in Portuguese, English and French and are not difficult to fill in; they can be requested on an initial trip to the office.**
- **Two recent and identical passport-type photographs in colour.**
- **Original and photocopy of work contract, in which the starting and finishing dates must be stated.**
- **Original and photocopy (of the relevant pages) of your passport.**
- **A fee of €2.54 is charged on making the application.**

Sole Traders and the Self-employed

Documents to be presented:

- **Application forms, as above.**
- **Two recent and identical passport-type photographs in colour.**
- **Documents proving that you have established a company as a sole trader or a declaration of having begun self-employment.**
- **Original and photocopy (of the relevant pages) of your passport.**
- **Document proving that you are covered for health care; this may be an insurance policy or a social security card.**
- **A fee of €2.54 is charged on making the application.**

Living off Your Own Means

Documents to be presented:

- **Application forms, as above.**
- **Two recent and identical passport-type photographs in colour.**
- **Documents proving that you have sufficient means to support yourself (normally proof of a pension being paid by bank transfer or of some other means of income or savings).**
- **Original and photocopy (of the relevant pages) of your passport.**

- **Document proving that you are covered for health care; this may be an insurance policy or a social security card.**
- **A fee of €2.54 is charged on making the application.**

Students

Documents to be presented:

- **Application forms, as above.**
- **Two recent and identical passport-type photographs in colour.**
- **Proof of sufficient means to support yourself, equivalent to or higher than the national minimum wage.**
- **Proof of being a registered student in the institution where you are studying.**
- **Original and photocopy (of the relevant pages) of your passport.**
- **Document proving that you are covered for health care; this may be an insurance policy or a social security card.**
- **A fee of €2.54 is charged on making the application.**

Family Members who are EU Citizens

Documents to be presented:

- **Application forms, as above.**
- **Two recent and identical passport-type photographs in colour.**
- **Spouses: marriage certificate issued less than one year ago.**
- **Children: birth certificate.**
- **Document proving that you are covered for health care; this may be an insurance policy or a social security card.**

Family Members who are Citizens of Third Countries

Documents to be presented:

- **A residency visa (*visto de residência*), applied for at a Portuguese consulate in the country of origin or current residence.**

Non-EU Citizens

Things are a lot tougher for citizens of non-EU countries, who may need a visa to enter Portugal even on a visit. For purposes of work and/or residency a visa will almost certainly be required, and many other requirements are made by the authorities. The best source of information is the Portuguese consulate in your own country. Information may also be found, in Portuguese, on the web page of the *Serviço de Estrangeiros e Fronteiras*, **www.sef.pt**. (At the time of writing, when you click on the button saying 'English Version', a window pops up with the message 'Available soon'.)

Where in Portugal: Profiles of the Regions

03

Despite its diminutive proportions – it is only slightly larger than Scotland – Portugal is remarkably diverse. With approximately 92,000 sq km of surface area (including Madeira and the Azores; continental Portugal covers 88,941 sq km) the country includes an enormous variety of landscapes, climatic zones and cultural diversity. Levels of development and sophistication in some parts are in stark contrast with others, where time seems to have stood still. As well as the contrasts to be found from one region to another, there is also considerable variation within each.

The north, with its wet climate, is green and lush, with forests, fast-flowing rivers, mountains and valleys. The characteristically chequered landscape is the result of the divisions and subdivisions of smallholdings, the main form of land ownership, over the generations. There are many contrasts even here. Porto (Oporto to English speakers), European City of Culture in 2001, has a gleaming new contemporary arts centre, lively nightlife, a top-notch football team and a work ethic that ensures its prosperity. Travel 90-odd km due east and you are in the province of Trás-os-Montes ('behind the hills'), where the sight of ox-carts and rudimentary agricultural techniques might lead you to suppose that a time-machine had deposited you back in the 17th century.

The southern coastline has stretches of dramatic, abrupt cliffs that seem to crash into the sea, spectacular sandy beaches and intimate little coves; the eastern end of the Algarve has flat, marshy land and a series of sand spits that accompany the coastline virtually to the Spanish border. Just inland from the coast are hills that contain an astonishing variety of flora and fauna and which are covered in wildflowers in February and March, followed by a carpet of orange blossom in April. Here, sophisticated resorts and fashionable golf and villa developments are in marked contrast with the quaint little inland villages which are just a short drive away.

Between these two extremes are the arid southern plains of the *Baixo* (lower) Alentejo region, which have a certain haunting beauty. This region covers about a fifth of the total surface area but accounts for no more than two per cent of the country's (approximately) 10 million inhabitants. With a landholding system of large *latifúndios* dating back to Roman times, as do cities like Évora, Elvas and Beja in the *Baixo*, this area could be in a completely different country from Trás-os-Montes.

Then there is central Portugal. Relatively well developed and more heavily populated, it includes the crumbling but unfailingly charming capital of Lisbon, plus a host of ancient cities that overflow with historic monuments. A long, straight coastline gives way to foothills and then verdant mountains offering a dazzling variety of views and experiences. Undeniably, Portugal packs a lot into one small package.

Yet, despite its diversity, Portugal also has many other aspects that make it a cohesive unit. Unlike neighbouring Spain, or France or the UK, there are no regional tensions apart from a certain local rivalry – generally expressed by chanting in football stadiums – between Lisbon and Oporto and between the north and south in general. There are no terrorist groups fighting for their region's independence. The nearest Portugal has ever come to that was a few hand grenades thrown at public buildings in Madeira during the heady days following the 1974 revolution, while the autonomy later granted to Madeira and the Azores (from 1976) has largely defused any pro-independence leanings there. Certain half-hearted proposals have been made for changing the political system and devolving power to the regions but even that has failed to come to fruition. Nor has Portugal had to face problems of different languages coexisting within its borders – a politically controversial issue in neighbouring Spain. Portugal is a small nation but one that has a feeling of being just that, a nation whose unity few would dispute.

Portuguese History

Portugal is one of Europe's oldest countries, with over nine centuries of history as a nation within the borders (more or less) that it has today. Until medieval times, there was little to distinguish historical developments on the western edge of the Iberian peninsula from the interior, so it is more accurate to talk of a common Iberian history until then. Portugal's long, complex, passionate history merits several volumes, but here is a brief snapshot.

Prehistory

There is evidence of early human settlements within the confines of present-day Portugal. Remnants of pottery and cave burials, found along the Tagus valley and in parts of modern Alentejo and Estremadura, are thought to be from around 8,000 to 7,000 BC. In the Beira Alta region, in Vila Nova de Foz Côa, the largest-known Palaeolithic 'art collection' was discovered in the 1980s. The late Neolithic period was to see some of the first cultural focal points that might be defined as having 'Lusitanian' characteristics, distinct from others in the peninsula: the construction of dolmens, and cromlechs. During the Bronze and Iron Ages the Celts and Iberians introduced a pastoral and agrarian culture to the whole area, while on the coast the Phoenicians, Greeks and Carthaginians established trading posts, exploited mines, and colonized much of the south. The first real permanent settlements in Portugal were the 'Castros', fortified hilltop villages whose construction and development were refined by Celtic peoples between 700 and 600 BC.

From the Romans to the Moors

Until the Middle Ages, Iberian history is defined by periods of invasion and colonization, first by the Romans, later the Moors and, between the two, the Visigoths. The Romans entered the stage after their victory over Carthage in the third century BC, and quickly made the former Carthaginian territory into a new province of their expanding empire. They met resistance from the Lusitanians, led by the warrior chieftain Viriato, Portugal's first national hero, who held up the Roman invasion for several decades – until he was betrayed and murdered in his bed. Viriato's death spelt the end of the Lusitanian resistance, and Rome quickly conquered the rest of the peninsula. Julius Caesar made Olispo (Lisbon) the administrative centre in 60 BC, a role it played until the founding of Emerita (nowadays Mérida, in Spain) in AD 25. A senate was established in Ebora (Évora), and other important towns such as Scallabis (Santarém) and Pax Julia (Beja) were founded. Romanization accentuated the differences between the two main regions. In the rugged northern mountains its impact was less felt but on the southern plains it led to the creation of large estates known as *latifúndios* and the introduction of olives, wheat, oats and vines. The Romans also imposed towns, *citânias,* into which they gradually forced the Lusitanian peoples to live. In the *citânias* the Lusitanians acquired Roman civilization and learned Latin, the basis of modern Portuguese. When the Romans converted to Christianity in the third century AD, so did the Lusitanians.

Roman cultural, economic and administrative influence would last for a long time throughout the entire peninsula – even the road network was used until well into the Middle Ages. Roman remains in Portugal are less impressive than those at Tarragona and Mérida in Spain but important sites are to be found in Évora and Conímbriga, southwest of Coimbra.

In AD 409, with Roman rule in decline, the first wave of barbarians invaded the peninsula. Vandals, followed by Alans, the Suevi and finally Visigoths, came and conquered. The Visigothic empire ruled most of the peninsula from AD 585 until the early eighth century but it was always a fragile alliance made up of differing factions, and when the first Moorish armies crossed from North Africa in AD 711, initially to help one particular Visigoth faction, the whole system collapsed. Within a decade the Moors had occupied practically the whole of the peninsula apart from the mountainous region of Asturias in northern Spain.

The Muslims, like the Romans, left their imprint on the peninsula long after their departure. Less influential in the north, a great civilization flourished in the south, under the rule of wise, tolerant governors who fostered the arts and sciences. The Arabs settled principally in what is nowadays the Algarve (the name derives from the Arabic *Al-Gharb* meaning 'the land beyond') though they controlled the Alentejo and the land up to Lisbon and the Tagus. In the mid-9th century a caliphate grew up around Shelb (nowadays Silves) which was independent of the main centre at Córdoba in Spain. The economy flourished. Roman irrigation techniques were improved upon, crop rotation was introduced, as were cotton, citrus fruits and rice, important products even today. Trading links with the north of Africa were established and urban centres such as Lisbon, Évora, Santarém and Beja grew and became more sophisticated. Decline started in the 11th century when rich, powerful local nobles began to carve up the caliphate into independent regional city-states (*taifas*), thus allowing small groups of Visigothic Christians to take the initiative from their mountain refuges in the northwest and launch the Christian reconquest of Iberia.

The reconquest had in fact originated in the eighth century and was a long-drawn-out campaign that culminated in Portugal in 1249 when Faro, the last enclave, finally fell. The Moors, even after that defeat, held on to much of *Al-Andalus* (southern Spain) until as late as 1492 when the Catholic kings finished the task. Throughout the southern Iberian peninsula the Moorish influence is still evident today, and in the Algarve, especially, it can be seen in place names such as Albufeira, Aljezur and Almancil, in ruined castles, in building styles and in some of the crops, notably citrus fruits. The Portuguese language also has some 600 words of Arabic origin.

Medieval Portugal

By the 11th century, *Portucale*, the Christian-held stronghold of northern Portugal, as it was known then, already had the status of a country despite the ever-shifting frontiers between lands reconquered and those still held by the Moors. Its rulers, though, were designated from the neighbouring kingdom of León in Spain. King Afonso VI gave the throne to his illegitimate daughter, Teresa, whose son, Afonso Henriques, continued the south-bound reconquest and proclaimed himself as the first king of Portugal, a title recognized by Alfonso VII of Castile-León in 1143 by the Treaty of Zamora. It was left to his successors, in particular Dom Dinis, to finish the reconquest and consolidate the country into a unified monarchy. Dom Dinis established the borders of Portugal in the Treaty of Alcañices, signed by King Fernando IV of Castile in 1297. He also founded the University of Lisbon and created the Order of Christ to replace the Knights Templar, who had been instrumental in the reconquest.

On the death of King Fernando I in 1383, his wife Leonor tried to enthrone the couple's only daughter, Beatriz, married to Juan I of Castile, which would effectively have ended Portugal's independence. The Portuguese bourgeoisie opposed the move and after Spanish forces were defeated João of Avis (Fernando's illegitimate stepbrother) occupied the throne as João I, the first of the House of Avis dynasty. Help from the English in defeating the Spaniards led in 1386 to the Treaty of Windsor, an Anglo–Luso alliance that would last until the 20th century.

Colonial Expansion

With Castile no longer a threat, Portugal started looking outwards. The early 1400s saw the beginning of Portugal's maritime expansion, especially after the Infante Don Henrique (Henry the Navigator) appeared on the scene, using the Order of Christ's wealth to finance maritime research and found a cosmography school in Sagres. Madeira and the Azores were discovered and the west coast of Africa was explored down as far as Sierra Leone. During the reigns of João II, Manuel I and João III, overseas expansion continued. Vasco da Gama reached India in 1497 and opened up important commercial routes, and Pedro Alvarez Cabral set foot in Brazil for the first time in 1500.

In 1494, the Treaty of Tordesillas established the shareout of the newly discovered territories between Portugal and Spain. The latter had also been busy in terms of maritime exploration, with Columbus first reaching America in 1492. An imaginary line drawn to the west of the Cabo Verde islands left in Portuguese hands anything that should be 'discovered' thereafter, resulting in Brazil becoming a colony shortly after. Portugal was by now the world's chief maritime power, with strategic posts in Goa, the Moluccas and Macao.

The Spanish

Decline was not far off. Throughout the Middle Ages, the country's finances had been in the hands of Jews, who had never been persecuted in Portugal as they were in the rest of Christendom. But during the reign of Manuel I, under pressure from Spain and Rome, they were expelled. It marked the beginning of the end of Portugal's imperial splendour. João III's successor, Dom Sebastião, then embarked on a costly crusade to the north of Africa which would result not only in the young king's death but also in the death of most of the Portuguese nobility. The power vacuum thus created allowed the Spanish to intervene in Portuguese affairs, with Felipe II being crowned Felipe I of Portugal in 1581, aided by the remnants of the Portuguese nobles. Spanish domination lasted little more than half a century, but was sufficient to create resentment for their eastern neighbours which many Portuguese still feel to this day, especially since so much of Portugal's overseas trading power was lost as a result.

Spanish rule ended in 1640, thanks to an uprising led by the Duke of Bragança who proclaimed himself João IV, thus beginning the rule of the House of Bragança, which would last until the proclamation of the Republic in 1910. By this time, gold had been discovered in Brazil, but much of the wealth would be wasted on megalomaniac projects such as the convent at Mafra, ordered by João V. He also signed a disastrous accord with England which effectively killed the flourishing Portuguese textile industry, giving preference to English imports.

The End of the Monarchy

The great earthquake that destroyed Lisbon in 1775 did further damage to the country's shaky finances, though Dom José I, by then on the throne, entrusted the rebuilding to his prime minister, the Marquis of Pombal, who applied the principles of enlightened despotism to get the country back on its feet. Dom José died in 1777, leaving the throne to his daughter, Dona Maria, who went mad in 1791 and delegated power to the Prince Regent, later to be called Dom João VI. The three Napoleonic invasions between 1807 and 1811 served to knock the country back yet again. The Portuguese royal family went into exile in Brazil while the fighting continued, leaving military affairs in the hands of British generals and the Portuguese army effectively in charge of the country. The French were finally pushed out of Portugal and Spain in 1814. Meanwhile, in Brazil, the Prince Regent had declared the colony an independent kingdom, leaving Portugal, technically, half a colony of Brazil and half a British protectorate. The military, in the absence of royal power and inspired by the liberal winds blowing throughout Europe, drew up a new constitution that the king, on his return from Brazil in 1821, was unwillingly forced to sign, thus spelling the end of absolutist monarchy.

The backlash came after Dom João died in 1826. Prince Pedro, his son and successor, drew up a new constitution and then abdicated in favour of his own seven-year-old daughter, Maria, naming his brother, Miguel, Prince Regent on the condition that Miguel would marry Maria when she came of age. Miguel did so but later backtracked on the constitution and returned to his absolutist convictions, nullifying Pedro's Constitutional Charter and suppressing all protests. What became known as the 'War of the Two Brothers', essentially between absolutist ideas – strong in the countryside – and enlightenment – strong in the cities – would divide Portuguese society for much of the 19th century, provoking a civil war in 1846. A two-party system of 'alternation' held things together for the rest of the century but the monarchy was practically bankrupt and republican ideas continued to grow stronger, especially among the army and the urban working-class. In 1908 King Carlos I and his son were assassinated and in 1910 a military uprising abolished the monarchy.

Parliamentary elections held in 1911 brought a republican triumph, the royal family went into exile and the provisional government of the First Republic took office. Political stability, however, was not to come. The ruling *Partido Democrático* was led by Afonso Costa, a man of a dictatorial bent who manipulated successive elections to keep power. The bureaucracy, a legacy of the monarchy, was corrupt and inefficient and the military took an ever greater role in governmental matters. Neither president nor prime minister ever had the authority to dissolve parliament and so military interventions – of which there were 45 between 1920 and 1926 – became the 'normal' way of changing governments.

The Republic

Finally, in 1926, General Carmona, a Catholic monarchist, led a coup and took power definitively, suppressing the republican constitution. Unsure how a restoration of the monarchy would be received, Carmona called elections in 1928, standing as sole candidate. In the same year he promoted an economics professor from Coimbra, Dr Salazar, to the post of tax minister. His strict control of the public purse would see him catapulted to the job of prime minister in 1932, a post he held until 1968. Ideologically it is difficult to paint Salazar and his '*Novo Estado*' as fascist but his methods certainly were. Parliamentarians were elected from a sole party, the *União Nacional*, trade unions were vertical and run by industry bosses, strictly controlled education fomented the Catholic religion, censorship was absolute and the political police, the PIDE, watched over everyone. The 'three F's' – Fátima, Football and Fado – were the regime's watchwords and its way of controlling the people.

Salazar's regime did create the infrastructure of a modern economy but the benefits did not filter down to the ordinary people, who continued to live in poverty, especially those in the countryside, which was largely abandoned. Discontent was rife but ultimately what caused the regime to fall had more to do with external factors than internal ones. Salazar's colonial wars cost the country dear and earned Portugal enemies in many places. Military officers, based in Africa, also began to realize how unjust their country's system was, and. when Salazar was incapacitated by a stroke in 1968, his successor, Marcelo Caetano, tried to make certain concessions towards democratization of the country. Too little, too late, for by 1974 military discontent had grown and the revolutionary *Movimento das Forças Armadas* (MFA), led by Otelo Saraiva de Carvalho, organized the overthrow of the government on 25 April. This moment of great change has since become known as the 'Revolution of the Carnations'.

Since then, Portugal's history has been, if not uneventful, at any rate one of progress towards liberty and democracy. The last quarter-century may be seen as two separate periods with a watershed in the middle. After the revolution, Portugal divested itself of its colonies, provoking an inrush of Portuguese citizens – many of them formerly residents of Angola and Mozambique. These *retornados* arrived at a moment of great economic chaos, which lasted until the mid-eighties. In 1986, however, Portugal gained entry to the European Economic Community (now European Union). This has resulted in massive investment in infrastructure as well as great changes in society – mostly for the better.

Today, Portugal, though still poor by the standards of most of its EU partners, is a prosperous, stable democracy that is finally beginning to look to the future instead of the past. Even relationships with neighbouring Spain, always strained, have become more fluid in recent years. Nobody knows exactly what the future holds, as EU subsidies (from which Portugal has benefited for the last

15 or 20 years) are channelled towards newer Member States. But the foundations at least have been laid for a tomorrow that will almost certainly be rosier than yesterday and the day before.

Which Portugal?

Despite its relatively small size, Portugal can offer a great variety of landscapes, weather patterns, geographical features and possible lifestyles to choose from. Do you, for example, want urban or rural living, to be on or near the coast, on the inland plains or in a mountain region? Would you rather live in a city, town or village? Most importantly, what can you afford? Or maybe, can you afford a second or holiday home *at all*? (This most basic of questions will be dealt with in **Selecting a Property**.) It is well worth asking yourself some serious questions before you start looking.

• **Is living by or close to the sea important?** Portugal has over 800km of coastline, and many beautiful beaches with soft, white sand. This means there are plenty of coastal destinations to choose from and many attractive locations that are not far from the sea. Beach properties are expensive these days, especially in the Algarve and those close to Lisbon. So, if your budget is limited, you may have little choice but to look at other coastal areas or else further inland. The interior of Portugal does, in any case, have many pretty towns and villages where properties are likely to be far more affordable and where you are never actually that far from the sea. The inland city of Évora in the Alentejo region, for example, is just over 100km from the coast.

• **Do you want a practically year-round sunny climate or would you be happy with seasonal variety?** If what you are seeking is a place in the sun with truly mild winters then it has to be southern Portugal, more especially the Algarve, or the island of Madeira. The Algarve enjoys around 3,000 hours of sunshine per year and it is only the rainy season (between October and late January or early February) that could remotely be classified as 'winter'. Even then, on days without rain, you may expect gorgeous blue skies. Madeira is subtropical and therefore mild all year, with warm, wet winters and hotter but not unbearable summers. If you like seasonal variety and do not mind, or even welcome, a little more rain then you may prefer to look further north, possibly inland.

• **How important is it for you to be close to a ready-made ex-pat community where most of your day-to-day affairs can be conducted in English?** There are English-speaking communities in many parts of Portugal, although they tend to be clustered in certain areas. These include the Algarve, where well over a third of all English-speaking residents choose to live, Lisbon and the Estoril coast, Oporto (both city and region) and Madeira. In many places you will be able to find English-speaking lawyers, doctors and dentists, as well as many other services staffed by English-speakers. In addition, there are international schools where the language of instruction is English. Moreover, wherever English-speakers get together, they tend to form clubs and associations – such as amateur dramatics societies, sports clubs, mother and toddler circles and even Alcoholics Anonymous groups – giving newcomers a ready-made social 'scene'. Living almost exclusively within the ex-pat community is a personal lifestyle choice that clearly suits many, especially those for whom learning Portuguese is not high on the list of priorities. On the Algarve, according to one resident, 'most locals speak English and because a lot of ex-pats live there the service economy is geared up for it. Portuguese is not necessary.' If this is not what you are looking for then maybe you should look to buy elsewhere.

• **Do you want to integrate into Portuguese society and take part in Portuguese social and cultural life?** If you want to merge into Portuguese society it is more a question of attitude than location, though it does help if you choose to live in a place that is not packed with foreign residents. In the Algarve, particularly, there are two separate, parallel societies. Though mutually dependent, the locals and the foreigners live apart, greatly respect each other and co-exist happily. Given the degree of separation between the two communities, therefore, the Algarve may not be the ideal place to look for integration. However, if you do want to integrate successfully then the first step is to get your Portuguese to a reasonable level of fluency. After that, it is a question of going where the locals go to eat, drink, dance or otherwise entertain themselves, join a sports club or some other association, get yourself invited to parties and take things from there. If you are naturally gregarious then you may be better off living in one of the larger cities, as they offer far more opportunities to develop an active social life. It will not necessarily be easy, since Portuguese society can be quite family-centred, especially in smaller towns and cities, and it can often take a while before you are invited to a Portuguese home. But, when you are, it is a sure sign that you have crossed an important barrier.

• **Are you planning to live in retirement or do you want to work?** If you plan to retire in Portugal then your choice of location should be influenced by where you want to be and what you can afford. If you want to work or set up a business then you should look very carefully at the labour market and economic conditions in the areas where you might like to live. Work is not easy to find and in some areas it is practically impossible to get a job, effectively excluding these places from your list. Tourist areas offer some opportunities for seasonal work, doing jobs created by the tourist industry itself, though out of season there may not be so many openings. Larger towns and cities are where you are more likely to find work. On the other hand, you could run a business practically anywhere, provided that it is viable, though finding this out usually requires thorough and exhaustive market research. *Whether you are seeking work or planning to run a business, a better than working knowledge of the Portuguese language is vital.*

• **Is access to golf courses an important factor in your choice?** Though not the most important reason for everybody's choice of location, for many people the possibility of playing golf in the sunshine (practically all year round) is an important factor. Known as golf's 'Golden Coast', the Algarve is the leading area for golf courses in Portugal; indeed, for most people this region is synonymous with the game. However, it is quite possible to play in other parts of the country, though the weather makes the season shorter. The country's first course was laid out and inaugurated in 1890 close to Espinho, a small town just south of Oporto, and there are many courses in that area. The greater Lisbon area also has a number of courses and there are several in Madeira and the Azores. Villa developments are often built adjacent to or very close to golf courses. However, this comes at quite a hefty price. For more on golf courses *see* **Settling In**, 'Sport', pp.262–4.

• **Do you want to escape from it all and live in rural solitude?** If this is what you want, then you might care to look inland at some of Portugal's lesser known and frequented areas. As homes on or near the beach in the Algarve have become scarcer and more expensive, many settlers are tending to look just inland in the hills but increased demand is beginning to push prices up there too. Offering more in the way of rural isolation are regions such as the Alentejo (huge and sparsely populated), central Portugal north of the Tagus and inland from the Costa de Prata (where many genuine bargains may still be found), and the rural area of Montanhas in the northeast (practically undiscovered). Properties may be found both in villages, offering some services, or way off the beaten track where the true hermit can find his longed-for isolation. Generally you will find that village and rural properties come cheaper but may require a lot of work and maintenance beyond what you would like to pay. Rural isolation has many pluses and not a few minuses; *see* 'Life in Rural Portugal', pp.45–6.

Life in the Big Cities

In Portugal, living in the 'big city' effectively means choosing between Lisbon and Oporto, as all other cities are really only small to medium-sized. Lisbon falls short of one million inhabitants, although the metropolitan area has more than two million, and Oporto barely reaches half a million. After that, no city comes even close to the 200,000 mark. Both offer some of the more positive aspects of urban living that you may not want to lose, and some of the downsides too.

Living in either of these cities implies having access to many things. For one thing, you have close at hand a huge range of cultural, leisure and entertainment possibilities. Lisbon has, for example, over 35 museums covering all manner of subjects, several excellent public exhibition spaces and a small but thriving private gallery scene. For music lovers there are auditoria and concert halls, music festivals in churches and other public spaces and a live music scene covering most non-classical genres. Perennially underfunded, the performing arts battle to provide theatre and dance buffs with many different options. Lisbon's nightlife and bar scene is vibrant and the range of dining possibilities is vast. There are also no fewer than four first division football clubs and lots of opportunities to take part in sport yourself. Living here also means having access to all manner of services – educational, legal, health, etc. – and, generally, a variety of experiences that cannot be found in small towns or villages, not least a cosmopolitan feel that is rare in provincial Portugal.

Oporto, being smaller, cannot match Lisbon's range but, as European City of Culture in 2001, the city does its best to live up to its second city status. Both cities are lower-key and more relaxed than, say, London, and because they are smaller and more compact, living even some way out of the centre of either does not mean you are condemned to a life of suburban boredom.

But big-city living has its downsides, too, especially the cost and types of accommodation available. If you choose to live in either Lisbon or Oporto then, unless you are very well off, you should expect to live in an apartment rather than a house. In Lisbon the demand for apartments at the cheaper end of the market is very high. In classified ads you may see apartments for around €400–500 a month but they are unlikely to be especially desirable. Anything decent, but not necessarily roomy, is likely to cost over €600 or €750 per month and you could well end up paying over €1,000 for a really nice apartment with all 'mod cons' in a good neighbourhood.

Oporto is only slightly less expensive. These prices may seem cheap in comparison with some other European capitals but remember that salaries in Portugal are very low indeed. To buy, expect to pay upwards of €150,000 for a nice apartment of 80 sq m in a good neighbourhood and considerably more for something bigger. Other annoying aspects of urban living include the inevitable traffic congestion (neither Lisbon nor Oporto's streets were laid out to cope with cars), street crime (pick-pocketing especially) and other aspects of urban decay such as drug use and visible prostitution, as well as access difficulties for the lesser-abled (both cities have steep gradients and cobbled pavements).

Life in Medium-sized Cities

If you choose not to live in Lisbon or Oporto, cannot afford the Algarve or other beach resorts and dislike the idea of rural isolation, then practically any Portuguese town or city falls into this category. After Oporto, Portugal's third largest urban area is Amadora, a satellite of Lisbon, with about 150,000 inhabitants. Only Braga, Coimbra and Funchal top the 100,000 mark and Portugal's 15th biggest city is Leiria, with a population of just over 50,000. After that, there are many towns with around 25–40,000 inhabitants. In short, it is almost the norm to live in a small city or town.

In one sense, wherever you live in Portugal you will never be that far from all the things you need. The country is small. Even living on a farmhouse in the Alentejo does not compare with rural isolation in the American mid-west (though still may not appeal). But there are degrees, and a medium-sized town or city might be just what you want.

Most Portuguese towns have a long history. This means that they have a centre that almost invariably boasts a few historical monuments ranging from churches to castles or monasteries – from Moorish to medieval in style. It is pleasant to have such history on your doorstep and to feel part of a place where many great moments have been lived by those who went before you. In the older parts of many towns there are often properties begging to be bought and done up. This may appeal to some purchasers.

Small-town life involves getting to know people you come across daily; it means you are familiar with them and they with you. If you can speak the language well enough you will find people to be hospitable and warm. This is not only pleasant, it can also give you someone to turn to in times of need. Good, friendly neighbours are of incalculable value and you are more likely to come across them in small communities. In small towns, everything is close to hand. The notorious, Kafkaesque Portuguese bureaucracy will be found as much in Beja or Leiria or Viseu as in Lisbon. But the offices where you deal with red tape may be a lot closer to your house – as will be the health centre, bank, shops, entertainment, friends, gymnasium, your favourite restaurant and local bar. On the other hand, many small towns do not have too much in the way of infrastructure and you may find some facilities lacking.

Your chances of getting mugged, assaulted or raped in a small town are probably much lower than anywhere else. Not that violent crime is especially a problem anywhere in Portugal, but the tranquillity of small town life is notable. If you are used to cities with a certain amount of 'action', do not expect to find it in small-town Portugal. Indeed, while most places have local festivities, plenty of local colour and the occasional 'big act' coming to town, if you love the performing arts or live music you may find boredom sets in after a while. For some, small-town life can be a bit too tranquil.

Weigh it all up. Spend some time in provincial towns and get a feel for life there. It may be what you want but, if it is not, then look elsewhere.

Life in Rural Portugal

Many people's dream, and certainly one that is sorely tempting if you have spent most of your time putting up with the stress and strain of urban living in a northern European country, is to buy a property in the middle of nowhere and retreat to a rural idyll. The chance to be away from crowds, noise, pollution and all the other ills of modern existence while enjoying uninterrupted views over the plains, the mountains or the distant sea is many people's idea of perfection. This is perfectly understandable and all very well as far as it goes – and as far as you are genuinely able to handle it. Not everybody is, and a good few find that after a while the attraction wears off.

The drawbacks are indeed many and should be taken into account before you plunge into the country adventure. For one thing, remember that all the services you may have been used to having close at hand may now be far away and only accessible by car. Shops, doctors, dentists, entertainment and sports facilities, schools (if you have children this will certainly be an issue to think carefully about) and, possibly most important of all, human company, may no longer be just up the road or around the corner. You may generally expect to find fewer English-speakers in rural areas, so your need to learn Portuguese will be correspondingly greater. Reliance on a car involves greater cost than if you are in a city, not to mention the inconvenience when it breaks down or the poorly maintained road that connects you to the rest of the world is cut off by bad weather. Communications in the more remote parts of rural Portugal may not be up to scratch. Getting a telephone may mean a long wait and you may have to pay a (very) large sum of money to get electricity and water connected. Many rural properties, in fact, have to generate their own electricity, draw their own water from a well and rely on using a septic tank. One important consideration (especially if you and your partner are elderly) is how well you will cope with the rural isolation in the event of being widowed.

Portugal Region by Region

Portugal comprises 11 mainland provinces, or *distritos*, but these divisions are administrative. For descriptive purposes it is therefore easier to follow the larger area groupings as used by the Portuguese National Tourist Office. These areas group together provinces that, broadly speaking, share climatic and geographical characteristics. Foreign house-buyers show a marked preference for certain areas and this is reflected in the space given to each in the description below.

The Algarve

Portugal's southernmost province has a south-facing coastline of about 150km (95 miles), stretching between Vila Real de Santo António in the east and Sagres in the west. As well as this there are a further 50km of wilder, west-facing beaches stretching north between the Cabo de São Vicente and Odeceixe on the border of the Alentejo region. For many tourists and potential property buyers, the very mention of the name 'Portugal' conjures up visions of the Algarve, such is the popularity this small province enjoys ahead of the rest of the country. In a recent survey some 35 per cent of would-be buyers expressed a preference for the region. This is perhaps unfair on other parts of Portugal, which also have much to offer visitors and residents. But the Algarve has an excellent climate – comparable with the Mediterranean or California – which is certainly one of the best, and healthiest, in Europe.

In addition to its many beautiful, unpolluted beaches and pretty coves, fishing ports, marinas and golf courses, the area has a picturesque interior, with greatly varied flora and fauna. Visitors and residents alike appreciate the range of outdoor pursuits available year-round both on the coast and inland. Add to that a relatively well-developed tourist infrastructure, much improved road connections with Lisbon and neighbouring Spain and the attractions of gastronomy and nightlife, include the international airport at Faro (destination of many budget airlines) and you can see why so many think the way they do. Nor are they alone. Some 50,000 British residents, it is estimated, have already made their home in the Algarve, with many more owning a second or holiday home in the area. Many of these may in turn decide to settle there once they have retired. They are being joined by Irish buyers, who are arriving each year in ever greater numbers, as well as people from other parts of northern Europe and, nowadays, as far afield as Russia.

The Algarve's history (and its present) has been shaped by various waves of invaders over the centuries. Phoenicians, Greeks, Carthaginians, Romans, Visigoths, Moors and the Spanish all invaded or colonized parts of Portugal at different times in the country's history. The Euro 2004 Football Championship may bring a different invasion, as the new stadium currently under construction just outside Faro is one of the tournament's designated venues.

In terms of the property market, the Algarve is anything but cheap. However, there are still many compelling reasons to buy there – starting with all the positive aspects (above), and the fact that a well-chosen property may have tremendous rental potential and prove an excellent investment in terms of resale value. Over the past few years, quality properties have been appreciating in value by almost 25 per cent annually. This trend looks likely to continue as strict building restrictions, which have now been in force for a decade, mean that practically the only new construction taking place is on plots where planning permission had been approved previous to the promulgation of the laws. The aim was to protect the environment and assure that 'quality of life' would remain the Algarve's main attraction. Consequently, there are ever fewer choice properties available, especially on or close to the beach, and property agents are now talking of a lack of supply, though they are not fearful of saturation point being reached quite yet. The Algarve may, for property purposes, be divided up into three areas:

- **The Central Algarve**: the area between Faro and Albufeira, which includes towns like Loulé, Vilamoura, Almancil, Santa Bárbara de Nexe and the five-star resorts of Quinta do Lago, Dunas Douradas and Vale do Lobo.

• **The Western Algarve**: between Armação de Pêra and Lagos, including the coastal towns and villages of Portimão, Alvor and Carvoeiro. The western Algarve also includes the stretch west of Lagos as far as Sagres and the coastline that faces west on to the Atlantic between. Apart from the luxurious Parque da Floresta estate, close to Budens and a couple of other inland villages, though, not many purchasers look this far west, as much of the coastline is protected parkland and fewer properties are available.

• **The Eastern Algarve**: between Faro and Vila Real de Santo António, the area that looks across the Guadiana river to Ayamonte, the first town in Spain, including places such as Moncarapacho, Tavira and Monte Gordo.

The Central Algarve (West of Faro to Albufeira)

Faro is the regional capital and administrative centre and the international airport is situated just to the west. Among the throngs of tourists who arrive on budget flights during the high season, few actually bother to stop here – which is a shame. Undoubtedly, Faro does have some appealing features that make it worth a short visit. There is an attractive harbour and, close by, a pedestrian shopping area where there are many places to eat and drink, offering both local and international cuisine. The old town, Cidade Velha, accessed via the Italian renaissance-style Arco da Vila, contains the Sé (cathedral) and nearby the Prince Henry Archaeological and Lapidary Museum (the best museum in the area) housed in a former convent. Faro is situated next to the Ria Formosa nature reserve, home to a vast number of birds that breed, winter and migrate there.

Although Faro itself seems to be of little interest to ex-pat housebuyers, you only have to go a little way out of town towards the west to find the most exclusive and expensive developments on the whole of the Algarve. There are three that practically merge into one another: Quinta do Lago (Lake Farm), Dunas Douradas (Golden Dunes) and Vale do Lobo (Valley of the Wolf). Collectively they are known as the 'Golden Triangle' and represent the ideal of a relaxed, opulent lifestyle in beautiful, sun-drenched surroundings – at a price.

Quinta do Lago, situated on the edge of Ria Formosa, is *the* most prestigious resort on the whole of the Algarve and boasts many luxury villas, standing in their own grounds, golf courses, tennis courts, shops, water sports and riding as well as beaches just a stone's throw away. This is the absolute top end of the housing market, and you should not even think about buying here unless you have a lot of money to spare. The cheapest property seen advertised in this area was a 70 sq m, one-bedroom apartment (not even on the estate) for about €215,000. The same money will get you a lot more elsewhere on the Algarve or in another part of Portugal. The other end of the price range for apartments here is over €900,000, which may buy you a three-bedroom and bathroom duplex. Luxury villas are a different matter altogether. About the cheapest you will find costs over €2 million. For this price you get 400 sq m of villa including three bedrooms and bathrooms, a living room and dining area, a barbecue area, covered swimming pool and garage all set in 2,000 sq m of land. If you have enough money to buy at the top end of the market, a little over €7 million gets you a palatial property, six bedrooms, six bathrooms, reception and dining areas, an overflow pool, an additional four-bedroom guest house, garage and 7,400 sq m of grounds. Quinta do Lago is not the place to buy unless you have plenty of money and want to flaunt it. Villas and apartments alike generally come with swimming pools, though in the latter they are communal.

Very close to Quinta do Lago, just a few minutes west by car, is the **Vale do Lobo**, Portugal's first purpose-built luxury resort, which recently celebrated its 35th birthday. Like its neighbours, Vale do Lobo places emphasis on high-quality, low-density developments, and its two golf courses are one of its key selling points. It, too, offers every type of water sport, tennis courts, a luxury health club and a range of restaurants and bars. Expect to pay similar prices here, also, though a researcher did come up with a small three-bedroom villa for €550,000 which (by comparison) is an absolute bargain.

Set between the other two, the third five-star resort in this area is **Dunas Douradas**, named after the golden sand dunes that separate it from the Atlantic Ocean. This holiday village blends into 77 acres of beautiful pine forest and boasts an unusual Roman-style swimming pool, tennis courts, and a pool bar. Poolside barbecues and live entertainment for all the family during the summer make it a child-friendly resort. Prices cover a large range: a ground floor apartment will set you back in the region of €240,000, and you can add on about another €30,000 for a first floor. Townhouses come with or without swimming pools and range from €300,000 to €425,000. A detached three-bedroom bungalow with swimming pool in the more exclusive end fetches almost €860,000 and thereafter the price of larger detached villas is 'negotiable'.

Close to these resorts are the towns of **Santa Bárbara de Nexe** and **Almancil**, a little inland, and **Quarteira**, on the coast. Here you may pick up something for a slightly lower price but, as properties are becoming fewer and further between, do not expect to find many bargains, especially if it is a villa you are looking for in the low hills just inland. A four-bedroom family villa in the much sought-after 'Almancil ridge' area now costs well over €1 million. A five-bedroom villa close to Santa Bárbara was recently advertised at €1,100,000 although a two-bedroom property was also spotted for just under €500,000. A little further inland (11km from the coast) is the town of **Loulé**, which is also becoming popular as coastal properties get ever scarcer. Loulé's Moorish past is evident in the ruined castle and agents in the surrounding hills also offer some villa developments at suitably inflated prices: €860,000 for one that includes five bedrooms, a pool and (somewhat distant) sea views.

Another private resort development – further to the west in the direction of Albufeira – is **Vilamoura**. It is a purpose-built resort and very much feels that way. Although it is not a place for those in search of quaint old back streets, cobblestones or Gothic churches, it does have a preserved Roman site, including the baths where the mariners used to perform their ablutions. During Roman times this was an important centre for the production of *garum* (fish paste), as can be seen in the interesting Cerro da Vila Museum. Nowadays, there is a king-sized marina for yachts, several top-notch golf courses, and facilities for many outdoor activities, including lawn bowling and a shooting range. With 6,000 permanent residents (a number that swells in the high season) Vilamoura offers lively nightlife, an active cultural scene, shopping and a great variety of restaurants. The company that owns the resort is also very conscious of its responsibilities towards the environment and Vilamoura hopes to become the first resort in southern Europe to achieve 'Green Globe' status. Property prices here cater for just about every budget. A three-bedroom, 110 sq m apartment with sea views, a wood-burning stove, with access to a communal swimming pool and close to all amenities may come for as little as €131,000. If your needs are more modest, for a real bargain, consider this: a furnished studio, 50 sq m in size, with balcony and fully fitted kitchenette, located in the centre of Vilamoura, for €72,325. Otherwise, apartments can cost anywhere between €125,000 and €225,000 depending on location and facilities. At the other end of the scale there are townhouses and villas which can go for between €330,000 and €1,200,000. Close by is the small village of Boliqueime where you may expect to pay a little (or a lot) more than in Vilamoura itself.

Albufeira, the last place in the central Algarve, contrasts hugely with all the resorts and towns mentioned above. This town, formerly a quiet fishing village, bases its prosperity on package holidays on a massive scale and offers the whole gamut of services you would expect. 'English pubs' abound, offering English beer, bottled or on tap, fried breakfasts, pub grub, live Premier League games on giant-screen TVs, karaoke and quiz nights, happy hours and more. There are also discotheques aplenty, street stalls selling woven bracelets, imported hippie clothes and leather crafts. There are apartments, townhouses and even villas galore both for sale and for rent. The market here is booming and prices are not yet in orbit. Studios and one-bedroom apartments can be as cheap as €55,000, and a two-bedroom villa with a built-in studio apartment in a private condominium development in nearby Armação de Pêra was recently advertised for as little as €160,000. Also, in Albufeira itself, villas with two to four bedrooms are currently going from a little over €115,000. One of Albufeira's advantages is that, being such a popular resort, it has good services and amenities. If (as well) you prefer not to mix with the crowds, then the town is particularly well situated, with unspoilt beaches – such as Praia da Falésia (towards Quatreira) – easily reached by car.

As you can see, prices in the five-star resorts do not give the overall picture; there is still a lot of less luxurious property to be found. It is true to say that the central Algarve is the most expensive of the three areas, partly because the infrastructure is better and partly because the facilities and amenities that foreign residents want are located there. The proximity of the five-star resorts also helps to increase prices in the area. In very general terms, and taking into account such factors as location, proximity to amenities, age and quality of construction, size (in square metres), the price range in the central Algarve may be summarized as follows:

- **Plots:** **€100,000–448,000**
- **Apartments:** **€100,000–600,000**
- **Townhouses:** **€175,000–350,000**
- **Villas:** **€200,000–1,750,000**

These prices do not include properties in five-star resort estates.

The Western Algarve

Until recently, buying a property to the west of Albufeira was not such an attractive proposition owing to poor communications. From the airport at Faro to Lagos is (as the crow flies) only about 70km. But the old two-lane *Estrada Nacional 125* simply could not cope with the traffic, and residents all have horror stories about how they would sit at a standstill in the most appalling tailbacks, slowly cooking in their own juices. The western Algarve remained a remote area despite the small distances involved. All that has now changed. In spring 2003 the A22 east–west motorway, known as the *Via do Infante*, finally reached Lagos. This means that you can drive to any point on the rest of the coast within, at most, an hour and a half, and puts Andalucía, in neighbouring Spain, within striking distance. Many Algarvians do in fact make day-trips to Sevilla (the Andalusian capital) to shop, see the sights or 'party'. In addition to this, the A2 motorway linking the greater Lisbon area with the Algarve was completed in 2002 – putting the capital between two and three hours' driving time. Both projects mean the western Algarve is now infinitely more accessible and it is foreseeable that prices will take an upturn in the near future – if they have not already begun to do so.

Even without decent communications, the western Algarve has always had a lot to recommend it. On offer are many small fishing villages that have not lost their character despite the tourist invasion, a wealth of intimate little coves and beautiful, clean beaches. Inland, there are towns such as **Silves**, once the capital of *Al-Gharb*, with its huge Moorish castle and 13th-century Gothic church (formerly a cathedral), **Caldas de Monchique**, a spa town, the market town of **Monchique** and **Fóia**, the highest point in the Algarve from where, on a clear day, there are splendid views of the whole coastline between Albufeira and Sagres. As elsewhere on the Algarve, golf-lovers are well catered for and there are several excellent courses in the area to the west of Lagos. Green fees tend to be cheaper than in the central Algarve and the courses are, for the time being, rather less crowded, though this may change as the area attracts more house buyers – and golfers.

Not far to the west of Albufeira are several small towns and villages that have become very popular with purchasers. **Armação de Pêra**, with its small 18th-century fortress and long sandy beach, has long been a haven for tourists. **Portimão** is the Algarve's second-largest town and its history goes back to the time of the Phoenicians, who established a trading post there – thanks to its excellent natural harbour. From the 19th century until the 1980s it had flourishing fishing and canning industries which disappeared in the economic recession. With a population of 35,000, it is still a commercial centre and was for a long time the Algarve's main shopping town. Little remains of the old town, except for the church that dates from 1476 although it has been altered many times over the past three centuries. Consequently, Portimão is not a pretty town but it does have an active cultural life, lots of excellent outdoor fish restaurants and a monthly market that brings people from all over.

It is the smaller towns and villages nearby that really attract the ex-pat buyer: **Praia da Rocha**, with its new marina; the charming picture-postcard beach village of **Carvoeiro**, with many villa developments in the surrounding area; **Alvor**, another beach village with a 16th-century parish church; **Ferragudo**, a delightful fishing village; and the pleasant administrative town of **Lagoa**, barely 5km inland, are all desirable locations these days. Then there is **Lagos**, extremely picturesque, quite laid-back and slow-moving, yet aware of its important role in Portugal's sea-faring past. Prince Henry the Navigator had his ships built and supplied here, while it was also a centre for the slave trade. Recently, Lagos has seen a lot of British, German and Dutch buyers moving in to the surrounding area.

Price-wise there is a reasonable range and a good number of properties available in this area, though recently the market has slowed down somewhat. The area around Carvoeiro and Ferragudo, and Silves inland, offers great rental potential for those hoping to buy and let. It is also popular with those who come to live, as there is a reputable international school in the area. Prices, consequently, tend to be quite high. Small apartments in Praia da Rocha were recently advertised from €65,000 – expect to pay another €10–15,000 in Alvor or Carvoeiro. Small villas (usually semi-detached) in Carvoeiro and Ferragudo go for upwards of €180,000 although if you want something large and on its own plot of land expect to pay well above €300,000, even as much as €500,000. In the Lagos area, popular places to buy are Meia Praia and Praia da Luz where two-bedroom apartments have recently been advertised for between €140,000 and €170,000, though something in a more select condo development could well cost half as much again. Semi-detached townhouses in the area go for upwards of €220,000 though, again, something a little more secluded can cost a lot more. An opulent villa in the Parque da Floresta golf and leisure resort can cost more than €500,000. Overall, prices in the western Algarve come more or less within the following range:

- **Plots:** **€75,000–225,000**
- **Apartments:** **€75,000–175,000**
- **Townhouses:** **€125,000–225,000**
- **Villas:** **€150,000–750,000**

The Eastern Algarve

Going east from Faro as far as Vila Real de Santo António, on the west bank of the Guadiana river (the Portugal–Spain border), the eastern Algarve has received much less attention from property developers, the tourist industry and visitors – so it is relatively undeveloped. A look at the range of properties on offer in any Algarve web-page or estate agent's brochure bears this out: the eastern towns simply do not feature as frequently; not so many properties are advertised. Consequently, prices on this side are much more affordable, if your resources are more modest. Some Germans have bought in this area in recent times but relatively fewer British purchasers have shown interest. Those who do buy here tend to be a little more 'alternative', seeking less spoilt, less developed locations – a slice of a more genuine Portugal, perhaps. This is an area in which to look for older properties, a village house or a farmhouse, though there are newer apartments, townhouses and a few luxury villas on the market. New coastal developments are unlikely to develop as most of this stretch of coast is taken up by the **Ría Formosa Nature Reserve**. Inland, no fewer than five golf courses have been constructed in recent years, which will probably help to kindle interest in property in the area. The eastern Algarve as a whole does offer plenty of attractions – though less infrastructure – and may become a growth area in the future as other parts of the coast become oversubscribed. A property here may be an interesting investment in the medium to long term, but not if you are hoping to make a quick return.

Heading east from Faro, the first town of any size is **Olhão**, a fishing port of about 30,000 inhabitants. In 1882, the first tuna and sardine canning factory was established here, quickly followed by others along the coast, as it became the Algarve's leading industry. The flat terraced roofs and straight, box-shaped chimneys characteristic of the town give it a Moorish feel and every morning the fish market is a noisy, colourful affair. Few buyers look in Olhão itself, but the inland villages of **Estói**, **Moncarapacho** and **Pechão** attract buyers. Another spot worth looking at might be the seaside village of **Fuseta** (a few kilometres to the east), though very little indeed is to be seen of this in property agents' brochures. One property advertised recently was a three-bedroom farmhouse in the hills near Estói, going for just under €175,000. In Moncarapacho an attractive two-bedroom country house, completely restored, may cost €245,000, though if you want to do the work yourself a 'semi-ruin' will cost significantly less. At the other end of the scale, a luxury villa in Pechão was advertised for almost €1,100,000! It has four bedrooms and bathrooms and over 400 m of space, a heated pool and huge grounds, but you could find something less splendid and perfectly habitable for a lot less money.

Towards the picturesque town of **Tavira**, which straddles the river Gilhão, foreign buyers are now beginning to show more interest. The town itself dates back to 400 BC, but like most other towns on the coast was practically flattened by the 1755 earthquake, so most of the interesting architecture is from the 18th century. The local economy combines tourism with an active tuna-fishing industry, though these days this is no longer the main source of income. Not surprisingly, there are many excellent fish restaurants, the most attractive on either side of the river. Fat tuna steaks are the standard fare. There are also many more basic, down-to-earth fishermen's bars and cafés where eating and drinking is still very affordable. Riverbank properties fetch the high prices here, and are very hard to come by. Most foreign buyers, however, are looking for places in the area surrounding Tavira, in the hills and in nearby villages like **Santo Estevão**, **Santa Catarina**, **Estorninhos** or **Vila Nova de Cacela**. A duplex apartment with two double bedrooms in **Cabanas** (just 3km from Tavira) was going recently for as little as €122,000 and a four-bedroom apartment in the town itself, needing a little work, for only €89,500. A rural property, 10km inland in **Marco**, comprising three bedrooms, two bathrooms, large dining and living areas and 10,000 sq m of land was also advertised recently for just €185,000. Further up the price range there are larger, renovated farmhouses of considerable size upwards of €225,000.

Further east, perched on the estuary of the Guadiana river, is **Vila Real de Santo António**, the last town before the Spanish border. Previously, the only way into the Algarve from Spain was on the little car ferry that still crosses from Ayamonte to Vila Real, though now it is nothing more than a unusual attraction, no longer a source of income. Sadly, the town has seen a decline, since the bridge was built across the river and the bulk of Algarve-bound traffic from Spain redirected along the bypass. Yet it is by no means an unpleasant place – originally a fishing village, with a history stretching back to Phoenician times. Vila Real's resort is down the river at **Monte Gordo**, a popular place with 14km of beach lined with pine trees. The property market here is not exactly booming, but it is anybody's guess as to what may happen in the future, especially since the opening in 2001 of the golf course at **Castro Marim**, just a little way inland.

If the prices in the central Algarve scare you off, you could do a lot worse than look in this area. Or even think about the following observation made by a property business insider who was consulted during research for this book: 'Many local Algarvians, increasingly priced out of their own region by foreign purchasers, are nowadays choosing to buy across the border in Ayamonte,

Spain.' They have many good reasons for doing so, not least the fact that newly constructed apartments cost anywhere between 30 and 40 per cent less. Since the bridge was built over the Guadiana estuary in 1991 and the international border has ceased to exist as such, a resident in Ayamonte who works in, say, Faro or Albufeira, can live in Spain and commute to work in Portugal, especially since the completion of the *Vía do Infante*.

In general terms, prices in the eastern Algarve may be summed up as follows:

- **Plots:** **€60,000–325,000**
- **Apartments:** **€75,000–125,000**
- **Townhouses:** **€100,000–225,000**
- **Villas:** **€100,000–600,000**

Planícies (The Plains)

One of Portugal's poorest and most backward areas, the Plains tourist region comprises most of the **Alentejo** and is also the largest, occupying almost a third of the surface area of continental Portugal. It is known as Portugal's 'bread basket' as most of the country's wheat (and other food) is grown on the large estates, *latifúndios*, which date from Roman times. From this area also come olives, cork and some excellent wines. The excellent Alentejo cuisine is famous throughout the country. As well as this, Arabian horses and bulls are bred here.

The name Alentejo means 'beyond the Tagus' (*Além do Tejo*) and the Alentejo comprises two districts, the *Alto* (upper) and the *Baixo* (lower) Alentejo, though in the Portuguese Tourist Board's definition of Planícies a slice of coastline that is administratively part of the Baixo Alentejo is included in the Lisbon Coast area (*see* pp.57–60). The Alto Alentejo is bounded by the Spanish border, to the east, the Tagus river to the north and west. A fairly straight line running east–west just to the south of the city of Évora marks the southern limits. From then on, and all the way to the Algarve, the imposing Baixo Alentejo plains take over. The Baixo is bounded to the west by the Lisbon Coast tourist region but has its own, unspoilt coastline starting just south of the industrial port of Sines as far as the limits with the Algarve. To the east, the frontier with Spain marks the limits and to the south the province borders on the Algarve. The inland plains are vast, flat, unrelenting and murderously hot in summer. They can also get quite cold in winter.

In the northern half there are a great many historic towns and villages, among them **Évora** (a UNESCO World Heritage site), a major political centre in Roman times, and Portalegre with its medieval castle. Then there are the so-called 'marble' towns of **Estremoz** and **Borba** (marble is not a luxury down here) and fortified hill villages such as **Elvas**, **Monsaraz** (another marble marvel) and **Marvão**, which was built to keep watch for Spanish incursions. **Beja**, further south, was another important Roman town, later a cultural centre in Moorish times. The charming little town of **Mértola**, close to the Guadiana river, has a Moorish watchtower still standing and now organizes an Islamic festival of music, dance and theatre every May. The area is also rich in archaeological remains from every period of Portuguese history.

For nature-lovers there are several natural parks. Between Portalegre and the Spanish border is the **Parque Natural da Serra de São Mamede**, in which are several fascinating medieval villages. Further south, crossed by the Guadiana river, is the practically uninhabited **Parque Natural do Vale do Guadiana**. To the west, the coastal strip that runs from the port of **Sines** down to **Cabo de São Vicente** (and beyond into the Algarve) is also a reserved area called the **Paisagem Protegido do Sudoeste Alentejano**.

The Alentejo does not at present attract foreign property-buyers, nor does it seem likely to in the immediate future. Only five per cent of those who took part in a recent survey said it was an area they would like to live in. However, this may change if the Algarve market ever reaches saturation point – especially since the completion of the A2 motorway from the Algarve to Lisbon, which passes through the Alentejo, and the recent construction of several dams aimed at easing the area's water problems.

The **Alqueva Dam**, a massive project, fiercely opposed by environmentalists, shut its sluice gates and began to fill up in February 2002. When it reaches full capacity it will be the largest artificial lake in Europe. Opposition to the project was based on the fact that it will drown 25,000 hectares of land, habitat of several endangered species, among them the golden eagle, the otter and the Iberian lynx. Over a million cork oaks were felled during the construction phase and a whole village, Luz, was built in replica two miles from the site it has occupied for hundreds of years. The original village will shortly disappear beneath the water, along with many valuable archaeological remains. Despite the opposition, politicians argued that the Alentejo's most endangered species was man, since poverty there has driven many young people to seek employment in the capital and beyond. The water (they claim) will help to regenerate the region, an argument denied by the opposition, who assert that the government's own secret reports say only 48 per cent of the irrigated land can be worked profitably, making the project a 'white elephant'. Whoever is right, the huge lake, including 146 'new' islands, is a potential goldmine for tourist operators. By May 2002, dozens of planning applications had been filed for golf courses, luxury hotels, health spas and island resorts. Given this, the question now is whether this area might become an 'inland Algarve'. Some estate agents already tout properties in the southern Alentejo as being in the 'Algarve hinterland'. If this proves to be the case, then the area may turn out to be interesting in terms of future investment.

The type of property currently on offer starts at small village houses that can cost as little as €35,000 but which may need some work doing on them. Another €10,000 will get you a 20,000 sq m plot of land with building permission. Farmhouses in attractive country locations (not far inland from the unspoilt Atlantic coast), often with a main building in good condition and outbuildings for conversion as guesthouses, can cost €75,000–90,000. For a similar price, you will find village houses in the area around Évora. As yet, there seems to be little available in the middle to upper middle bracket, except perhaps for a farmhouse in the Évora area for around €160,000. More than €750,000 will get you a huge manor house, often consisting of a main building and two or three others. The idea here is to live in one and turn the rest of the property into 'upmarket' rural hotels. This may be a risky or sensible investment, depending on future developments in the southern Alentejo.

Costa de Lisboa (The Lisbon Coast)

The Lisbon Coast, whose northernmost point is the small fishing village of Ericeira, comprises **greater Lisbon**, the southern parts of the provinces **of Estremadura** and **Ribatejo** (meaning 'beside the Tagus') and the coastal part of what administratively is the **Baixo Alentejo**, finishing at the ugly industrial port of Sines. The area has many beautiful resort towns, charming villages and towns both on the coast and inland, a wealth of 'iced-cake' palaces, fairytale castles, historic monuments and other sights. Although property does not come cheap, there is a range of prices available. The presence of the capital here also means a well-developed infrastructure, with good transport and communication, both of which have improved immensely in recent years.

Lisbon

Lisbon, capital of the republic and once the metropolis of a huge ocean-going empire, is a city that enchants most visitors. Straddling seven hills along the northern side of the Tagus estuary, Lisbon presents many of the contradictions and contrasts to be found all over Portugal, all concentrated in one city. Dilapidated and tumbledown in parts, furiously modern in others, Lisbon had its heyday many centuries ago, went through a time of apparently terminal decline, but is now enjoying a period of revitalization. Electric trams – many of them built around 1900 (in the UK's industrial midlands) – still clank their way up and down the impossible slopes of the medieval neighbourhoods of Alfama and Mouraria (a maze of streets that is a map-maker's nightmare), while only a couple of kilometres away is the brashly ultra-modern Amoreiras shopping mall. On the north side of town, shanty towns huddle in the shadow of glass-fronted office blocks. The narrow streets of the Bairro Alto (upper neighbourhood) are quiet by day, where women in nylon dressing gowns and slippers hang out washing and children play in the narrow streets. By night these same streets are taken over by a throng of 'up-for-it' clubbers, bar-hoppers and diners. The dining experience in this city runs the whole gamut from shabby little family-run *tascas*, to trendy, post-modern establishments that would not be out of place in London or New York. Quaint, quirky museums are to be found not far from the state-of-the-art Expo '98 site with its impressive aquarium.

With it being the capital, property does not come cheap in Lisbon. For some sample prices, *see* 'Life in the Big Cities', pp.43–4.

West of Lisbon

Central Lisbon is not everybody's ideal of a place to live, as its noise, traffic and cramped conditions are far from the peace and quiet sought by many would-be buyers. The suburbs and the coastal areas to the west, though, are extremely attractive.

Before you get out of Lisbon, you come to the western suburb of **Belém**, from where Vasco da Gama embarked on his 1497 voyage to India. Here is a fabulous Manueline-style monastery, a UNESCO World Heritage site and arguably the best custard tart shop in the whole country. About 20km to the west of Lisbon lies the resort of **Estoril**, nowadays somewhat faded but once a magnet for aristocrats and dethroned 'royals'. Ian Fleming based his James Bond novel *Casino Royale* on the town's gambling house and during the Second World War, owing to Portugal's neutrality, both Allied and Axis spies hung out here. Just along the coast lies the smart resort of **Cascais**, complete with its new marina, an abundance of restaurants, watering holes and nightlife, and several architectural gems.

Around the Cabo Raso (facing out on to the Atlantic) are many fine beaches and coastal villages favoured by sun-seekers, bathers and surfers alike, **Praia do Guincho**, **Praia da Adraga**, **Praia Grande** and **Praia das Maças** are among the most popular.

The inland part of this coast has many other pleasant towns and villages. **Sintra**, another World Heritage site, described by Lord Byron as 'this glorious Eden', was once the summer residence of the Portuguese royal family and before that of the Moorish rulers. Here there are a series of palaces that could well have served as the setting for Disney cartoons.

Queluz (closer to Lisbon itself) is a bit shabby but has a wildly Baroque/rococo palace built for Prince Dom Pedro in the mid-18th century. Overall, the area has much to recommend it. Apart from the tourist attractions and the beaches, there are plenty of golf courses and a sprinkling of English schools. Not surprisingly, therefore, there is a small but prosperous English-speaking ex-pat community firmly established here.

Prices vary hugely in this area, so it is a good idea to look around and then look around again. What you pay for an apartment in one place may get you another twice as big, or even a house, just a few kilometres away. For example: a two-bedroom, 45 sq m apartment in Cascais was recently advertised for €150,000. A brand-new two-bedroom apartment of twice the size was advertised by the same agents for exactly the same price in nearby **Estoril**. At the lower end of the market is a studio apartment in Cascais – where €73,000 buys you 38 sq m. Between €150,000 and €200,000 there are a lot of apartments, generally with two bedrooms in both Cascais and Estoril. Going further up the scale, there are large duplex apartments in the Cascais area for around €250,000 and up to €300,000 buys a very pleasant apartment. Once over that limit, houses with gardens start becoming available, and the extra €25,000 or so may well be worth it. Closer to the €400,000 level there are some large houses with swimming pools included, often a little inland with views of the mountains and down to the sea. For €4–500,000, spacious villas are available and €1 million will get you something bordering on the palatial.

South of Lisbon

About 50km south of Lisbon, on the other side of the Tagus estuary, lies the city of **Setúbal**, Portugal's third port and an important industrial centre. Setúbal is not itself particularly interesting for the ex-pat tourist or home buyer, but the surrounding area has a lot to recommend it. West of the city is **Sesimbra**, a picturesque fishing village complete with medieval castle. The town of **Palmela**, in the nearby **Parque Natural da Arrábida**, also has a splendid castle. To the south is the **Rio Sado** estuary and natural park which includes the **Tróia peninsula**, Setúbal's own beach resort, nowadays somewhat overrun with high-rise developments. To the west is the **Costa da Caparica**, more attractive and much favoured by 'Lisboetas' at weekends, a continuous row of beaches and clapboard houses.

This area is not nearly as popular with foreign buyers as the Estoril coast, since communications with the capital are more difficult. Properties are cheaper, but the difference may not warrant choosing this side of the Tagus estuary. A brand new two-bedroom apartment may cost less – around €100,000 – and a family house in Palmela around €190,000. A very large house with spacious garden can cost around €475,000 or more and a manor house more than €750,000.

South to Sines

From the Tróia peninsula on the Sado estuary, going south to Sines, the 'Costa de Lisboa' is technically part of the **Baixo Alentejo** and has only low-key resorts and towns but some fine beaches. However, there is the pleasant little town of **Santiago do Cacém**, with a Moorish castle that was later rebuilt by the Knights

Templar and, nearby at **Miróbriga**, some fascinating Roman ruins. Santiago do Cacém is inland but the coast is close and there are two lagoon beaches at **Santo André** and **Melides**. Beyond that are the Atlantic-facing beaches that stretch in a continuous swathe between Comporta in the north and Sines in the south. As yet, this is not an area that has been discovered by foreign property buyers but it is probably worth researching.

Costa de Prata (The Silver Coast)

So-called because of the silvery sheen of the sun reflecting on the sea, the Costa de Prata stretches from just north of Ericeira almost all the way to Oporto. It comprises most of the provinces of **Estremadura** and **Ribatejo** as well as the province of **Beira Litoral**. This area of central Portugal is economically well developed, with good communications, and has many lovely beach resorts plus forest-clad hills and mountains inland. It also has a great wealth of historical monuments, castles, palaces and monasteries, an abundance of pretty towns and cities and is easily accessible from both Lisbon and Oporto. Popular with Portuguese and Spanish holidaymakers alike, in recent years many foreign property buyers have begun to home in on the area, not least because it offers cheaper alternatives to the Algarve and the Lisbon coast while enjoying many of the same advantages that make those areas such a magnet.

The main urban centre is **Coimbra**, the capital of Portugal in the 12th and 13th centuries and a university city since the mid-1500s. A medium-sized city of approximately 100,000 inhabitants, Coimbra is steeped in history, and has a lively café and nightlife scene during the academic year owing to the presence of the traditionally black-capped student population. It was also the birthplace of the northern variant of *fado*, a rival to the Lisbon style of this traditional form of song. Close by is **Óbidos**, a wonderfully preserved medieval village, completely walled-in, with whitewashed walls framed in deep blue. The village was once the traditional present given to their brides by Portuguese kings.

The coast has resort after resort. **Figueira da Foz**, with long, sandy beaches and plenty of facilities for water sports, is one. **Nazaré** is another attractive spot. Here the brightly coloured fishing boats still ply their trade, though they now dock in the new port instead of being dragged in to shore by oxen. The fishermen's wives still sport the local costume including several layers of skirts. Not far south of Nazaré is **São Martinho do Porto**, a charming little town with one of the safest beaches on the whole stretch of coast – a bay that forms three-quarters of a circle, protected by two headlands that practically meet at the entrance. A little further south is the fishing port of **Peniche**, not especially attractive but home to a large fleet and departure point for the **Ilhas Berlangas**, an island nature reserve 12km out to the sea. Close by is a new resort, **Praia do Rei**, a golf and country club development with villas arranged around the championship-level course, rated second in the country. At the far northern end of the Silver Coast is **Aveiro**, famous for its lagoon and the canals that crisscross the town, hence its nickname as 'Portugal's Venice'.

Inland from the coast, apart from Coimbra and Óbidos, there are many other places of note. **Caldas da Rainha** (6km north of Óbidos) is a spa resort, first put on the map in 1484 by Queen Dona Leonor, who was impressed by the sulphuric waters; it reached the peak of its popularity during the 19th century. **Alcobaça** and **Batalha** both have a World Heritage monastery, and there are many other local sights worth seeing, such as the Roman ruins at **Conimbriga**. Near to Coimbra is the sanctuary of **Fátima**, which comes a close second to Lourdes in terms of the number of annual visits from pilgrims, and the city of **Viseu** which maintains part of its Gothic walls and its 15th-century gates. This is a land of castles and palaces – and some quite cheap property.

Prices here cover a huge range with big differences between coastal resort prices, those in inland, rural locations and those in cities. Inland, in villages around Coimbra, going in the direction of the Serra da Estrela (and approaching the Montanhas region as defined here), there are properties going for as little as €22,500 – but do not expect much for that price and be prepared to pay a lot more for restoration work. Between €40,000 and €100,000 there are all manner of rural properties available. On the coast, smallish apartments in resorts such as Figueira da Foz can cost more than of €100,000 and there are villas, admittedly not of the Algarve type, starting at about €300,000. Expect fashionable resorts such as Praia do Rei to be vastly more expensive.

Costa Verde (The Green Coast)

There are no prizes for guessing why this area is so named. Portugal's far northern coastal area is just that – a deep emerald green colour. It comprises two provinces, **Minho** and the minuscule **Douro Litoral**, and also includes Oporto and Braga (Portugal's ecclesiastical capital) as well as a good many picturesque fishing villages and inland market towns. Fortunately, the coast remained remarkably unscathed after the *Prestige* (an unseaworthy tanker) sank in November 2002 off the coast of Vigo in neighbouring Spain. The thousands of tons of crude oil that spewed from the hull affected the Galician coast but did not reach Portuguese beaches.

Oporto, the English translation of Porto, was the cradle of the modern Portuguese state, the city from which the Christian reconquest began in the eighth century. Nowadays, it is Portugal's second city but in many ways it leads the field, certainly in terms of sophistication and economic development. There is much rivalry between Oporto and Lisbon, evident particularly in football games between FC Porto and either Benfica or Sporting. *Lisboetas* refer to *Portuenses* as '*tripeiros*', 'tripe-eaters', a reference to the northern preference for offal, while locals refer to the capital city-dwellers as '*alfacinhas*', 'lettuce-nibblers'. But *Portuenses* are proud of their work ethic and prosperity, 'Lisbon shows off, Porto works,' they claim. The city has always known that its prosperity would be assured so long as it kept up its role as a crossroads for world trade and as a manufacturing centre. The port wine trade, too, is what the city is famous for and is another mainstay of the local economy. No visit is complete without a tour of one – or several – of the wine lodges in **Vila Nova de Gaia** (a separate municipality), on the southern bank of the Douro. Traditions apart, Porto is also forward-looking and dynamic. In 2001 it was European City of Culture, acquiring a gleaming new arts centre in the process. Architecturally it is a mix of the old and the ultra-modern, though the former still prevails and the city, built on a slope, has many picturesque streets, an assortment of elegant bridges and fine monuments. There are also beaches right in the city and others just up and down the coast.

The region as a whole is certainly one of the country's most colourful and generally agreed to be among the most beautiful. Four rivers flow from east to west: the Douro, which crosses Castilla–León in northern Spain and reaches the sea at Oporto; the Cavado, which flows just past **Braga**; the Lima, which comes out at the coastal town of **Viana do Castelo**; and the Minho, which is part of the border between northern Portugal and Galicia in Spain. Into each flow many tributaries, meaning that the terrain is hilly and carved up by deep verdant valleys. The area is dotted with villages that have hardly been touched by modern development and where age-old agricultural methods still hold their own. The rural areas are poor (but proud) and traditional village festivities can often trace their roots back to pre-Christian times. For lovers of hill walking, bird-watching and similar pursuits, this area is unbeatable.

On the coast there are pretty fishing villages aplenty. Worth visiting are **Caminha**, on the banks of the Minho, sheltered from the sea and **Esposende** and **Ofir**, either side of the mouth of the Lima river. In addition, there are several resort towns on the coast, among them **Espinho** (site of Portugal's first-ever golf course), **Póvoa do Varzim**, a fishing port that has turned into a resort, and nearby **Vila do Conde**.

This area is a wonderful place to visit and perhaps look for a place to buy though as yet foreign property buyers seem not to have discovered its charms. Very few properties are advertised either in brochures or on websites and those that are tend to be in or around the city of Oporto, where apartments can go for around €70,000 for a small studio, €100,000 for a two- or three-bedroom flat in an average suburb and considerably more for something a little more luxurious in a good neighbourhood. A little further afield, apartments in places such as Póvoa do Varzim and Vila do Conde fetch between €130,000 for three bedrooms and €175,000 for four bedrooms. A large, detached house with garden in the same area goes for around €270,000.

Montanhas (Mountains)

Poor and backward, more so than anywhere else in Portugal, the Montanhas area is made up of **Trás-os-Montes** (meaning 'Behind the Hills') province, **Beira Alta** and **Beira Baixa**, and the upper part of the **Douro**. It is a large, sparsely populated area, the least-discovered part of Portugal, but nevertheless offers some fantastic, rugged countryside, ancient traditions, hearty cuisine and unspoilt peace and quiet – hard to find anywhere else in Europe.

The province of Trás-os-Montes itself is a place that time, aided and abetted by central government, has all but forgotten. Hemmed in by three mountain ranges that have ensured its isolation, the province has a climate that locals describe as 'nine months of winter and three months of hell'. Mechanization on farms is rare; it is far more common to see wooden-wheeled ox-carts and leathery-faced old men working the land by hand. Animals are slaughtered in the old-fashioned way and every scrap of them is used. Women may be seen washing out pigs' entrails in a stream before smoking them, marinading them in wine and garlic and mixing them with meat to make *chouriço*, a form of sausage. The local costumes, dances and songs give away the region's pre-Roman, pre-Christian, Celtic past. Religion here is deeply felt. Catholic rituals were adopted but grafted on to a much older pagan heritage. It is said that the people prefer to consult medicine men about life's important issues. While city types see *transmontanos* as primitive, the proud, fiercely independent locals, whose dialect is closer to *Galego* (Galician), spoken on the other side of the border, do not care a jot.

Montanhas certainly justifies its name and offers some absolutely stunning mountain scenery, much of it protected natural parkland. Any decent map shows *serras* (mountain ranges) all over the place. The **Parque Natural da Peneda-Gerês**, which continues over the border into Galicia, comprises four: the Serras da Peneda, do Soajo, do Gerês and do Larouco, and there are several more serras on the borders of the park. In the very northeastern corner of Portugal, close to the provincial capital of Bragança, is the **Parque Natural de Montezinho**, comprising the Serras de Montezinho and da Caroa. The river Douro, watched over by the Serra do Mogadouro, forms, for many kilometres, Portugal's eastern border (where it is called the 'Duero') and on either side lies the **Parque Natural do Douro Internacional**, shared with Spain. Further south, and to the east of Coimbra, is the **Parque Natural da Serra da Estrela**, more accessible and therefore popular with walkers, canoeists, climbers and anglers than the parks to the north.

The area also has some fine cities and towns and many unspoilt villages. **Bragança**, a majestic city with a medieval castle and walls, was the seat of the royal family that occupied the throne from the mid-17th century until the declaration of the Republic in 1910. It boasts a *Domus Municipalis* which is a unique example of civic Romanesque architecture in Portugal. **Vila Real** also has some impressive ecclesiastical architecture.

While as yet almost unknown so far as property buyers are concerned, this region holds many great surprises. Even if you have no intention of buying here, at least pay the region a visit. You will not be disappointed, since it can be most rewarding. You never know, you might stumble across a lovely little old stone farmhouse and change your ideas about buying in Portugal completely. The prices quoted above for the inland part of Costa de Prata are much what you might expect to pay here.

Offshore Portugal

For some strange reason best known only to the Portuguese, the offshore island provinces of Madeira and the Azores are referred to collectively as the *Adjucentes*, meaning the 'Adjacent Islands' – which clearly they are not. Madeira is almost 1,000km away from mainland Portugal and the Azores are about a third of the way to North America. Then again, as one of the first and foremost colonial powers, Portugal's overseas empire included territories as far away as Brazil, Mozambique, Goa, Timor and Macau. So perhaps – when viewed in these terms – these islands are indeed relatively 'adjacent'.

Madeira

Situated some 1,000km southwest of Lisbon and 800km from the northwest coast of Africa, Madeira (Portuguese for 'wood' or 'timber', pronounced 'Mah-DAY-rah' not 'Mah-DEER-ah') has various nicknames, among them 'Pearl of the Atlantic', 'Flor do Oceano' ('Ocean Flower') and the 'Garden of the Atlantic'. Such is the outstanding beauty of the archipelago and its eternally subtropical climate that it always feels like spring. Madeira and its neighbouring islands were 'undiscovered' until 1419 when Portuguese navigators first landed there, though it is probable that other seafaring peoples knew of their existence previously – the Phoenicians among them. The island was first colonized by emigrants from the Algarve and prisoners from Lisbon's jails. The steep slopes of the interior valleys were a challenge to these early settlers who had to work hard to terrace the hillsides and make agriculture first possible and then profitable. This was done with the aid of an intricate system of carefully channelled irrigation ducts, known as *levadas*. They have never really looked back since then. Madeira is now a prosperous producer of grapes, for Madeira wine, sugar and fruit. Barely an inch of surface area goes to waste and the original landscape has been transformed into something that has an attractiveness all of its own.

The group of islands comprises Madeira itself, which is the largest and most populated and where the capital Funchal is situated, the island of Porto Santo, and two groups of uninhabited islands, *Ilhas Desertas* (Deserted Isles) and *Ilhas Selvagens* (Wild Isles). Both are bird sanctuaries. The archipelago's exceptional climate – temperatures range between 16°C and 25°C (61°F and 76°F) – and

Profiles of the Regions

The Algarve

<< see page 46

Far and away the most popular part of Portugal for foreign homebuyers, the Algarve has, by means of strict planning laws, managed to avoid much of the blight of overdevelopment found in some coastal areas in neighbouring Spain. Enjoying a climate that is practically unbeatable, with over 3,000 hours of sunshine per year, it has no winter to speak of. But the attractions go far beyond the weather: excellent facilities for golf and watersports, beautiful beaches and coves, good air links from northern Europe, a reasonable cost of living and a certain level of peace and quiet are factors that mean people keep coming, even though quality properties are becoming scarce.

1 Albufeira coastline
2 Villa and pool
3 Near Tavira
4 Golfing, Vale do Lobo
5 Quinta do Lago
6 Carvoeiro coastline
7 Pottery

8
9
10
11
12

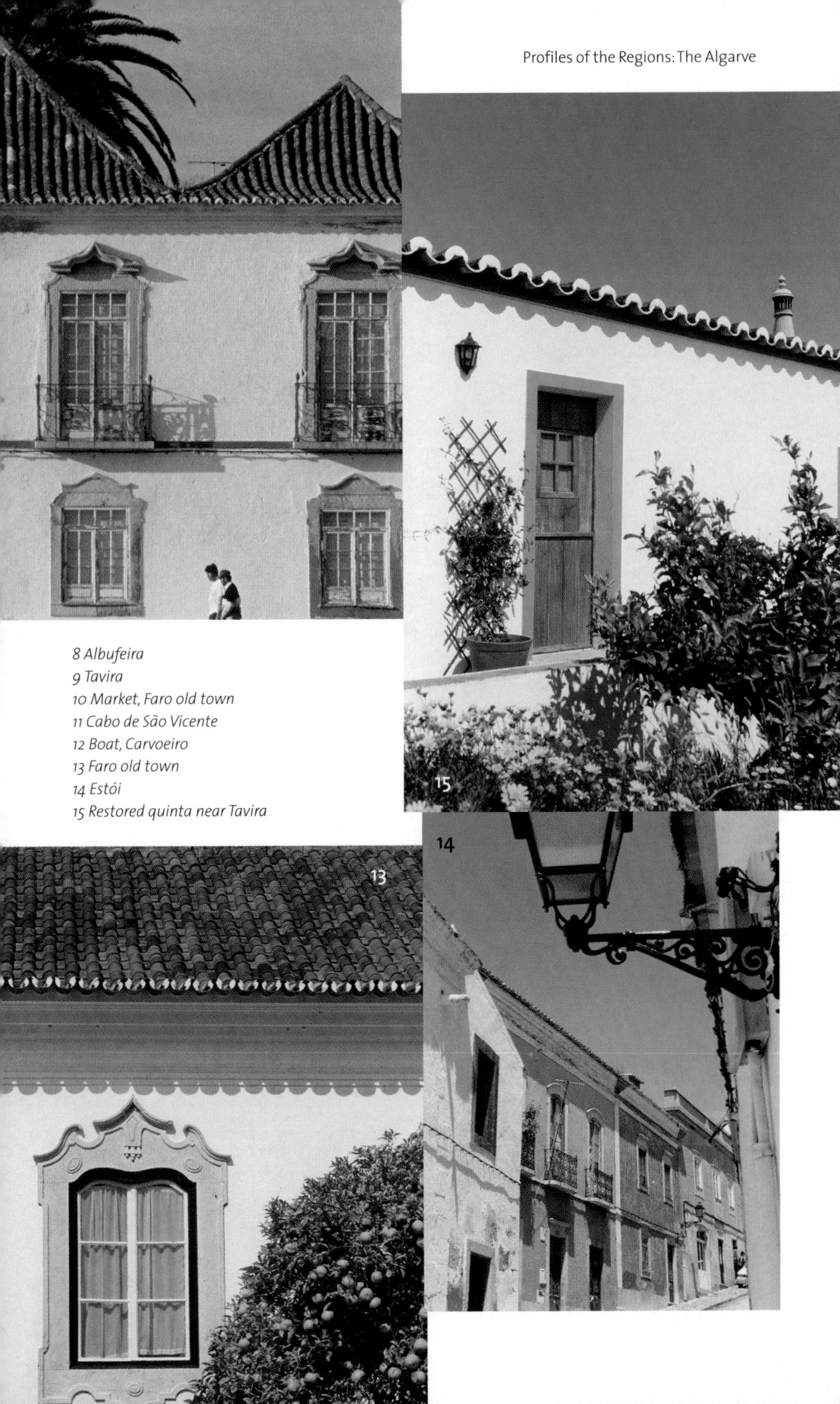

8 Albufeira
9 Tavira
10 Market, Faro old town
11 Cabo de São Vicente
12 Boat, Carvoeiro
13 Faro old town
14 Estói
15 Restored quinta near Tavira

Alentejo

<< Planícies, see page 55;
Costa de Lisboa, see page 57

Long a forgotten backwater, which is possibly what makes it so attractive, the Alentejo is one of Portugal's least-visited regions. The name comes from 'Além do Tejo' ('Beyond the Tagus') and the Alentejo is often called 'Portugal's Bread Basket', as most of the country's wheat and other foodstuffs are grown on the region's undulating plains. Alentejana cuisine is thought by many to be Portugal's finest, and the region's wines also rank among the country's best. The region offers much unspoilt rural beauty and a wealth of pre-Christian, Roman and Moorish history, including the stunning city of Évora, a UNESCO World Heritage site. As the Algarve becomes oversubscribed, the Alentejo may well be the next area for foreign homebuyers to explore. There are still plenty of rural properties going cheap.

1 Monsaraz
2 Alentejo landscape
3 Monsaraz
4 Roman temple, Évora
5 Évora street

3
4
5

6
7

9

6 Vineyards
7 View from Monsaraz
8 Alentejo landscape
9 Évora

8

The Azores

<< *see page 66*

No longer thought to be the remains of Atlantis, this archipelago of volcanic outcrops is another of Portugal's best-kept secrets and is, as yet, relatively undiscovered for foreign property-buyers. Lying about 700 miles west of continental Portugal, and consisting of nine islands in three groups, the Azores take their name from '*açor*', the Portuguese word for 'vulture', of which the island has none! Few visitors to the islands fail to be impressed by their outstanding beauty; one six year-old once asked his parents, 'Is this God's home?' For the outdoor type, the Azores remain one of Europe's last remaining totally unspoilt playgrounds. As air travel gets cheaper, more people may start looking at this area as an offshore alternative for holidays and second homes.

1 Pico, from São Jorge
2 Traditional house, Fajã, João Dias
3 Lago das Furnas valley, São Miguel

Beiras

<< Montanhas, see page 63;
Costa de Prata, see page 60

Consisting of three provinces, Beira Alta and Beira Baixa (both in the Montanhas region) and Beira Litoral (on the Silver Coast), Portugal's heart offers white sandy beaches, charming fishing villages, Atlantic pine forests and the forbidding mountains of the Serra da Estrela. There are also university cities like Coimbra, steeped in history, and others such as Aveiro, sitting on a lagoon and criss-crossed by canals. Add the scores of historic villages, churches and castles, convents and abbeys, and spa towns where the stressed come to take the natural healing waters with which the region is blessed, and it all forms a remarkably rich area.

1 Monsanto
2 Serra da Estrela
3 Beiras landscape

3

4
5
6
144

7

8

9

4 Cottages
5 Cheese, Serra da Estrela
6 Aveiro
7 Tiled house, Aveiro
8 Salt flats, Aveiro
9 Beach houses, Aveiro

Estremadura

<< Costa de Lisboa, see page 57; Costa de Prata, see page 60

The relatively prosperous and developed region of Estremadura occupies a small area to the northwest of Lisbon and has several appealing resorts plus a good many engaging towns on the green, fertile hinterland, which also produces some excellent wines. The region's important role in Portugal's history is evident in the splendid little medieval walled village of Óbidos, the monastery at Batalha, the abbey at Alcobaça and the shrine at Fátima. Along the coast, which is the lower half of the Silver Coast, are fishing villages such as Nazaré that have developed into resorts.

1 Windmill
2 Ericeira
3 Óbidios
4 Palácio Nacional, Sintra
5 Palácio de Pena, Sintra

6

7

8

9

6 Óbidos
7 Óbidos
8 Óbidos
9 Mafra
10 Alcobaça Abbey
11 Sintra

10
11

Lisbon

<< see page 57

Recaptured from the Moors in 1147 and Portugal's capital since 1255, Lisbon stretches along the banks of the Tejo (Tagus) and straddles several hills which make for a dazzlingly rich, delightfully quirky cityscape. Inland from the Praça do Comércio, the lower, central area, Baixa, rebuilt after 1755's devastating earthquake, follows a rational 18th-century layout. To the east, the one-time Moorish neighbourhoods of Alfama and Mouraria, with their maze of narrow, irregular alleyways, huddle on the hill that is topped by the castle of São Jorge (St George). West of the Baixa, up similar gradients, is the Bairro Alto (the 'upper neighbourhood') where black-clad widows and clubbers people the same narrow streets by day and night respectively. Clanking old trams, elegant shopping districts, grubby taverns and smart restaurants all have their place in this marvellous, crumbling but enchanting capital.

1 Alfama district
2 View from Largo das Portas do Sol
3 Monument to the Discoveries
4 Café A Brasileira
5 Torre de Belém

6 Elevador de Santa Justa
7 Praça do Comércio
8 Praça do Comércio

Madeira

<< *see page 64*

Closer to Africa than it is to Lisbon, the subtropical archipelago of Madeira ('timber' in Portuguese) and its neighbours, Porto Santo, the Deserted Isles and the Wild Isles, is most famous for its fortified wines, but has many other attractions besides. Of volcanic origin, discovered in 1419 and initially colonized by immigrants from the Algarve and jailbirds from Lisbon, Madeira's fertile combination of volcanic soil and potash (the result of burning the dense forests that once covered the island) produces abundant crops of tropical fruits and grapes to this day. In Funchal, the capital, the manors and gardens that descend into the ocean evoke a natural nativity scene. With rich ecclesiastical and civil architecture, stunning inland landscapes, excellent cuisine, golf and other leisure facilities, tranquillity and nightlife for the stressed and the restless respectively, Madeira is an attractive destination for the discerning homebuyer.

1 Funchal Old Town
2 Cabo Girão
3 Tropical Gardens, Monte

The North

<< Montanhas, see page 63; Costa Verde, see page 61

Mostly known for port wine, the grapes for which are cultivated along the steep, terraced valleys of the Douro river, northern Portugal's attractions go far beyond the pleasures associated with the drink. This is the cradle of the country itself, and the magnificently preserved city of Guimarães is considered Portugal's birthplace. But the whole of the north is steeped in history: there are ancient cave paintings in Vila Nova de Foz Côa and scores of medieval castles, convents and Romanesque churches in cities such as Braga, Bragança, Chaves, Barcelos, Viana do Castelo or Lamego. Undiscovered, unspoilt, the region is perfect for hill-walking, canoeing, fishing, surfing or simply relaxing and enjoying the plentiful and rich local cuisine.

1 Ponte de Lima
2 Douro Valley
3 River Lima
4 Harvest time

5 Barcelos market, Minho
6 Espigueiros, Lindoso, Minho
7 Barcelos cockerel, Minho
8 Douro Valley

legendary natural beauty long ago made it a popular holiday destination and the local authorities there have made sure the infrastructure is in place to deal with it. Two international airports receive flights from Lisbon and many other European capitals – London is about three and a half hours away – and there is also good communication between the main island and Porto Santo, with its 9km of white sandy beaches. The population is nowadays about a quarter of a million, with around half living in Funchal, while the rest are scattered in small towns and villages throughout the main island and, in much smaller numbers, on Porto Santo. Politically, Madeira has enjoyed a certain level of autonomy since 1976 and certain sectors of society have flirted with the idea of total independence, but apart from a few hand grenades tossed at public buildings in the heady days following the 1974 revolution there has been no violence. The current tax regime means Madeira is a magnet for offshore investment, adding to its prosperity, while being part of Portugal means it is also a full member of the EU with all the advantages that implies for locals and residents alike.

Considering its tiny size – it measures just 57km in length and 22km across – Madeira offers much for the visitor to do, as well as an incredibly relaxed lifestyle for the resident. The more popular activities tend to be gentle in nature, which is possibly why Madeira has become known as a place for the retired. However, serious hill-walkers should not miss a trek along the *levadas*. Since there are no beaches on the main island, beach-lovers must go instead to **Porto Santo** to laze around on soft, white sand. The journey takes 15 minutes by plane or three hours by the boat service for which foot passengers do not need to make a reservation. Golf is available – with two championship standard courses on Madeira. **Funchal** has a fairly active nightclub scene for the young, its own casino, as well as a good selection of restaurants serving both local and international cuisine. Also worth seeing are the Flemish and Portuguese 16th-century art, gold objects and collection of statues in the museum of Sacred Art, the furniture and decorative arts in the Quinta das Cruzes museum, the 19th-century photo studio in the Vicentes Photographic Museum. On Porto Santo is Christopher Columbus' house, which has now been turned into a museum. Churches, of which there are plenty, cover a range of styles. Trips to Madeira wine-producers are also not to be missed. Throughout the year there are several festivals, for example the flower festival in April and the music festival in June. Above all, it is the island's beauty and serenity that make Madeira so attractive.

The housing market is not as active as in parts of mainland Portugal and houses do not come that cheaply. However, there are some interesting properties to be had. Prices are relatively high, though there are some bargains, but they compare favourably with the more expensive parts of the Algarve. About the cheapest currently on offer is a small but newly built cottage on the unspoilt north coast, going for around €80,000. For the same price you may get a two-bedroom apartment close to the surfers' beach in Porto Santo. Between

€100,000 and €150,000 there are some quite interesting properties on offer such as a renovated stone cottage for €100,000 or a traditional Madeiran country house with two large bedrooms for about €132,000. Between €200,000 and €300,000 might buy you an architect-designed, semi-detached triplex in Funchal, listed at €214,000, a spacious townhouse in the village of Garajau, with sea views for €235,000, or a sky-lit designer home in Caniço for €240,000. A large family home with 'awesome' (according to the advertiser) sea views in Calheta costs around €265,000, and €300,000 buys you a home in Camacha, lovingly built by its current owners. Above this price level and rising to well over €1 million, there are any number of luxury properties – for example a Scandinavian-built (and styled) three-bedroom property with views of the bay and city of Funchal, a minute's walk from the golf course and with a built-in sauna. This was advertised at €400,000. An English-style *quinta* (farmhouse with land) can cost as much as €750,000 – so too may a dream villa complete with swimming pools and gymnasium. For €1,750,000, you could get over 5,500 sq m of Funchal's most prime real estate, overlooking the harbour and with spectacular views.

Açores (The Azores)

This is the province with the fewest foreign residents in the whole of Portugal, which is hardly surprising given the Azores' remote location, some 1,460km from the European coast and 3,750km from North America. Much mystery surrounds the actual date of their discovery by Portuguese navigators, though they were certainly aware of the islands' existence in the late 1300s. The archipelago's correct Portuguese name is *Açores*, which means vultures, as the first colonists to arrive in the 15th century erroneously believed those were the birds circling overhead. They were in fact hawks – but the name stuck anyway. The archipelago consists of nine islands, all the result of now-extinguished volcanic activity, which belong to three separate groups. The 'Grupo Oriental' (eastern group) is formed by two islands: São Miguel and Santa Maria; the 'Grupo Central' (central group) comprises five: Terceira, Graciosa, São Jorge, Pico and Faial; while the 'Grupo Occidental' (western group) is made up of Corvo and Flores. Apart from the international airports of Santa Maria, Ponta Delgada (on São Miguel) and Angra (on Terceira), the regional airline SATA operates flights to all the islands and there are boat services between all of them.

No longer believed to be the remains of the lost continent of Atlantis, this archipelago of sapphire-blue and emerald-green lakes, fertile prairies, volcanic cones and craters, colourful hydrangeas and azaleas, 15th-century churches and majestic manor houses still retains an aura of mystique and legend. With year-round mild temperatures of between 14°C and 22°C (57°F and 71°F), the 250,000 inhabitants of this mid-Atlantic paradise do not know the meaning of words like 'stress' and 'pollution'. Like Madeira, the Azores has been an autonomous region since 1976 though still remains part of the Portuguese Republic and, as such, members of the EU with all that membership entails.

Many Azoreans have had to emigrate over the generations owing to the relative poverty of their region. Aggressive farming, especially the cultivation of tea, tobacco, red peppers and fruit such as pineapples, without crop rotation, has left much of the once highly fertile land spent, and now cattle-raising is the main agribusiness. The Azores are now no longer an important stop-off point for transatlantic shipping. The whaling industry died on its feet in the mid-1980s, though the boat owners now take tourists whale-watching or big-game fishing. Sizeable communities of Azoreans are to be found in the USA and elsewhere. However, the tourist boom that has brought so much prosperity to other parts of Portugal has yet to reach the islands – not necessarily a bad thing, since the challenge for the authorities and the community is perhaps to encourage a different style of tourism that is more respectful of the environment. Tour operators have begun to show an interest, though for the moment it is the specialist traveller or the solitude-seeker who tends to come here. Although large groups on package deals are not much in evidence, there are groups of golfers who fly in from Boston in springtime.

There are many attractions that make the islands worth visiting, including a wide variety of sporting activities. There are two good golf courses on São Miguel and a third, less well maintained, on the island of Terceira. None of them is oversubscribed – even in the months of July and August – and green fees are very low when compared with those on the mainland. As well as this, there are activity sports such as bicycle tours, deep-sea fishing, trekking, diving and underwater exploration, freshwater fishing, horseback riding, hunting, rock climbing, para-sailing and hang-gliding, rock fishing, sailing and wind surfing, surfing, tennis, volcano climbing and yachting. In many towns and cities splendid chapels, churches, manor houses, palaces and forts are to be found. Religion is something that Azoreans feel very deeply, and throughout the year there are regular festivals that even bring émigrés home from abroad. Wonderful local food, a range of crafts products and the spectacular beauty of the islands mean that, as one visitor put it, 'if you are thinking of going to either Yellowstone or Hawaii for a vacation, consider the Azores and you will have the best of both.'

But few, as yet, come to live. For one thing, work and business opportunities are limited, although the more enterprising may be able to set up some kind of business that caters to such tourism as there is – a rural hideaway hotel for bird-watchers and hill-walkers, perhaps, or a restaurant. Rugged, self-sufficient types in the style of *The Good Life* could do well here too. The property market, though, is geared almost totally towards locals and the lack of information about properties for sale in the islands is indicative of this. De-luxe villas are not advertised, and there is no sign of private condo developments or *urbanizações* with communal swimming pools or horse-riding facilities. You are unlikely to be accosted by hopeful timeshare salespeople when walking the streets of Ponta Delgada. A simple search on Google using 'azores+real estate' or 'azores+property' as your search criteria throws up few results and usually directs you to property sites specializing in other parts of Portugal (mainly in the Algarve), which can be most frustrating. If you can read Portuguese you are better off making your search in the language. Try, for example, 'açores+imoveis' (or maybe leave out the 'c cedilla' and type in 'acores' as this letter is not always recognized by search engines). You might then get some more promising results. Two locally based sites that give some indication of what you might be able to pick up are **www.rbg-imob.com** and **www.amachado.pt**.

Most of the apartments and newer houses on offer in the Azores seem to be in **Ponta Delgada**, or the surrounding areas, on the island of **São Miguel**. Apartments in relatively unspectacular blocks are quite inexpensive, ranging from just over €100,000 for one-bedroom flats with garage space to around €180,000 for a fairly luxurious three-bedroom, two-bathroom and two garage apartment in a new development. Houses with land come in all shapes and sizes and with prices ranging correspondingly. As little as €72,000 buys a small, two-storey house with a main bedroom and a small extra room upstairs in Ribeira Grande while across the other side of the island, close to Furnas, for just under €85,000, in 2,400 sq m of garden is a two-up-two-down with an attached garage. Newer housing developments around Ponta Delgada offer suburban-style family homes spread over two or three floors with three or four bedrooms, at least two bathrooms, a garage and some garden space, usually with a barbecue area, for between €225,000 and €275,000. On the much less-known and developed island of Pico, where Portugal's highest mountain is to be found, there is quite a range of modest little stone cottages going for between €25,000 and €40,000, though they may need some work; there are larger ones costing up to €70,000. There are also bigger country houses to be found in the €180,000–250,000 price range. Take a look at **www.picopage.com.pt** and see for yourselves. To buy here would really be to get away from it all.

Selecting a Property

04

One of Portugal's great advantages is its size, at least as far as getting there, getting around and searching for a property is concerned. It is a very small country, though one with an amazing amount of variety, and different areas have cultural, culinary, geographical and climatic characteristics that set them apart from the rest. Apart from the Alentejo no region is especially extensive so house-hunting, once you have narrowed down your choice to a particular area, does not mean having to cover huge distances in an endless quest for the perfect spot. Likewise, changing your mind in favour of a neighbouring area if you do not find what you are looking for in your first-choice location does not mean going back to square one. It is a question of just shifting focus a little. But you still should try to identify roughly where you want to be and the type of property you want before you go on a house-hunting trip, if nothing else to eliminate all the places and properties that you *don't* want.

Having made the decision to buy in Portugal, it is important to get things sorted out in your mind even before you travel. You need a research strategy to work out how you are going to find out all you need to know in order to make an informed decision. While you should never be in a rush to buy – precipitate decisions are rarely the best – you do need to have a good, clear, overall view of the property market in your chosen area, because when you least expect it the apparently 'perfect' property (price, type, location, everything you wanted) may suddenly become available and you could be under pressure to make a quick decision about whether to buy or not. Thorough research beforehand will equip you to make a quick decision, but one based on sound information. Apart from acquiring 'the knowledge', it is also important to be aware of the intricacies involved in the actual purchasing process. As this is complicated you are advised to seek the advice, and contract the services of, a reliable, reputable lawyer who is experienced in Portuguese property law and proceedings and can help steer you through from the beginning to the end. The particular issues involved are discussed at length – *see* **Making the Purchase**.

Some of the other issues that you ought to have clear from the beginning:

- How much do you want to spend?
- How much can you spend (if it comes to it)?
- Why are you buying?
  - A holiday getaway?
  - An eventual retirement home?
  - A place in which to make a new start?
  - An investment?
- How easy or difficult will it be to get to and from your Portuguese property and your home country (assuming regular or frequent travel is on your agenda)?

Fixing the Budget

As soon as you have decided that you are going to buy a house in Portugal you should try and fix a budget for the whole operation and decide on the maximum you are prepared to spend to end up with a house ready to live in. This means adding up the cost of the property itself plus estimates of any essential repairs or improvements and the taxes and fees that are payable.

If you are buying a new property or one that is in good condition and needs little repair work done, this is quite simple. But if you are buying a ruin to be restored or a house that needs a lot of repair work, fixing your budget is more difficult. Nobody ever estimates the cost of the repairs accurately; the tendency is to underestimate, and few jobs ever finish exactly within the budget or even on time. This is true almost everywhere. Buyers, however, make life difficult for themselves by not being realistic when costing out the work. Repair work often turns out to be more extensive than was apparent on a first viewing. If you are buying a property that needs major work, do not commit yourself until you have had a survey done and builders' estimates for the necessary work. If you are told that there is no time for this and that the 'other person' interested in the property is ready to hand over the cash if you can't sign today/this week/before Easter, let that other person have it.

In any case, fixing a budget is not something you can do just on the basis of perusing a few property magazines, looking in a couple of estate agent's windows or looking at properties on the internet. Obviously your budget must be adjusted to the amount of money you have at your disposal, so it is necessary to look at what is available within that range. Further on in this chapter, issues such as carrying out exhaustive research, spending time reconnoitring and even a season or two in rented accommodation prior to buying are discussed at length. This cannot be stressed enough as without an in-situ fact-finding mission you will not get a clear idea of what is available within your budget and may end up stretching your resources too far.

Unless you are fortunate enough for money to be no object, do not go over budget by any serious amount without careful thought and consultation with your financial adviser. It is too easy, after a good lunch and in the company of a silver-tongued estate agent, to throw your financial plans to the wind. 'Only another £30,000' is a statement you may later come to regret.

- How much space do you need for yourself and how much extra for your expected visitors?
- How much are you prepared to spend on improvements? How much of that will be taken up by labour costs? Can you do repairs yourself?
- What do you want to do when you are at your Portuguese property? What type of entertainments, hobbies, forms of relaxation, sports and so on are important to you? Will you be able to pursue them there?

Travelling to Portugal

Ease of travel to and from your Portuguese property may be as important an issue when choosing where to buy as the climate and facilities available in the local area. This is clearly the case if you plan to travel back and forth fairly regularly, but also if you are expecting frequent visits from family and friends and (especially) if you hope to let the property. You may take the opposite view, of course, and want a property that is as inaccessible as possible, as perhaps you do not want anybody visiting you. Either way, Portugal, or most of it, is accessible these days, and not only from London, as there are flights from a number of UK and Irish airports, especially to the Algarve. Central Portugal is well served by flights to Lisbon and most of the northern end of the country is fairly accessible from Oporto. Inland and mountain areas can be less easy to reach, since communications within Portugal are not universally good, and investment in road building has been unevenly distributed. Some areas are still practically as remote as they ever were.

Madeira, though much further away, still has regular connections both from continental Portugal and northern Europe, and only the remote Azores Islands are relatively poorly served. Few people think of the Azores as the ideal location for buying property, however, and there is only a small community of foreign residents based on the archipelago – which you might see as a bonus.

Air

Portugal is easily reached by air from the UK and Ireland. There are international airports at Lisbon, Oporto, Faro (in the Algarve), Funchal in Madeira and Ponta Delgada on the island of São Miguel in the Azores. **Lisbon**, being the capital, is the main Portuguese destination for many top airlines and is just over two and a half hours from London. The airport is also the hub for international air traffic into and out of Portugal and is only a short drive or bus ride from the city centre, from where there are road, rail and coach connections with the whole of the country.

Flying to **Oporto** takes marginally less time than flying to Lisbon; the airport is well situated for travellers making for the north and central Portugal. It is much the same whether you fly to Oporto or to the Lisbon if you are headed for certain destinations in central Portugal such as Coimbra, the Costa de Prata or the inland area approaching the Serra da Estrela.

Faro, just under three hours from the UK, is the only airport in the Algarve but is close to the new *Via do Infante* motorway which runs from the Spanish border all the way to Lagos. This means that few Algarve destinations should be much more than an hour from the airport. The southern part of the Alentejo is also within striking distance of Faro, although destinations in the middle and north of this extensive region are perhaps just as easily reached from Lisbon. Some travellers headed for the Costa de la Luz (between Huelva and Ayamonte) in Andalusia also use this airport because of the number of budget flights to Faro.

Madeira is more than three and a half hours from London but from Funchal airport travelling times anywhere on Madeira are short as the island is so small.

Reaching the **Azores** will take you more than four hours but between the islands you can use the local airline SATA or a network of ferries.

Scheduled Flights

In terms of cost, the variety of scheduled flights available to all Portuguese airports (especially to Faro), together with seasonal variations and special deals, make any figure that could be quoted here meaningless. However, it is possible to give an idea of approximate minimum and maximum prices. British Airways recently launched a new low-cost service from London Heathrow to Lisbon for just over £99 one-way if you book online at **www.ba.com**. From London Gatwick to Oporto, Faro and Funchal there are deals, again booking online, to Lisbon from £129, to Oporto from £119, to Faro from £149 and to Funchal from £189. All these flights are operated by GB Airways and prices are subject to availability at the time of booking. One-way flights start creeping up in price from there. British Airways has a scheduled flight to Lisbon for a little over £125. TAP Air Portugal, Lufthansa, Swiss and BA have a variety of flights for about £150, while Alitalia and Air France have flights for about £170. Prices to Oporto show a similar range with about the cheapest scheduled flight being BA's from London Gatwick for £113 and the most expensive being Air France's from London Heathrow for £250, with plenty of fares in between. Faro can cost between about £110 (with Monarch Airlines) and £170 (with TAP Air Portugal) and there are many flights costing about £150 with several other airlines.

Funchal is more expensive with fares ranging from TAP Air Portugal's £172.30 to British Airways' £222.30. Most, however, cost in the region of £190. Not surprisingly, Ponta Delgada (given its more distant location) is a far more expensive destination. TAP Air Portugal will get you there from London for £310 and after that prices range from about £340 to £420 – though a recent quote from TAP Air Portugal showed that you could pay as much as £1,418.50.

Of course, fares are subject to seasonal variations and special offers, whether paid for online or via a travel agent, and other factors such as purchasing a return ticket. The fares quoted above are for one-way flights; economy round-trip fares tend to work out substantially cheaper except during high season, so should be taken as guidelines only. There is no substitute for shopping around, either through the internet, travel agencies, the travel sections of the main daily or Sunday newspapers and magazines with good travel pages. Searching around will almost certainly lead to better deals than those cited above.

'No-frills' Budget Airlines

The budget charter flight market is in a state of flux at the moment with several new players entering the game. Until quite recently EasyJet (**www.easyjet.com**) appeared to dominate the UK–Algarve market, which is by far the most popular Portuguese destination for British travellers. In the spring of 2003, however, the company announced heavy losses, resulting perhaps from its acquisition of Go. Despite pessimistic forecasts for tourism worldwide resulting from the September 11 attacks, the war in Iraq and fears of further terrorism, the Algarve is just about holding its own and three new options for cheap travel to the region have been announced as this book is in its final stages of preparation. MyTravelLite (**www.mytravellite.com**) started a daily service from Birmingham to Faro in June 2003 for the trifling sum of £28, including taxes, possibly the cheapest deal possible going from any UK airport. Only a pound dearer is the offer of charters to Faro from Manchester from Thursday to Sunday announced by air2000.com (**www.air2000.com**) as of 1 July 2003. For the winter, starting on 4 September 2003, Jet 2 (**www.jet2.com**) plans to fly daily from Leeds Bradford for £39. However, with the market constantly changing, new deals may become available at any time from airlines such as Ryanair (**www.ryanair.com**), who bought out Buzz in January 2003, or Bmibaby (**www.flybmi.com**). The travel sections of major daily newspapers, as well as their websites, are always full of information on new and last-minute deals, as is the London listings magazine *Time Out*, and other locally based listings magazines and newspapers.

Major Air Links – Britain to Portugal

Not all places in Britain are equally served when it comes to flying to Portugal, and not all places in Portugal are readily accessible. Getting to Madeira and the Azores is a lot easier if you are prepared to change in Lisbon as TAP and SATA (the Azorean airline) both run flights out of that airport.

From	To	Operator
Birmingham	Faro	Monarch, MyTravelLite
	Lisbon	TAP Air Portugal
Bristol	Faro	Air2000, easyJet
Cardiff	Faro	Bmibaby
Dublin	Faro	Aer Lingus, Portugalia, Ryanair
	Lisbon	Aer Lingus, Portugalia
East Midlands	Faro	Air2000, Bmibaby, easyJet
Edinburgh	Lisbon	TAP Air Portugal (change in London)
Glasgow	Faro	Air2000, Britannia Airways
Leeds Bradford	Faro	Jet2
London Gatwick	Faro	British Airways, Britannia Airways, Excel Airways, Flyjet, GB Airways, Monarch, Thomas Cook Airlines

Airline Contact Details

Aer Lingus	t 0845 084 444	www.aerlingus.com
Air2000	t 0870 240 1402	www.air2000.com
Air France	t 0845 359 1000	www.airfrance.co.uk
Alitalia	t 0870 544 8259	www.alitalia.co.uk
Bmibaby	t 0870 607 0555	www.flybmi.com
Britannia Airways	t 0870 801 4155	www.britanniadirect.com
British Airways	t 0845 773 3377	www.britishairways.com
easyJet	t 0870 600 0000	www.easyjet.com
Excel Airways	t 0870 000 2468	www.excelairways.com
Flyjet	t 0870 000 2468	www.flyjet.com
GB Airways	t 0845 773 3377	www.gbairways.com
Jet2	t 0870 737 8282	www.jet2.com
Monarch	t 0870 040 5040	www.monarch-airlines.com
MyTravelLite	t 0870 156 4564	www.mytravellite.com
Portugalia	t 0870 755 0025	www.pga.pt
Ryanair	t 08 18 30 30 30	www.ryanaircom
TAP Air Portugal	t 0207 828 0262	www.tap.pt
Thomas Cook Airlines	t 0870 243 0416	www.thomascook.co.uk

From	To	Operator
London Gatwick	Funchal	Air2000, British Airways, Excel Airways, GB Airways, MyTravelLite, Thomas Cook Airlines
	Lisbon	Air France, Alitalia, British Airways, TAP Air Portugal,
	Oporto	British Airways, GB Airways, TAP Air Portugal
London Heathrow	Faro	British Airways, TAP Air Portugal
	Funchal	British Airways, TAP Air Portugal
	Lisbon	British Airways, TAP Air Portugal
	Ponta Delgada	TAP Air Portugal (via Lisbon)
	Oporto	British Airways, TAP Air Portugal
London Luton	Faro	easyJet, Monarch
London Stansted	Faro	Air2000, easyJet
Manchester	Faro	Air2000, Monarch
	Lisbon	TAP Air Portugal, Portugalia
	Oporto	Portugalia

Road

Portugal, by road, is a long way from the UK or Ireland and, given the distances involved and the time taken up in covering them, far fewer people undertake the journey this way than go by air. Some second-home owners, though, do like to have their car for use while in Portugal and if staying permanently may decide to import it. Having bought a holiday home, or if moving there permanently, you may at some point need to make a road trip anyway. If you are taking a lot of household items to your Portuguese house it is unlikely you will be able to take them with you if you travel by air, so at least one long-haul road trip may be necessary. However, if you are travelling frequently between your main home and a second home you are probably better advised to make use of a rented car or even buy one for use in Portugal. A right-hand drive car may be an additional source of danger when driving in Portugal where accident statistics are alarmingly high.

There is no direct ferry from any UK port to Portugal so travelling by this means involves a considerable drive at the other end, whichever port you sail to. If you take a car to Portugal from the UK you have two choices:

- **A fairly rapid channel crossing to any of France's northern ports** followed by a long journey through France and Spain. From the Channel ports to Portugal, depending on the route you take, approximate distances are as follows: Oporto about 1,800km; Lisbon over 1,900km; the Algarve 2,200km.
- **A longer crossing, either the P&O ferry from Portsmouth to Bilbao (about 27hrs) or the Brittany Ferries route from Plymouth to Santander** (about 24hrs). This means the drive at the other end is reduced by between 1,000 and 1,200km. From Spain's northern ports the distance are as follows: Oporto about 800km; Lisbon about 1,000km; the Algarve about 1,300km.

Deciding which option to choose means juggling four main factors: cost, distance, time and fatigue. Cost does not only mean the price of the cross-Channel trip versus the price of the longer ferry trip. It also includes petrol, road tolls, food and accommodation en route. Distance means the extremely long drive from the French channel ports as compared with the lesser, but still not inconsiderable, journey from the ports in northern Spain. Time means time spent driving – much longer if you choose option 1 – and time spent on the ferry if you choose option 2. Fatigue is the result of the time spent driving, more in the case of option 1, less (but not much) in the case of option 2.

The **long-haul ferries** between Plymouth and Santander and Portsmouth and Bilbao have an extremely varied fare structure that depends on the time of year, the length of your vehicle, the type of cabin you choose, any special offers at a given time and whether or not you are a frequent user. Booking is generally done online these days (**www.poportsmouth.com** for P&O and **www.brittany-ferries.com** for Brittany Ferries). A frustrating aspect of both company's websites is that when booking you cannot see a full list of fares and extras. Instead, you have to choose a date for sailing, complete a form with the number of passengers, the length of the car and the type of berth you want and proceed from there. You will be given a price and then have to choose whether to purchase or not. What you cannot know, without repeating the whole procedure, is whether sailing a few days earlier or later will save you a lot of money.

P&O say they are redesigning the online booking system at present. Hopefully it will be more user-friendly when finished, but in the meantime contact the reservations centre (**t** 08705 202 020). A family of four with a medium-sized saloon car occupying a four-berth cabin travelling both ways can pay in the region of £1,200 for the return trip during the high season, to which the cost of food and drinks and on-board entertainment should be added. Sailing is a pleasant way of travelling provided the sea is not too rough and it avoids a very long trip through France. You may, though, prefer option 2 and decide to sample the joys of France on your way.

There are many **cross-Channel services** to France:

- **Dover and Folkstone to Calais**:
  Eurotunnel (**t** 08705 353 535, **www.eurotunnel.com**)
  Hoverspeed (**t** 0870 240 8070, **www.hoverspeed.com**)
  P&O Stena (**t** 0870 600 0600, **www.post.com**)
  Seafrance (**t** 08705 711 711, **www.seafrance.com**)
- **Newhaven to Dieppe**:
  Hoverspeed (**t** 0870 240 8070, **www.hoverspeed.com**)
  Transmanche Ferries (**t** 0800 917 1201, **www.transmancheferries.com**)
- **Portsmouth to Le Havre**:
  P&O Portsmouth (**t** 0870 242 4999, **www.poportsmouth.com**)
- **Portsmouth to Caen**:
  Brittany Ferries (**t** 08705 665 333, **www.brittany-ferries.com**)
- **Portsmouth to Cherbourg**:
  P&O Portsmouth (**t** 0870 242 4999, **www.poportsmouth.com**)
  Condor Ferries (**t** (01305) 761 551, **www.condorferries.com**)
- **Poole to Cherbourg**:
  Brittany Ferries (**t** 08705 665 333, **www.brittany-ferries.com**)
- **Portsmouth to St Malo**:
  Brittany Ferries (**t** 08705 665 333, **www.brittany-ferries.com**)
- **Poole and Weymouth to St Malo**:
  Condor Ferries (**t** 01305 761 551, **www.condorferries.com**)
- **Plymouth to Roscoff**:
  Brittany Ferries (**t** 08705 665 333, **www.brittany-ferries.com**)
- **Cork to Roscoff**:
  Brittany Ferries (**t** 08705 665 333, **www.brittany-ferries.com**)
- **Rosslare to Cherbourg and Rosslare to Roscoff**:
  Irish Ferries (**t** 00353 01890 313 131, **www.irishferries.com**)

Whichever you choose, it is a long way so be prepared and set aside at least three days for the trip. Depending on your schedule and urgency you may, rather than rushing it, decide to make a pleasant, relaxed trip of the journey, especially if you are to drive through France. If you are going alone you will need to take plenty of breaks to fight fatigue. If there are two people who can share the driving while the non-driver takes some time off to relax or sleep then you can get there more quickly. If cost is an issue, remember that both France and Spain have many toll roads (*autoroutes* and *autopistas* respectively) which can work out expensive. So you might like to travel on other roads and look at the scenery, stop for relaxing meals and stay in hotels along the way. What you spend on these items could work out to be more or less what you do not spend on tolls. Both the French and Spanish road authorities have websites with regularly updated information about the state of the roads, weather conditions as they affect driving, roadworks and tolls. For France, check out **www.autoroutes.fr**, the site of the company that manages the *autoroutes* with toll charges and maps, and there is also **www.bison-fute.equipement.gouv.fr**, the site of the French National Traffic Centre, which has lots of good information on potential hold-ups, alternative routes and so on. For Spain visit **www.dgt.es**, which has information in English.

Rail

Travelling by train to Portugal inevitably means going through Paris and the whole of France and Spain, with different options along the way depending on your final destination. Wherever you are headed and whichever route you choose, it is a long trip (about a day and a half) but a pleasant one for those who enjoy rail travel. From the UK, Eurostar (via Paris) is the best option, taking the French high-speed train (TGV) from the Gare d'Austerlitz to the Basque border at Irún/Hendaye. There you have to change trains, since the bright sparks that built the first Spanish railways in the 19th century decided to use a wider gauge than the rest of continental Europe. From Irún, the Rápido Sud-Expresso takes you across northern Spain and enters Portugal at Vilar Formosa going on to Pampilhosa (southeast of Coimbra – where you can change for Oporto) and finally on to Lisbon. The trip takes about 18hrs in total. From Lisbon there are train and coach links to the rest of Portugal. An alternative, for real train buffs, is to go via Madrid and take the eight-hour trip on the overnight Lusitânia Express to Lisbon. If you are going to the Algarve, another possibility is to take the Spanish high-speed train, the AVE, to Sevilla (2 hours 25 minutes) and pick up the coach to Faro operated by Eva Bus. There are two trains a day, early morning and mid-afternoon. Going by rail from the UK to Portugal is likely to cost you more than a budget flight. Expect to pay upwards of €150 just from Paris. It is more an option for the nostalgic train-traveller.

- **Eurostar** (**t** 08705 186 186, **www.eurostar.com**)
- **Rail Europe** (**t** 08705 848 848, **www.raileurope.co.uk**). Reservation and information service run by French Railways in the UK.

- **SNCF** (French Railways) (**www.snfc.com**)
- **RENFE** (Spanish Railways) (**www.renfe.es**)
- **CP** (Portuguese Railways) (**t** 808 208 208, **www.cp.pt**)

Coach

Not many second or holiday home-owners choose to travel by coach from northern Europe to Portugal. For one thing it is a very long journey. From Victoria Station (London) to Lisbon takes approximately 40hrs and takes almost two days to reach the Algarve. Secondly, the fare is likely to cost more than a budget flight added to which is the cost of food and drinks along on the way. (Stops tend to be beside motorways and can be expensive.) Coaches are a lot more comfortable than they used to be but most travellers get swollen ankles and are hobbling for a day or two after the trip. Only use this means if you like international coach travel and there are absolutely no flights available.

- **Eurolines**, Victoria Coach Station, Buckingham Palace Road, London SW1 (**t** (020) 7730 0202, **www.eurolines.co.uk**)

Travelling Around Portugal

One of Portugal's virtues, from the point of view of getting around, is its compact size. This means that, apart from journeys from the far north to the south coast, travelling from A to B for business or pleasure is usually quite manageable – whether you go by car or public transport. Public transport infrastructures have improved considerably in recent years and between the main cities and the most developed tourist areas connections are fairly frequent, reasonably quick and not too expensive. As well as this, EU funding has helped to improve the main road and motorway network immensely and there are now more motorways under construction. There are, however, parts of the country that the government seems to have overlooked in terms of public transport, often leaving the traveller with few options other than getting there by car. Unfortunately, these also tend to be the areas where road improvements have been least in evidence. Moreover, not all newly built roads are up to scratch and even some of the smart new motorways have come in for criticism for poorly designed signposting.

Bus (*Autocarros*)

The most popular and fastest form of intercity travel in Portugal, the bus network, has tentacles that reach just about everywhere, although in out-of-the-way rural areas services are not as frequent as they might be. Until recently, all intercity bus travel was operated by the state-owned *Rodoviária Nacional* network whose vehicles were easily recognized by their bright orange paintwork. This monopoly has now been broken up and several private companies have stepped in to operate many lines. Still remaining in state hands is the *Rede Nacional de Expressos*, the National Express Network, whose buses are white with an orange–red stripe along the side. This network is fast, covers a huge number of destinations and is not expensive. For example, the price from Albufeira (Algarve) to Lisbon is €14 one-way. Fares can be found and tickets booked on **www.rede-expressos.pt**, which is in Portuguese only and not as fast as the buses. If your Portuguese is up to it and you are a mobile telephone enthusiast, it is possible to get timetables and to buy tickets by SMS. Several private companies now operate other former RN routes in different regions. *Eva Bus* operates services throughout the Algarve and also connects the southern coastal region to Lisbon and other points. The company also runs luxury coaches (*Alta Qualidade*) on some routes, complete with toilets and movies, often in English with Portuguese subtitles. Again, fares are reasonable and are generally comparable with those of *Rede Expressos*. One advantage of travelling around by bus is that most towns and cities have a centrally located bus station, something that the trains do not. However, this is not always the case since the break-up of the RN monopoly has meant that some of the newcomers use alternative terminals which may be in a different part of town from the company to which you are connecting.

Rail

The history of Portuguese railways stretches back almost a century and a half since the inaugural rail journey took place on 26 October 1856. Throughout the early part of the 20th century several companies operated different lines but in 1951 they were merged into the Companhia dos Caminhos de Ferro Portugueses (Portuguese Railway Company), a name that was shortened in 1975 to Caminhos de Ferro Portugueses, or simply CP as it is known today. Every year CP transports around 178 million passengers and 9.3 million tons of freight throughout its 3,100km network. This network reaches almost all major towns and cities but many rural areas in the interior have no service. Stations are often situated some way from the centre of many small- and medium-sized towns and passengers often have no choice but to take a taxi, as there may be no bus into the centre. For the first-time visitor, many stations are a feast for the eyes, frequently adorned with the blue tile-work that is so much a feature of Portugal, and a good many stations are well kept, boasting colourful, carefully cultivated flower beds. As a rule, travelling between the main cities by train is slightly slower than going by bus, but a little cheaper, and the relaxed comfort and greater safety of trains really does make it worth your while.

Travelling by rail in Portugal is usually a pleasant experience as the trains are generally well maintained, clean, rarely late and tickets are almost ridiculously cheap when compared with prices in northern European countries. CP has invested in new rolling stock in recent years and the sleek, streamlined, comfortable ***Alfa Pendular*** (**AP**) trains cover the Lisbon–Porto route. This service is known as the *rápido* and, owing to a shift in terminology, passengers no longer travel in first or second class but in *conforto* and *turística*. With a journey time of 3 hours 25 minutes it is just about possible to travel from one to the other, do a day's business or sightseeing and return the same evening. Other major cities are reached by the ***Intercidade*** (intercity, known as **IC**) trains, which are only slightly inferior to the *Alfa Pendular* model and offer a comparable level of comfort.

As well as this there are ***Interregional*** trains (**IR**), not as fast as the *Intercidade* ones and with more stops, but efficient nevertheless, covering a large part of the network. These trains keep the old denominations of first and second class. Finally come the ***Suburbano***, otherwise known as ***Regional*** services (**R**), which, as their name suggests, stop at every town, village and halt and make no class distinctions – one price only is available. A rather battered-looking small fleet of trains chug the length of the Algarve from Vila Real de Santo António to Lagos. For long trips, such as from Faro to Oporto, the night train, with sleeping cars, is an option and it is also possible to send your car by rail.

Tickets and Prices

Prices are cheap by comparison with those in the UK. You can travel from Lisbon to Porto in tourist class for a mere €21 or pay the difference and do it in *conforto* style for €31. From the capital to Faro, on the Algarve, a second-class ticket costs as little as €12 and first-class will only set you back €16.50. **Do be sure to buy your ticket before departure, as you will be fined for travelling without one unless you have boarded the train at some tiny rural station where the ticket office was closed, in which case you can pay the conductor.**

Tickets can be bought at stations, travel agents and by telephone **t** 808 208 208; open 7am–11pm. For *Alfa Pendular* and *Intercidade* services tickets may be bought up to 30 days in advance from any train station. They can be obtained through **www.cp.pt**, or from ATM machines up to 21 days in advance and as late as 15mins before departure. Note that only full-price tickets (as opposed to discount tickets, details of which figure below) may be bought through this method.

There are several discount schemes which can make rail travel cheaper still.

- **Groups of 10 or more: 20 per cent discount.**
- **Children under the age of four: free if they do not occupy a seat. Ages 4–11: half-price.**

- **Young persons aged 12–26 benefit from the *Cartão Jovem* (youth card): 30 per cent discount on full prices for certain journeys on some lines.**
- ***Bilhete Turístico* (tourist ticket), valid for 7, 14 or 21 days at €100, €170 or €250 days, respectively; half-price for the 4–11s and senior citizens.**
- ***Cheque Trem* (train cheque) allowing you to buy pre-paid travel up to a certain price for a 10 per cent discount.**

All discounts are subject to restrictions on certain days and times and it is advisable to check for details on **www.cp.pt** or at a CP information centre in the major railway stations.

Portuguese train travel centres on Lisbon, which has four mainline stations. The neo-Manueline style Rossio has trains departing for Sintra and other places to the west of the capital. The old but refurbished Santa Apolónia serves the north and east and is also where trains to and from Spain depart and arrive. Cais do Sodré, on the river bank, is for Estoril and Cascais and other points along the Lisbon coast. Barreiro, across the Tagus estuary and reached by means of a ferry, serves all points south. As well as this there is the flashy new Gare de Oriente, built to serve the Expo '98 complex and, with its good metro connections, a convenient halt on north- and east-bound lines as well as international trains. It is, in fact, easier to get to than Santa Apolónia, which still lacks the metro link originally scheduled for early 2000. Construction work on the line from Cais do Sodré has been abandoned for the time being after part of the Praça do Comercio caved in.

Road

A glance at any literature available on Portugal, travel guides especially, makes for depressing reading when it comes to the section dealing with motoring in Portugal. All, without fail, make some reference to the 'normally placid Portuguese' turning into 'raving lunatics' once behind the steering wheel. If you take a look at road accident statistics then you begin to see why. Portuguese roads are, statistically, the most dangerous in Europe, if only marginally more so than those in Greece, and your chances of dying on the roads are three times higher in Portugal than in the UK, Sweden or Holland. Statistics regarding pedestrians killed by car drivers also make for scary reading.

Why is this? Opinions vary but there seems to be a general consensus that it is a combination of several factors, namely bad driving habits, bad roads, poor signposting, inadequate policing of the roads, sanctions which are often not enforced and a lack of political will on the part of the authorities to recognize that the problem exists and deal with it, though, to be fair, efforts have been made in recent times.

Regarding drivers, several bad habits are cited as causes of problems on roads and highways. These are: excess speed (87 per cent of drivers are thought to break speed-limits habitually); unpredictable driving (lane-hopping especially); driving while under the influence of alcohol or drugs; reckless overtaking on bends, solid yellow lines or in the middle of no-overtaking zones such as residential areas or outside schools; parking anywhere and everywhere, on the pavement or other places that pose a hazard to moving traffic; use of fog headlights at night; not keeping the correct distance from the car in front; speeding up when traffic lights are about to change to red or directly jumping them, and chatting on mobile telephones while driving. All of these habits are common fare on Portuguese roads.

Car ownership on a massive scale is a fairly recent phenomenon. This means that many people are first-generation drivers who have not benefited from a road culture built up over the generations. Many drivers quite simply have had no parental role model to copy.

The roads themselves, or rather those in charge of building and maintaining them, must take their share of the blame. Motorists have levelled all manner of criticisms at the abandoned state of back roads. These roads are:

- **often riddled with potholes.**
- **poorly illuminated.**
- **often congested due to slow-moving repair and agricultural vehicles.**
- **poorly signalled when under repair.**
- **often dangerous because of hairpin bends with no warning signs.**
- **poorly signposted. Signs are often misleading, covered in graffiti, situated out of drivers' sight-lines or behind trees, or are simply inadequate for their functions.**

National highways also come in for their fair share of criticism:

- **They are often no more than two-lane roads.**
- **Overtaking lanes are a rarity, and where one is available is it often on a hill where both descending and ascending cars can overtake simultaneously. Head-on collisions often result as there is frequently no central division.**
- **They are subject to back-ups owing to slow-moving heavy lorries, something that encourages the reckless and impatient to try dangerous overtaking.**

Economic growth in the past few years has led to a dramatic rise in car ownership, which, in turn, has served to increase congestion on smaller roads, especially since the new motorways are generally expensive toll roads, so that much of the intercity traffic for which they were designed and built tends to stay on the national highways.

Some claim there is little chance of things improving until the police start taking a more active role and clamp down on offenders on the roads. Accusations that the police are either never there when needed or turn a blind eye to reckless driving are common in the Portuguese and ex-pat press. One Algarve-based journalist consulted reckoned that there was only ever one set of radar equipment in operation at any one time in the region. Worse, it seems that some officers are open to bribes when they stop drivers breaking the speed limits or who have been drinking. Moreover, penalties for offences such as drink-driving, while stiff, are very often not enforced as they should be. More than one blatant offender has got off with nothing more than a warning. There is also a widely held view that many people 'buy' their driving licences rather than actually pass the test.

Portuguese road classifications can be confusing, as can their respective speed limits. Note that the Portuguese road system is undergoing permanent improvement work so try to get the latest road map. The *Turinta* series is widely available at petrol stations. Be prepared for surprises!

- **Urban areas: the speed limit is 50kph.**
- ***Estradas Municipais*, main roads between towns and villages in country areas: speed limit is 90kph. These roads are usually narrow and often have no painted lines or guard-rails but are fairly safe as there is not a huge amount of traffic using them.**
- ***Estradas Nacionais* (national highways): speed limit is 100kph, reduced to 80kph when pulling a trailer. These roads often have only two lanes. Similar, but slightly higher in grade than these roads, are the *Itinerários Complementares* (principal routes), which often become four-lane roads and pass directly through towns and villages, and *Itinerários Principais* (which you would think should translate as main roads but which are actually 'highways' of near-motorway status), usually having three lanes. These are subject to the same speed limits as the *Estradas Nacionais* and in many cases are ENs which have been upgraded and widened recently.**
- ***Autoestradas* (motorways): speed limit is 120kph, reduced to 100kph if you are pulling a trailer. Most motorways are of recent construction and are usually quite good but the tolls are high; as a result few drivers use them and they are considered to be safer. Motorists are therefore faced with either expensive, safe motoring (where available) or overcrowded roads that do not always come up to scratch.**

The most important *autoestradas* (some of which are considered to have dangerous stretches) are:

- **The A1, from Lisbon to Oporto (Portugal's first toll road and probably the most used).**
- **The A2, from Lisbon to the Algarve, completed in 2002.**

- **The A3, from Valença do Minho, on the northern border, to Porto.**
- **The A4, from Porto to Amarante, heading east towards Bragança; after Amarante it becomes the IP-4.**
- **The A6, from Lisbon to Elvas and the Spanish border close to Badajoz. As this road crosses flat plains it is not considered to be especially dangerous.**
- **The A15, from Santarém to Óbidos.**
- **The A22, *Via do Infante*, completed in spring 2003, crossing the Algarve from Vila Real de Santo António to Lagos. The most recently inaugurated motorway.**

Motorway users are required to pay **tolls** to help pay for their upkeep. Penalties for avoiding payment or inability to pay on arrival at a toll gate are stiff. There is an automatic payment scheme known as the *Via Verde*, the 'Green Way', which enables drivers to avoid long queues at toll gates. In order to subscribe to this system you need a bank account and a Multibanco card.

In addition to tolls on the main stretches of *autoestradas*, it is worth remembering that there is a toll on southbound vehicles crossing the 25 de Abril Bridge which links Lisbon with the south bank of the Tagus River at the end of the Vila Franca de Xira expressway.

The *Direcção Geral de Viação* (DGV), the Portuguese Highway Authorities, make the following recommendations.

Drivers must carry a **valid driving licence** and **photographic identity** (i.e. passport, identity card or residency card) in addition to the following information relating to the vehicle (these are supplied with hire cars but if you are using your own car you must have them with you):

- **Registration document.**
- **Ownership registration document (where applicable).**
- **Insurance certificate and if insured outside Portugal the green card valid in Portugal.**
- **Vehicle inspection certificate (where applicable).**
- **Written permission to drive if you are not the owner (car hire contract or owner's declaration).**

Note: Children under 12 years are not allowed to sit in the front. Car seat belts must be worn in both the front and the rear seats; failure to do so may earn you an on-the-spot fine.

Other compulsory items to carry in the car are:

- **A red warning triangle and a first-aid kit. If you hire a car make sure that the vehicle has these and that you know where they are, as you may face a fine if you cannot show them immediately during a spot-check.**
- **You must also carry a spare wheel and a tool-kit for changing the wheel if necessary.**

When driving, there are certain precautions you can take to avoid inflating the accident statistics; above all you should concentrate and be on the defensive when you are driving in Portugal.

- **All traffic coming from the right has priority; always give way if you are not sure who has right of way.**
- **On roundabouts, traffic approaching from the left has priority and the traffic goes in a clockwise direction.**
- **Stay out of bus and taxi lanes. They will often be obstructed by illegally parked cars anyway, so you will not gain anything by using them.**
- **Do not use your horn at night unless you are in an emergency.**
- **Use your headlamps at night and in foggy conditions. Dip them as well.**
- **If a driver flashes his headlights at you he may be warning you of a police speed-trap up ahead.**
- **Solid single lines or two solid lines mean no overtaking.**
- **A single broken line means overtaking is permitted. A double line, broken on your side of the road, also means you can overtake. Be extra careful if you are driving a trailer.**
- **The international sign depicting two cars side by side, one red, one black, also means no overtaking.**
- **Traffic lights (*sinais de tráfico*) follow a red, green, amber, red sequence. Many Portuguese drivers go through on amber even though they are not supposed to. Flashing amber means proceed but with caution, possibly be careful of pedestrians.**
- **Be especially cautious at railway crossings, particularly those with no barrier.**
- **Be careful of youths on mopeds; many ride without lights at night. Be extra careful when overtaking them.**
- **In rural areas, watch out for domestic and farm animals on the roads.**
- **Park only where it is legally permitted (not always so easy); illegally parked cars may be clamped or towed away.**
- **Wear a crash helmet if you ride a bicycle or a motorbike.**
- **If you are caught speeding or otherwise driving illegally you may have to pay the fine on the spot. Residents have up to 15 days to pay.**
- **Do not drink and drive, penalties can be stiff –** ***see*** **opposite.**

Accidents and Breakdowns

The *Automóvel Clube de Portugal* (ACP) (**www.acp.pt**) has reciprocal agreements with most foreign automobile organizations and is the most useful body to contact in case of breaking down, provided you are a member of the AA or the RAC.

Drinking and Driving – What To Expect if You Get Caught

blood alcohol level	considered to be	fine	additional sanction
0.5–0.8 g/l	serious	€240–1,200	Minimum: 1-month ban Maximum: 1-year ban
0.8–1.19 g/l	very serious	€360–1,800	Minimum: 2-month ban Maximum: 2-year ban
1.2 or more g/l	not rated on DGV website	Imprisonment of up to 1 year *or* fine + imprisonment of up to 120 days	Minimum: 3-month ban Maximum: 3-year ban

A minor bump with no consequences does not require you calling the police if both drivers involved are in agreement as to who was to blame. Both of you should move your vehicles out of the way of other traffic and then complete the European Accident Statement (known in Portugal as the *Declaração Amigável de Acidente Automóvel*) and you must each send a copy to your respective insurance companies, who will sort the matter out. In the case of a more serious accident, or if you and the other driver cannot agree who was to blame, then the police must be called. Do not move your vehicle until the police come, you could be removing evidence; but display the red warning triangle to warn other cars. When the police come, both parties must make a declaration – so too must any witnesses. Copies of the police reports are sent to the respective insurance companies and they argue it out between them. If you do not have the correct insurance (*see* **Settling In**, 'Insuring Your Car', p.218), you could be in serious trouble. If you were not at fault and the other driver was uninsured there is a compensation board for claims; the police and your insurance company will tell you how to proceed.

Petrol Stations (*Postos de Gasolina*)

Larger filling stations on motorways and in urban areas are usually open 24 hours a day. Smaller, individually owned petrol stations tend to be open 8am–7pm midweek and on Saturdays 9am–1pm. The different types of petrol are *normal* (equivalent to 2 star), *super* (equivalent to 4 star), *sem chumbo* (unleaded) and *gasóleo* (diesel). Expect to pay between €0.85 and €0.90 for a litre of unleaded and about €0.70 for diesel. **Credit cards are not universally accepted so always have some cash on you when filling up.**

Climate

Clearly one of the features that makes Portugal so attractive for so many people is the weather. Generally speaking it is mild all over and the south is said to have weather comparable to that of the Mediterranean (although Portugal does not actually have one centimetre of Mediterranean coast) or more accurately that of California. It does, of course, vary from season to season and from one region to another.

The Atlantic and the Gulf Stream exert a major influence on Portugal's climate so that summer temperatures in the Algarve and the western coastal areas of Costa de Prata and Costa Verde do not differ greatly. Faro's average summer midday temperature, for example, is 28°C and Oporto stays at around 25°C, a small difference. The Costas de Plata and Verde, further to the north, get a lot more rainfall throughout the year, and winter temperatures are lower, though not that much, Oporto averaging around 13°C at this time. Along the still barely exploited Alentejo coastline, stretching south of Lisbon to the Algarve, the opposite occurs: winters are progressively drier and warmer. The Algarve itself is the warmest region in Europe during the winter, if 'winter' can really apply to a place where temperatures in January average around 15°C. It can, at times, get quite a lot colder but this is rare. Snow and ice would be a freak phenomenon there. This is what draws so many people to the Algarve and, though in summer it can get very hot, with daytime temperatures averaging 28°C and often climbing to well above 30°C, the breezes that come in off the Atlantic keep things bearable. In all of continental Portugal the winter means rain, quite a lot of it from the central region to the north and somewhat less to the south. Lack of rain is in fact the major problem faced by the Alentejo and Algarve regions, and drought is not uncommon.

Inland is where you get more variation in temperature and rainfall. The Montanhas region, comprising the upper and lower Beiras and Trás-os-Montes, may experience extremely hot summers with temperatures getting up to almost 40°C in the Douro valley, though spring and summer showers are frequent in the higher areas such as the Serra da Estrela. These areas can be very cold and very wet indeed in winter; freezing temperatures are not unknown and the city of Bragança averages only 8°C in winter. Rainfall in the Montanhas area is five times more than that of the Algarve. It is in the Serra da Estrela, in fact, where Portugal's only winter sports facilities are to be found. The interior of the Alentejo also suffers from extremes, with summers that are very hot – from 35 to 40°C is common in Évora and Beja – and while winter temperatures average around 12°C it can often be a lot colder.

Lisbon enjoys a fortunate climate owing to its position a little to the south of central Portugal and its proximity to the sea. In summer, which lasts practically from June to October, temperatures average 27°C, but sometimes hit almost

40°C; in winter the thermometer sits around the 14°C mark and rarely drops below 10°C, though the wind chill factor should be borne in mind when choosing what to wear. Apart from the summer, which is very dry, Lisbon is quite a wet city, especially in spring and autumn when there are frequent showers and in winter when downpours are not infrequent.

Madeira has a subtropical climate and so does not suffer too much from thermal extremes; the range is from about 16°C in winter to upwards of 22°C in summer. The island boasts 2,000 hours of sunshine annually though there is a rainy season, from October to March, and August is famous for the misty season, known as the *capacete*. Otherwise, the island gets warm winds known as the *leste* coming off the Sahara, which sometimes bring deposits of sand and the odd tropical storm. The Azores, a third of the way across the Atlantic, enjoy a mild climate, perhaps surprisingly given their location. Winter temperatures rarely drop below 14°C and in summer average around 21°C. Rainfall is frequent but it comes more in the form of showers than downpours.

For a regional temperature and rainfall chart, *see* 'Climate Charts', p.308.

Choosing a Location

It might seem like a cliché, trotted out by property experts everywhere, but it is true: location is all when it comes to buying a home anywhere, not just in Portugal. Apart from the area around Lisbon, Oporto and choice beach locations in the Algarve, there is still a wealth of property available in Portugal, at affordable prices. When choosing where to buy, much depends on your long-term plans. You may be buying with the idea of selling later on and making a tidy profit. You may be thinking of buying a property to let out to holidaymakers, even if you intend to spend some time there yourself. You may be looking to buy a place to settle down in comfortable, relaxed retirement. You may also be planning to work or run a business and live full-time in Portugal.

Whatever your long-term plan may be, choosing the right location is vital. The wrong choice could be a cause of serious disappointment and disillusionment. If you want to sit back and watch as your property soars in value then you are much better off buying in a popular location where prices are guaranteed to rise. If you want to let a property out then the existence of good communications and proximity to services, entertainment and beaches is highly important. If you neither care about making money nor wish to let your property, preferring to live the rest of your life in peace and quiet, then you are freer to choose something more remote and maybe more to your taste, though do bear in mind the possible drawbacks of rural isolation in later life; *see* **Where in Portugal**, 'Life in Rural Portugal', pp.45–6.

Getting to Know your Area

A good many people decide to buy in a given area on the strength of a much-enjoyed holiday. It could be that you especially liked the landscape, the nightlife, the tranquillity, the cuisine, the proximity of a golf course or marina, the weekly travelling market or any combination of these things. Deciding to move permanently, however, does entail recognizing and understanding a number of important factors, since within any area there are likely to be dozens (perhaps hundreds) of different locations where day-to-day reality may differ greatly from holiday impressions or memories. Before committing yourself it is therefore vital to go beyond mere familiarity and achieve a certain intimacy with your chosen region. Apart from being an important step before to buying, it can be a lot of fun and a voyage of discovery. Spending some time in the area during different seasons is also very important. Your view could be overly influenced by glorious summer weather, only to find that winter is a very different story indeed. Or it could be the other way around: you may have had a pleasant, quiet week or two somewhere during the autumn, winter or spring with sunny but agreeable weather only to find that summer is frankly unbearable, with temperatures beyond what you can stand and the tranquillity transformed by lager-fuelled mayhem.

During a holiday you cannot possibly hope to exhaust all of an area's sightseeing, cultural, culinary or leisure activities, still less its climatic range. You think you know the area but really you have only scratched the surface. So, it is now time to become intimate with it. To get started, find a general guide book to Portugal to set the area within the national context (*see* pp.303–305). Then take a look at some publications that are more specifically about the region in question. Look up information on the internet; most regions of Portugal have their own websites with texts in English. You will probably find that there is a whole lot more to the place than you had gleaned from your last holiday.

Once you have read up on the area, it is time to take a trip or two, not conceived of as holidays but as 'reconnaissance'. This is a good chance for you to focus on all those aspects that you would not normally consider when on a holiday per se and when all that you have read about starts to fall into place. Rent a car, get a detailed map of the area, cover as much ground as possible, stay in inexpensive hotels, eat at a variety of restaurants, explore those country lanes that you always wondered about, drive to the top of that hill you had previously only admired from a distance, brave the shops and markets, go to a show or concert if there is one nearby. Above all, make copious notes of your impressions of everything and do not be worried about defacing the map (make notes there too). Take a camera with you and do not skimp on film, though do try to note down to which place exposure number 12, or 20 or 31 corresponds. Pick up local newspapers and magazines, whether in English or Portuguese – they will give you an idea of what is going on in the area. By all means take a look at properties advertised in local estate agents' windows and cut out and keep the 'For Sale' columns from the classifieds in the papers you have picked up. But remember, *the purpose of this trip is to get to know the area, not to buy a property yet*. You are here, first and foremost, to see whether this is a place that you really see yourself living in full-time. If you start looking at individual properties and thinking about the need for double-glazing here, how poky the kitchen is there, what a pretty patio you might lay behind this house, then you are focusing on details rather than on the general picture. Location is at this point far more important than the merits or defects of individual properties. If after a couple of week's exhaustive reconnoitring you are convinced that this is the area for you, then the actual property search is the next stage.

When you get back home, look over your notes again, get the films developed, make a list of all the towns and villages you visited and note down the pluses and the minuses you appreciated in each. Then take another trip, and even a third if you can, each one at a different time of year, and spend some time living in one of the top two or three from your list. While you can start exploring the property market in a little more detail now, make do with temporary, rented accommodation, for the time being. *See* 'Temporary Accommodation', pp.117–19.

Setting Your Priorities

In combination with all the impressions you noted down in the reconnaissance trips recommended above, you might like to consider the following specific points. While much emphasis has been placed on location, it should not be forgotten that location means different things to different people and what is important for one person's needs might be completely irrelevant to somebody else's. If you are young and single and want to be out on the nightlife scene then your choice of the 'right' location will probably be markedly different from that of a retired couple. If you have school-age children then your priorities will differ from those of the childless or the couple whose children have grown up. If you want golf, Guinness, fried breakfasts and satellite Premiership football in a pub in the company of other football fans then your location priorities will likely contrast with those of the hill-walker, the museum-goer or the Baroque church enthusiast. Some considerations are universal and would apply whether you are planning to buy in Portugal or just about anywhere else but others are important when it comes to choosing a specific location.

Town versus Country

One of the basic choices you have to make is urban versus rural, deciding just how close to or far from the crowd you want to be. Getting some 'away-from-it-all' peace and quiet, or at least the illusion of it, might not actually mean finding a farmhouse in the back end of the Alentejo or Trás-os-montes as there are places to be found that offer a countrified idyll while only being 45 minutes' or an hour's drive from good facilities. Conversely, an urban location does not mean that access to the country is limited. Far from it, there are plenty of towns and cities with all the joys of the country just a short drive or bus-ride away.

Gardens and Neighbours

If a garden (or some space around the house) and privacy are important factors then you are restricted to the country or a villa development – with a price to match. A large proportion of properties on offer in Portugal (especially purpose-built second and holiday homes) are apartments, often inside *urbanizações*, where gardens are communal and neighbours practically on top of one another. *Urbanizações* also have a tendency to grow, filling in unused spaces with more apartments, so today's cosy community might get unwieldy in two or three years' time.

Local Amenities

Consider how well stocked local shops are, and how they compare with others (i.e. supermarkets and hypermarkets) elsewhere, how close and accessible they are, whether you can walk to them or are obliged to use a car just to buy some tomatoes.

Public Transport

Consider how close the nearest public transport is and the service offered, and also whether it gets you anywhere worth going! How close are the major transport links (e.g. train hubs, bus stations with good connections and airports)?

Beaches

If access to a beach is important this is one question you will need to consider carefully. Remember that proximity to a beach can have a substantial impact on prices. Also do not forget that there are beaches and beaches, some of them a delight all year round, others horrifically overrun during the season.

Schools

If you have children of school age this is a vital issue. The Portuguese education system is currently in crisis (*see* 'Education', pp.227–9) although the one in your area might not be in too bad a state. If your plan anyway is to send your children to a fee-paying international school where the language of instruction is English, then this limits your choice of area as these schools are fewer in number – unless of course you do not mind your children becoming commuters at an early age. Think about what they may or may not like themselves and how much pressure they would be under with a long trip to and from school.

Work

If you are planning to live and work in Portugal, proximity to sources of jobs is important if you are not going to pre-arranged employment. The security of your job and alternatives if it should fall through may determine choice of area. Similarly, ideas and prospects for the success of a business are factors that limit and determine where you move to. *See* pp.19–23, and pp.198–209.

Health and Social Services

Proximity to and quality of health services may be more or less important to you depending on your age, condition and whether or not you have children. The Portuguese health system, like education, is currently in bad shape, although the quality of service again depends on where you are. Reports of mismanagement, waiting lists, shortages of professionals and poor standards of patient treatment are frequent. The system is going through a process of review, rethinking and redesigning with some degree of privatization as one solution proposed by government. Things may improve over the next few years if not sooner. Generally speaking, though, in most medium-sized towns there will be a *centro de saúde* (health centre), open 8am–8pm for less important complaints and minor accidents. You also need to know how far the nearest emergency department is, as the health centres may not be equipped to deal with anything too serious. The availability of English-speaking doctors and dentists may be a priority for you. If so, you will almost certainly be better served in an area with a high number of ex-pats, though private health coverage is essential unless you don't mind paying astronomical fees. Other foreign residents and local English-language publications will provide useful information.

Golf and Other Sports Facilities

For many people, the main point of going to live in Portugal is being able to play golf most of the year round. If this applies to you, you will need to focus on a location from where courses are easily reached. As most people know, the Algarve is about as close you can get to a golfer's paradise, with over 25 courses, many in stunning settings. Greater Lisbon is also well served and in the area around Oporto there are several courses. For other sports, facilities vary considerably in terms of availability and quality. Portugal is not a country that is renowned for its sports infrastructure. Large multi-use sports centres and athletics tracks are not common outside the major cities and participation in sports clubs is statistically low compared with other European countries. Better facilities for sports other than golf are to be found in the large towns and cities or in the areas most frequented by tourists. Anywhere on the coast is certain to offer a reasonable range of facilities for watersports. If you want to do activity sports, check out nearby facilities before deciding on an area.

Arts and Entertainment

If arts and entertainment are important to you, it is advisable to look at the proximity of cinemas, theatres and facilities for live music as well as museums and galleries. Look at the events listings in local newspapers to see the frequency, range and content of cultural events programmed.

Young People

If you have pre-teens or teenage children, take a good look at what the local area offers them in terms of entertainment and active participation in sports, clubs and other pursuits. Avoiding boredom is important as is making sure they do not turn into TV-watching 'couch potatoes' or addicted to computer games. Larger cities usually have a wider choice of possibilities to suit adolescents and coastal areas also have more facilities for active sport and entertainment.

Where the Expatriate Communities Are

It should be emphasized that choosing to live in a largely ex-pat community or completely away from it is a factor that largely determines (and limits) where you buy and where you don't. There are large concentrations of British and, increasingly, Irish residents in certain parts of Portugal, not to mention Germans, Dutch and Scandinavians. This is certainly true of the Algarve, Greater Lisbon, to a lesser extent in the Oporto area and Madeira. There are many people, British people particularly, whose only real contact with Portuguese life is when they eat and drink (and not always then) and when they deal with civil servants, that is if they do not entrust their bureaucratic dealings to an English-speaking solicitor. Many do not get beyond the most elementary level of Portuguese and know little about the country's culture, history or present. The Algarve has two parallel societies (natives and incomers) that live apart and with very little mixing. Choosing to live like this is entirely a personal decision but it is one that should be taken knowing what it implies. Even if you are interested in integrating with locals, you might find that in an area so full of ex-pats they will show little interest in getting to know you, since it is assumed that you are just as much an alien as the rest. Furthermore, while there are year-round ex-pat areas, there is the danger of your chosen location being overly busy during the season and too quiet (with hardly any shops, restaurants or bars open) for the rest of the year.

Other people choose to do things a different way, to accept the challenge of the language, try to get to know their Portuguese neighbours and take an interest in their adopted country. This choice also affects where you may or may not buy as your chances of making inroads into Portuguese society are greatly enhanced if you choose an area that is mostly unaffected by ex-pat culture.

Neighbours

Apart from the wider community in which you are to live, it also helps if you get an idea of what your prospective neighbours are like. If you plan to buy in an apartment or condominium complex this is especially important as walls may be thin and you may get to know all about your neighbours' private life without really wanting to. When buying a community property there are also a whole series of issues of common importance – such as paying community fees and looking after communal areas – that can be easier or more difficult to handle depending on how pleasant and reasonable, or not, the other neighbours are. It pays to know this beforehand.

Tourism and Tourists

Popular tourist areas are attractive for obvious reasons: beaches, weather, summertime entertainments and so on. Areas that are popular with foreign residents tend to share these characteristics – they are often the same areas. Year-round residents, consequently, often feel swamped during the season and have to put up with the racket of discotheques, rowdy holidaymakers, increased traffic and packed shops, bars and restaurants. If you cannot face this, look elsewhere.

Parking

The availability or lack of parking facilities may influence your decision. If you buy a villa or country house this will not be a problem, but if you buy an urban property or in an apartment block it may be. Some apartment complexes come with underground parking, though this must usually be paid for, either by rental or purchasing the space. Sometimes apartments are sold with the parking space all together in one package. In towns and cities the lack of off-street (or any) parking can be a particularly acute problem and car crime is increasing in Portugal, especially if the car is known to be foreign.

Crime

While Portugal is not, in general, a country with especially high crime rates and violent crime is rare, it is still worth checking out some statistics on criminality in the area you hope to buy in. Villas, especially those known to belong to foreigners or which are isolated, are common targets. Areas with a large foreign resident population may also suffer higher rates of burglary and petty crime. Higher or lower rates, apart from the 'bother' factor, could also affect insurance premiums.

Planning Permission

This is a thorny issue if you are hoping to buy a plot and build your own house, rebuild a ruin or even put extensions on to an existing property. Obtaining planning permission, like any other bureaucratic process in Portugal, can be a long and tortuous process, especially in an area such as the Algarve where there are severe restrictions in place. There are good reasons for these restrictions, the intention being to avoid the blight of over-development and to protect the natural areas that still exist. When buying with the intention of building you have to know whether the plot has a project approved *previous* to the promulgation of the current laws. A good lawyer is essential if you are buying with this in mind.

Local Authorities

Some towns are run by efficient, professional teams of functionaries and technical staff; others suffer from municipal incompetence or even corruption. Things can change when there are elections but it is in your interest to know who is in charge, how well they carry out their functions, what services you get in return for your local rates and what redress you have if you are not satisfied.

Rural Services

Rural properties may not be connected to water and electricity supplies. Getting them connected may cost fantastic sums or oblige you to look at alternatives such as wells and generators.

Water Shortages

This is a problem in the southern half of the Iberian peninsula which also affects the Alentejo and Algarve. Water is a serious issue and a precious resource. Shortages can become acute in the tourist season and restrictions or even cuts in supply can be the result. Choosing to live in these areas can necessitate investing in a back-up system to ensure water all year-round. Water quality can also be a problem – many people rely on drinking bottled water. The Alqueva Dam project in the Alentejo may provide a solution to water shortages in some areas but is regarded by its critics as a 'white elephant'.

Portuguese Homes

Depending on your spending power and needs, the range of properties on offer runs the full gamut, from one-bedroom studio apartments to luxury villas in their own grounds. There is a whole series of in-betweens including duplex apartments, townhouses, country houses and ruins. There may even be the odd castle. Then there are old houses in need of renovation, still older ones needing a complete rebuilding job and plots where there is no building at all (yet). In contrast with this there are brand new places where the paint is still tacky, golf developments where houses and apartments blend in with the greens, the fairways and the rough – where the promoters insist the 'quality of life' is unbeatable. Your choice of type of property will be conditioned by your budget and your desires; it is to be hoped that you will find something that suits both.

Apartments, Townhouses, *Urbanizações* and Community Properties

An apartment or flat, within a block of apartments, is by its very nature a 'community' property. This is because there are many areas which are common to and the responsibility of all of the owners: the entrance hall, stairways, lifts, landings, the façade, the patio and maybe the area of garden or grounds in which the block stands and the fence and gate. Some fittings (such as satellite dishes) are also considered common elements. But it is not only apartments that may be considered community properties; practically any property that is situated in an *urbanização* (purpose-built estate), even a townhouse or villa, will share some elements with the rest. If you own a property in an *urbanização* your responsibilities do not begin or end on your own doorstep. Community elements might include a swimming pool, tennis courts, roads, play areas and parking facilities. The more luxurious the community, the more common facilities there will be. Top-range *urbanizações* may offer householders a golf course (with membership sometimes included in the price of the property), a gymnasium, riding stables and even a bar or restaurant. All this, of course, must be paid for.

When you buy a property that is part of a community (as about two-thirds of all foreign property-owners in Portugal do), you are buying more than just the square metres of your apartment, house or villa. You are in fact buying proportional ownership of all the common elements. The only properties that cannot be said to belong to a community are single houses on private plots of land, whether in the country or in a town or city. The rest are community properties, a form of ownership that has several pluses and not a few minuses. It should also be noted that many *urbanizações* are geared towards holidaymakers.

On the plus side, buying into a community implies joining a ready-made social network with neighbours close by. The common facilities such as the pool or other sports installations, as well as a garden, play area and garage space, are all just about on your doorstep. You do not have to take personal responsibility for their maintenance, though you will pay for this in your community fees. Property taxes are generally lower than they would be for an individual property and you also may get to live in a relatively privileged location which would otherwise be beyond your reach. Check the prices of a beachside villa on its own plot of land and you will understand this!

Of course, the ready-made social network might be made up of people with whom you have nothing in common or, worse still, whom you find disagreeable. You might like to hold rowdy parties and your neighbours might not. Or it might be the other way around. The very proximity of neighbours and the lack of privacy can be a source of irritation. If peace and quiet is high on your agenda and you have bought in an *urbanização* that is primarily geared towards holidaymakers, you could find that the constantly changing stream of visitors who are there to have a good time becomes extremely irritating. Neighbours, whether permanent or transitory, can also have many annoying habits and be downright antisocial at times. Everybody should pay community fees but not all members always do, and it can take a long time, and much acrimony, to squeeze the money out of the slow payers or eventually embargo their property, which can happen with repeating long-term offenders. Remember, you might have to pass these people on the stairs every morning. As well as this, the fees might be higher than the services provided would warrant; not all communities are well administered and, while you have the right to vote on fee increases and all other policy matters, if you are in a minority your voice will not be heard.

By law, all apartment blocks and *urbanizações* must have an officially constituted owners' community (*comunidade de proprietários*) which must draw up and vote on its set of statutes (*estatutos*). These statutes should define very clearly what constitutes communal property and what proportion of the maintenance costs corresponds to each owner. This is usually proportionate to the size of each owner's property. If you own a 38 sq m one-bedroom apartment, for example, your share of the cost as reflected in your fees should be considerably lower than the neighbour whose apartment occupies 120 sq m. Six owners of six identical flats, on the other hand, should all in theory pay exactly the same.

Voting rights are similarly proportional. You should know exactly what your share is to be, and this should be in the deeds of the property, before buying in any given community. If there is no legally constituted community, refrain from buying in that particular apartment block or *urbanização*. The money you pay in fees contributes to the costs of cleaning, decoration, maintenance of all facilities and much more besides, depending on what communal facilities there are. It may include the salary of the porter or concierge (*porteiro*) if there is one and those of the security staff on estates where such a service is provided. You are usually charged monthly, quarterly or six-monthly and you should be given an annual breakdown of expenditure. The annual accounts should be approved at an annual meeting of all community members and minutes of previous years' meetings should be made available to a prospective buyer. Ask to see them. If you are not convinced by them, consider looking elsewhere. Community meetings can be fairly stressful affairs especially if there are difficult, confrontational neighbours in the community and if there are some controversial issues to be debated. There may, at times, be 'cliquey' lobby groups or even majorities who force the approval of motions that suit their interests but not yours. Fees range enormously and correspond to the level of services that are provided to the members. Expect to pay a lot if you buy into a five-star golf community on the Algarve, much less if you buy a flat in a small apartment block with no pool or gardens.

Buying 'Off-plan'

Very often, would-be foreign buyers who attend property exhibitions in the UK or Ireland are attracted to the artist's impression and plywood model of an *urbanização* that is yet to be built or is in the construction stage. These developments often combine apartments and semi-detached or terraced townhouses. On the building site itself there is always a show flat or house (*casa modelo*) for potential buyers to look around. This is known as buying 'off-plan'. What attracts buyers to this option is that everything, when completed, will be brand-new and, if built to modern standards and regulations, will have none of the defects found in re-sale or old properties and none of the costs of refurbishing. You have the possibility of choosing the décor and fittings such as the kitchen furniture, the bathroom tiles, taps, plugs and sockets, and the wallpaper or colour of the paint on the walls. The property, if your specifications are followed, will be entirely to your taste and not require you to do anything other than move your possessions in when it is ready.

Beware, though, of certain drawbacks with 'off-plan' purchasing. For one thing, initial payments may be quite substantial. It is often the deposit paid by the buyers that helps the builder to keep at work even though financing for the whole project should have been secured before construction begins. Further payments are made as stages of the construction process are completed but it is important to be sure that these stages are in fact completed, and finished on time. Before embarking on an 'off-plan' adventure you should look for certain guarantees. You need to get as much information as possible from the developer and agents and in addition you must get a 'termination guarantee' which commits the developer to finish *every* phase of the project. That means not only your apartment or townhouse with the bathroom tiles and taps as requested, but also the external elements such as the beautiful landscaped gardens, access roads or driveways, connection to all utilities and so on – as portrayed in the artist's impression. This should all be backed by a full insurance policy.

Also you need to check whether the image and model you see is the full extent of the project as you may find later to your cost that it is actually only 'Phase I' and that 'Phase II' (planned for next year) is to be built right between your terrace and the sea. Further guarantees you need refer to things like the quality of the materials employed and the standard of workmanship. Standards of new buildings have gone up in recent years as legislation and consumer demand have exerted an influence.

If you are not there to oversee matters, you may care to pay for the services of an architect or structural engineer to keep an eye on things and report back to you. Make sure that this person has no professional links with the developer. Overseeing the standards of construction and finishing are very important as quite a high proportion of new developments are found to have structural defects, fittings that are not of the promised standard and poor finishing. These problems often become apparent only after the property has been occupied for a few months and, while the developer and the builder are accountable, it is usually quite difficult to get them to rectify defects after the fact. As with every other aspect of property-buying in Portugal, your lawyer's advice is important from the outset and throughout the process.

Many new developments come complete with a range of communal facilities that you cannot expect to find elsewhere. These may include a gymnasium, tennis courts, swimming pools (both indoor and outdoor for year-round use), a golf course, access to a marina and more besides. More modest developments may not offer so many facilities but will be much more accessible in price. In some cases, the developer also continues on the *urbanização* after construction has finished – converting himself into the estate manager – meaning that he then has a vested interest in quality and post-sales service. Many new developments offer buyers management services as part of the deal, which may be advantageous if those services are provided properly and well run. Another advantage, from an investor's point of view, is that, in areas where prices are rising rapidly, the initial purchase price might well be overtaken by resale price even before the keys are handed over. Some buy with this in mind and there have been cases, exceptional perhaps, of people who have made a 50 per cent capital gain on the sale of a recently completed property.

Villas

Villas are what many people are after – for good reasons. A villa in its own grounds represents prestige and exclusivity. A villa enjoys privacy, can be rented out for a very substantial sum of money in the high season (and the rest of the year too) and is almost guaranteed not to fall in value. This is especially true in areas where there is no more room to build or where restrictions on granting planning permission mean that the scarcity value of a quality villa increases year after year. Villas come in all shapes and sizes, both old and new. Some of them are splendidly restored old properties with many modern fittings now incorporated. Others, despite a traditional look, are of very recent construction and built to the highest standards. Top villas fetch incredible prices in the Algarve, the Lisbon coast area, Madeira and, little by little, on the coastline extending north of Lisbon. A really large, quality-built-and-fitted villa commands a high price anywhere. In fact, there are even some in remote areas of the Alentejo going for around a million euros. In the more popular areas expect to pay a lot more than that.

Townhouses

A 'townhouse', in the Portuguese context, does not mean exactly the same thing as it might in London or Manchester, where the word conjures up the image of a Victorian or Georgian terraced house. When you are looking at property brochures or websites the word does crop up a lot. It usually refers to a newish property, built within an *urbanização*, that falls somewhere between the apartment or duplex and the villa. In the property business jargon they are sometimes referred to as 'linked villas'. Townhouses are often built over two or three floors and may have a small amount of garden space either at the front or at the back, although often the front door opens directly onto the street. They are generally conceived of as single-family dwellings and are of a size that is sufficient for the average, nuclear family consisting of two parents and two children with a spare bedroom, possibly a main bathroom and small toilet plus shower or second bathroom. Kitchens are usually quite generous in size and may be part of a larger kitchen and diner space or even of a open-plan lower floor that includes the living area too. Full-size swimming pools do not usually come with a townhouse but a plunge-pool might be included in the garden area. Balconies and terraces are often part of the design as is a barbecue area. Forming part of an *urbanização*, townhouse ownership usually implies access to and use of all facilities that are on offer. Prices are for those who cannot contemplate buying a villa but want something more than an apartment and can pay for it.

Houses in Towns and Villages

A 'townhouse' should not be confused with a 'house in a town' (or village) which may well be something of much less recent construction (old, in fact) and offering fewer, if any, mod-cons unless it has been renovated by a previous owner. Like their near-namesake, houses in towns are not usually detached or in their own grounds but may be in a row of terraced dwellings. You do not find so many of these properties in popular resort areas as much of the stock for sale consists of purpose-built holiday apartments, townhouses or villas. However, in towns and villages that were once small fishing communities but have become resorts over the last 20–30 years it is possible to find more traditional houses still – though their prices will inevitably have been pushed up by the existence of villa developments, *urbanizações* and other tourist facilities nearby. Bargains are to be found in smaller, inland towns and villages though in the Algarve this is less likely, since the scarcity of quality properties there means that buyers are increasingly looking at village properties that previously were of little interest.

As they tend to be older, village houses and townhouses may have quite quirky layouts but this could be part of their charm. Traditionally families were much bigger than nowadays so there may be a lot of small rooms that modern buyers prefer to knock through to create larger spaces. Older properties may also have structural problems that require a considerable outlay to put right (a survey is needed here) and the wiring and plumbing will almost certainly need to be ripped out and replaced. Not all village properties, in fact, have electricity, so you will need to install this. The same may apply to sanitary installations as well. Taking all of this into account, as well as any other renovation work that might be needed, an apparent bargain may turn out to be an expensive adventure as full renovation of an old property could amount to double, or more, the purchase price. This may not be a problem for you if you want to redesign an old house to your taste and have the money to pay for it. You will certainly end up with a unique, one-off home that is far more original and individual than you will ever get in an *urbanização* or apartment complex.

The problem comes when you decide to sell it. Renovated older properties rarely fetch much in terms of resale value. Bearing in mind what you have spent on the house and the cost of the work involved, and adding in factors like capital gains tax on an eventual sale, profit is likely to be slight. Not many Portuguese people would think of buying an old property, however beautifully restored, and if your house is a considerable distance from the areas that are most popular with foreign buyers you may not be able to attract them either. From an investment point of view, a new or near-new house is probably a better option. It remains to be seen how the market develops over the next few years. If the Algarve reaches something like saturation point, and planning and building restrictions mean fewer new properties becoming available, buyers and investors may begin to train their sights on older village-type properties but, in the current situation, only think of buying such a property if it is primarily for your enjoyment.

Farmhouses and Rural Properties

Much of what has been said in the previous section also applies to farmhouses and rural properties in general. The market for old homes in the country is quite limited in Portugal, unlike across the border in Spain where rural *fincas* have been gaining in popularity and price owing to saturation on the coasts. As with small village properties, farmhouses often have structural problems and may not be connected to water or electricity supplies. If situated in a remote area, getting connected may be extremely expensive and can add a major cost to the purchase price. Equally, as many Portuguese people leave the land to try their luck in the cities, there are more abandoned rural properties, especially in the interior. There are a small but growing number of people that have bought up an old *quinta* and turned it into a unique house, at a cost. Some have made a successful business by providing accommodation, either with the family or by making self-catering apartments within the structure of the house. Their customers are not the typical sun-seeking tourist that goes to the Algarve. There is a small but well-defined market for rural tourism and more people are seeking out the delights of the undiscovered Portugal. The Alentejo and Montanhas regions, for example, are beginning to attract visitors who are more interested in architecture, nature, bird-watching, hill-walking, cycling holidays, etc., and who may be less inclined to stay in hotels. A different type of accommodation is needed, and a gorgeously restored farmhouse may well satisfy that demand. It should be stressed that this is still a small market and not everybody can expect to turn an abandoned farmhouse into a money-spinning rural hotel. Still, it is worth thinking about if you are not interested in buying in the Algarve or other popular areas. At the same time, never underestimate the outlay, budget very carefully, and check thoroughly all possible restrictions about rebuilding and usage before getting involved in a project of this nature. With luck and good planning, you could end up with a very special property which will provide you with a great deal of pleasure.

Other Forms of Ownership

The advantages and disadvantages of buying a second or holiday home that is to be used part-time but which also may be let (or stand idle for many months) have already been mentioned. If you cannot go to live full-time in a Portuguese property and also have no guarantee of being able to make some rental income from one, then you may be reluctant to buy in the first place, since you may see it as wasting money that could be better invested elsewhere. One way around this problem is to look at the various forms of shared ownership. These include co-ownership, leaseback and timeshare. All have their advantages and disadvantages and you are well advised to look very carefully at the financial aspects of such a deal before committing yourself or money.

Co-ownership is an arrangement by which the ownership of a whole property (as opposed to just the common elements – as in a community) is shared between several people who can make use of it for an amount of time proportional to their share each year. All the individuals involved appear as owners on the deeds and in the property register. The chief attraction of such a scheme is that it gives the co-owners a chance to enjoy, part-time, a property that would ordinarily be way beyond their reach, since they are effectively only buying a quarter, or a fifth, or a smaller fraction of it. Co-ownership can turn out to be an ideal solution for a family or group of friends who wish to have a holiday home for several weeks a year but cannot contemplate buying on their own. After all, a share in a family-sized townhouse or villa could well cost less than an entire apartment (depending on location).

Many *urbanização* developers promote these schemes. A common deal offered is the quarter or four-part ownership, which gives you the right to a quarter of a year's occupancy. Do be aware, though, that developers selling quarter shares will almost certainly be selling each at above 25 per cent of the value of the property, that is to say, their return on the package is greater than it would have been had they sold the entire property to just one owner. Depending on the contract conditions, co-owners may agree among themselves who gets which period, normally some form of rotation occurs and the quarter does not necessarily have to be one solid block of time. Alternatively, some groups of friends organize their own co-ownership schemes independently of developers and there is nothing to stop anybody trying it. You could club together with a group of friends and/or family members and buy the house all together or you could go ahead and buy it yourself and then invite people to come in on the deal and purchase shares to defray your original costs. These need not be of equal size; five different owners might end up with, for example, a 30:20:20:15:15 per cent stake. The more complex it gets, though, the more difficult it might be to share the usage time and how well this works depends greatly on the group dynamics involved. If anyone opts to sell his share, the remaining co-owners are normally offered first refusal and they may opt to split the share between them, thus reconfiguring the ownership breakdown, or look for a new buyer. As always, a lawyer's advice on co-ownership is recommended.

Leaseback allows people to buy a property at considerably below the market price, maybe by as much as 30 or 40 per cent, on the condition that they only occupy it for a specified number of weeks a year, generally between six weeks and two months. They then 'lease it back' to the developer, who lets it out to holidaymakers the rest of the time. The deal is usually for a fixed number of years, generally 10 or thereabouts, after which the purchaser gains full and unrestricted ownership. During the years in which the leaseback deal is in force, the developer usually takes responsibility for management of the property. It is in his interests to do so, since he needs to attract people willing to rent. The advantage to the buyer is that he gets a holiday home for part of the year without having to worry about finding rental income or pay for management and he eventually assumes full ownership anyway. There are some drawbacks. For instance, a good many leaseback deals are available only at the upper end of the market so even at the discount price the property may be beyond the reach of many ordinary buyers. Make sure that on expiry of the agreed leaseback term there is no hidden 'redemption charge' or other fee for getting full possession.

Much has been written and spoken about **timeshares** – a lot of it negative. This is mainly because the timeshare business has gained notoriety owing to the well-publicized scams that have taken place over the years. It is now, apparently, illegal to 'tout' timeshares in Portuguese resorts but it still goes on and it is the hard sell techniques which have contributed most to the negative reputation of the timeshare as a form of ownership. But what is it? Timeshare can take two forms in Portugal. One is full, real ownership of a property, or fraction thereof, with the right to sell. The other is the right to occupy a property for a certain period (a week, two weeks, etc.) over a specified length of time, which may range from as little as a couple of years up to about 15. Timeshares tend to be found in larger resorts and in apartment complexes and despite all the bad press they remain a popular way of buying a slice of sunshine.

The selling methods have attracted much of the criticism. Young foreigners are employed to go around looking for tourists who are then invited to clubs and bars, given all manner of 'freebies' and asked to attend a 'presentation' (effectively a sales talk aimed at a captive audience). In Portugal a timeshare presentation may by law only take place on the timeshare premises, whereas in other countries would-be buyers are taken for lunch and given the sales 'pitch' afterwards when they are in a more relaxed state. But the aggressive technique is still applied and some people cannot resist it. Among the inducements offered are a 'discount', a free week in the first year, no legal fees and other bait as well. It takes a very cool head to work out the figures on the spot but if you think about it carefully, there may be many reasons not to buy. Supposing the apartment in question has a market value of €120,000. The company may offer you a week's timeshare for a little more than €15,000. If the company sells nearly all the weeks available in the year, say 50 of them, you do not have to be a genius to see how much income they generate. (€750,000 plus, for those who cannot be bothered to get the calculator out.) If you have €15,000 to spare you may care to invest it elsewhere and pay for part of your annual holiday with the interest. You can also then go somewhere different each holiday!

You may think that a timeshare is not necessarily the best investment or even particularly good value for money, especially if you add on the fact that there are management fees to be paid annually on top of your initial outlay. If you do decide on this form of ownership, logically, you need to be very well-advised by your lawyer who should check over the contract and all other documents for any 'hidden extras' which are, by all accounts, common.

Timeshare slots are also notoriously difficult to sell and many of the companies involved often do not fulfil their pledge to buy them back at market price. You are likely to lose out on the deal. To find out more about timeshares in general, look at the following:

- **www.timeshare.org.uk** – the site of the Timeshare Consumers' Association (**t** 0901 607 0077).
- **www.hpb.co.uk** – the site of Holiday Property Bond (**t** 0800 66 54 90), a scheme which gives you access to properties in European countries.
- **www.marriott.co.uk** – the site of Marriott Vacation Club International, whose worldwide timeshare organization allows you to use your slot in their resorts around the world.
- **www.crimeshare.com** – a site for those who have been ripped off to name and shame the perpetrators and generally criticize the worst offenders. Some strong language may be found on this site!

New Property in Portugal

Advantages

- **The technical specification and design will be better than in an older property. This is particularly so in areas such as insulation and energy-efficiency.**
- **It will have been inspected and built to known standards.**
- **Most people prefer new kitchens, which get more sophisticated each year.**
- **It will probably have a reasonable heating system.**
- **Electrical and plumbing installations will be to a superior standard.**
- **Provision will probably have been made for parking.**
- **You may share the cost of expensive common resources such as pools or tennis courts with other people.**
- **The building will require a lot less maintenance than an older property, certainly for the first few years.**
- **It should be cheaper to run.**
- **You can design your own property or, at least, often fine-tune the design to your special requirements.**
- **The fabric will be guaranteed.**
- **If you buy 'off plan' you may see some pre-completion growth in value.**

Disadvantages

- **The building will be new and brash, not mellow.**
- **It can be hard to envisage what you are going to get from a plan and specification.**

• You will have to sort out all the small snags inevitable in any new building.You may spend all your holidays chasing the builder or doing this. You probably don't speak Portuguese.

• You will have to sort out the garden.

• You may have to decorate.

• Although technical design may have improved the aesthetic appeal may be less than that of an older property and the detailed workmanship less rewarding than that of a time when labour was cheap.

• As a rental property most (British) people prefer either a property with close access to golf or entertainment or a villa with a pool.

Older Property in Portugal

Advantages

• The property has 'character'. Its design may be classically beautiful and the detailed workmanship will probably be superior to today's product.

• The garden will be mature.

• It may occupy a better site than a newer property – on the basis that the best were often built on first.

• It may be a more attractive rental proposition than a new property, especially in rural areas.

• You will feel that you are living in a property in Portugal.

• What you see is what you get. You turn on the taps, there is water. You can see the room sizes and how the sun lies on the terraces. You can see the views and the distances to adjacent properties.

• It may be cheaper than a comparable new property.

• It will probably have more land than acomparable new property.

Disadvantages

• Older properties can need a lot of maintenance and loving care.

• It will be more expensive to heat and run.

• You may need to spend significant sums on, say, the kitchen and bathrooms to bring the property up to modern standards.

Research and Information Sources

There is no substitute for a reconnaissance trip to Portugal with the aim of looking at properties *in situ*, and at some stage in the process you will almost certainly do this. It would be most unwise to buy a property *without* having seen it and here it is assumed that readers are sufficiently sensible not to buy blind. This, however, does not exclude looking around via other sources before planning a trip. Indeed, exhaustive pre-research will help you to get a good overall picture of the market. From there, further research will help you to whittle down your search to a particular geographical area, a specific type of property and a price range that you can afford. With this information to hand, a week or two spent in Portugal is likely to be far more profitable than it would be if you just went on 'spec'. In this 'information age' there is so much data available that it is difficult to sift through it all. There are lots of sources of information, which fit broadly into three groups: internet, print media and property exhibitions.

The Internet

Despite the recent dot.com boom-to-bust story, the internet has its place though it should be approached with caution. Apart from buying flights, books or other products online, you should not view the internet as a marketplace for properties and only the criminally reckless would ever contemplate actually buying a property through this medium. Look on it as a shop window, a valuable research tool that can help you form a clear idea of possibilities before you look further. The trick is to refine your search and specify towns or provinces in which you might be interested. It can also help if you include the type of property in the search. So, if you want that farmhouse in Coimbra try 'rural+properties+coimbra' or 'farmhouses+central+portugal'; among what comes up will be some sites that meet your criteria. Most property sites offer you the chance to click on sample prices and properties that they have for sale.

For more regionally specific information it can also pay to do a search in Portuguese, keying in a search criteria such as 'imoveis+costa+prata' or whichever region you are interested in. You will not find them too difficult to use, after all, an image of a property and a price in euros is fairly understandable for all. Many Portuguese sites do in fact have a little Union Jack symbol which, if clicked on, leads you to the information in English anyway. This is the case with **www.imoregioes.com**, which you might find useful. There are also many websites that are not specific to Portugal but which deal in properties worldwide and offer you the chance to choose from a list of countries.

Apart from websites that are dedicated to property, many printed publications also have an online edition so the distinction between the two media becomes a little blurred. This is the case with *The News*, Portugal's main English-language weekly, which is available on news stands throughout the Algarve and other parts of Portugal but which can also be found at **www.the-news.net**. Every week there are downloadable property pages in PDF format. You can sign up to receive the online edition of the paper and 'alerts' about property, flights, golf, gardening, schools and special supplements on specific themes.

For an extensive list of websites that specialize in Portuguese properties, *see* **References**, 'Internet Sites', pp.302–303.

Print Media

The main daily and Sunday newspapers all have travel and property sections and can be a useful place to start, especially as they also have articles on overseas property-buying in general, aspects of living abroad, and sometimes articles specifically about Portugal or a region of the country. There are also specialized glossy property magazines that are crammed full of adverts, usually arranged by country. In addition, there are property advertising magazines in English but published in Portugal, predictably with a strong Algarve bias.

- ***Homes Overseas*** (**t** (020) 7939 9888, **www.homesoverseas.co.uk**). A lively, colourful monthly with a worldwide scope but some space given over to Portugal. They also organize property exhibitions (*see* below).
- ***World of Property*** (**t** (01323) 726 040, **www.outboundpublishing.com**). A bi-monthly publication with worldwide scope which also organizes property exhibitions. Portugal features in the magazine and in the exhibitions.
- ***International Homes*** (**t** (01245) 358 877, **www.international-homes.com**). A glossy magazine with an international perspective, as the name suggests, but there may be some Portuguese properties featured.
- ***Private Villas*** (**t** (020) 8329 0120, **www.privatevillas.co.uk**). A glossy magazine mainly used by those looking to rent a holiday villa or apartment but also has a 'For Sale' section. Most of the advertisers there are estate agents.
- ***Dalton's Weekly*** (**www.daltonsholidays.com** – operative from October 2003). Carries ads for Portuguese properties and the new website, which will be operated jointly with Private Villas (above), will carry ads mainly for holiday lets but also for sales.

Local Press

- ***Algarve Property Advertiser*** (**t** 00351 282 343 088). A bimonthly property magazine specializing in the Algarve but also branching out into the Costa de la Luz, across the border. Many private properties and estate agents are featured among the advertisements. Cost: €2. Two other magazines are published by the same editorial group, Vista Ibérica, and carry property advertising: ***Destination Algarve***, on sale at WH Smith's for £2.50, and ***Algarve Golf Guide***, golf and property all in one.
- ***The News*** (**t** 00351 282 341 100, **www.the-news.net**). A weekly newspaper, centred mainly on the Algarve but with news and occasional property ads, both for estate agents and private sales from other parts of Portugal. A good publication to place your own 'wanted' ad if you are looking privately.

- ***The Anglo-Portuguese News*** (**t** 00351 214 661 423). Based in Estoril, Lisbon, and so less Algarve-centred in terms of its advertisers.

Property Exhibitions

As foreign property-buying has become popular, so has the paraphernalia that goes with it. Property exhibitions are symptomatic of this and there are several held in different parts of the UK and the Irish Republic throughout the year. They are usually run in association with major internationally aimed property publications. None of them feature Portugal specifically but most include stands and information about Portuguese property, alongside those promoting Spain, France, Italy, Florida, the Caribbean. At these events you will find representatives of many different companies working in the field, specialized lawyers, financial advisers, estate agents and developers. You probably cannot expect to find the property you are looking for at one of these exhibitions but you will get an idea of what the market is like, how things function and maybe some names, addresses and leads that will put you on the track.

- **The International Property Show** (**t** 01962 736 712, **www.internationalpropertyshow.com**) organizes several shows a year in London, Manchester and other venues.
- **The Evening Standard Homebuyer Show** (**t** (020) 8877 3636, **www.homebuyer.co.uk**) is held in London in late February to early March. It focuses more on the home market but also has stands dedicated to properties in several countries, among them Portugal.
- **The World of Property Show** (**t** (01323) 745 130, **www.outboundpublishing.com**) is currently held three times a year, twice in the south of England, and once a year in the north. It is believed to be the largest overseas property exhibition in Europe, featuring thousands of properties and up to 140 exhibitors.
- **Homes Overseas Exhibitions** (**t** (020) 7939 9888, **www.homesoverseas.co.uk**) provides buyers of second homes, relocation or investment, guidance on where to buy, how to buy, plus advice on legal and financial matters, travel, even pet care. The exhibitions provide information on new and resale property in many countries. In 2003 some 25 exhibitions were held in London, Birmingham, Manchester, Glasgow, Brighton, Exeter, Leeds, Edinburgh, Cardiff, Belfast, Dublin and Stockholm.
- **World Class Homes** (**t** 0800 731 4713, **www.worldclasshomes.co.uk**) organizes its own exhibitions in hotels throughout the UK. Several exhibitions are held every month.

Lawyers

Not everybody likes lawyers, but you will probably have noticed that this book regularly advises you not act without first consulting your lawyer. You should get your lawyer involved from the outset, rather than calling him or her in towards the end of the process or when things start going 'pear-shaped'. One reason for this is that if you feel nervous about the legal side of buying a property at home, where you know the lie of the land, are familiar with the terminology and speak the language, how are you going to feel when buying in another country? There are so many areas about which you cannot be expected to know anything unless you have a background in law yourself. For detailed information about the legal aspects of buying your property, *see* **Making the Purchase**. The financial side of property ownership (tax, investments, inheritance, wills, etc.) are covered in **Financial Implications**.

The services of a good lawyer, with experience in foreign property, preferably with particular experience in Portuguese transactions, will cost you between one and three per cent of the overall price of your property depending on the services provided.

Estate Agents

Most foreign people who buy a property in Portugal do so through an estate agent. Estate agents may be based in the buyer's home country or in Portugal. Some home-based agents work hand in hand with Portuguese agents; others have branches in both countries.

Portuguese-based Agents

Many Portuguese agents advertise in the UK and Irish property press and in English-language publications in Portugal itself. Then there are agents that are foreign-owned and -run but based in Portugal. In Portuguese they are known as *inmobiliárias* or *mediadores inmobiliários*. If you go to an area where the property market is booming, on any given street you are just as likely to walk past the offices of a *mediador inmobiliário* as you are a bar, a restaurant or a grocer's shop. In essence, the role of the estate agent in Portugal is the same as anywhere else, namely to attract potential buyers of properties that sellers have entrusted to them. Some specialize in different segments of the market, maybe luxury villas or rural properties; others are experts in second homes and holiday properties; still others cover the whole range. Some are large concerns with branches all over. Others are small businesses that only handle properties within a small geographical area. Within Portugal a good many undertake tasks that go beyond the usual scope of an estate agent such as providing management services for absentee owners or organizing viewing trips from abroad for potential purchasers. As in any country, there are agencies which are highly professional, extremely competent and thoroughly reliable, others that are slapdash and shoddy.

In Portugal, estate agents must, in theory, hold professional qualifications and be licensed to operate. An agent thus authorized, a *mediador autorizado*, should also be a member of the appropriate professional association, in this case the *Associação de Mediadores Inmobiliários* (AMI), the *Associação Portuguesa de Empresas de Mediação Inmobiliários* (APEMI) or the *Associação dos Mediadores do Algarve* (AMA). An agent may also be affiliated to the *Associação das Mediadoras Imobiliárias de Portugal*, which itself is a member of the *Confédération Européenne de l'Immobilier.*

Most agencies display the sticker of one or more of these bodies on their shop door or window and have their certificate in a frame on the wall. This may not be guarantee enough, as the agent could have left (or been asked to leave) the association and not removed the sticker. You should not be shy about asking to see proof of an agent's registration, since if they are bona fide they will have no problems in showing it to you. If you have sought the services of a good, independent lawyer or solicitor, he should be able to check out the agent's credentials for you as well. While legislation has tightened up in recent years and there are proportionally fewer rogues than there used to be, you still have to be careful as unnoticed errors in the conveyancing process may have far-reaching and costly consequences further down the line. A further problem is that customers who have paid for incompetent service have serious difficulty in obtaining redress as agents are not necessarily subject to legislation protecting consumers and may not have sufficient insurance to cover compensation, even if you were to lodge a successful lawsuit (which could take years to resolve). So, be careful.

In the end, it is less important which *type* of estate agent you choose (provided they deal in the sort of property you are after) as long as they do their job properly, leave nothing in a state of legal limbo and give you the correct service for the fee charged.

It is the seller who pays the estate agent's commission. It is illegal for the agent to take commission from both parties. These fees are usually between 5 and 10 per cent of the price of the property. The amount will depend on the value of the property, whether it is new or old and the area where it is located. Cheaper properties generally pay more commission than more expensive properties and properties in main tourist areas tend to pay more commission than in less sought after (and generally poorer) areas.

Beware of hidden commissions. These arise where the agent agrees with the seller that the seller will receive a fixed amount from the proceeds of sale and that the generous agent will forgo charging his normal commission but will, instead, retain everything that he obtains over and above the guaranteed amount. The agent has a much better idea of the value of the property than the seller. This can mean that the seller, instead of receiving, say, €300,000 out of which he pays, say, €18,000 commission, received his guaranteed €200,000 – leaving the agent to pocket €100,000 – and the buyer paying far more than is necessary for the house. These commissions are generally illegal, but still exist.

In order to protect his substantial commission the agent may ask you to sign a document before he takes you to see the property. This is a statement that it is he who has introduced you to the property, so avoiding later arguments about who should be paid the commission due.

There are other significant differences from English practice. Generally agents are rather less proactive than they are in the UK. This is particularly true in rural areas, especially non-tourist rural areas. You will seldom find printed property particulars or be supplied with photographs. Still less will you find plans or room dimensions in most estate agents' offices. They see their role as capturing property to sell and then showing buyers around that property. Many agents are either 'one-man bands' or in small firms with a limited range of property on their books. This is, again, especially true in rural areas, but if you walk down any street in any town on the coast of Portugal you will see evidence of the large numbers of small agents offering services to the public. This can make it difficult to get a comprehensive view of what is on the market in a locality. In addition, there are few local or national groupings of agents.

You are probably best off starting to look for property by using an estate agent in the immediate vicinity of the place you are interested in. Many rural agents will only cover an area about 40km in diameter. If you are still uncertain where precisely you intend to buy, try several adjoining agents or, if there is one in your area, one of the big chains such as Century21. Local newspapers will give you an indication of which agents are advertising, and so active, in your area. You can also get names out of the Portuguese Yellow Pages (under AMI). The Yellow Pages for popular areas are kept in many city libraries in the UK. Some agents also advertise in both the Portuguese and UK specialist property press.

Aside from taking a holiday or reconnaissance trip on your own, with the express purpose of viewing properties, there is also the chance that an estate agent may offer you the chance of a trip to Portugal to view a specific property. If you end up buying it they usually pay your travel expenses for you. This is a legitimate practice but could mean that you have to make the decision on whether to buy or not based on one two-day trip, which may not be advisable.

UK-based Estate Agents

There are growing numbers of people based in the UK who sell property in Portugal. Most popular areas are covered. Although, under English law, they are entitled to call themselves estate agents, it is important to note that, in most cases, they are not licensed Portuguese estate agents. They very often work in association with one or more Portuguese agents, generally covering a wider area than a single Portuguese agent would cover. They advertise or market the properties through exhibitions, etc., and then act as an intermediary between the potential buyer and the Portuguese estate agent – who may not speak English. Because they deal with British buyers all the time they should be able to anticipate some of the common problems that can arise and smooth the progress of the transaction.

Generally, they should share the commission of the Portuguese agent – who is very pleased that they can expand his potential buyer base by introducing foreign buyers. Thus their services should cost you nothing extra.

These people can be very useful, particularly if you have little experience of dealing with Portugal and don't speak Portuguese.

Unfortunately, it is not as simple as that. Some charge substantial amounts of extra commission for their services. Often they do not disclose that commission to the buyer. There is nothing wrong with paying someone who is doing a useful job some commission, but you should be told that you are expected to do so. You can then decide whether the convenience of dealing with someone in Britain is worth the extra cost. Always ask for confirmation that the price you will be paying is exactly the same as you would have paid in Portugal or, if there is an extra charge, the amount of the charge.

Some UK-based agents advertise their prices as a global price including the price of the property, tax, notary's fees and all commissions. This can be very useful for the British buyer unused to these transactions but it can also, in the hands of the unscrupulous, be a way of hiding a large element of hidden commission. Mr Silva has agreed to sell his apartment for €150,000 (about £100,000). Commission has been agreed at five per cent (€7,500). Notary's fees and taxes will amount to about 12 per cent (€18,000). An all-inclusive price of €250,000 therefore gives an extra hidden charge of €74,500 – or over £50,000. If you are offered property on this basis, check what the price includes.

Many of these UK-based sellers are highly experienced and very reputable. Before deciding which to use, ask about their level of experience. It is more difficult to assess whether they are reputable. A good starting point is to see whether they are members of FOPDAC (the Federation of Overseas Property Developers, Agents & Consultants, Lacey House, St Clare Business Park, Holly Road, Hampton Hill, Middlesex TW12 1QQ, **t** (020) 8941 5588, **f** (020) 8941 0202, **info@fopdac.com**, **www.fopdac.com**). This is a non-profit organization that agents and developers can join if they are experienced in the field, are prepared to be scrutinized and willing to abide by its code of conduct.

DIY Sales

In Portugal, especially in big cities and rural areas, far more property is sold 'person to person' than in the UK. There are a variety of different sources of information about such properties for sale.

Vende-se (For Sale) Signs

As you drive around you will see a number of DIY 'For Sale' signs. They normally give a contact telephone number. To take advantage of property offered in this way, you obviously have to be in the area and you will probably need to speak Portuguese. If you do not speak Portuguese it is worth a trial phone call. If the person who answers doesn't speak English there may be a local English-speaking person – perhaps in your hotel – who would make contact on your behalf. As a last resort phone your lawyer. He should be able to find out the necessary details for you and, if you wish, make arrangements to view. He will, of course, charge for this work, but the saving of estate agent's fees will make his charges look cheap.

Local Newspapers

Individuals place advertisements in the 'For Sale' section of the local paper. Once again, the ability to speak Portuguese is an advantage. There is also a reasonable classifieds website, **www.classificados.iol.pt/inmobiliario**. Similarly the English-language press comes with property ads, many of them placed by private individuals. You could also place one yourself, either in the English publications or Portuguese ones.

Auctions

Property in Portugal can be bought at auction, just as in the UK. Some auctions are voluntary, others run by court order.

Prices can be very attractive. A few years ago, at the height of the last recession, there were incredible bargains with prices, perhaps, 30 per cent of 'value'. Now auctions usually offer less spectacular bargains but can still be attractive because, particularly in many judicial auctions, the process is intended first and foremost to recover someone's debt. Once that and the considerable costs have been covered there is little reason to press for a higher price, even though the owner will ultimately receive the excess.

Buying a property at auction is not simple for someone who does not live in the area and it is vitally important that you have taken all the normal preparatory steps – including seeing a lawyer – before you embark on the process.

The procedure leading up to the auction is basically the same whether the auction is a judicial auction or a voluntary auction.

- **You must know that the auction is taking place.** They are usually advertised six to eight weeks in advance. Auctions ordered by the court will be advertised by order of the court in the local press. Notices will also be posted in the area.
- **You must find out what is in the auction.** Brief details of the property to be sold are published. These details of the property will mean nothing to you. The place could be derelict or next door to a nuclear power station – or both. You will need to inspect the property and decide whether it is of interest. This is a time-consuming and potentially costly process. Remember that you might have to inspect 20 properties to find three you might like and then you might be outbid on all three. An alternative to personal inspection is to get someone to do it for you. This is not as satisfactory but a local estate agent will, for a fee, go to look at the property and give you a description of it. If you're lucky he might post or email you some photographs. The fee, about £200 if the property is close to the office, will probably be less than the cost of travel. Some people buy blind. This is for real poker players.
- **You will need to check out the legal situation of the property before the date of the auction.** Most of the steps needed in an ordinary purchase will be required (*see* **Making the Purchase**).
- **Many properties on sale by auction are not in the best of condition. You will therefore need to get estimates as to the likely cost of repairs or improvements** so as to make sure that the price you bid is not so high as to make the project non-viable.
- **You will have to appoint a lawyer to act on your behalf at the auction.** You would be brave or foolish not to be represented. The lawyer will explain precisely what will need to be done for this particular auction. You will have to tell him the maximum price you want to offer and pay him the bidding deposit – a refundable deposit levied by the auctioneer in order to allow you to enter a bid. You will also have to give him your personal details (marital status, occupation, nationality, passport number, etc.) and a deposit of (usually) 10 per cent of the price you are offering, less the bidding deposit. The full deposit is paid across at the time your bid is accepted.

You do not need to attend the auction – the lawyer will be able to do so for you. He will probably require a power of attorney for that purpose. He will, of course, charge you for this work. Get an estimate. Even though you do not need to be present, an auction (especially a judicial auction) is a most interesting event, so you might want to go along.

Although the prices at auction can be very attractive you must bear in mind that you will face additional costs over and above those on a normal purchase. These are likely to raise the overall costs of buying from the normal 12–13 per cent of the price to perhaps 15–17 per cent of the price paid. The extra costs include the fees paid to your lawyers for dealing with the auction.

It is also possible to buy a Portuguese property at auction in the UK. This is very rare. The auction acts simply as a preliminary sale of the property. The sale will need to be formalized in Portugal in the usual way (*see* **Making the Purchase**).

Temporary Accommodation

Renting while house-hunting is by far the best form of accommodation. However, not everybody has time to look for a place to rent on top of looking for a place to buy. If time is really short it should still be possible to find a week, 10-day or fortnight-long holiday let at a reasonable price, especially in the low season. That is, of course, if you are looking for a property in a resort area. The location is less important as resort towns usually have good communications so if you make your base camp in one, getting around to look for a property to buy is not that much of a problem. Out of season there are also many cheap hotel deals in resort areas. If you are looking in a city, however, there is usually a dearth of holiday-let type accommodation so you have to look elsewhere. Hotels are practically the only option and can prove expensive in larger cities, though there is always the budget end if you are not too fussy. There is a small market for apartments that can be rented for days, weeks or longer periods in Lisbon. Expect to pay around €50 per night or more for a two-bedroom apartment that is relatively central. Weekly rates can range between €350 and €500 for others. This compares favourably with hotel prices and may be a more attractive option for the freedom it offers and the fact that it gives you an insight into apartment-living in the city. One source of information on short-term self-catering lets that covers both resort areas and others worldwide is **www.nomorehotels.com**, where many Portuguese apartments are listed.

Renting Before Buying

It is a good idea to rent a place to live in for a reasonable period before committing yourself to buying. You will get to know the area thoroughly, in all the seasons, and you will learn to appreciate its positive and negative points. If the positive outweigh the negative by a fairly clear margin then you will know that you want to stay. You will also have time to look calmly at the property market and get a well-informed view of what you can afford. When you come to take that final step and buy a place to move into permanently you will be doing so fully conscious of the implications and reconciled to them. Renting could also save you money, especially if you decide that this is not the life you wanted after all. If, instead of renting, you had rushed into buying a property only to discover after a few months that you hated the place and wanted to get out, you would then have to sell, and maybe at a loss. Your property almost certainly would not have appreciated sufficiently in value for you to recuperate the fees you have paid to your lawyer, the SISA (property transfer) tax and all the other costs involved. Placing it on the market with an estate agent would now mean that, in the event of a sale, you have to pay them their cut as well. And if the house has increased in value then you may be liable for capital gains tax.

As well as this, if you rent in a relatively cheap area and are planning to start up a business, it may be in your interests to continue renting. Maybe at this delicate early stage you do not want to tie up too much capital in a property, freeing it up to invest in your company, or just keeping it somewhere else gaining interest while you see if the business is going to work or not.

Renting can work both in your favour and against you – depending on where you go. If the area you have chosen to live and rent in is cheap, this is because it is not one of the areas most in demand, so property prices are unlikely to rise especially fast. If you do intend to buy eventually, it will not hurt you too much financially to wait a few months or even longer before taking the plunge. On the other hand, if you choose one of the more fashionable areas, the rent will not be so cheap to start with (and there are fewer long-term rents to be had) and property prices tend to rise a lot more over shorter periods of time.

Renting, then, can be a double-edged sword. It can save you grief and money in the short term if you are being wise and cautious but it can also hamper your entry into the property market if that is where you want to go.

Assuming you want to rent relatively long-term, you will probably want to look at some places first, just as you would if you were buying. Before you can do that you have to sort out some temporary accommodation while you are viewing rental properties. The easiest thing to do for this purpose is to rent a holiday apartment for a couple of weeks while you are looking. Newspapers and magazines, both national and locals carry classified ads with houses and apartments for rent; look in the classifieds under *imobiliário – aluga-se*. The English-language press also has rental ads, but expect them to be considerably more limited in number. You can of course place your own 'wanted' advert as well. You may also look for a long-term rental through an estate agent as some also deal in this side of the business. You might have to pay a fee. In resort areas, especially the Algarve, there tend to be fewer long-term rentals as the market is geared up either for sales or for short-term holiday lets. However, out of season a landlord or management agency might be quite happy to rent for, say, six months, at a reasonable price as you are providing guaranteed income which they may or may not get from holidaymakers.

Outside tourist areas, in small towns and cities, long-term rentals are easier to find and at far more reasonable prices. In the larger cities, though, Lisbon especially, rents can be quite high. Rental properties may be furnished (*mobiliado*) or unfurnished (*sem mobília*); in tourist areas furnished is the norm while in a city you may find either.

Rentals, both long- and short-term, are subject to a contract (*contrato de arrendamento*) and this should clearly state the rights and obligations of the two contracting parties. Traditionally, rental laws have favoured tenants, a fact that has held back the development of the rental sector, since many landlords are wary of renting to anyone – fearing that they may not be able to get rid of them. A standard long-term rental contract is for one year and then may be renewed for further periods if both parties are happy to do so. Utilities bills will usually be paid by the tenant. Like renting anywhere, it is a good idea to have an expert (such as your lawyer) check over the contract before you sign it, especially for the clauses relating to repairs for damage (as opposed to wear and tear) and any community charges that the landlord expects you to pay (which he should not). You may have to pay a deposit of two months as a guarantee in case of any serious damage or breakages, and the landlord may also require a guarantor (*fiador*) who will be liable if you fail to pay the rent and abscond, or wreck the place. Questions such as the way in which rent is to be paid should be made clear from the beginning.

Short-term rentals are much more the norm in resort areas, for the simple reason that there are so few long-term arrangements available. There are specific laws governing these agreements, the contract clearly states the rental period and, because it is understood that occupation is temporary, there are usually no problems on either side.

Building from Scratch or Renovating

If there is nothing on the market to your taste or to meet your requirements you can buy a plot of land (*lote*) and build your own house. If you look in many estate agent's windows or in property magazines, you will often see vacant plots for sale as well as existing homes. It is very tempting. Who would not want a property built exactly to their own specifications and incorporating all their whims and fantasies? Given the price and scarcity of quality villas in many of the more popular areas, building from scratch is another way of fulfilling the villa dream. Fewer and fewer people are looking for 'just' a summer house these days; ever more people want quality. Good materials are far more easily sourced than they used to be so it is possible to build a real home from home. You will certainly not be the first to embark on such an adventure. Recently the market for plots in areas such as the Algarve has begun to heat up. However, building your own home is not a matter to be taken lightly, as there are numerous problems, pitfalls and stumbling blocks along the way. Not the least of the problems typically encountered is obtaining planning permission, which can be a long, slow, frustrating process. In some areas, the Algarve particularly, there are restrictions in force regarding where and what can be built, and how high and so on. Then you have to seek the services of a reliable architect and a reputable building company and be on top of the project from start to finish. Consult your lawyer on all the legal aspects of buying a plot and building.

Some plots are available with planning permission already approved. This might have gone through a long time ago but the owner never got around to building for whatever reason. Some sellers of plots never have intentions of building themselves, or the financial means to do so; just obtaining permission to build is sufficient for them to sell a piece of land that would otherwise be worthless to them. If there is no approved planning permission you have to know whether or not you will ever be able to get it, because if not you could be on the point of buying a couple of totally useless hectares. Be careful, though. 'Cowboy' operators have been known to sell plots where no permission was ever approved, assuring the buyer that it would be, and the buyer has innocently believed them. In order to be sure you have to go to the town hall and find out whether permission has already been granted or is likely to be. The town hall will only issue permission *licença de utilização* within the limits laid down by the local land usage plans, *planos directores municipais*. These usage plans may be interpreted more, or less, strictly according to where you are (and who you are, sometimes). If the possibilities of obtaining permission are good, and you proceed with the purchase, insist on a clause in the purchasing contract that allows you to back out if the local authorities should unexpectedly turn down the project. (This is not unknown in the shifting sands of local politics.) Assuming the plot has an approved project, check that it is actually suitable for building on. If it is on a steep hillside or in the bottom of a valley it may be difficult, and more expensive than it is worth, to dig out the foundations or even allow lorries access. You also have to look at the question of water supply. If it is not close to the local network it can be extremely costly to get connected. The alternative would be to tap into subterranean supplies by means of a well or a borehole. If this is not possible either, then you are advised not to buy that particular plot. The same goes for electricity. Getting connected to the network can also be very expensive and you may have to include a generator in with your building plans. Other aspects to look into before buying the plot might be whether any rights of way across the land may limit exactly where you can situate the house, whether any adjoining vacant plots are susceptible to having a building project approved (restricting your view) and whether there are any road-building or other infrastructure plans proposed affecting adjacent land. Finally, make sure that the demarcation of the plot in the land registry is exactly as it appears in the deeds, as the last thing you want is a later dispute with a neighbour over whether half a field is his or yours.

In many cases, the seller of a plot is also a builder who is offering a package deal in which both the land and the cost of building your house are included. Whether or not you want to buy the land from the same builder is up to you, though you might care to look at other builders' prices in combination with those of plots just on their own. You might find that you get a better deal by elsewhere. But if you decide on the 'combi' deal, dig your heels in and demand two separate contracts, one for the land and another for the building. Sign the contract for the building work only once you have the title deed to the land – this guarantees your right to the land even if things go awry with the builder. If you are a first-time buyer it also means paying less tax.

Having gone ahead with your project, the next step is to find a professional architect. Only contract an architect whose work you have seen and who has been recommended to you by other clients or trustworthy people in the area. The architect should be a registered member of the official Architects' Association – ask to see a certificate. It is also important that you have a common language in which you can communicate. You need to ask for a detailed quotation for all the sketches, calculations, finished plans and supervisory work that the architect will undertake to do. This should be from the start of the project until the very end. Expect to pay in the region of 10 per cent of the total costs of the building project in architect's fees.

Apply the same criteria when choosing a builder – communication being equally important. Builders should be officially registered and be able to show you examples of other projects that they have previously undertaken. They should also be solvent (more than one has gone bust before completing a project). Make sure that the builder is insured against this and that the insurance is included in the building contract (*see* below). Get two or three quotes and make sure that not only the price is included but also the building schedule and the instalments by which you are to pay. The cheapest quotation is not necessarily the best. When you have two or three, consult somebody else who has had a house built and see what their opinion is. The architect may be able to recommend a builder but be cautious as you do not want them to be in cahoots. Remember, the architect has been contracted by you to design and oversee the construction of your house. The builder has also been contracted by you to carry out the construction work, overseen by the architect. There should be a certain amount of healthy tension between them, not a relationship of camaraderie which could lead to neither of them working in your interests. As you are the one paying the money, you have the right to be picky, to insist on your specifications being carried out to the letter and within the times agreed upon in the contract.

Make sure that the contract is watertight, specifies everything and provides you with guarantees if things do not go as planned. Your specifications should include every little last detail, even the make and type of fittings, correct insulation (cavity walls), the exact dimensions, location and orientation of the house as well as the materials that are to be employed in its construction. Be careful to ensure that the connection costs of utilities, water and electricity, to the house and not just to the building site, are also included. All of these details should figure in the architect's plans.

The contract should also state clearly what each stage of the construction process is and on what date each of these should be complete (not just the final date for completion of the whole house). These will most likely coincide with the dates on which you are to pay your instalments to the builder. There should also be a built-in penalty clause by which you can retain a percentage of the price for late completion. As well as this you should contractually be able to retain a small percentage of the building costs as a guarantee against defective work or materials. The contract should also establish an agreed court of arbitration where any disputes will be resolved should they arise. Once the building has been completed you should organize an inspection by a structural engineer who should also prepare a report. If all is not well you must be very persistent to ensure any deficiencies are rectified. The builder is liable for minor defects up to a year after construction is complete and up to five years in the case of structural defects, which may appear after the building has 'settled down', especially if the builder has skimped on materials. The contract should also state clearly that building work may only be considered complete, and the final payment made, when the habitation licence (*licença de habitação*) has been issued by the local authorities who in turn will only issue this document on satisfactory inspection of the finished house. If it has not been built according to the plans or following building regulations, the licence will not be issued and alterations will have to be made. If the project has been supervised adequately from day one this should not be the case.

Every step of the drawing up of the above contract should be overseen by your lawyer to make sure that there are no get-out clauses embedded in the wording.

What if It Doesn't Work Out?

Most people take up the challenge of moving abroad and making a new life for themselves with gusto and launch themselves into the adventure with enthusiasm and optimism. The most successful are usually those who are best prepared and who have researched their area, pondered everything carefully, left no stone unturned in looking for the right property in the right location and mentally readied themselves for all the changes and challenges involved. But not everybody adapts or fits in. Some find that family, friends, a familiar culture and way of life is too much to give up and that their new surroundings by no means make up for such things. Others, while happy, may find that circumstances beyond their control back home make staying on impossible. Others are unlucky, lose the job that took them to Portugal in the first place, lose the partner they came with, or lose their money in unwise business or property deals. There can be so many reasons why a return to the home country becomes necessary that it is probably wise to have a plan 'B' or at least not to burn your bridges totally.

This is not necessarily easy as not everyone is in a position to keep options open back home, usually for financial reasons. Clearly, the lucky person who can buy the Portuguese dream home without having first to sell up at home is in an enviable position if things go wrong and returning becomes necessary. Those who have not fully committed themselves anyway and live part-time in both countries have always got an escape route too. But those who have sold up and moved lock, stock and barrel only to find themselves obliged to return some time later may be in a difficult position. For one thing they will be used to living on their income – a pension say – at Portuguese prices. For another, their Portuguese property, while it may have increased in value since purchase, will almost certainly not have kept pace with property prices in the UK or Ireland. In this case, selling and returning means settling for something less than that which they left behind. If the Portuguese property was bought fairly recently, selling it may mean they are hit by a hefty capital gains tax bill. Owners of exclusive Algarve or Lisbon Coast villas may not fare so badly when selling and buying anew, but anyone with a more modest property will simply have to accept that they will be re-entering the property ladder back home on a lower rung.

It all depends on the funds you have available. If you can keep some money aside or avoid selling up at home (and are able to rent out your house there), then you should try to do this, at least until you are absolutely sure that going to Portugal was the right move. If you have any doubts about this move, think again before you move or at least rent before getting involved in property buying.

Making the Purchase

John Howell
Solicitor and International Lawyer
John Howell & Co

05

Buying a property in Portugal is as safe as buying a property in the UK. On reading a book such as this – which must explain the potential pitfalls if it is to serve any useful purpose – it can seem a frightening or dangerous experience. If you go about the purchase in the right way, it is not dangerous and should not be frightening. The same or similar dangers arise when buying a house in the UK. If you are in any doubt, look briefly at a textbook on English conveyancing and all of the horrible things that have happened to people in the UK. You do not worry about those dangers because you are familiar with them and, more importantly, because you are shielded against contact with most of them by your solicitor. The same should be true when buying in Portugal. Read this book to understand the background and why some of the problems exist, ask your lawyer to advise you about any issues that worry you – and leave him to avoid the landmines!

Law

This book is intended primarily for people from England and Wales. For this reason I have drawn comparisons with English law. Scots law is somewhat different. Where the points apply also to Scots law I have tried, depending on the context, to refer to either UK or British law. The law is, except where otherwise stated, intended to be up to date as at 1 January 2003.

Disclaimer

Although we have done our best to cover most topics of interest to the buyer of a property in Portugal, a guide of this kind cannot take into account every individual's personal circumstances, and the size of the book means that the advice cannot be comprehensive. The book is intended as a starting point that will enable people who are thinking of buying property to understand some of the issues involved and to ask the necessary questions of their professional advisers. **IT IS NO SUBSTITUTE FOR PROFESSIONAL ADVICE.** Neither the author nor the publishers can accept any liability for any action taken or not taken as a result of this book.

Finding a Property in Portugal

At the moment we are in a property 'boom'. It is, in most popular areas, a seller's market. Property – and, in particular, attractive, well-located and well-priced property – sells very quickly. A few years ago it was fairly simple to go to Portugal, look around, see a few properties and then come back to England to ponder which to buy. Today someone doing this could well find that the house they wanted to make an offer on had sold to someone else in the few days since they saw it.

As a result of this, people who are serious about buying property in Portugal should do some research and make some preparations *before* they go on a visit to look at property. When they visit they should do so with the intention that, if they see something they really like, they will make an offer and commit themselves (at least in principle) to the purchase while they are still in the area.

What Preparation Should You Make?

Understand the System

The system of buying and selling property in Portugal is, not surprisingly, different from the system of buying property in England or Scotland. On balance, neither better nor worse – just different. It has many superficial similarities, which can lull you into a false sense of familiarity and overconfidence. *The most important thing to remember is that buying a home in Portugal is just as safe as buying a home in Cardiff – providing you take the right professional advice and precautions when doing so.* If you do not, there are many expensive traps for the unwary.

See a Lawyer

See your lawyer *before* you find a property. There are a number of preliminary issues that can best be discussed in the relative calm before you find the house of your dreams rather than once you are under pressure to sign some document to commit yourself to the purchase.

These will include:

- **Who should own the property, bearing in mind the Portuguese and British tax consequences of ownership.**
- **Whether to consider mortgage finance and if so in which country.**
- **What to do about buying the euros needed to pay for the property.**
- **How to structure your purchase to minimize taxes and cost.**
- **If you are going to be living in Portugal, sorting out the tax, pension and investment issues that will need to be dealt with *before your move* if you are to get the best out of both systems.**

Only UK lawyers who specialize in dealing with Portugal will be able to help you fully. Your normal English solicitor will know little or nothing of the issues of Portuguese law and a Portuguese lawyer is likely to know little or nothing about the British tax system or the issues of English or Scots law that will affect the way the transaction should be arranged.

The lawyer may also be able to recommend estate agents, architects, banks, surveyors, mortgage lenders and other contacts in the area you are looking.

A physical meeting is still the best way to start an important relationship. It allows you to show and be shown documents and to wander off more easily into related topics. Most importantly, it is usually easier to make certain that you have each understood the other in a face-to-face meeting. But, these days, 'seeing' your lawyer does not need to involve an actual meeting. If it is more convenient to you it could be done by telephone conference call, by videoconference or over the internet.

Decide on Ownership

Who should be the owner of your new home? This is the most important decision you will have to make when buying a property. Because of the combination of the Portuguese and British tax systems, getting the ownership wrong can be a very expensive mistake indeed. It can lead to totally unnecessary tax during your lifetime and on your death. Even on a modest property this can amount to tens of thousands of pounds. This subject is dealt with more fully later.

Get an Offer of Mortgage/Finance

These days, with very low interest rates, more and more people borrow at least part of the money needed to buy their home in Portugal. Even if they don't need to do so, for many it makes good business or investment sense.

If you want to borrow money to finance your purchase, it is better to get clearance *before* you start looking at property. Your lawyer should be able to get a preliminary mortgage offer within about two to four weeks.

Estate Agents

The role of the Portuguese estate agent is similar to the role of the British estate agent. Their job is to find buyers for properties entrusted to them by a seller. But there the similarity ends.

In the UK, a person can be a plumber today and, without any qualifications or experience, set up an estate agency tomorrow. They cannot do this in Portugal. In Portugal, in order to practise as an estate agent, you must hold a licence. Only people who devote the large majority of their time to estate agency can be licensed. Check that your proposed estate agent is registered with the Institute of Dealers in Private and Public Works and in Real Estate (*Instituto de Mercados de Obras Públicas e Particulares e do Imobiliário*). This is a state-run organization that is responsible for the supervision and control of real estate agents. All this is partly an example of the generally greater paperwork and red tape prevalent in Portugal and partly a useful consumer protection measure. Agents must be licensed, insured and bonded. This means that their clients should be able to obtain compensation in the event of any improper or negligent conduct on the part of the agent. Be aware, however, that the minimum values of the bonds and insurance policies are very low. The bond – guaranteeing payment to the client in the case of any improper action such as taking a commission from both parties – need be only €2,493.99 (about £1,700) and the insurance against negligence need only give cover up to about £100,000. Many agents have much higher cover. Licensed agents are identified by the initials AMI (*Actividade de Mediação Imobiliária*).

There are quite large numbers of agents operating in Portugal without a licence. That is, illegally. Many are foreigners servicing the foreign buyer. British selling to British, Germans to Germans, etc. Some of these 'illegals' are excellent, skilled people who offer a service at least as good as many of their legal agents. Despite this, you are better dealing with a 'proper' agent or his genuine employee as you will then be covered by the legislation and the codes of conduct to which the agents must adhere.

You can tell whether the agent is licensed because he must display details of his licence in his offices and he must give details of his licence in all correspondence and contracts. If you are dealing with the agent by telephone, fax or e-mail he will not take offence if you ask to see proof of these documents.

Property Inspection

Whatever property you are thinking of buying you should think about having it inspected before you commit yourself to the purchase. It costs just as much and causes just as much disruption to repair property in Portugal as in the UK, so you don't want any surprises. In fact – foolishly – very few buyers of property in Portugal do this.

A new property will be covered by a short guarantee running from the date of handover and covering minor but not trivial defects in a new property. The property will also benefit from a guarantee in respect of major structural defects that will last for 10 years. As a subsequent purchaser you assume the benefit of these guarantees. After 10 years you are on your own. For property more than 10 years old (and, arguably, for younger property too) you should consider a survey.

If you decide on a survey, there are a number of options available to you.

Do-it-yourself

There are several things that you can do yourself. These will help you decide when to instruct a surveyor to do a proper survey and help direct him to any specific points of interest, *see* 'Checklist' in 'Appendix 1', pp 308–13.

Estate Agent's Valuation and 'Survey'

It may be possible to arrange for another local estate agent to give the property a quick 'once over' to comment on the price asked and any obvious problem areas. This is far short of a survey. It is likely to cost about £200. It is also possible to have a valuation (*avaliação*) carried out by an official valuer (*técnico avaliador*). This is also likely to cost about £200 for a simple property, but can sometimes be less helpful and practical than the estate agent's valuation.

Mortgage Lender's Survey

This is no substitute for a proper survey. Many lenders do not ask for one and, where they do, it is normally fairly peremptory, limited to a check on whether it is imminently about to fall over and whether it is, on a forced sale at short notice, likely to be worth the money the bank is lending you.

Portuguese Builder

If you are going to do a virtual demolition and rebuild, then it might make more sense to get a builder to do a report on the property. A reputable and experienced builder will also be able to comment on whether the price is reasonable for the property in its existing state. Make sure you ask for a written quotation for any building work proposed. As in any country, it is as well to get several quotes, though this can be tricky. There is a lot of work for builders at the moment.

Portuguese Surveyor

Your lawyer can put you in touch with the right people. In most rural areas there will be limited choice. If you prefer you can select 'blind' from a list of local members supplied by the surveyors' professional body. The cost of a survey is typically £500–1,500.

You will find that the report is different from the sort you would get from an English surveyor. Many people find it a little 'thin', with too much focus on issues that are not their primary concern. It will, hardly surprisingly, usually be in Portuguese. You will need to have it translated and have access to a technical dictionary. Translation costs amount to about £60–100 per thousand words, depending on where you are located and the complexity of the document. Incidentally, always use an English native speaker to translate documents from Portuguese into English. An alternative to translation of the full report would be to ask your lawyer to summarize the report in a letter to you and to have any areas of particular concern translated.

A few Portuguese surveyors, mainly in the popular areas, have geared themselves to the non-Portuguese market and will produce a report rather more like a British survey. They will, probably, also prepare it in bilingual form or at least supply a translation of the original Portuguese document. A few produce the report in English. Sometimes the English is not very good. Sometimes, coupled with the technicalities involved, the report is almost unintelligible.

UK-qualified Surveyor Based in Portugal

A number of UK surveyors – usually those with a love of Portugal – have seen a gap in the market and have set themselves up in Portugal to provide UK-style structural surveys. As in this country, they usually offer the brief 'Homebuyers' Report' or the fuller 'Full Structural Survey'. This is not as simple as it would first appear. To do the job well they must learn about Portuguese building techniques and regulations, which are different from those in the UK. Without this knowledge, the report will be of limited value. Prices are generally slightly more expensive than for a Portuguese report, but it will be in English and so avoid the need for translation costs. Your UK lawyer should be able to recommend a surveyor able to do a survey in your area. Alternatively, look for advertisers in the main Portuguese property magazines.

Check they have indemnity insurance covering the provision of reports in Portugal. Check also on the person's qualifications and experience in providing reports on Portuguese property and get an estimate. The estimate will be an estimate because they will not know for sure the scope of the task until they visit the property and because travelling time means that visits just to give estimates are not usually feasible.

UK-based Surveyor

Some UK surveyors provide reports from a base in the UK. These can be very good but travelling time often makes them impractical – especially in remote areas – and expensive. Make the same checks as for a UK surveyor based in Portugal, *see* above.

Timescale

Most surveys can be done in seven to ten days.

Contracts 'Subject to Survey'

This is unusual in Portugal. Legally, there is nothing to stop a Portuguese preliminary contract containing a 'get-out clause' (*condicion resolutoria*) stating that the sale is conditional upon a satisfactory survey being obtained. It is unlikely to meet with the approval of the seller or his agent unless the transaction is unusual. In an ordinary case, the seller is likely to tell you to do your survey and then sign a contract.

General

Get a recommendation before deciding which type of surveyor and then which surveyor to use. Your lawyer is probably the best person to ask. For obvious reasons, be very careful before taking a recommendation from the estate agent selling the property.

Whichever report you opt for, its quality will depend in part on your input. Agree clearly and in writing the things you expect to be covered in the report. If you do not speak Portuguese (and the surveyor does not speak good English) you may have to ask someone to write on your behalf. Your UK lawyer would probably be the best bet. Some of the matters you may wish to think about are set out below. Some of these will involve you in additional cost. Ask what will be covered as part of the standard fee and get an estimate for the extras.

Checklist – Things You May Ask Your Surveyor to Check

- **Electrical condition and continuity.**
- **Drains, including assessment of drain to point where they join mains sewers or septic tank.**
- **Septic tank.**
- **Rot.**
- **Cement quality in a property constructed out of cement.**
- **Underfloor areas, where access cannot easily be obtained.**
- **Heating and air-conditioning.**
- **Pool and all pool-related equipment and heating.**
- **Wood-boring insects. Roughly half of Portugal is infested with termites, so this is important.**

Raising Finance to Buy a Property in Portugal

In these days of low interest rates, many more people are taking out a mortgage in order to buy property abroad.

If the property is viewed simply as an investment, a mortgage allows you to increase your benefit from the capital growth of the property by 'leveraging' the investment. If you buy a house for £200,000 and it increases in value by £50,000 that is a 25 per cent return on your investment. If you had put in only £50,000 of your own money and borrowed the other £150,000 then the increase in value represents a return of 100 per cent on your investment. If the rate of increase in the value of the property is more than the mortgage rate, you have won. In recent years, property in most popular areas has gone up in value by much more than the mortgage rate. The key questions are whether that will continue and, if so, for how long.

If you decide to take out a mortgage you can, in most cases, either mortgage (or extend the mortgage on) your existing UK property or you can take out a mortgage on your new Portuguese property. There are advantages and disadvantages both ways.

Many people buying property in Portugal will look closely at fixed-rate mortgages so they know their commitment over, say, the next 5, 10 or 15 years. Again there are advantages and disadvantages.

Mortgaging Your UK Property

At the moment there is fierce competition to lend money and there are some excellent deals to be done, whether you choose to borrow at a variable rate, at a fixed rate or with one of the hybrid schemes now on offer. Read the Sunday newspapers or the specialist mortgage press to see what is on offer, or consult a mortgage broker. Perhaps most useful are mortgage brokers who can discuss the possibilities in both the UK and Portugal.

It is outside the scope of this book to go into detail about the procedures for obtaining a UK mortgage.

Advantages

- **The loan will probably be very cheap to set up.**

You will probably already have a mortgage. If you stay with the same lender there will be no legal fees or land registry fees for the additional loan. There may not even be an arrangement fee.

If you go to a new lender many special deals mean that the lender will pay all fees involved.

- **The loan repayments will be in sterling.**

If the funds to repay the mortgage are coming from your sterling earnings, then the amount you have to pay will not be affected by fluctuations in exchange rates between the pound and the euro.

Equally, if sterling falls in value, then your debt as a percentage of the value of the property decreases. Your property will be worth more in sterling terms but your mortgage will remain the same.

- **You will be familiar with dealing with British mortgages and all correspondence and documentation will be in English.**
- **You can take out an endowment or PEP mortgage or pension mortgage or interest-only mortgage, none of which is available in Portugal.**

Normally only repayment mortgages are available in Portugal.

- **You will probably need no extra life insurance cover.**

If you had to take out more cover this could add considerably to the cost of the mortgage, especially if you are getting older.

Disadvantages

- **You will pay UK interest rates which, at the time of writing (summer 2003), are higher than Portuguese rates.**

UK rates are about 4.5 per cent variable. Portuguese rates are about 3.75 per cent variable. Note that rates, at the moment, are changing frequently.

Make sure you compare the overall cost of the two mortgages. Crude rates (which, in any case, may not be comparable as they are calculated differently in the two countries) do not tell the whole tale. What is the total monthly cost of each mortgage, including life insurance and all extras? What is the total amount required to repay the loan, including all fees and charges?

- **If the pound increases in value against the euro, a mortgage in euros would become cheaper to pay off.**

Your loan of €60,000 (now worth about £40,000 at £1.00 = €1.50) would cost only about £30,000 to pay off if the euro rose 20 per cent.

- **If you are going to let the property, it will be difficult or impossible to get Portuguese tax relief on the mortgage interest.**
- **Many people do not like the idea of mortgaging their main home – which they may only just have cleared after 25 years of paying off an earlier mortgage!**
- **Some academics argue that, in economic terms, debts incurred to buy assets should be secured against the asset bought and assets in one country should be funded by borrowings in that country.**

All in all, a UK mortgage is generally the better option for people who need to borrow relatively small sums and who will be repaying it out of UK income.

Portuguese Mortgages

A Portuguese mortgage is one taken out over your Portuguese property. This will either be from a Portuguese bank or from a British bank that is registered and does business in Portugal. You cannot take out a mortgage on your new Portuguese property from your local branch of a UK building society or high street bank.

The basic concept of a mortgage to buy property is the same in Portugal as it is in England or Scotland. It is a loan secured against the land or buildings. Just as in the UK, if you don't keep up the payments the bank will repossess your property.

The Main Differences Between an English and a Portuguese Mortgage

- Portuguese mortgages are almost always created on a repayment basis. That is to say, the loan and the interest on it are both gradually repaid by equal instalments over the period of the mortgage. Endowment, PEP, pension and interest-only mortgages are not known in Portugal.
- There are often restrictions or penalties or the ability to impose penalties for early payment of the loan.
- The formalities involved in making the application, signing the contract subject to a mortgage and completing the transaction are more complex and stricter than in the UK.
- Most Portuguese mortgages are usually granted for 15 years, not 25 as in the UK. In fact, the period can be anything from five to (in a few cases) 30 years. Normally the mortgage must have been repaid by your 70th (sometimes 65th) birthday.
- The maximum loan is generally 80 per cent of the value of the property and 75 or 66 per cent is more common. As a planning guide, you should think of borrowing no more than two-thirds of the purchase price. This allows for the value placed upon the property by your bank – a conservative figure intended to reflect what they might get for the property on a forced sale – being less that the price you are paying.
- Fixed rate loans – with the rate fixed for the duration of the loan – are more common than in the UK. They are very competitively priced.
- The way of calculating the amount the bank will lend you is different from in the UK. As you would expect, there are detailed differences from bank to bank, but most banks are not allowed to lend you more than an amount the monthly payments on which amount to 30–33 per cent of your net disposable income. *See* 'How Much Can I Borrow?', p.136.
- There will usually be a minimum loan (say £20,000) and some banks will not lend at all on property with less than a certain value. Some will not lend in rural areas.
- The way of dealing with stage payments on new property and property where money is needed for restoration is different from in the UK. *See* below.
- The paperwork on completion of the mortgage is different. There may be a separate mortgage contract (*contrato de mútuo com hipoteca*). Alternatively, the mortgage can be reflected solely in the *escritura*, which is prepared by and signed in front of a notary public (*notário*).

How Much Can I Borrow?

Different banks have slightly different rules and different ways of interpreting the rules.

Generally they will lend you an amount that will give rise to monthly payments of up to about 30–33 per cent of your net available monthly income.

The starting point is your net monthly salary after deduction of tax and National Insurance but before deduction of voluntary payments such as to savings schemes. If there are two applicants, the two salaries are taken into account. If you have investment income or a pension, this will be taken into account. If you are buying a property with a track record of letting income, this may be taken into account. If you are buying a leaseback, then the leaseback rental income will usually be taken into account. If you are over 65, your earnings will not usually be taken into account, but your pension and investment income will be. If your circumstances are at all unusual, seek advice, as approaching a different bank may produce a different result.

e.g.	Mr Smith – net salary per month, after tax and NI	£3,000
	Mrs Smith – net salary per month, after tax and NI	£2,000
	Investment income per month	£1,000
	Total income taken into account	£6,000 per month

The maximum loan repayments permitted will be 30 per cent of this sum, less your existing fixed commitments

i.e. Maximum permitted loan repayment £6,000 x 30% = £1,800 per month

Regular monthly commitments would include mortgage payments on your main and other properties, any rent paid, HP commitments and maintenance (family financial provision) payments. Repayments on credit cards do not count. If there are two applicants both of their commitments are taken into account.

e.g.	Mr and Mrs Smith – mortgage on main home	£750
	Mr and Mrs Smith – mortgage on house in Portugal	£400
	Mrs Smith – HP on car	£200
	Total pre-existing outgoings	£1,350 per month

Maximum loan repayment permitted = £1,800 – £1,350 = £450 per month. This would, at today's rates, equate to a mortgage of about £60,000 over 15 years.

If you are buying a property for investment (rental) the bank may treat this as commercial lending and apply different criteria.

Applications for a Portuguese Mortgage

Once again, the information needed will vary from bank to bank. It will also depend on whether you are employed or self-employed.

Applications can receive preliminary approval (subject to survey of the property, confirmation of good title and confirmation of the information supplied by you) within about two to four weeks.

The Mortgage Offer

Allow four weeks from the date of your application (the date on which you supply the bank with all of the documentation needed to support your application) to receiving a written mortgage offer. It can take longer.

Once you receive the offer you will generally have 30 days from receipt of the offer in which to accept it, after which time it will lapse.

Have the mortgage explained in detail by your lawyer.

Payments for New Property

In Portugal, when buying a new property one normally makes payments as the development progresses and takes title at the end. This can pose problems for banks as you do not own anything you can mortgage until you make the final payment and take title. In most cases the mortgage will therefore only be granted to cover the final payment. As this is often 60 or 70 per cent, this is seldom a problem. In some cases if the earlier payments are more substantial the banks will offer a credit facility to make the earlier payments. Once the property has been delivered to you (and thus the full loan has been taken) the normal monthly payments will begin.

Property Needing Restoration

Not all banks will finance such property.

If you have enough money to buy a property but need a mortgage to renovate it, you *must* apply for the mortgage before buying the property as it can otherwise be difficult to find a lender.

The Cost of Taking Out a Mortgage

This will normally involve charges amounting to about four per cent of the sum borrowed. These charges are in addition to the normal expenses incurred when buying a property, which usually amount to about 12 per cent of the price of the property.

You will probably be required to take out **life insurance** for the amount of the loan, though you may be allowed to use a suitable existing policy. You may be required to have a medical. You will be required to **insure the property** and produce proof of insurance – but you would probably have done this anyway.

The offer may be subject to **early payment penalties**. Early payment penalties are of particular concern in the case of a fixed-rate mortgage.

Make sure you understand what you are signing up for. If in any doubt, get your lawyer to advise you.

The Exchange Rate Risk

If the funds to repay the mortgage are coming from your sterling earnings, then the amount you have to pay will be affected by fluctuations in exchange rates between the pound and the euro. Do not underestimate these variations. Over the last 15 years – a typical period for a mortgage – the Portuguese escudo has been as high as escudos 180 = £1 and as low as escudos 350 = £1. This means that sometimes the amount in sterling you would have had to send to Portugal to pay the mortgage would have been almost double the amount at other times. This is less of a worry if you have income in euros, for example from letting the property.

Mortgaging Your Portuguese Property: Summary

Advantages

• **You will pay Portuguese interest rates, which at the time of writing (summer 2003) are lower than UK rates.**

British rates are about 4.5 per cent variable. Portuguese rates vary from about 3.75 per cent variable.

Make sure you compare the overall cost of the two mortgages. Crude rates (which, in any case, may not be comparable as they are calculated differently in the two countries) do not tell the whole tale. What is the total monthly cost of each mortgage, including life insurance and all extras? What is the total amount required to repay the loan, including all fees and charges?

• **If you are going to let the property you will usually be able to get Portuguese tax relief on the mortgage interest.**

• **The loan repayments will usually be in euros.**

If the funds to repay the mortgage are coming from rental income paid to you in euros this will give you something to spend them on!

• **Many people do not like the idea of mortgaging their main home – which they may only just have cleared after 25 years of paying a mortgage!**

• **Some academics argue that, in economic terms, debts incurred to buy assets should be secured against the asset bought and assets in one country should be funded by borrowings in that country.**

Disadvantages

• **The loan will probably be expensive to set up.**

Arrangement fees, inspection fees, notary's fees and land registry fees will come to about four per cent of the amount borrowed.

• **You will incur further fees to clear the record of the mortgage of your title once it has been paid off.**

This will usually only be a problem if you want to sell the property during the two years following paying off the mortgage.

- **The loan repayments will usually be in euros.**

If the funds to repay the mortgage are coming from your sterling earnings then the amount you have to pay will be affected by fluctuations in exchange rates between the pound and the euro.

Equally, if the pound falls in value then your debt as a percentage of the value of the property increases in sterling terms. Your property will be worth more in sterling terms but your mortgage will also have increased in value.

- **You will be unfamiliar with dealing with Portuguese mortgages and all correspondence and documentation will be usually be in Portuguese.**

- **Normally only repayment mortgages are available – i.e. mortgages where you pay off the capital and interest over the period of the mortgage.**

- **You will probably need extra life insurance cover.**

This can add considerably to the cost of the mortgage, especially if you are getting older.

Generally speaking, Portuguese euro mortgages will suit people letting their property regularly.

Saving Money on your Euro Repayments

Your mortgage will usually be paid directly from your Portuguese bank account. Unless you have lots of rental or other euro income going into that account, you will need to send money from the UK in order to meet the payments.

Every time you send a payment to Portugal you will face two costs. The first is the price of the euros. This, of course, depends on the exchange rate used to convert your sterling. The second cost is the charges that will be made by your UK and Portuguese banks to transfer the funds – which can be substantial. There are steps that you can take to control both of these charges.

As far as the exchange rate is concerned, you should be receiving the so-called 'commercial rate', not the tourist rate published in the papers. The good news is that it is a much better rate. The bad news is that rates vary from second to second and so it is difficult to get alternative quotes. By the time you phone the second company the first has changed! In any case, you will probably want to set up a standing order for payment and not shop around every month.

There are various organizations that can convert your sterling into euros. Your bank is unlikely to give you the best exchange rate. Specialist currency dealers will normally better the bank's rate, perhaps significantly. If you decide to go through a currency dealer you must deal with one that is reputable. They will be handling your money and, if they go bust with it in their possession, you could lose it. Ask you lawyer for a recommendation.

Another possibility for saving money arises if you 'forward-buy' the euros that you are going to need for the year. It is possible to agree with a currency dealer that you will buy all of your euros for the next 12 months at a price that is, essentially, today's price. You normally pay 10 per cent down and the balance on delivery. If the euro rises in value you will gain, perhaps substantially. If the euro falls in value – well, that's life! The main attraction of forward-buying is not so much the possibility of gaining on the exchange rate – though at the moment this seems highly likely – but the certainty that the deal gives you. Only enter into these agreements with a reputable and, if possible, bonded broker.

Bearing in mind the cost of conversion and transmission of currency, it is better to make fewer rather than more payments. You will have to work out whether, taking into account loss of interest on the funds transferred but bank charges saved, you are best sending money monthly, quarterly or every six months.

Foreign Currency Mortgages

It is possible to mortgage your home in Portugal but to borrow not in euros but in sterling – or US dollars or Swiss francs or Japanese yen.

There may be some attractions in borrowing in sterling if you are repaying out of sterling income. The rates of interest will be sterling rates, not euro rates. This will currently mean paying more. Usually the rates are not as competitive as you could obtain if you were re-mortgaging your property in the UK as the market is less cut-throat. You will have all the same administrative and legal costs as you would if you borrowed in euros – i.e. about four per cent of the amount borrowed.

This option is mainly of interest to people who either do not have sufficient equity in their UK home or who, for whatever reason, do not wish to mortgage the property in which they live.

Who Should Own the Property?

There are many ways of structuring the purchase of a home in Portugal. Each has significant advantages and disadvantages. The choice of the right structure will save you possibly many thousands of pounds of tax and expenses during your lifetime and on your death. Because, in Portugal, you do not have the total freedom that we have in the UK to deal with your assets as you please on your death, the wrong choice of owner can also result in the wrong people being entitled to inherit from you when you die. This is a particular problem for people in second marriages and unmarried couples.

The Options

Sole Ownership

In some cases it could be sensible to put the property in the name of one person only. If your husband runs a high-risk business, or if he is 90 and you are 22, this could make sense. It is seldom a good idea from the point of view of tax or inheritance planning.

Joint Ownership

If two people are buying together they will normally buy in both their names. Your half is yours and your fellow owner's is theirs. On your death, your half will (subject to the requirement of your matrimonial regime) be disposed of in accordance with Portuguese law. Generally, if you are British, this allows you to do as you please with your assets on your death. A person who owns in this way, even if they own by virtue of inheritance, can usually insist on the sale of the property. So if your stepchildren inherit from your husband they could insist on the sale of your home.

If you decide to buy together then, in certain cases, it can make sense to split the ownership other than 50/50. If, for example, you have three children and your wife has two, then to secure each of those children an equal share on your death, at the lowest possible tax rates, you might think about buying 60 per cent in your name and 40 per cent in your wife's name.

It is very important to seek clear advice from your lawyer about the form of ownership that will suit you best, both with regard to the consequences in Portugal and the consequences in the UK.

Adding Your Children to the Title

If you give your children the money to buy part of the property and so put them on the title now, you may save quite a lot of inheritance tax. On your death you will own only (say) one-fifth of the property rather than one-half. Only that part will be taxable. It may be of such small value as to result in a tax-free inheritance. This only works sensibly if your children are over 18. Of course, there are drawbacks.

Putting the Property in the Name of Your Children *Only*

If you put the property only in the name of your children (possibly reserving for yourself a life interest – *see* below) then the property is theirs. On your death there will be little or no inheritance tax and there will be no need to incur the legal expenses involved in dealing with an inheritance. This sounds attractive. Remember, however, that you have lost control. It is no longer your property. If your children fall out with you they can insist on the sale of the property – which you still (wrongly) think of as yours – and on receiving their share. If your children divorce, their husbands or wives will be able to claim a share. If they die before you without children of their own, you may end up inheriting the property back from them and having to pay inheritance tax for the privilege of doing so.

A life interest (*usufructo*) is the right to use the property for a lifetime. So, on your death, your rights would be extinguished *but* your second wife or partner, who still has a life interest, would still be able to use the property. Only on their death would the property pass in full to the people to whom you gave it years earlier. This device can not only protect your right to use the property but also save large amounts of inheritance tax, particularly if you are young, the property is valuable and you survive for many years. As ever, there are also drawbacks, not least being the fact that after the gift you no longer own the property. If you wish to sell, you need the agreement of the 'owners', who will be entitled to their share of the proceeds of sale and who would have to agree to buy you a new house.

If you wish to do this you must structure the gift carefully. Otherwise it could be taxable *at once* in Portugal. This would lead to gift tax – payable *now* – at up to 50 per cent of the value transferred. Ask you lawyer for detailed advice.

Limited Company

For some people, owning a property through a limited company can be a very attractive option. You own the shares in a company, not a house in Portugal. There are various types of company.

Portuguese Commercial Company

Ownership through a company will mean that the income from letting the property is taxed in the way usual for companies – basically, you pay tax only on the profit made – rather than at the flat rate applicable in the case of an individual owner who is not tax resident in Portugal. This can reduce your tax bill. Ownership in the form of a company also gives rise to certain expenses: accountancy, filing tax returns, etc.

Buying through a Portuguese company gives rise to a host of potential problems as well as benefits. The plan needs to be studied closely by your advisers so that you can decide whether it makes sense in the short, medium and long term.

UK Company

It is rare for a purchase through a UK company to make sense for a holiday home or single investment property. This is despite the fact that the ability to pay for the property with the company's money without drawing it out of the company and paying UK tax on the dividend is attractive.

Following a decision in the Inland Revenue's favour in the House of Lords in October 2001, the Revenue is now able to contend that if an individual owns shares in a UK company and that company owns a property which the individual used, he would be regarded as a shadow director of that company and, accordingly, be liable to be charged tax on the benefit for occupying that property.

The taxable benefit for offshore companies is the annual value, i.e. what the property would be let for on the open market. This is normally taken as eight per cent of the capital value. Therefore, on a £1 million property this is the equivalent to a rent of £80,000 per annum. The effect of an £80,000 per annum benefit in kind is (for most UK tax residents) a tax bill in the UK of £32,000 per annum. Ouch!

Do take careful legal advice before buying in the name of a UK company.

Offshore (Tax Haven) Company

There are tax problems for people who buy through an offshore company. They arise both in the UK and in Portugal.

Historically, many people have bought properties in Portugal in the name of limited companies, based 'offshore' – i.e. in a tax haven – and which they control. By controlling the company they, of course, control the house.

Advantages

- **Resale**

A company does not die unless it is 'struck off' the register of companies. This is, normally, either because you ask for it to be removed, it is wound up on the application of a third party or because it did not file its annual paperwork. Therefore, generally, provided your company is up to date with its filing requirements, it always remains the registered owner of the property.

There is no saving when buying the property in the name of a company but, when you decide to sell the property, if the buyer chooses (or can be persuaded) to buy the company rather than the house itself, he is not required then to pay property transfer tax (SISA), land registry fees or notary's fees. There may also be a possible saving in legal fees. These could, together, amount to a saving of between 13 and 15 per cent of the price and thus prove a much more attractive proposition to a buyer. So, it is argued, the buyer might be prepared to pay a bit more for the house.

- **Succession**

As a company does not die, there is no requirement for the Portuguese equivalent of probate on the 'owner's' death. This may lead to the non-payment of inheritance tax in Portugal. Whether probate is needed or Portuguese inheritance tax is payable will depend on the legal requirements of the country where the company is registered and whether the shares of the company are officially registered in your name.

- **Capital Gains Tax**

Depending on the jurisdiction governing the company, capital gains will not normally be payable on the sale of the property either in Portugal or in the country where the company is resident, unless you bring the proceeds of sale into the UK or the country where you are tax resident.

Disadvantages

- **Cost**

  The annual cost of maintaining the company, which varies from jurisdiction to jurisdiction but is typically £500 per year, amounts to a lot of money if you own the property for, say, 20 years.

- **Sale**

  The intended buyer may not want to buy the property in the name of the company. The cost is then, largely, wasted.

UK Tax

For the person who is tax resident in the UK, essentially the same UK tax problems arise as in the case of a UK company. *See* above. In the case of an offshore company there *may* be ways out of the UK tax problem, but they need careful thought and planning before you buy.

Portguese Tax

In Portugal there is the added disincentive that you will have to pay a special additional tax *every year*. This is to compensate the Portuguese for all the inheritance and transfer taxes that they will not receive when the owners of these companies sell them or die. This tax treatment has more or less killed off ownership via such companies, yet they still have a limited role to play. A 93-year-old buying a £1 million property, or someone who wishes to be discreet about the ownership of the property, might think the extra tax is a small price to pay for the avoidance of inheritance tax or privacy respectively.

About two years ago, the Portuguese government got a fixation about tourist property rentals. Many owners let out their houses for the summer, often for quite sizeable sums. While they are meant to declare this income to the Portuguese tax authorities, it was suspected, quite correctly, that many owners didn't bother. The government was also upset at the amount of tax it was missing out on when property was transferred and on inheritance. So it was decided that this tax evasion by overseas property owners should be targeted. To do this, they needed to look no further than France and Spain, which had both taken similar steps – very successfully – several years previously. They raised billions of euros in extra tax – and, remember, you don't lose votes by taxing foreigners. It was irresistible.

1. A tax will be payable on deemed rentals. A legally very doubtful decision has been made to assume that all offshore companies established in more favourable tax regimes (tax havens) are renting out their villas. An annual tax charge of up to 40 per cent of the deemed rental income is then levied. This is based on a deemed rental income of one-15th of the official (rateable) value of

the property. This step is subtly combined with an imminent and long overdue revaluation of rateable values. Together they will amount to a huge increase in the cost of running a property through an offshore company. While some tax deductions are available, all the bills have to be properly documented. No account is to be taken of the actual amount of any rentals, nor of whether the villa is occupied full-time by its real owner, who may be legally and resident in Portugal.

2. The annual property rates – which presently range between 0.8 and 1.3 per cent of the (currently very low) rateable value of the property – are to be reduced for ordinary 'non-company' owners to between 0.2 and 0.8 per cent of the new, revised value. This will probably still mean a steep increase in the amount actually payable for most people, as it is so long since the properties were revalued. But offshore company owners will pay five per cent of the new valuation. This will increase the average bill for a four-bedroom house on the Algarve from, say, €1,000 to perhaps €10,000.

In short, if you are thinking of buying a home in Portugal, the 'offshore company' route probably isn't a great idea.

If you already own a property in this way, take immediate and detailed legal advice. There are a number of options available to you – none hugely attractive. You can transfer the 'home' of the company to a better tax jurisdiction. There are potential legal problems in this, and of course associated costs. Many owners are therefore thinking about transferring the property back into their personal names. This is easy but expensive. SISA tax will be payable; this is typically 10 per cent of the value of the property transferred. Add on to this legal costs and the usual notary and land registry fees. In addition, you are faced with capital gains tax on the gain in value of the property from the date you bought it until the date upon which it is transferred back to you. This can be as high as 25 per cent of the gain.

There may be a limited window of opportunity to reduce the transfer costs. See your lawyer and accountant without delay.

The Use of Trusts

As a vehicle for owning a property, trusts are of little direct use.

Portuguese law does not fully recognize trusts and so the trustees who are named on the title as the owners of the property would be treated as private individual owners, having to pay all of the income, wealth and inheritance taxes applicable in their case. In a few cases this could still give some benefit but there are probably better ways of getting the same result.

This does not mean that trusts have no place for the owner of property in Portugal. A trust could still, for example, own the property via a limited company if this fitted the 'owner's' overall tax and inheritance planning objectives. Again, careful specialist advice is essential.

Which is Right for You?

The choice is of fundamental importance. If you get it wrong you will pay massively more tax than you need to, both during your lifetime and on your death. The tax consequences arise not only in Portugal but also in the UK.

For each buyer of a home in Portugal, one of the options set out above will suit you perfectly. Another might just about make sense. The rest would be an expensive waste of time and money.

The trouble is, it is not obvious which is the right choice. You need *in every case* to take advice. If your case is simple, so will be the advice. If it is complex, the time and money spent will be repaid many times over.

The Process of Buying a Property in Portugal

The Law

As you would expect, the law relating to the ownership of property is complicated. A basic textbook on Portuguese property law might extend to 500 pages. There are certain basic principles that it is helpful to understand.

1. The main legal provisions relating to property law are found in the civil code, which was introduced in 1867 but modified since, most notably in 1967. The analysis of rights reflects the essentially agrarian society of late 18th century Portugal and pays limited attention to some of the issues that, today, would seem more pressing. That has only partly been remedied by the later additions to the code.
2. The civil code declares that foreigners are to be treated in the same way as Portuguese people as far as the law is concerned.
3. Portuguese law divides property into two classes – moveable property (*bienes muebles*) and immovable property (*bienes inmuebles*). The whole basis of ownership and transfer of ownership depends on which classification property belongs to. The distinction is similar to the English concept of real and personal property *but it is not exactly the same*. Immovable property includes land and buildings, but not the shares in a company that owns land and buildings.
4. The sale of real estate located in Portugal must always be governed by Portuguese law.
5. The form of ownership of land is always absolute ownership. This is similar to what we would call freehold ownership.
6. It is possible to own the buildings – or even parts of a building – on a piece of land separately from the land itself. This is of particular relevance in the case of flats, which are owned 'freehold'.

7. Where two or more people own a piece of land or other property together they will generally own it in undivided shares (*pro indiviso*). That is to say the piece of land is not physically divided between them. Each owner may, in theory, mortgage or sell his share without the consent of the others – though the others might have certain rights of pre-emption – that is the right to buy the property in preference to any outsider.
8. Where a building or piece of land is physically divided between a number of people a condominium (*condomínio*) is created. The land is divided into privately owned parts – such as an individual flat – and communally owned areas. The management of the communally held areas is up to the owners of the privately held area, but can be delegated to someone else.
9. Transfer of ownership of real estate is usually by simple agreement. This must be in writing. That agreement binds both the parties to it but is not effective as far as the rest of the world is concerned, who are entitled to rely upon the content of the land register. Thus ownership of land can be transferred between buyer and seller, for example, by signing a sale contract even if the seller remains in possession and some of the price remains unpaid. But that ownership would not damage the interests of someone other than the buyer or seller (such as someone owed money by the seller) who is entitled to take action against the person named as owner in the land registry. Ownership can also be acquired by possession, usually for 30 years.
10. Other rights – short of ownership – can exist over land. These include rights of way, tenancies, life interests, mortgages and option contracts. Most require some sort of formality in order to be valid against third parties but they are always binding between the people who made the agreements.
11. There are two land registers. Each area maintains a tax register (*registo predial*). In this all the land in the district is divided into plots and assessed for tax purposes. The second register is the deed and mortgage register (*registo de propriedade*). Not all land is registered here. The entries (size, boundaries, etc.) do not necessarily correspond in the two registries.

General Procedure

The general procedure when buying a property in Portugal seems, at first glance, similar to the purchase of a property in the UK. Sign a contract. Do some checks. Sign a deed of title. This is deceptive. The procedure is very different and even the use of the familiar English vocabulary to describe the very different steps in Portugal can produce an undesirable sense of familiarity with the procedure. This can lead to assumptions that things that have not been discussed will be the same as they would in the UK. This would be a wrong and dangerous assumption. *Work on the basis that the system is totally different.*

Choosing a Lawyer

The Notary Public (*Notário*)

The notary is a special type of lawyer. They are in part public officials but also in business, making their living from the fees they charges for their services. Notaries also exist in England but they are seldom used in day-to-day transactions.

Under Portuguese law, only deeds of sale (*escrituras públicas de compra e venda*) approved and witnessed by a notary can be registered at the land registry. Although it is possible to transfer legal ownership of property such as a house or apartment by a private agreement not witnessed by the notary, and although that agreement will be fully binding on the people who made it, it will not be binding on third parties. Third parties – including people who want to make a claim against the property and banks wanting to lend money on the strength of the property – are entitled to rely upon the details of ownership recorded at the land registry (*registo de la propriedade*). So if you are not registered as the owner of the property you are at risk. Thus, practically speaking, all sales of real estate in Portugal must be witnessed by a notary.

The notary also carries out certain checks on property sold and has some duties as tax enforcer and validator of documents to be presented for registration.

His fee is fixed by law, and is modest. For each signatory to the title, he is paid €11 plus a fee for the deed of a fixed €175, irrespective of value. Notaries are challenging this level of fees and they have threatened to go on strike to secure better payment.

Notaries are strictly neutral. They are more a referee than someone fighting on your behalf. They are usually someone who checks the papers to make sure that they comply with the strict rules as to content and so will be accepted by the land registry for registration.

Many Portuguese notaries, particularly in rural areas, do not speak English well enough to discuss complex issues. Very few will know anything about English law and so will be unable to tell you about the tax and other consequences *in the UK* of your plans to buy a house in Portugal. In any case, it is not their job to do so and the buyer will, anyway, seldom meet the notary before the signing ceremony and so there is little scope for seeking detailed advice. It is, in any case, rare for notaries to offer any comprehensive advice or explanation, least of all in writing, to the buyer.

For the English buyer the notary is no substitute for also using the services of a specialist UK lawyer familiar with Portuguese law and international property transactions. This is the clear advice of every guidebook, of the Portuguese and British governments and of the Federation of Overseas Property Developers, Agents and Consultants (FOPDAC). It is therefore baffling why so many people buying a property in Portugal do not take this necessary step.

Portuguese Lawyers (*Advogados*)

Most Portuguese people buying a home in Portugal will not use the services of a lawyer (as opposed to the notary public (*notário*)) unless there is something unusual or contentious about the transaction.

English Lawyers (Solicitors)

For English people, the services of the notary are unlikely to give them all the information or help they need to buy a home in Portugal. They will often require advice about inheritance issues, the UK tax implications of their purchase, how to save taxes, surveys, mortgages, currency exchange, etc. which is outside the scope of the service of the notary. They should retain the services of a specialist UK lawyer familiar with dealing with these issues. The buyer's usual solicitor is unlikely to be able to help as there are only a handful of English law firms with the necessary expertise.

The Price

This can be freely agreed between the parties. Depending on the economic climate, there may be ample or very little room for negotiating a reduction in the asking price. At the time of writing (summer 2003) the scope is limited for popularly priced properties in the main cities and tourist areas, which are in short supply.

How Much Should Be Declared in the Deed of Sale?

For many years there was a tradition in Portugal (and other Latin countries) of under-declaring the price actually paid for a property when signing the deed of sale (*escritura*). This was because the taxes and lawyers' fees due were calculated on the basis of the price declared. Lower price, less property transfer taxes for the buyer and less capital gains tax for the seller. Often the price declared was only a quarter of the price actually paid. The days of major under-declarations have now largely gone. In rural areas you can still sometimes come under pressure to under-declare to a significant extent, but it is now rarer. In many areas the seller will still suggest some more modest form of under-declaration. Large under-declaration is illegal and foolish. There are severe penalties. There are fines and penalties for late payment. In addition, unless when you sell your buyer under-declares, you create an entirely artificial capital gain for yourself – taxed, typically, at 25 per cent.

At the moment most buyers are declaring values of between 66 and 80 per cent of the true value. The more enlightened are pressing for higher amounts.

Nonetheless, you may find that you have little choice but to under-declare. The seller will often refuse to sell unless you do. Fortunately, there is a semi-legitimate 'grey area' for manoeuvre over declared price, rather like doing 40 mph in a 30 limit. It is wrong but you will not get into serious trouble. It is better not to go there at all, though. Apart from the tax issues, there are other practical problems. In a world of anti-money laundering legislation and terrorism such irregular transactions may well be reported to the authorities, with the result that (at best) you are forever branded a 'dodgy person'. You cannot, these days, simply place £50,000 in someone's bank account – or even take it out of your own – without generating paperwork that you might not want to generate, but people have been mugged or killed while dealing with cash, and the exchange rates for cash are very poor. You cannot take cash freely from one country to another. If you try and are caught, the money may be confiscated. At best, you will have to file the necessary declarations and pay the necessary tax to get it back. Increasingly, lawyers and others are refusing to touch 'black' money. Seek advice from your lawyer.

Where Must the Money Be Paid?

The price, together with the taxes and fees payable, is usually paid by the buyer to the seller in front of the notary. This is the best and safest way. You can, in fact, agree to pay in whatever way and wherever you please. So, for example, in the case of a British seller and a British buyer the payment could be made in sterling by bank transfer.

Try to avoid arrangements, usually as part of an under-declaration, where part of the money is handed over in cash in brown-paper parcels. Apart from being illegal, it is dangerous at a practical level; buyers have lost the bundle – or been robbed on the way to the notary's office. Sometimes there is a suspicion that the seller, who knew where you were going to be and when, could be involved.

General Enquiries and Special Enquiries

Certain enquiries are made routinely in the course of the purchase of a property.

These include, in appropriate cases, a check on the planning situation of the property. This inquiry will reveal the position of the property itself but it will not, at least directly, tell you about its neighbours and it will not reveal general plans for the area.

If you want to know whether the authorities are going to put a prison in the village or run a new motorway through your back garden (both, presumably, bad things) or build a motorway access point 3km away (presumably a good thing) you will need to ask. There are various organizations you can approach but, just as in the UK, there is no single point of contact for such enquiries. If you are concerned about what might happen in the area then you will need to discuss the position with your lawyers at an early stage. There may be a considerable amount of work (and therefore cost) involved in making full enquiries, the results of which can never be guaranteed.

Normal enquiries also include a check that the seller is the registered owner of the property and that it is sold (if this has been agreed) free of mortgages or other charges.

In order to advise you what special enquiries might be appropriate, your lawyer will need to be told your proposals for the property. Do you intend to let it out? If so, will you do this commercially? Do you intend to use it for business purposes? Do you want to extend or modify the exterior of the property? Do you intend to make interior structural alterations?

Agree in advance the additional enquiries you would like to make and get an estimate of the cost of them.

The Community of Owners (*Comunidade de Proprietários*)

This is a device familiar in continental Europe but most unusual in the UK.

The basic idea is that when a number of people own land or buildings in such a way that they have exclusive use of part of the property but shared use of the rest, then a *comunidade* is created. Houses on their own plots with no shared facilities will not be a member of a *comunidade*.

In a *comunidade*, the buyer of a house or an apartment owns his own house or apartment outright – as the English would say, 'freehold' – and shares the use of the remaining areas as part of a community of owners. It is not only the shared pool that is jointly owned but (in an apartment) the lift shafts, corridors, roof, foundations, entrance areas, parking zones, etc.

The members of the *comunidade* are each responsible for their own home. They collectively agree the works needed on the common areas and a budget for those works. They then become responsible for paying their share of those common expenses, as stipulated in their title.

The community is managed by an elected committee and appoints a president and secretary – both of whom are residents in the community.

Day-to-day management is usually delegated to an administrator, who need not be a resident in the community.

The charges of the *comunidade* are divided in the proportions stipulated in deed creating the *comunidade*. You will pay the same *comunidade* fees whether you use the place all year round or only for two weeks' holiday. Of course, your other bills (water, electricity, etc.) will vary with usage.

The *comunidade* should provide not only for routine work but, through its fees, set aside money for periodic major repairs. If they do not – or if the amount set aside is inadequate – the general meeting can authorize a supplemental levy to raise the sums needed.

The rules set by the *comunidade* (the *regulamentos do condomínio*) are intended to improve the quality of life of residents. They could, for example, deal with concerns over noise (no radios by the pool), prohibit the use of the pool after 10pm, ban the hanging of washing on balconies, etc. More importantly they could ban pets or any commercial activity in the building. These regulations are an important document. Every buyer of a property in a *comunidade* should insist on a copy of the rules. If you do not speak Portuguese you should have them translated, or at least summarized in English.

Initial Contracts

In Portugal, most sales start with a preliminary contract. The type of contract will depend upon whether you are buying a finished or an unfinished property. Signing any of these documents has far-reaching legal consequences, which are sometimes different from the consequences of signing a similar document in the UK. Whichever type of contract you are asked to sign, always seek legal advice before signing.

Generally, the preliminary contract is prepared by the estate agent – who is professionally qualified in Portugal – or by the developer. Estate agents' contracts are often based on a pre-printed document in a standard format.

Some contracts originating from estate agents – especially the unqualified and, therefore, illegal agency – are legally muddled and not properly thought through. They can blur or mix different types of contractual obligation, often referring to mutually exclusive concepts in the same document – for example, referring to it as a contract of sale and an option contract.

Sometimes the contracts are extremely one-sided, giving their client – the seller – all the rights and taking away all the rights of the buyer.

It is very important that these contracts are not just accepted as final. In every case they will need to be modified, in some cases extensively.

If You Are Buying a Finished Property

You will be invited to sign one of two different documents. Each has different features. Each has different legal consequences. Each is appropriate in certain circumstances and inappropriate in others.

Reservation/Option Contract

This is a written document in which the seller offers to take a stated property off the market for a fixed period and to sell it at a stated price to a stated person at any time within a stated period.

Sellers will usually require that any person taking up their offer pays them a deposit. Once they have received this deposit, the seller must reserve the property for you until the end of the period specified in the contract.

You will see that this is similar to an English 'option contract'. If you want to go ahead and buy the property, you can, but you are not obliged to do so. If you do not go ahead you lose your deposit.

The contract could contain special 'get-out clauses' stipulating the circumstances in which the buyer will be entitled to the refund of his deposit if he decides not to go ahead. The drafting of these clauses is of vital importance. See your lawyer.

If you do want to go ahead, you can exercise the option at any point up to the end of the agreed period. If the seller refuses to go ahead the buyer is entitled to claim compensation. If you do not go ahead with the purchase the seller will keep the reservation fee.

Full Contract (*Contrato Promessa*)

In most parts of Portugal this is the most common type of document.

It is called a *contrato promessa* (promissory contract) not because it is secret but because it is not recorded in the public register kept by a notary.

It is an agreement that commits both parties. The seller must sell a stated property at a stated price to a stated person on the terms set out in the contract. The buyer must buy.

This is the more far-reaching of the documents and so it is particularly important that you are satisfied that it contains all of the terms necessary to protect your position. Take legal advice. Remember that under Portuguese law by signing and completing this contract you become, in some senses, the owner of the property, although you will need to sign a deed of sale (*escritura*) and register your ownership to be safe as far as third parties are concerned.

The contract will contain a variety of 'routine' clauses.

- **The names of the seller and buyer should both be stated fully.**
- **The property should be described fully, both in an everyday sense and by reference to its land registry details.**
- **A date for the signing of the deed of sale (*escritura*) will be fixed or the contract will permit either party to require the signing of the *escritura* at any point by giving notice to the other.**
- **A statement will be made as to when possession will take place – normally on the date of signing the title.**
- **The price is fixed.**
- **A receipt for any deposit is given.**
- **The property should be sold with vacant possession.**

- **The property should be sold free of any charges, debts or burdens and all bills should be paid up to date before signing the *escritura*.**
- **It will provide for who is to pay the costs of the purchase.**
- **It may confirm the details of any agent involved and who is to pay his commission.**
- **It will set out what is to happen if one or both of the parties break the contract.**
- **It will establish the law to cover the contract and the address of the parties for legal purposes.**

If the buyer or seller drops out of the contract or otherwise breaks it, various arrangements may be made. A deposit (*sinal*) is payable by the buyer. This is typically 10 per cent, occasionally more. If the buyer fails to complete, he will lose the deposit. If the seller fails to complete he will have to return (usually) double the deposit paid.

Alternatively, the contract may provide for a deposit to be paid as a simple part of the price of the property. The contract can provide for all or part of this deposit – and any other sums paid up to the relevant moment – to be lost if the buyer does not proceed.

If the parties fail to comply with their obligations there is the ultimate remedy of seeking a court order. As in any country, this is very much a last resort, as it is costly, time-consuming and (as in any country) there is no guarantee of the outcome of a court case. If a court order is made in your favour, this order can be registered at the land registry.

If You Are Buying an Unfinished Property

Full Contract

There are three possible types of contract in this case.

- **Contract for immediate sale of the land.**

You sign a contract agreeing to sign title deed in respect of the land – and anything the seller has so far built on it – now. This involves paying for the land and work so far undertaken in full at this stage. At the same time you enter into a contract to build your house on the land.

As the building continues, it automatically becomes the property of the buyer. The buyer, of course, is under an obligation to pay the agreed price, usually by instalments dependent upon the progress of the building work.

This has the great advantage of securing the money you pay to the builder. If the builder goes bust, you own the land and everything built on it. It only really works for property built on its own plot rather than, say, apartments. It can be tax- and cost-inefficient.

- **Contract 'on plan'.**

You agree to buy a property once it has been built and agree to make payments in stages as the construction progresses. Sometimes the payments are dependent upon the progress of the building works. On other occasions they are due on set dates. The latter are now the more common, though less attractive to the buyer.

Once the property has been built, you will sign the deed of sale and pay the balance of the price. It is only then that you become the owner of the property and register your title. Until then, if the builder goes bust you are simply one of many creditors.

The law requires that the contract must give details of a guarantee to secure completion of the construction in the event, for example, that the seller goes bust. In most parts of Portugal, these guarantees are furnished with no problems. In other places, builders simply refuse to give the guarantee. 'I am your guarantee. I am a man of honour. I have been building for over 30 years!' This is part of the commonplace experience in Portugal of the law saying one thing but people blatantly doing something entirely different. Why do they do it? They think that they save money (guarantees have to be paid for and the bank will probably not release all the money until the property is finished) and they think the law is a bureaucratic imposition. Most of these areas were poor and backward. The peasant mentality of 'build now, paperwork later' still prevails although the peasants are now multi-millionaires! Remember that big companies and honourable men go bust: Rolls-Royce, Barings Bank, Enron.

- **Contract to buy once the property has been built.**

You agree to buy a plot of land and building. You agree to pay once it has been built. Simple! You take title and pay the money at the same time. This is really the same as buying a resale property. This type of contract is little used.

Reservation Contract

Usually in these cases there is a preliminary contract. This is the reservation contract (*see* p.153 above). This allows you to reserve a plot when you see it and allows you time to sign one of the other types of contract when you have made the necessary enquiries.

Other Documentation

Has the property got planning permission/a building licence?

You should be given a full specification for the property, a copy of the community rules and constitution if the property shares common facilities, and a copy of any agreements you have entered into regarding ongoing management or letting of the property. All are important documents. Pay particular attention to the specification. It is not unknown for the show flat to have marble floors and high quality wooden kitchens but for the specification to show concrete tiles and MDF.

Checklist – Signing a Contract

<table>
<tr><th>Property in the Course of Construction</th><th>Existing Property</th></tr>
<tr><td colspan="2">Are you clear about what you are buying?</td></tr>
<tr><td colspan="2">Have you taken legal advice about who should be the owner of the property?</td></tr>
<tr><td colspan="2">Have you taken legal advice about inheritance issues?</td></tr>
<tr><td colspan="2">Are you clear about boundaries?</td></tr>
<tr><td colspan="2">Are you clear about access?</td></tr>
<tr><td colspan="2">Have you seen the seller's escritura (title)?</td></tr>
<tr><td colspan="2">Have you seen an up-to-date nota simple (land registry extract)?</td></tr>
<tr><td></td><td>Are you sure you can change the property as you want?</td></tr>
<tr><td></td><td>Are you sure you can use the property for what you want?</td></tr>
<tr><td></td><td>Is the property connected to water, electricity, gas, etc.?</td></tr>
<tr><td></td><td>Have you had a survey done?</td></tr>
<tr><td colspan="2">Have you made all necessary checks or arranged for them to be made?</td></tr>
<tr><td colspan="2">Have you included 'get-out' clauses for all important checks not yet made?</td></tr>
<tr><td colspan="2">Is your mortgage finance arranged?</td></tr>
<tr><td colspan="2">Is the seller clearly described?</td></tr>
<tr><td colspan="2">If the seller is not signing in person, have you seen a power of attorney/mandate to authorize the sale?</td></tr>
<tr><td colspan="2">Are you fully described?</td></tr>
<tr><td colspan="2">Is the property fully described? Identification? Land registry details?</td></tr>
<tr><td colspan="2">Is the price correct?</td></tr>
<tr><td colspan="2">Are there any possible circumstances in which it can be increased or extras described fully?</td></tr>
<tr><td>Are the stage payments fully described?</td><td>Does the contract say when possession will be given?</td></tr>
<tr><td>Are arrangements for stage payments satisfactory?</td><td>Is there a receipt for the deposit paid?</td></tr>
<tr><td>Is the date for completion of the work agreed?</td><td>In what capacity is the deposit paid?</td></tr>
<tr><td>Does the property have planning permission/licence to build?</td><td>Does the property have a habitation licence?</td></tr>
<tr><td colspan="2">Is the date for signing the escritura agreed?</td></tr>
<tr><td colspan="2">Does the contract provide for the sale to be free of charges and debts?</td></tr>
<tr><td colspan="2">Does the contract provide for vacant possession?</td></tr>
<tr><td colspan="2">Which notary is to act?</td></tr>
<tr><td colspan="2">Is the estate agent's commission dealt with?</td></tr>
<tr><td colspan="2">What happens if there is a breach of contract?</td></tr>
<tr><td colspan="2">Are all the necessary special 'get-out' clauses included?</td></tr>
</table>

Steps between Signing the Contract and Signing the *Escritura de Compra e Venda*

Provisional Registration

This notifies any other person that a purchase is in progress. Anything that person does is done subject to whatever rights ultimately flow from the contract to buy. Once registered it lasts for six months, within which time the *escritura* should be signed and presented for registration.

You need to weigh up the additional cost of this process against the benefits that flow from it.

Power of Attorney (*Poder Geral na Procuração*)

Very often it will not be convenient for you to go to Portugal to sign the *escritura* in person. Sometimes there may be other things that, in the normal course of events, would require your personal intervention but where it would be inconvenient for you to have to deal with them yourself.

Just as often you will not know whether you will be available to sign in person. Completion dates on Portuguese property are notoriously fluid and so you could plan to be there but suffer a last-minute delay to the signing that makes it impossible.

The solution to this problem is the power of attorney. This document authorizes the person appointed to do whatever the document authorizes on behalf of the person granting the power.

The most sensible type of power to use will be the Portuguese style of power that is appropriate to the situation. The power will be signed in front of a notary either in the UK or in Portugal. If it is signed in front of a UK notary, it has to be ratified by, of all people, the Foreign and Commonwealth Office for use overseas. This sounds very grand but is actually quick and simple.

The type of Portuguese power of attorney that you will need depends on what you want to use it for. Your specialist English lawyer can discuss your requirements with you and prepare the necessary document. Alternatively, you can deal directly with the Portuguese notary who will ultimately need the power.

In theory, an English-style power should be sufficient, but in practice the cost and delay associated with getting it recognized are likely to be unacceptable.

Even if you intend to go to Portugal to sign, it is sensible to think about granting a power 'just in case'. It is not something that can be done at the last moment. From decision to getting the document to Portugal will take at least seven and more likely 10 days. If you are able to go, the power will not be used.

Even if you have granted a power of attorney, if you get the opportunity to go to Portugal at the time of the signing it is worth doing so. It is quite interesting but, more importantly, you will be able to check the house to make sure that everything is in order before the *escritura* is signed.

Tax Identification Number

To own a property in Portugal you need to obtain a NIF (*número de identificação fisca*) – tax identification number. This is obtained from any Portuguese tax office – usually from the tax office near to where you are buying your property. You will need to fill in a simple form and produce your passport and two passport photographs. Alternatively, your lawyer can obtain this for you.

Getting the Money to Portugal

There are a number of ways of getting the money to Portugal.

Electronic Transfer

The most practical is to have it sent electronically by SWIFT transfer from a UK bank directly to the recipient's bank in Portugal. This costs about £20–35, depending on your bank. It is safest to allow two or three days for the money to arrive in a rural bank, despite everyone's protestations that it will be there the same day.

Europe has introduced unique account numbers for all bank accounts. These incorporate a code for the identity of the bank and branch involved as well as the account number of the individual customer. These are known as IBAN numbers. They should be quoted, if possible, on all international currency transfers.

You can send the money from your own bank, via your lawyers or via a specialist currency dealer.

For the sums you are likely to be sending you should receive an exchange rate much better than the 'tourist rate' you see in the press. There is no such thing as a fixed exchange rate in these transactions. The bank's official inter-bank rate changes by the second and the job of the bank's currency dealers is to make a profit by selling to you at the lowest rate they can get away with! Thus, if you do a lot of business with a bank and they know you are on the ball you are likely to be offered a better rate than a one-off customer. For this reason it is often better to send it via your specialist UK lawyers, who will be dealing with large numbers of such transactions. This also has the advantage that their bank, which deals with international payments all the time, is less likely to make a mistake causing delay to the payment than your bank for which such a payment might be a rarity.

You or your lawyers might use a specialist currency dealer to make the transfer of funds instead of a main UK bank. Such dealers often give a better exchange rate than an ordinary bank. Sometimes the difference can be significant, especially compared to your local branch of a high street bank. The author recently carried out a spot check. His secretary, anonymously, asked a major high street bank to convert £50,000 into euros and send it to Portugal. They offered a rate of 1.6125. A currency dealer offered 1.6311 (a saving of €930 – or £575).

Although these dealers use major banks actually to transfer the funds, you need to make sure that your dealer is reputable. Your money is paid to them, not to the major bank, so could be at risk if the dealer was not bonded or otherwise protected.

However you make the payment, make sure you understand whether you or the recipient is going to pick up the receiving bank's charges. If you need a clear amount in Portugal, you will have to make allowances for these, either by sending a bit extra or by asking your UK bank to pay all the charges. Make sure you have the details of the recipient bank, its customer's name, the account codes and the recipient's reference precisely right. Any error and the payment is likely to come back to you as undeliverable – and may involve you in bearing the cost of it being converted back into sterling.

The bank in Portugal will make a charge – which can be substantial – for receiving your money into your account.

Bankers' Drafts

You can arrange for your UK bank to issue you with a banker's draft (bank certified cheque) which you can take to Portugal and pay into your bank account. Make sure that the bank knows that the draft is to be used overseas and issues you with an international draft.

Generally this is not a good way to transfer the money. It can take a considerable time – sometimes weeks – for the funds deposited to be made available for your use. The recipient bank's charges can be surprisingly high. The exchange rate offered against a sterling draft may be uncompetitive as you are a captive customer.

Cash

This is not recommended. You will need to declare the money on departure from the UK and on arrival in Portugal. You must by law do this if the sum involved is over €8,000. You are well advised to do so for smaller amounts. Even then, if you declare £200,000 or so they will think you are a terrorist or drug dealer. That suspicion can have far-reaching consequences in terms of listings in police files and even surveillance. To add insult to injury, the exchange rate you will be offered for cash (whether you take sterling and convert there or buy the euros here) is usually very uncompetitive and the notary may well refuse to accept the money in his account. Don't do it.

Exchange Control and Other Restrictions on Moving Money

For EU nationals there is no longer any exchange control when taking money to or from Portugal. There are some statistical records kept showing the flow of funds and the purpose of the transfers.

When you sell your property in Portugal you will be able to bring the money back to the UK if you wish to do so.

Final Checks about the Property

All of the points outstanding must be resolved to your satisfaction, as must any other points of importance to you.

Fixing the Completion Date

The date stated in the contract for signing the *escritura* could, most charitably, be described as flexible or aspirational. Often it will move, if only by a day or so. For this reason it is not sensible to book your travel to Portugal until you are almost sure that matters will proceed on a certain day.

Checklist – Steps Before Completion

Property in the Course of Construction	**Existing Property**
Prepare power of attorney	
Check what documents must be produced on signing the *escritura*	
Confirm all outstanding issues have been complied with	
Confirm all other important enquiries are clear	
Confirm arrangements (date, time, place) for completion with your lender if you have a mortgage	
Confirm arrangements (date, time, place) for completion with notary	
Send necessary funds to Portugal	
Receive rules of community	
Insurance cover arranged?	
Sign off work or list defects	Proof of payment of community fees
	Proof of payment of other bills

Paying the Taxes

Before the deed is signed, the SISA (property transfer) tax must be paid. A receipt for the payment is produced to the notary who witnesses the *escritura*.

The Deed of Sale (*Escritura*)

This must be signed in front of a Portuguese notary either by the parties in person or someone holding power of attorney for them.

It will contain a statement that the notary has advised you of your fiscal obligations arising out of the sale. Because it is rare for notaries actually to perform this important part of their duty it is worth setting out some of these sanctions.

1. The right to raise a supplemental demand for tax not paid plus interest plus penalty.

2. If the amount declared is less than 80 per cent of the value as assessed by the tax office – or the apparent under-declaration exceeds €12,000 – to treat the balance as a gift from the seller to the buyer. This is a *taxable* gift.
3. If there is a clear and intentional understatement, the right to buy the property at the price stated.

There are other consequences of under-declaration, referred to above.

Formalities

Certain procedures are followed at the signing of the *escritura*.

The parties are identified by their passports or identity cards. This will normally be done, initially, by the notary's clerk and then also by the notary.

The notary's clerk may also go through the content of the *escritura* with the parties. This tends to be very superficial and often the person concerned will have limited English.

The parties will then be ushered into the presence of the notary. In addition to the buyer and seller, the group could also comprise the notary's clerk, your lawyer, a translator, a representative of your mortgage lender, the estate agent and any sub-agent appointed by the estate agent. Most of these people are there to receive money. Needless to say, if they all turn up it can get a little loud and confusing.

If you do not speak Portuguese an interpreter should be present when you sign the *escritura*. The attitude of notaries when it comes to assessing when an interpreter is necessary varies enormously. No written translation is provided as a matter of course.

After the *Escritura* Has Been Signed

Your title and any mortgage should be presented for registration at the land registry. This should be done as quickly as possible. He who registers first gets priority. After several months the land registry will issue a certificate to the effect that the title has been registered.

The Cost of Buying a Property in Portugal

There are fees and taxes payable by a buyer when acquiring a property in Portugal. They are sometimes known as completion expenses or completion or closing costs. They are impossible to predict with total accuracy at the outset of a transaction. This is because there are a number of variable factors that will not become clear until later. We can, however, give a general guide.

These costs are calculated on the basis of the price that you declared as the price paid for the property in the *escritura*. The size of these expenses, coupled with the Portuguese dislike for paying tax, has led to the habit of 'accidentally' under-declaring the price in the *escritura*. These days are now largely over and it is recommended that the full price of the property is declared. *See* 'How Much Should be Declared in the Deed of Sale', pp.149–50.

Notary's Fees

These are fixed by law, so are not negotiable. They are modest.

Property Transfer Tax (SISA)

This is charged instead of VAT on properties bought from private individuals. The rate is usually 10 per cent, depending on the type of property and its value.

SISA Tax Rates

Property Value	Tax Rate	Deduct from Sum Payable
Up to €60,015.49	0%	Nil
From €60,015.49 to €82,207.38	5%	€3,000.77
From €82,207.38 to €109,678.18	11%	€7,933.22
From €109,678.18 to €137,097.72	18%	€15,610.69
From €137,097.72 to €166,054.81	26%	€26,578.51
Over €166,064.81	10%	Nil

e.g. Property value €70,000.
Tax rate 5%
Tax due €3,500
Deduct €3000.7.
Pay €499.33

Since drafting this book, the SISA tax rules have been replaced. It is not yet clear from which date the new rules will take effect; it could be any time up to December 2003. The new rules, which have yet to be finalized, can be summarized as follows:

- **SISA will be replaced by what will be known as a municipal tax over transactions or IMT.**
- **Several uncertainties remain as to the finer details of the new tax.**
- **Properties valued at €80,000 or under will be exempt from any initial taxes.**
- **In addition, the maximum rate will be dropped from 10 per cent of the value of the property to 6 per cent, while this top rate will only be applied to properties whose value exceed €500,000 (currently, any property priced at**

€170,000 or more was liable to pay the maximum rate).

Value of the Transaction	Tax Rate	Deduct from Sum Payable
Under €80,000	0%	€0
From €80,000 to €110,000	2%	€1,600.00
From €110,000 to €150,000	5%	€4,900.00
From €150,000 to €250,000	7%	€7,900.50
From €250,000 to €500,000	8%	€10,400.00
Over €500,000	6%	€0

Rates will also drop for the annual municipal tax (*contribuição autárquica*). Currently, this annual tax is charged at a rate varying between 0.7 and 1.3 per cent of the property's value. The new system will discriminate between new and old homes, with newer homes being charged between 0.2 and 0.5 per cent of their respective values, while older properties will be subjected to a rate that varies between 0.4 and 0.8 per cent.

Enforcement of the new municipal tax, previously the sole responsibility of the local tax department, will now be passed on to city and town halls, who will be granted the authority to evaluate a property and adjudicate on potential tax benefits, such as the 10-year exemption from paying municipal tax.

Land Registration Fees

This is normally 0.8 per cent of the price of the property.

Mortgage Costs (if Applicable)

If you are taking out a mortgage, there will be additional costs. *See* 'Raising Finance to Buy a Property in Portugal', pp.132–40. These typically amount, altogether, to about 4 per cent of the amount borrowed.

Miscellaneous Other Charges

Architect's fees, surveyor's fees, UK legal fees (typically 1 per cent), first connection to water, electricity, etc. Most of these will be subject to Portuguese IVA at 19 per cent, but your UK lawyer's fees will be outside the scope of English VAT.

Key Points

Property Under Construction

When buying a new property the key points to look out for are the following:

- **Make sure you understand exactly what you are buying. How big is the property? What will it look like? How will it be finished? What appliances are included? What facilities will it enjoy?**
- **Think about who should own the property so as to minimize tax and inheritance problems.**
- **Make sure the contract has all of the necessary clauses required to protect your position.**
- **Make sure there is a bank guarantee if you are buying 'off plan'.**
- **Be clear about the timetable for making payments.**
- **Think about whether you should forward-buy currency.**
- **When you take delivery of the property, consider carefully whether it is worth incurring the expense of an independent survey to confirm that all is in order with the construction and to help draft any 'snagging list'.**

Resale Properties

When buying a resale property, the key points to look out for are the following:

- **Make sure you understand exactly what you are buying. Are the boundaries clear? What furniture or fittings are included?**
- **Think about whether to have the property surveyed, especially if it is nearly 10 years old and your statutory guarantee will soon be expiring.**
- **Think about who should own the property so as to minimize tax and inheritance problems.**
- **Make sure the contract has all the necessary clauses required to protect your position.**
- **Think about whether you should forward-buy currency.**
- **When you take delivery of the property, make sure that everything agreed is present.**

Special Points – Old Properties

When buying an old property – by which is meant a property built more than, say, 50 years ago – there are one or two additional special points to look out for:

- **Are you having a survey? Not to do so can be an expensive mistake.**
- **Are you clear about any restoration costs to be incurred? Do you have estimates for those charges?**

• Are there any planning problems associated with any alterations or improvements you want to make to the property?

• When you take delivery of the property, make sure that everything agreed is present.

Special Points – Rural Properties

• Such properties have often acquired a number of rights and obligations over the years. Are you clear about any obligations you might be taking on?

• You are probably buying for peace and quiet and the rural idyll. Are you sure that nothing is happening in the vicinity of your property that will be detrimental?

• If you have any plans to change the property or to use it for other purposes, will this be permitted?

• If you intend to build on the site, be very clear about minimum permitted plot sizes – which can vary up to 25,000m² – and other planning limitations.

Special Points – City Properties

• City properties will usually be apartments, *see* further below.

• Unless you are used to living in a city – and, in particular, a continental city – do not underestimate the noise that will be generated nearby. If you are in a busy area (and you are likely to be) this will go on until late at night. How good is the sound insulation?

• Are your neighbouring properties occupied by full-time residents, are they weekday-only '*pied-à-terre*'s or are they holiday homes? Think about security issues.

• If you intend to use a car, where will you park?

Special Points – Apartments and Houses Sharing Facilities

• Have you thought about having a survey of the property? Will it include the common parts? This can be expensive.

• Make sure you understand the rules of the community – *see* below.

• Make sure you understand the charges raised by the community.

• Make contact with the property's administrator. Ask about any issues affecting the community. Are there any major works approved but not yet carried out? Make sure that the contract is clear about who is responsible for paying for these.

• Make contact with owners. Are they happy with the community and the way it is run? Remember that no one is ever fully happy!

- **Understand how the community is run. Once you are an owner, try to attend the general meetings of the community.**

Other Things to Do When You Buy a Property

- **Insure the property and its contents.**
- **Make a full photographic record of the property. This is useful in the event of an insurance claim and for your scrap book.**
- **Make arrangements for your bank to pay your local property tax, water and electricity bills, etc.**
- **Make a will in the Portuguese form covering your assets in Portugal. This will usually mean making small changes in your existing UK will as well.**
- **Appoint a fiscal representative. This is your point of contact with the Portuguese tax office. He will also usually complete and file your annual tax return. Your lawyer may provide this service or should be able to suggest a suitable person.**

Financial Implications

John Howell
Solicitor and International Lawyer
John Howell & Co

06

Taxation

Introduction

All tax systems are complicated. The Portuguese system is no exception. The Portuguese would say that it is nearly as complex as ours. Fortunately, most people will only have limited contact with the more intricate parts of the system. For many owners of holiday homes in Portugal their contact with the system will be minimal.

It is helpful to have some sort of understanding about the way the system works and the taxes that you might face. Be warned: getting even a basic understanding will make your head hurt. You also need to be particularly careful about words and concepts that seem familiar to you but which have a fundamentally different meaning in Portugal. Of course, just to confuse you, the rules change every year.

There are several points in this book where it is emphasized that the contents are only a general introduction to the subject. Nowhere is this more true than in this section. Books (and lengthy ones at that) have been written about the subject of Portuguese taxation. This general introduction does little more than scratch the surface of an immensely complex subject. It is intended to allow you to have a sensible discussion with your professional advisers and, perhaps, to help you work out the questions you need to be asking them. It is *not* intended as a substitute for proper professional advice.

When you have a foot in two countries, and particularly when you are moving permanently from one country to another, your situation involves the consideration of the tax systems in both countries with a view to minimizing your tax obligations in both. It is not just a question of paying the lowest amount of tax in, say, Portugal. The best choice in Portugal could be very damaging to your position in the UK. Similarly the most tax-efficient way of dealing with your affairs in the UK could be problematic in Portugal. The task of the international adviser and his client is to find a path of compromise which allows you to enjoy the major advantages available in both countries without incurring any of the worst drawbacks. There is no perfect solution to most tax questions. That is not to say that there are not a great many bad solutions into which you can all too easily stumble.

What should guide you when making a decision as to which course to pursue? Each individual will have a different set of priorities. Some are keen to screw the last ha'penny of advantage out of their situation. Others recognize that they will have to pay some tax but simply wish to moderate their tax bill. For many the main concern is a simple structure which they understand and can continue to manage without further assistance in the years ahead. Just as different clients have different requirements, so different advisers have differing views as to the function of the adviser when dealing with a client's tax affairs. One of your first tasks when speaking to your financial adviser should be to discuss your basic philosophy concerning the payment of tax and management of your affairs, to make sure that you are both operating with the same objective in mind and that you are comfortable with his approach to solving your problem.

Are You Resident or Non-resident for Tax Purposes?

The biggest single factor in determining how you will be treated by the tax authorities in any country is whether you are resident in that country for tax purposes. This concept of tax residence causes a great deal of confusion.

Tax residence can have different meanings in different countries.

Let us first look at what it does not mean. It is nothing to do with whether you have registered as resident in a country or whether you have obtained a residence permit or residence card (although somebody who has a card will usually be tax resident). Nor does it have anything to do with whether you have a home (residence) in that country – although a person who is tax resident will normally have a home there. Nor is it much to do with your intentions.

Tax residence is a question of fact. The law lays down certain tests that will be used to decide whether or not you are tax resident. If you fall into the categories stipulated in the tests then you will be considered tax resident whether you want to be or not and whether it was your intention to be tax resident or not.

It is your responsibility to make your tax declarations each year. The decision as to whether you fall into the category of resident is, in the first instance, made by the tax office. If you disagree with the decision you can appeal through the courts.

Because people normally change their tax residence when they move from one country to another the basis upon which decisions are made tends to be regulated by international law and to be fairly, but not totally, consistent from country to country.

The Rules that Determine Residence

You will have to consider two different questions concerning tax residence. The first is whether you will be treated as tax resident in the UK and the second is whether you will be treated as tax resident in Portugal.

UK

It is outside the scope of this book to go into any details about UK taxation but some basic points will have to be dealt for the explanation of Portuguese taxation to make any sense.

In the UK there are two tests that will help determine where you pay tax. These assess your domicile and your residence.

Domicile

Your domicile is the place that is your real home. It is the place where you have your roots. For most people it is the place where they were born. You can change your domicile but it is often not easy to do so. Changes in domicile can have far-reaching tax consequences and can be a useful tax reduction tool.

Residence

Residence falls into two categories. Under English law there is a test of simple residence – actually living here other than on a purely temporary basis – and of ordinary residence.

A person will generally be treated as resident in the UK if he spends 183 or more days per year in the UK. A visitor will also be treated as **resident** if he comes to the UK regularly and spends significant time here. If he spends, on average over a period of four or more years, more than three months here he will be treated as tax resident.

A person can continue to be **ordinarily resident** in the UK even after he has actually ceased being resident here. A person is ordinarily resident in the UK if his presence is a little more settled. The residence is an important part of his life. It will normally have gone on for some time.

The most important thing to understand is that, once you have been ordinarily resident in this country, the simple fact of going overseas will not automatically bring that residence to an end. If you leave this country in order to take up permanent residence elsewhere then, by concession, the Inland Revenue will treat you as ceasing to be resident on the day following your departure. But they will not treat you as ceasing to be ordinarily resident if, after leaving, you spend an average of 91 or more days per year in this country over any four-year period.

In other words, they don't want you to escape too easily!

Until 1993 you were also classified as ordinarily resident in the UK if you had accommodation available for you use in the UK even though you may have spent 364 days of the year living abroad. This very unfair rule was cancelled but many people still worry about it. It is not necessary to do so provided you limit your visits to the UK to less than the 91 days referred to above.

Portugal

Tax residence in Portugal is tested by a number of rules, the main ones of which are as follows:

- **If you spend more than 183 days in Portugal in any tax year, you are tax resident in Portugal. This time can be in one block or in bits and pieces through the year. The tax year runs from 1 January to 31 December. You are then generally treated as tax resident from 1 January in that year unless your country's double taxation treaty provides otherwise.**

• If you have accommodation available in Portugal (owned or rented) on 31 December and the Portuguese tax authorities have reasonable grounds for assuming that you intend to use it in the following year as your principal residence, you will be treated as tax resident in Portugal.

• If your centre of economic interests is in Portugal you are tax resident in Portugal. Your centre of economic interests is where you have your main investments or business or other sources of income and, usually, where you spend much of your money.

• If the head of your family is resident in Portugal you will be *assumed* to be resident in Portugal unless you show the contrary. If you satisfy the taxman that you are not resident in Portugal then you will pay tax on your income and assets as a non-resident but your husband or wife will pay taxes on their income and assets as a resident. *See* below for details.

Tax Residence in More than One Country

Remember that you can be tax resident in more than one country under the respective rules of those countries. For example, you might spend 230 days in the year in Portugal and 135 days in the UK. In this case you could end up, under the rules of each country, being responsible for paying the same tax in two or more countries. This would be unfair so many countries have signed reciprocal 'Double Taxation Treaties'. The UK and Portugal have such a treaty. It contains 'tie breakers' and other provisions to decide, where there is the possibility of being required to pay tax twice, in which country any particular category of tax should be paid. *See* 'Double Taxation Treaty', pp.182–3.

Decisions You Must Make

The most basic decisions that you will have to make when planning your tax affairs is whether to cease to be resident in this country, whether to cease to be ordinarily resident in this country and whether to change your domicile to another country. Each of these has many consequences, many of which are not obvious.

The second consideration is when in the tax year to make these changes. Once again, that decision has many consequences.

For many ordinary people getting these decisions wrong can cost them tens of thousands of pounds in totally unnecessary taxation and a great deal of irritation and inconvenience. It is vital that you seek proper professional advice before making these decisions. You will need advice from specialist lawyers, accountants or financial advisers, all of whom should be able to help you.

Taxes Payable in the UK

The significance of these residence rules is that you will continue to be liable for some British taxes for as long as you are either ordinarily resident or domiciled in the UK. Put far too simply, once you have left the UK to live in Portugal:

- **You will continue to have to pay tax in the UK on any capital gains you make anywhere in the world for as long as you are ordinarily resident and domiciled in the UK.**
- **You will continue to be liable to British inheritance tax on all of your assets located anywhere in the world for as long as you remain domiciled here. This will be subject to double taxation relief (see pp.182–3). Other, more complex rules apply in certain circumstances.**
- **You will always pay UK income tax (Schedule A) on income arising from land and buildings in the UK – wherever your domicile, residence or ordinary residence.**
- **You will pay UK income tax (Schedule D) on the following basis:**
  - **Income from 'self-employed' trade or profession carried out in the UK (Cases I & II) – normally taxed in the UK in all cases if income arises in the UK.**
  - **Income from interest, annuities or other annual payments from UK (Case III) – normally taxed in the UK if income arises in the UK and you are ordinarily resident in the UK.**
  - **Income from investments and businesses outside UK (Cases IV & V) – normally only taxed in the UK if you are UK domiciled and resident or ordinarily resident in the UK.**
  - **Income from government pensions (fire, police, army, civil servant, etc.) in all cases.**
  - **Sundry profits not otherwise taxable (Case VI) arising out of land or building in the UK are always taxed in the UK.**
- **You will pay income tax on any income earned from salaried employment in the UK (Schedule E) only in respect of any earnings from duties performed in the UK unless you are resident and ordinarily resident in the UK – in which case you usually pay tax in the UK on your worldwide earnings.**

If you are only buying a holiday home and will remain primarily resident in the UK, your tax position in the UK will not change very much. You will have to declare any income you make from your Portuguese property as part of your UK tax declaration. The calculation of tax due on that income will be made in accordance with UK rules, which will result in a different taxable sum than is used by the Portuguese authorities. The UK taxman will give you full credit for the taxes already paid in Portugal. On the disposal of the property you should disclose the profit made to the UK taxman. He will again give full credit for

Portuguese tax paid. Similarly, on your death the assets in Portugal must be disclosed on the UK probate tax declaration but, once again, you will be given full credit for sums paid in Portugal.

Should You Pay Tax in Portugal?

Under Portuguese law it is your responsibility to fill in a tax return in each year when you have any taxable income.

The tax office is generally known as *Finança*. It is organized by province.

There are three key points to remember:

- **Lots of Portuguese people don't pay the taxes they owe – and view with mild derision the fact that the British do so!**
- **The rules are applied more strictly every year.**
- **If you are caught not paying the taxes you owe the penalties are substantial and the irritation can be even more substantial.**

The tax office provides a lot of help and advice – including tax forms and guidance notes – over the internet. It is, not surprisingly, almost all in Portuguese.

Local Taxes (*Contribução Autárquica*)

Both residents and non-residents pay these taxes. They are levied by the municipality where your property is located. They apply to urban and rural property and whether the property is rented out or not.

The tax rates vary according to the type of property and its value. Rural property is taxed at a lower level (0.8 per cent of the registered value) than urban property and building plots. Town halls are free, within the permitted range of 0.7–1.3 per cent of the official value of the property, to fix whatever tax rate they think appropriate for urban property.

Each property has an official value (*valor patrimonial or valor tributável*), which is recorded in the tax register (*matriz predial*). These values are, generally, very low compared with the true market value for the property as there has not been a revaluation for many years. There is likely to be a revaluation soon. This will, of course, tend to increase the level of taxes payable.

If you have bought a property that you intend to use as your own residence or to let out and you have paid SISA (property transfer tax) you will be allowed a period free of local property tax. This can be up to 10 years, depending on the *valor tributável*.

Official Tax Value of the Property	Tax Free Period (Years)
Up to €111,266.97	10
From €111,266.97 to €139,199.03	7
From €139,199.03 to €168,258.62	4
Over €168,258.62	0

Each year you will be sent a bill. If it is more than €250 you can pay in two instalments in April and September of the following year.

Other Taxes Payable in Portugal – Non-residents

In general a person who is non-resident for tax purposes has few contacts with the Portuguese tax system and they are fairly painless.

Please bear in mind the complexity of the Portuguese tax system. What follows can can only be a very brief summary of the position.

Income Tax – *Imposto sobre o Rendimento das Pessoas Singulares (IRS)*

As a non-resident you will generally only pay tax on:

- **Income generated from land and buildings located in Portugal. If you own a building in Portugal and rent it out, the Portuguese government collects the first wedge of tax from you.**
- **Income from Portuguese securities and capital invested in Portugal.**
- **Income from business activities in Portugal.**
- **Earned income if you are employed or self-employed in Portugal.**

Income tax is calculated on these amounts. Before calculating the tax due, you are allowed to deduct any social security payments made and various types of expenses. In particular, in the case of rental income, repair and maintenance costs and certain administrative expenses will be tax deductible provided they are supported by documentation.

Note that if you own your home in the name of an offshore company the company will generally pay tax at a fixed rate of 25 per cent on a notional income of 6.67 per cent of the official value of the property *whether or nor the property is actually let*. If it *is* let and the tax on the lettings would exceed this notional sum, then the larger sum is payable.

Certain withholding taxes are collected to ensure payment of what is due. For example, if you let your property the agent should keep back 25 per cent of the rent received and send it to *finanças*. You should, therefore, file your tax return and claim the appropriate allowances so as to be able to claim back any refund due.

The tax rates applicable are on a sliding scale.

The tax is calculated in tranches (*see* box, opposite). That means the tax is calculated separately on each portion.

e.g. Income €20,000
Tax payable on first €15,683 = €3,047.78
Balance of €4,317 at 34% = €1,467.78
Total payable €4,515.56
This equates to an overall rate of 22.6 per cent.

Income Tax Rates – 2003 (payable 2004)

Taxable Income	Rate	Cumulative Tax to Top of Band
Up to €4,182	12%	€501.84
From €4,182 to €6,325	14%	€801.86
From €6,325 to €15,683	24%	€3,047.78
From €15,683 to €35,071	34%	€9,639.70
From €35,071 to €52,277	38%	€16,177.98
Over €52,277	40%	

Tax on your income for the year 1 Jan–31 Dec 2003 is declared and paid in 2004.

Corporation Tax

A company will pay tax on the profits it makes from activities in Portugal but not its activities elsewhere.

The tests of company residence and these taxes are not considered further here.

Taxes on Wealth

There is no Portuguese wealth tax.

Tax on Real Estate Owned by 'Foreign' Companies in Portugal

First, a tax will be payable on deemed rentals. A legally very doubtful decision has been made to assume that all offshore companies established in more favourable tax regimes (tax havens) are renting out their villas. This is most such companies. An annual tax charge of up to 40 per cent of the deemed rental income is then levied. This is based on a deemed rental income of one-15th (6.67 per cent) of the official (rateable) value of the property. This step is subtly combined with an imminent and long overdue revaluation of rateable values. Together they will amount to a huge increase in the cost of running a property via an offshore company. While some tax deductions are available, all the bills have to be properly documented. No account is to be taken of the actual amount of any rentals, nor of whether the villa is occupied full-time by its real owner, who may be legally and resident in Portugal.

Secondly, the annual property tax – which presently ranges between 0.7 and 1.3 per cent of the (currently very low) rateable value of the property – is to be reduced for ordinary 'non-company' owners to between 0.2 and 0.8 per cent of the new, revised value. This will probably still mean a steep increase in the amount actually payable for most people as it is so long since the properties were revalued. But offshore company owners will pay five per cent of the new valuation. This will increase the average bill for a four-bedroom house on the Algarve from, say, €1,000 to perhaps €10,000: a major hit.

British companies do not have to pay this tax but 'tax haven' companies, including Channel Islands and Isle of Man companies, do.

There may be a limited window of opportunity to reduce the transfer costs. See your lawyer and accountant without delay. If your property is owned in a way that attracts this tax it is probably worth seeking advice as to how to restructure the ownership to avoid the tax.

Taxes on Capital Gains – *Imposto de Mais Valias*

You will pay tax on the capital gain you make on the sale of real estate in Portugal bought after 1989 or on any other capital gain made from property or a business in Portugal.

The apparent gain (the difference between the sale price and the purchase price) is subject to various allowances. These include the costs of purchase and sale and the **documented** value of any improvements made to the property. The resulting figure is then adjusted, effectively to reflect inflation. For these purposes there is a scale of coefficients which are applied to the price you paid for the property, depending on the year in which it was bought.

Year Bought	Coefficient
1989	1.82
1990	1.64
1991	1.45
1992	1.35
1993	1.25
1994	1.19
1995	1.14
1996	1.10
1997	1.08
1998	1.05
1999	1.03
2000	1.00
2001	1.00

Tax is payable on 50 per cent of the gain calculated in accordance with these rules. The taxable gain is treated as income in the year in which it was made and taxed at the appropriate rate.

Example

Property bought in 1995 for:	£100,000
Sold in 2001 for:	£200,000
Gain	£100,000
Adjusted by coefficient (£200,000 – (£100,000 x 1.14))	£86,000
Costs of acquisition	£12,000
Costs of disposal	£10,000
Documented improvements	£20,000

Taxable gain (£86,000 – £42,000)	£44,000
Tax payable on 50 per cent of the gain	£22,000

There is no withholding tax in respect of capital gains, so gains made by people selling and leaving Portugal have, in the past, often not actually been collected. There are indications that this will change shortly.

Taxes on Death or on Gifts – *Imposto sobre Sucessões e Doações*

Inheritance tax is paid in Portugal on the value of any assets in Portugal as at the date of your death. This includes real estate, cars and boats registered in Portugal and shares registered in Portugal.

The tax is an inheritance tax rather than, as in the UK, an estate tax. That means the tax is calculated by reference to each individual's inheritance rather than on the basis of the estate as a whole. Thus, two people each inheriting part of the estate will each pay their own tax. Even if they each inherit the same amount, the tax they pay may be different, depending on their personal circumstances.

All of the assets will have to be declared for the purposes of UK taxation. Again, double taxation relief will apply so you will not pay the same tax twice. UK tax is not further considered in this book.

The overall value of the part of the estate you inherit is calculated in accordance with guidelines laid down by the tax authorities. Assets are generally valued as at the date of the death. This valuation is declared by the person who inherits but can be challenged by the tax authorities. The death must be declared to the tax office within 30 days if the deceased lived in the area; 60 days if the person lived elsewhere in Portugal; and 180 days if the person lived overseas – e.g. in the UK. The deceased's assets must be listed and declared within 60 days of notification. The amount due can be paid at once or by instalments – but in that case interest is then charged on the amount due.

Any debts (including mortgage or overdraft) are deducted from the assets' value as are medical bills and funeral costs.

The tax payable depends, in part, on the amount you inherit and in part on your relationship to the deceased. There are four groups of relationships of the person receiving the gift:

- **Class I – minor children and grandchildren under 21 years of age.**
- **Class II – spouse, children and grandchildren over 21 years of age.**
- **Class III – parent and grandparents, brothers and sisters.**
- **Class IV – other (including same sex and common law partners).**

The tax is calculated in tranches. *See* tax rates on p.178.

The tax is paid by the person who inherits and not (as in the UK) by the estate as a whole.

Inheritance Tax Rates

The tax rates on the taxable amount of any gift are as follows:

Value	**Class I**	**Class II**	**Class III**	**Class IV**
Up to €3,641	**–**	**7%**	**13%**	**16%**
€3,641–14,625	**3%**	**10%**	**17%**	**20%**
€14,625–36,212	**6%**	**13%**	**21%**	**25%**
€36,212–71,328	**9%**	**16%**	**25%**	**30%**
€71,328–178,968	**13%**	**21%**	**31%**	**36%**
€178,968–€355,343	**17%**	**26%**	**38%**	**43%**
Over €355,343	**24%**	**32%**	**45%**	**50%**

If these figures alarm you, there are many legal ways of limiting the amount of tax payable in Portugal. Do seek advice before you buy a home there.

Taxes Payable in Portugal – Residents

Bear in mind that the Portuguese tax system is very complex. What follows can only be a very brief summary of the position. The detail is immensely complicated and is made worse because it is so different from what you are used to. This section is written with reference to the person retiring to Portugal. Issues arising out of employment or self-employment are not considered in detail.

Income Tax – *Imposto sobre o Rendimento das Pessoas Singulares (IRS)*

Types of Income

Income is divided, as in the UK, into various categories. Each category of income is subject to different rules and allowances.

For a married couple income tax is generally assessed by reference to the income of your household, rather than on your sole income. Unmarried couples are assessed as two households – which is, generally, a disadvantage. When assessing the income of the household the income of any dependent children is also included. Dependent children are, generally, children under 18 although the definition can include older children in certain circumstances.

As a tax resident you will generally pay tax in Portugal on worldwide income.

Remember that Portugal is (taken overall, not just in relation to income tax) a high tax society. Whether for this reason or out of an independence of spirit many people suffer from selective amnesia as far as the tax man is concerned and significantly under-declare their income. Probably 30 per cent of Portuguese people and 50 per cent of foreign residents do this. This is dangerous. There are severe penalties. There are, however, quite legitimate tax-saving devices that can be used to reduce your tax liabilities. These issues are best addressed *before* you move to Portugal as there are then many more possibilities open to you.

Income Tax Rates – 2003 (payable 2004)

Taxable Income	Rate	Cumulative Tax to Top of Band
Up to €4,182	12%	€501.84
From €4,182 to €6,325	14%	€801.86
From €6,325 to €15,683	24%	€3,047.78
From €15,683 to €35,071	34%	€9,639.70
From €35,071 to €52,277	38%	€16,177.98
Over €52,277	40%	

Deductions from Taxable Income

From your gross income you can deduct:

- **any payments made to the Portuguese social security scheme**
- **your (or your family's personal allowances**
- **payments to an ex-wife or child as a result of matrimonial proceedings.**

There may be other deductions too. See your adviser.

Tax Rates

The tax payable is calculated using the following table. The tax is calculated in tranches. That is, you calculate the tax payable on each complete slice and then the tax at the highest applicable rate on any excess.

Taxes are paid partly to the national government and partly to the regional government. The table above shows the combined total.

Tax Credits

Various tax credits are available. These are deducted from the tax otherwise payable as calculated above. The rules are complex. They include credits for

- **a personal allowance of €208.80 for a single taxpayer, €348.00 for each married taxpayer.**
- **an allowance of €139.20 for each child.**
- **mortgage interest and other housing costs in certain cases – usually 30 per cent of applicable amounts – up to €1,536.30 or rental payments up to the same amount.**
- **health care, education and life insurance expenses up to certain limits.**
- **personal taxes paid in another country – up to the amount that would have been paid in Portugal in respect of that income.**

See your adviser for the up-to-date list of credits.

Payment of Tax Due

You will be sent a tax form in January. You must complete your tax form and submit it by the dates applicable in your case. If you have only a pension or income from employment it must be filed between 1 February and 15 March. If you have other income as well you must file your return between 16 March and

30 April. You will then be sent a tax bill – usually within two months – and you must pay it within one month. Late payment incurs a penalty.

Income Tax Based on Apparent Wealth

If you do not file a tax return – or if the amount of income you disclose is out of kilter with your apparent wealth – the tax office can assess you for income tax based on your visible wealth.

There are detailed rules as to how your assets should be viewed for this purpose. For example, the taxman will expect your declared income to be no less than 20 per cent of the cost of your home plus, if you have an expensive car (over €50,000), 50 per cent of the price of the car. This provisional assessment can be challenged, so if you can show that the assets were acquired by gift or loan or prior to your retirement, the tax office will not take them into account.

Corporation Tax

These taxes are not considered further here.

Taxes on Wealth

There is no wealth tax in Portugal.

Taxes on Capital Gains

You will pay tax on your worldwide gains.

Gains are generally only taxed when the gain is crystallized – e.g. on the sale of the asset. Gains are, generally, taxed as part of your income for the year in which the gain occurred.

Real Estate

Real estate is treated differently.

If a resident sells his main residence and then uses the money to buy another, then the gain will not be taxed provided the new purchase is made within three years. If a gain on the sale of real estate is taxable then only 50 per cent of the taxable gain is taxable.

The method of calculating the tax payable on the sale of real estate is complicated. You will pay tax on the capital gain you make on the sale of real estate in Portugal bought after 1989 or on any other capital gain made from property or a business in Portugal.

The apparent gain (the difference between the sale price and the purchase price) is subject to various allowances. These include the costs of purchase and sale and the *documented* value of any improvements made to the property. The resulting figure is then adjusted, effectively to reflect inflation. For these purposes there is a scale of coefficients which are applied to the price you paid for the property, depending on the year in which it was bought.

Year Bought	Coefficient
1989	1.82
1990	1.64
1991	1.45
1992	1.35
1993	1.25
1994	1.19
1995	1.14
1996	1.10
1997	1.08
1998	1.05
1999	1.03
2000	1.00
2001	1.00

Tax is payable on 50 per cent of the gain calculated in accordance with these rules. The taxable gain is treated as income in the year in which it was made and taxed at the appropriate rate.

Example

Property bought in 1995 for:	£100,000
Sold in 2001 for:	£200,000
Gain	£100,000
Adjusted by coefficient (£200,000 – (£100,000 x 1.14))	£86,000
Costs of acquisition	£12,000
Costs of disposal	£10,000
Documented improvements	£20,000
Taxable gain (£86,000 – £42,000)	£44,000
Tax payable on 50 per cent of the gain	£22,000

Stocks, Shares and Bonds

If these have been held for more than 12 months the gains are tax-free; if owned for less than 12 months they bear tax at a maximum of 10 per cent.

Taxes on Death

The taxes are similar to the taxes paid by non-residents (*see* pp.174–8). Even for residents tax is paid only on your assets located in Portugal as at the date of your death.

If your only asset in Portugal is a bank account it is tax free in Portugal.

The proceeds of life policies are only taxable in Portugal if paid in Portugal to a Portuguese resident.

Remember that, as long as you remain domiciled in England, you will be liable to pay UK inheritance tax on your worldwide estate. It is well worth seeking advice to see whether that link can be broken.

VAT

VAT is a major generator of tax for the Portuguese. Detailed consideration of VAT is outside the scope of this book.

Other Taxes

There is a miscellany of other taxes and levies on various aspects of life in Portugal. Some are national and others local. Individually they are usually not a great burden. They are outside the scope of this book.

New Residents

New residents will be liable to tax on their worldwide income and gains from the date they arrive in Portugal, and possibly back dated to 1 January of the year in which they arrive. Until that day they will only have to pay Portuguese tax on their income if it is derived from assets in Portugal.

The most important thing to understand about taking up residence in Portugal (and abandoning UK tax residence) is that it gives you superb opportunities for tax planning and, in particular, for restructuring your affairs to minimize what can otherwise be penal rates of taxation in Portugal. To do this you need good advice at an early stage – preferably several months before you intend to move.

Double Taxation Treaty

The detailed effect of double taxation treaties depends on the two countries involved. Whilst treaties may be similar in concept they can differ in detail. Only the effect of the Portugal–UK treaty is considered. This treaty dates from 1969 and covers income tax, capital gains taxes and corporation taxes. It does not specifically cover inheritance tax.

The main points of relevance to residents are:

- **Any income from letting property in the UK will normally be outside the scope of Portuguese taxation and, instead, will be taxed in the UK.**
- **Pension received from the UK – except for government pensions – will be taxed in Portugal but not in the UK.**
- **Government pensions will continue to be taxed in the UK but are neither taxed in Portugal nor do they count when assessing the level of your income or when calculating the rate of tax payable on your income.**
- **You will normally not be required to pay UK capital gains tax on gains made after you settle in Portugal except in relation to property located in the UK.**

- **You will pay Portuguese capital gains tax on the disposal of moveable (personal) property in Portugal.**
- **If you are taxed on a gift made outside Portugal then the tax paid will usually be offset against the gift tax due in Portugal.**
- **If you pay tax on an inheritance outside Portugal the same will apply.**

Double tax treaties are detailed and need to be read in the light of your personal circumstances.

Tax Planning Generally

Do it and do it as soon as possible. Every day you delay will make it more difficult to get the results you are looking for.

There are many possibilities for tax planning for someone moving to Portugal. Here are some points worth considering.

- **Time your departure from the UK to get the best out of the UK tax system.**
- **Think, in particular, about when to make any capital gain if you are selling your business or other assets in the UK.**
- **Arrange your affairs so that there is a gap between leaving the UK (for tax purposes) and becoming resident in Portugal. That gap can be used to make all sorts of beneficial changes to the structure of your finances.**
- **Think about trusts. Although the Portuguese system has more restrictions on their effective use than many continental systems they can still be very effective tax-planning vehicles.**
- **Think about giving away some of your assets. You will not have to pay wealth tax on the value given away and the recipients will generally not have to pay either gift or inheritance tax on the gift.**

Inheritance

The Portuguese Inheritance Rules

The Portuguese cannot do just as they please with their property when they die. Inheritance rules apply.

These rules *for Portuguese people* are much more restrictive than the rules under English law. Certain groups of people have (almost) automatic rights to inherit a part of your property.

Fortunately, if you are *not* Portuguese you can dispose of your property in whatever way your national law allows. For British people this is, basically, as they please.

Making a Will

It is always best to make a Portuguese will. If you do not, your UK will should be treated as valid in Portugal and will be used to distribute your estate. This is a false economy as the cost of implementing the UK will is much higher than the cost of implementing a Portuguese will and the disposal of your estate set out in your UK will is often a tax disaster in Portugal.

If you are not a resident in Portugal your Portuguese will should state that it only applies to immovable property in Portugal. The rest of your property – including movable property in Portugal – will be disposed of in accordance with English law and the provisions of your UK will. If you are domiciled in Portugal (as to the meaning of which *see* pp.169–71) you should make a Portuguese will disposing of all of your assets wherever they are located. If you make a Portuguese will covering only immovable property in Portugal you should modify your UK will so as to exclude any immovable property located in Portugal.

Always use a lawyer to advise as to the contents of your will and to draft it. Lawyers love people who make home-made wills. They make a fortune from dealing with their estates because the wills are often inadequately drafted and produce lots of expensive problems.

What if I Don't Make a Will of Any Kind?

A person who dies without a will dies intestate.

This gets complicated. Will the UK rules as to what happens in this event apply (because you are British) or will it be the Portuguese rules? This gives rise to many happy hours of argument by lawyers and tax officials – all at your (or your heirs') expense.

It is much cheaper to make a will.

Investments

The Need to Do Something

Most of us don't like making investment decisions. They make our head hurt. They make us face up to unpleasant things – like taxes and death. We don't really understand what we are doing, what the options are or what is best. We don't know whom to trust for advice. We know we ought to do something, but it will wait until next week – or maybe the week after. Until then our present arrangements will have to do. But if you are moving to live overseas you *must* review your investments. Your current arrangements are likely to be financially disastrous – and may even be illegal.

What Are You Worth?

Most of us are, in financial terms, worth more than we think. When we come to move abroad and have to think about these things it can come as a shock.

Take a piece of paper and list your actual and potential assets. A suggested Checklist can be found in 'Appendix 2', p.314.

This will give you an idea of what you are worth now and, just as importantly, what you are likely to be worth in the future. Your investment plans should take into account both figures.

Who Should Look After Your Investments?

You may already have an investment adviser. You may be very happy with the service you have received. However, your adviser is unlikely to be able to help you once you have gone to live in Portugal and will almost certainly not have the knowledge to do so. He or she will know about neither the Portuguese investment that might be of interest to you nor, probably, of many of the 'off shore' products that might be of interest to someone no longer resident in the UK. Even if your adviser has some knowledge of these things, he or she is likely to be thousands of miles from where you will be living. Nor is it a simple question of selecting a new local (Portuguese) adviser once you have moved; he or she will usually know little about the UK aspects of your case or about the UK tax and inheritance rules that could still have some importance for you.

Choosing an investment adviser competent to deal with you once you are in Portugal is not easy. By all means seek guidance from your existing adviser. Ask for guidance from others who have already made the move. Do some research. Meet the potential candidates. Are you comfortable with them? Do they share your approach to life? Do they have the necessary experience? Is their performance record good? How are they regulated? What security/bonding/guarantees can they offer you? How will they be paid for their work: fees or commission? If commission, what will that formula mean they are making from you in 'real money' rather than percentages?

Above all, be careful. There are lots of very dubious 'financial advisers' operating in the popular tourist areas of Portugal. Some are totally incompetent. Some are crooks, seeking simply to separate you from your money as cleanly as possible.

Fortunately there are also some excellent and highly professional advisers with good track records. Make sure you choose one.

Where Should You Invest?

For British people the big issue is whether they should keep their sterling investments. Most British people will have investments that are largely sterling-based. Even if they are, for example, in a Far Eastern fund they will probably be denominated in sterling and they will pay out dividends, etc. in sterling.

You will be spending euros.

As the value of the euro fluctuates against sterling the value of your investments will go up and down. That, of itself, isn't too important because the value won't crystallize unless you sell. What does matter is that the revenue you generate from those investments (rent, interest, dividends, etc.) will fluctuate in value. Take, for example, an investment that generated you £10,000 per annum. Rock steady. Then think of that income in spending power. Let's use Portuguese escudos as an example because the euro does not yet have a sufficient track record to illustrate the point. In the last few years the Portuguese escudo has varied in value from £1 = 310 escudos to £1 = 200 escudos. Sometimes, therefore, your income in Portuguese escudos would have been 3,100,000 escudos per year and at others it would have been 2,000,000 escudos per year. This is a huge difference in your standard of living *based solely on exchange rate variations*.

This is unacceptable, particularly as you will inevitably have to accept this problem in so far as your pension is concerned.

In general terms, therefore, investments paying out in euros are preferable if you live in a euro country.

Trusts

Trusts are an important weapon in the hands of the person going to live in Portugal. Trusts offer the potential benefits of:

- **allowing you to put part of your assets in the hands of trustees so that they no longer belong to you for wealth tax or inheritance tax purposes.**
- **allowing you to receive only the income you need (rather than all the income generated by those assets) thus keeping the extra income out of sight for income tax purposes.**
- **allowing a very flexible vehicle for investment purposes.**

So how do these little wonders work?

After leaving the UK (and before moving to Portugal) you reorganize your affairs by giving a large part of your assets to 'trustees'. Trustees are normally a professional trust company located in a low tax regime. The choice of a reliable trustee is critical.

Those trustees hold the asset not for their own benefit but 'in trust' for whatever purposes you established when you made the gift. It could, for example, be to benefit a local hospital or school *or it could be to benefit you and your family*. If the trust is set up properly in the light of the requirements of Portuguese law then those assets will no longer be treated as yours for tax purposes.

On your death the assets are not yours to leave to your children (or whomever), and so do not (subject to any local anti-avoidance legislation) carry inheritance tax.

Similarly, the income from those assets is not your income. If some of it is given to you it may be taxed as your income, but the income that is not given to you will not be taxed in Portugal and, because the trust will be located in a nil/low tax regime, it will not be taxed elsewhere either.

The detail of the arrangements is vitally important. They must be set up precisely to comply with Portuguese tax law. If you do not do this they will not work as intended.

Trustees can manage your investments in (virtually) whatever way you stipulate when you set up the trust. You can give the trustees full discretion to do as they please or you can specify precisely how your money is to be used. There are particular types of trusts and special types of investments that trusts can make that can be especially beneficial in Portugal.

Trusts can be beneficial even to Portuguese resident people of modest means – say £350,000. It is certainly worth investing a little money to see if they can be of use to you, as the tax savings can run to many thousands of pounds. If you are thinking of trusts as an investment vehicle and tax-planning measure you must take advice early – months before you are thinking of moving to Portugal. Otherwise it will be too late.

Keeping Track of Your Investments

Whatever you decide to do about investments – put them in a trust, appoint investment managers to manage them in your own name or manage them yourself – you should always keep an up-to-date list of your assets and investments and tell your family where to find it. Make a file. By all means have a computer file but print off a good old-fashioned paper copy. Keep it in an obvious place known to your family. Keep it with your will and the deeds to your house. Keep in it either the originals of bank account books, share certificates, etc. or a note of where they are to be found.

As a lawyer it is very frustrating – and expensive for the client – when, after their parents' death, the children come in with a suitcase full of correspondence and old cheque books. It all has to be gone through and all those old banks contacted lest there should be £1 million lurking in a forgotten account. There never is, and it wastes a lot of time and money.

Conclusion

Buying a home in Portugal – whether to use as a holiday home, as an investment or to live in permanently – is as safe as buying one in the UK.

The rules may appear complicated. Our rules would if you were a Portuguese person coming to this country. That apparent complexity is often no more than lack of familiarity.

There are tens of thousands of British people who have bought homes in Portugal. Most have had no real problems. Most have enjoyed years of holidays in Portugal. Many have seen their property rise substantially in value. Many are now thinking of retiring to Portugal.

For a trouble-free time you simply need to keep your head and to seek advice from experts who can help you make the four basic decisions:

- **Who should own the property?**
- **What am I going to do about inheritance?**
- **What am I going to do about controlling my potential tax liabilities?**
- **If I am going to live in Portugal, what am I going to do about investments?**

If you don't like lawyers, remember that they make far more money out of sorting out the problems you get into by not doing these things than by giving you this basic advice!

Settling In

07

Finally, after all that searching for a property, raising finance, taking hard decisions and waiting for the seemingly interminable bureaucratic processes to be resolved, the papers have changed hands and you now have the keys to your dream home in Portugal. Now for the really interesting part: moving there and settling in. This chapter takes a look at many of the issues involved from moving to arrival, getting connected up to utilities, dealing with the administration, finding work, setting up a business or learning to enjoy retirement. Many aspects of life in Portugal are also considered, from looking after yourself, your family, your property and your pet to enjoying the country's exquisite cuisine and learning its language. You will also be taught how to serve port 'properly'...

Making the Move

In this section it is assumed that you are planning on moving permanently to Portugal and are therefore making a 'complete' move. This does not necessarily mean the same thing to everyone. You may only be taking a few essential items, others of value (sentimental or real) and planning to furnish your new home from scratch. On the other hand, you may want to take just about everything – 'lock stock and barrel'. Most people end up settling for a happy medium.

Your decision on what to take and what to leave behind will affect how you organize the removal. If you are taking only the essentials they may fit into a small to medium-sized van, either borrowed or rented, or even into a trailer, and you can transport them there yourself. If you are making a substantial move then it is in your interests to look for a removal company that specializes in overseas removals. Choosing a good company is important and it is advisable to get at least three itemized, written quotes (doing it over the telephone is not enough) and also to compare the small print regarding every aspect of the removal process.

If you are moving the contents of an average three-bedroom house, do not expect to get much change from €5,000 and do not be surprised at having to pay half as much again or even double for a large houseful including some valuable items. If you are not especially in a hurry and not shipping a full lorry-load, you can get a cheaper deal by booking a 'part load' whereby your goods are put in storage until the company gets enough orders from other customers to make up a complete truckload. You can still make an agreement by which the company undertakes to deliver your load within a certain period.

Once you have chosen a company, you should provide it with as much information as possible concerning your new home. This should include a room plan, a local map and any peculiarities involved in accessing the property. Make sure the driveway is big enough to accommodate the lorry and that there will be no parking problems. If your new property is an apartment, inform the company of the size of the lift (or lack of one) and of any narrow, twisting stairways or other hazards. If you have bought a farmhouse with small doors or windows, do not expect the removal men to come up with a solution for getting your grand piano in on the spur of the moment!

For peace of mind, always insure the property to be moved. The remover will usually offer cover, specially designed to include risks specific to removals. However, you may prefer to look for an independent insurer in case of conflicting interests if a claim is made. This is not generally a problem with reliable companies, especially those affiliated to the organizations mentioned below in 'Removal Companies'. Most all-risk policies include breakages and damage in transit but may not provide cover if you have done the packing yourself. Some policies actually specify that packing should be done by the removers. Valuable items should be photographed before packing and a full inventory of all items drawn up and checked on unloading.

If you are coming from an EU country you do not have to worry about customs duties and can import any personal belongings you like. Furniture, household goods, tools, bicycles, camping equipment and more besides can all be imported provided they have no particular commercial value and you have used them for six months prior to your departure. If there are any formalities to be dealt with, then the removal company should be able to deal with them, which is yet another reason why it is important to use an experienced international remover, better still one that has experience in removals to Portugal and an office there. If you have any doubts you should contact your nearest Portuguese consulate or the *Direcção Geral da Alfândega*, the Portuguese Customs and Excise Authority, at Rua da Alfândega, 1100-016, Lisboa (**t** 00351 218 813 700; **www.dgaiec.min-financas.pt**). This is also strongly recommended if you are moving your possessions from outside the EU, as the red-tape is likely to be considerably more complicated.

Removal Companies

Top international removal companies should be affiliated to the British Association of Removers and/or one of the international associations, such as the International Federation of Furniture Removers (FIDI) or the Overseas Moving Network International (OMNI). All three have websites: **www.bar.co.uk**; **www.fidi.com** and **www.omnimoving.com**, respectively. Members offer the user certain guarantees including completion of the removal by another affiliated member should the contracted company not finish the job. If you contract a Portuguese company, it helps if it is also a member of FIDI and/or OMNI and it should be licensed to do removal work in Portugal. For a list of specialist removal companies, *see* p.301.

The Move

Careful forward planning is essential to ensure that the move goes smoothly and causes you minimal stress. Unless the move is a sudden event, you should book the moving day with the chosen company at least a month ahead. Here are just some of the things to consider.

- **If you have children, especially small ones, arrange for them to be taken care of on the day of moving. You should also ask their school for educational records to be made available or sent to the new school if you have already chosen one.**
- **Inform all authorities, health, tax, social security, that you are moving and obtain any relevant leaflets and other information useful to you as a soon-to-be resident abroad.**
- **Notify banks, credit companies and insurance companies where you have policies.**
- **Make arrangements for your pets to be moved.** ***See*** **'Taking Your Pet to Portugal', pp.240–41 for details on regulations concerning vaccinations.**
- **Start using up food in the deep freeze and the freezer; both will need to be disconnected and defrosted a couple of days before transportation, otherwise they might get damaged in transit.**
- **Around a fortnight before the big day, arrange for meter readings to be done on the day of your move and for utilities to be disconnected or else put in the name of the person who is buying or taking over your home. You also need to arrange for utilities to be connected in your home in Portugal ready for your arrival.**
- **Ask for your telephone to be cut off on the day of your removal unless you want to put it into the name of the new occupant. Get the telephone company to send the outstanding bill to a trustworthy neighbour or, if you pay by standing order, make sure to keep the account open long enough – you will probably want to leave it open anyway.**
- **Arrange for your mail to be redirected to another address, that of a family member or the same trustworthy neighbour. Inform all your regular correspondents of your new address from the date you are moving in.**
- **If you are going to take your washing machine, cooker or gas fires, arrange for a technician to come and disconnect them properly as close a time as possible before the move. You should have checked beforehand if they will be compatible with the fittings in your house in Portugal, if they are not, try to sell them or include them in the sale price of the house.**
- **Two days or so before the move, disconnect the fridge and freezer if you are taking them.**
- **Cancel deliveries such as newspapers or milk.**

• Start the packing process (if you have not already) by arranging items into piles or designated areas so that the removal company can make up boxes of similar items, clothes, books, ornaments and so on.

• Do not fill chests of drawers or trunks with books as they will be too heavy to move.

• Make sure that all containers of inflammable liquids (such as paraffin stoves or petrol motors) have been emptied as no removal company will transport potentially explosive items.

• If any furniture, such as bunk beds, needs to be dismantled before moving, try to do it the night before.

• Curtains are not normally included in the removal contract so you should take them down yourself. Leave items that are not to be moved in clearly marked piles.

• Houseplants may or may not travel well and adapt to the climate at your new home. The removal company may have a policy on transporting them but may not offer any guarantee of safe arrival or later health owing to variations of temperature. It may be better to give them to a friend!

• Attach small furniture keys to the item of furniture itself, otherwise they will get lost.

• Jewellery, trinkets and other valuable items should be packed separately. Take them yourself, as few companies will take responsibility for them.

• Make sure, before the lorry disappears, that you have exchanged contact details with the removal crew and fixed an approximate time for the rendezvous in Portugal. Do try to get there before the lorry does, as waiting time will cost more. If you cannot guarantee this, make sure someone is on hand to receive them and oversee the unloading.

• When you set off yourself, make sure to lock up securely having turned off water, gas and electricity. Drop the keys off with the estate agent if the house is still on the market or arrange to hand them over to the new owner.

In general, be as prepared as possible, as something is bound to go wrong on the day of the move itself. Good planning and preparation means there will be time left over for any unforeseen problems that may arise.

Leaving and Arriving

If your possessions have departed without a hitch, it remains for you to get yourself to Portugal without problems and to settle in as smoothly as possible. *There are certain things that you ought to have done before travelling to ensure this and there are some things you can only do once you have arrived.* Some may seem obvious, others not so.

Beforehand...

- **Make sure that your passport and those of your family are in order and not on the point of expiring.**
- **Make sure to take all important documents with you.**
- **Organize travel and health insurance that will cover you in Portugal.**
- **Make sure your pet is covered by the PETS scheme.**
- **Make sure your credit and debit cards can be used in Portugal.**
- **Get enough euros to get you through the first two or three days.**
- **Arrange schools for your children.**
- **Tell people your new address.**

Once there...

- **Open a bank account as soon as you can and arrange for utilities bills to be paid from it.**
- **Rent or buy a car if you have not brought one with you.**
- **Apply for the fiscal card, social security card and residency permit.**
- **Get signed up with a doctor and dentist.**
- **Get to know your neighbours.**

Bureaucracy – How to Deal with It

Portuguese bureaucracy, as every one will tell you, is *infernal*! The good news is that it is considerably less awkward than it used to be. Since Portugal joined the European Community in 1986 there has been a sustained attack on the worse aspects of an administrative system that seemed designed to make life difficult for everybody. Whatever needed dealing with, there was always another document to find, another office to visit, another queue to stand in and an army of unhelpful bureaucrats. This was the legacy of centuries of authoritarian and unrepresentative government, which is now slowly being replaced by a system in which citizens have more control over their own lives and access to those who govern them. It is definitely getting easier nowadays, though nobody should expect things to be straightforward. Foreign investors, for example, no longer have to seek permission to invest (formerly a long process). Nowadays they only have to register for statistical purposes.

For ordinary citizens, one of the most important steps has been the establishment of the *Loja do Cidadão*, the 'Citizens' Shop', a one-stop office where practically every arm of the administration is present. Here most bureaucratic processes can be dealt with without needing to go to several offices spread throughout the city. A wide range of procedures can be dealt with at the *lojas*, including all civil registry matters, enquiries and payment of utility bills, postal

Saudade

One of those words that compilers of bilingual dictionaries always have problems with, *saudade* has been defined as 'nostalgia', 'loss', 'yearning', 'melancholy', 'fatefulness' or 'homesickness' but none of these quite do the word justice. Portugal's geographical position, stuck on the western edge of the Iberian Peninsula (and always back-to-back with Spain), with only the sea on the horizon, meant that the country was destined to become a nation of seafarers, fishermen and, eventually, the builder of a vast overseas empire. During its period as a major world power, then when the empire went into terminal decline and until quite recently, millions of Portuguese have emigrated in search of richer pickings elsewhere. Some four and a half million Portuguese still reside abroad and the cash they send back to their families represents a considerable economic contribution even today.

But few émigrés, no matter how well life treats them in their places of adoption, ever give up their dream of coming home and settling in their birthplace which they believe to be the most blessed place on earth. *Saudade* is what the émigré feels when thinking of home and what those left behind feel when thinking of those that left. *Saudade* is what fishermen feel when out at sea, often for weeks on end, and what the fishermen's wives feel when waiting anxiously for the fleet to return. *Saudade* is what many people feel when remembering Portugal's illustrious, long-gone past which, many feel, will always overshadow the present. *Saudade* is part of the Portuguese character and is perfectly expressed in the tone and themes of *fado*, the sorrowful form of song that has been described as Portugal's blues. But times are changing and after a decade and a half of EU membership, sweeping changes and a new-found prosperity, the Portuguese are beginning to look more to the future than to the past. Young people, especially, seem to have had enough of longing, yearning and being sad and now want to get on with having some fun.

services, social security, taxes, pensions (for Portuguese pension entitlement), road tax and driving licences and more besides. For the moment there is only an information service for questions relating to foreigners' matters and residency. Actual applications must still be made at the *Serviço de Estrangeiros e Fronteiras*. Currently there are *lojas* in Lisbon (two branches), Oporto, Aveiro, Braga, Coimbra, Setúbal and Viseu. The *loja* has also opened many mini-branches known as *Postos de Atendimento ao Cidadão* (PAC) in these cities and others too. The Algarve, the Alentejo and the offshore islands still do not have the benefit of their services. However, as with most parts of the administration these days, it is possible to make enquiries online at **www.lojadocidadao.pt**. The information is, at present, in Portuguese only and there is no sign of when services will be available in English. Many ministries, such as *Finanças* (tax), do now have information and downloadable forms available in English, although their information can sometimes be inadequate or completely out of date.

When dealing with those aspects of Portuguese bureaucracy that involve spending or saving large amounts of money (e.g. the tax office) you are always advised to seek the assistance of a reliable lawyer or financial adviser.

Retirement

Living in Retirement

There is a good chance that some of those reading this book will be planning to retire to Portugal. Many have gone before you (4,700 UK pensioners live in Portugal) and most are perfectly happy. The attractions are obvious and have been pointed out elsewhere. The climate, especially in the south, makes healthy outdoor activities possible for most of the year, while the (relatively) low cost of living that means your pension will stretch a little further than if you stay in the UK. Overall, the environment is far less stressful. For EU citizens, there are many added advantages.

There is much evidence to show that the majority of pensioners who retire abroad (Spain, Italy and Portugal are the most popular destinations) are generally content with their decision. The happiest are those who have thought everything through very carefully, particularly the financial and tax implications. Such things as health, location, access to facilities and ease of travelling home are also important considerations. It pays to think about these issues before jumping in at the deep end. Your conclusions should help you decide whether this is what you really want and, if it is, where and how you should live.

Cost of Living

Portugal is cheaper, yes, but not that much cheaper, and prices are going up. It is very difficult to make sweeping statements about how cheap or expensive a country is and anyway your spending depends on how expensive or frugal your tastes are.

A recent *Sunday Times* cost of living table compared a basket of groceries containing 22 basic items and showed that these cost more or less the same in Portugal, Holland and Belgium – around £50 (or roughly €71). The same items could easily cost up to £10 more in Italy and £30 more in the UK. Eurostat figures (reported recently in the *Guardian*) partially contradict this. They show a basket of basic supermarket goods to be more expensive in Portugal than either Spain (not surprising), France (surprisingly) or Italy (the contradiction!). However you measure it, Portugal is not as cheap as it was, and since nobody can predict future inflation rates or currency exchange fluctuations, it is difficult to say how far a pension will stretch.

Pensions

Your state pension will be paid in the way described in 'Welfare Benefits', pp.231–6.

If you have a company pension, it will be paid wherever the pension scheme rules dictate. Some permit the administrators to pay the money into any bank anywhere and others (ostensibly for security reasons) insist on the money being paid into a UK bank account. If this is the case for your pension, you can of course simply ask the bank to send it on to you in Portugal. Bank transfer costs mean that is probably best to do this only three or four times a year. You can also make an annual arrangement with some currency dealers whereby they will send the money at a fixed exchange rate for the whole year. This provides certainty of income.

Portugal has no problems granting residency to pensioners as they bring their money into the local economy without putting strains on the job market, providing that the pension is worth more than the official minimum wage, which currently stands at just over €356 a month. This applies both to those in receipt of a pension from any EU state and to non-EU pensioners too. If your pension does not reach the minimum wage, look for another, cheaper country, as you will be destitute!

Tax

If you spend more than 180 days in Portugal you must become a resident. If you become a resident and receive your pension in Portugal then the money is considered a source of income and is, therefore, taxable. The tax threshold for pensions in Portugal is just over €7,000a year, though it is to be hoped you will get more than that.

State pensions in the UK are not taxable but government pensions (army, civil service, police, etc.) are, as are any other sources of income, so you have to be careful not to end up paying tax at both ends. You can get leaflet (IR121) 'Income tax and pensioners' from the Inland Revenue, or, for further information, take a look at **www.inlandrevenue.gov.uk**. Alternatively, contact the Inland Revenue Inspector of Funds, Lynwood Road, Thames Ditton, Surrey KT7 0DP. When in Portugal, talk to other resident pensioners and find out how they have dealt with this issue. *See* 'Taxation', pp.168–83, for more information.

Other Issues

Once the financial issues have been dealt with, you have to look at where you are going to live and think about settling in. Living abroad does not suit everyone, especially those who have not considered the issues involved. Culture shock is not to be underestimated. Ask yourself just how open you are to new ways and a different lifestyle. Moving away from a close circle of family and friends can turn out to be a bigger shock to the system than you originally thought. After the initial thrill of arriving, it is not uncommon for retirees to feel isolated, especially if they have little understanding of the language and culture. Also – without something to do, boredom can easily set in. It depends on each person's level of adaptability.

Being alone or accompanied can also influence how well you adapt. This is why retirees are warned of possible problems that can arise when choosing to live in a rural setting. Lack of access to services, entertainment and company can seriously affect your health and state of mind. Before moving, you should try to spend some time in the area that you plan to retire to, rent a place, and test the lifestyle for more than one season. That way, if things are not as rosy as you thought, you have not invested money in a property or burnt any bridges. There is always the chance then of trying the same experiment in a different setting.

One reason why so many people are happy living on the Algarve or the Lisbon coast is precisely the existence of a ready-made community with its clubs, societies and social life. This does not mean you cannot learn Portuguese or integrate – a stimulating, challenging proposal at any age – to the extent that you want but it is always helpful to have familiarity to fall back on.

As a retired person (over 65 for a man and. currently, 60 for a woman) you are entitled to the full use of the Portuguese health care system on the same basis as a Portuguese person. *See* 'Health and Emergencies' pp.229–31 for more information.

Burial and Cremation

If you die in Portugal, your death must be registered within 24 hours. Like everything else, this is done at the town hall. As a British person you should also record the death at the British consulate.

Burial is much more common in Portugal than cremation. Land is plentiful, crematoria are expensive to build. Crematoria are usually only found in large cities and towns. Funerals are as ridiculously expensive in Portugal as they are in the UK – maybe even more so. Having your body taken back to the UK, however, is possible but complex and even more expensive.

Working and Employment

If you are an EU or EEA (European Economic Area) citizen you enjoy the same rights and obligations as any Portuguese worker or entrepreneur. Citizens from outside the EU can expect many more restrictions. Those who wish to work in Portugal or get involved in running a business (whatever their legal position) also face a number of difficulties.

During the mid to late 1990s, the employment situation was quite healthy. Unemployment figures fell to around 4 per cent in 2001, but have subsequently increased, reaching 7 per cent in 2003, and are currently predicted to rise further. Though still in line with the EU average, the situation nevertheless does not look particularly promising. Portugal has suffered a recession over the last couple of years, accentuated in the last two or three quarters, and the factors that contributed to the near-miraculous growth of the '90s will soon no longer apply. In reality, the economic miracle was achieved by keeping wages low (the minimum wage is now only just over €356 a month, which represents about 57 per cent of the average wage) and the injection of European development funds, invested in large infrastructure projects such as motorways, bridges, dams and the Expo '98 in Lisbon. Such projects are now largely finished and the EU money that benefited Portugal is likely in future to be channelled towards new countries joining as part of the EU's 2004 enlargement programme. Unless Portugal is able to find other sources of revenue, it is unlikely that more employment will be generated and it is hard to see wages rising.

The Euro 2004 football championship has attracted massive investment and created short-term jobs in stadium-construction and services related to the organization of such an event. The government is confident that an increasingly well-qualified but low-paid workforce remains an incentive to investors and insists that the EU's expansion eastwards will open up new markets for Portuguese exporters. The tourist sector continues to bring in money and provide jobs, but still the big question remains – how much investment will continue to flow to Portugal and how much will turn eastwards?

There is now much talk of reform in the labour market, of introducing greater flexibility and mobility, making hiring and firing easier and reducing the financial burden on companies. Taxes on corporations, it is hoped, will be down to somewhere around 25 per cent by mid-2004. Whether this will lead to a more dynamic economy or to one in which thousands of workers will be forced into the uncertainty of short-term contracts is anybody's guess. Many experts think that Portugal is still not ready for fundamental reform of the labour market, as the social cost will prove too high.

For the foreigner hoping to find a job, this means that, while there is work available, wage expectations should be realistic. Most foreigners, other than those recruited at a management level to work in large multinational companies, are likely to end up being paid very little. This may not be a problem for people for whom going to live in Portugal is more about enjoying quality of life, relaxing and getting away from the 'rat race'. But if your aim is to make serious money, you should think about getting qualifications that will help you find a well-paid job or else reconsider going to Portugal.

Finding Work

Think carefully about your prospects before going to Portugal as it is unlikely that you will instantly be able to find a job. Unless you are going to work directly with and for other ex-pats it is essential that you have a good level of Portuguese. Even then you will not be competing on equal terms, since local workers are more familiar with conditions, know the rules of the game and have contacts. The Portuguese have a word, *cunha*, which translates literally as 'wedge' but which means knowing people in the right place who can help you get your foot in the door. No newly arrived foreigner can hope to have *cunha*. It is something that Portuguese people have – thanks to the country being so small and traditionally introspective.

Sources of Work

Start looking before you set off for Portugal. There are various ways of doing this. In all EU countries you can visit your local employment office (Job Centre in the UK) and look at the database of the EURES scheme, on which job vacancies are posted Europe-wide. Alternatively look at the website: **http://europa.eu.int/jobs/eures** where jobs are advertised in all EU countries. This may not be especially productive, since very few jobs are posted there for Portugal. None in fact at the time of going to press!

Portuguese Job Centres (*Centros de Emprego*)

If you are already in Portugal, you are entitled to sign up as a jobseeker with a local job centre, or *Centro de Emprego*. They are operated by the *Ministério do Emprego e Segurança Social* and have offices in most towns and cities. Do not expect them to be that helpful if you do not speak Portuguese, or even if you do. They may, however, have jobs posted on the noticeboard and since it is your right to accept training you can ask about possible courses. To find the address of your nearest office, look in the telephone book, ask at the town hall or go to **www.iefp.pt/Quem_Somos/Centros/ce.html**. A map appears; click on the town and the address appears. The main regional delegations have the following addresses:

- **Delegação Regional de Lisboa e Vale do Tejo**
  Rua das Picoas 14, 1069-003 Lisboa (**t** 00351 213 307 400)
- **Delegação Regional do Centro**
  Avendia Fernão de Magalhães 660, 3001-174 Coimbra (**t** 00351 239 860 800)
- **Delegação Regional do Alentejo**
  Rua do Menino Jesus 47–51, 7000-601 Évora (**t** 00351 266 760 500)

- **Delegação Regional do Norte**
  Rua Engº Ezequiel Campos 488, 4149-004 Porto (**t** 00351 226 159 200)
- **Delegação Regional do Alagarve**
  Rua Dr Cândido Guerreiro 45 – 1º, Edíficio Nascente, 8000-318 Faro (**t** 00351 289 890 100)

Press Advertisements

Portuguese jobs rarely appear in the UK press, though it always pays to keep an eye on the job pages of the major dailies, particularly for senior management jobs or teaching posts. Portuguese newspapers, of course, have plenty of job advertisements but you cannot expect to understand them, still less apply, if your Portuguese is not up to scratch. Advertisements do occasionally appear in English, usually when companies are recruiting senior managers and do not want to limit their search to Portugal. The English-language press in Portugal, *The News* and *The Anglo-Portuguese News* (see details below), can both be useful though the jobs section can be limited. Bear in mind that servicing the ex-pat population has become something of an industry in itself. Apart from the general press, it is a good idea to look at trade magazines if you are looking for a job in any given sector.

Advertising Yourself

It often helps to take the initiative. Make yourself known by advertising and put yourself in contact with potential employers. This applies whether you are seeking employment or looking for work as a self-employed person.

Chambers of Commerce and other business organizations are worth contacting. They may not be able to help you find work directly, but they do have a lot of useful information concerning companies that operate in Portugal and which are likely to recruit foreign staff. They may know of companies with vacancies that fit your profile. At the very least, they will be able to provide you with a list of companies worth applying to. The *Câmara de Comércio Luso-Británica* (British–Portuguese Chamber of Commerce) is a starting point – Rua da Estrela 8, 1200-699 Lisboa (**t** 00351 213 942 020, **f** 00351 213 942 029, **info@bpcc.pt**; **www.bilateral.biz**).

If you have a specific skill to offer (e.g. hairdressing, translating, IT trouble-shooting, shiatsu massages, tennis-coaching, child-minding) and are looking for a job (or self-employment), you may find one within the ex-pat community, since many residents feel more comfortable hiring an English-speaker than a local. Advertisements offering your services can be placed via the English-language press in Portugal. Contact *The News*, an Algarve-based weekly, at Apartado 13, 8401-901 Lagoa (**t** 00351 282 341 100, **ClassAds@The-News.net**). *The Anglo-Portuguese News* also accepts advertisements, which must be submitted in writing (by mail, fax or e-mail), stating whether you want a box or normal classified. They will then confirm the price. Contact APN, Apartado 113, 2766-902 Estoril (**t** 00351 214 661 423, **f** 00351 214 660 358, **apn@mail.telepac.pt**).

Using the Internet

These days there are many websites dedicated to bringing together potential employees and employers. There are international sites with links to the country you want to work in and there are also some Portugal-specific sites. Here are a few:

- **www.overseasjobsexpress.com** – register online to view vacancies and receive the electronic magazine.
- **jobera.com/international_resume/portugal/portugal.htm** – help with Portugal-specific CV and application letters.
- **www.anyworkanywhere.com/jobsearch.html** – most jobs currently offered are with tour operators.
- **www.net-empregos.com** – Portuguese-language site where you can file a CV and view and apply for jobs on-line.
- **www.stepstone.pt/home_fs.htm** – Portuguese page of the international www.stepstone.com.
- **http://superemprego.sapo.pt/pt/index_emprego.htm** – Portuguese-language site with a similar structure to net-empregos.
- **www.des.min-edu.pt/estia/lab/vacancies.html** – Portuguese Education Ministry site with links to some of the above plus pages in English on the job market and related questions.

Temporary Work Agencies

There are many such organizations. The majority are based in Lisbon and Oporto and are worth contacting. As before, it is not much use applying if your Portuguese is not up to scratch, but if it is they may help you to get a temporary placement. Look in the Yellow Pages under *Pessoal Temporário* or *Recrutamento e Selecção*.

Teaching English

Many English-speakers, originally trained for something else, find work teaching English as a foreign language (TEFL). The sector has grown in line with economic progress over the past 20 years and many people now send their children to private English classes. There is also demand for business English. Schools are concentrated in commercial and industrial central and northern Portugal more than in the Algarve. Business English is taught year-round, although lessons for children and teenagers start up with the school term in September or October.

A TEFL certificate is not absolutely necessary but helps you find work, as does a degree and maybe some experience. A driving licence may be an additional requirement. Full-time teaching contracts generally last nine months with three weeks' paid holiday. Pay can range between €720 and €950 per month. Some contracts may include flights and/or accommodation. Tax and social security deductions account for roughly 23 per cent of your salary.

Getting Qualified and Finding Work

It is a good idea to do get some training before looking for work. Many centres both in the UK and Portugal run training courses leading to the TEFL or CELTA certificates; once you have experience you can upgrade your qualifications by doing the full RSA Certificate. A good starting point for training is International House, 106 Piccadilly, London W1J 7NL (**t** (020) 7518 6950, **f** (020) 7518 6951, **www.ihworld.com**).

Another useful institution for jobseekers is the British Council, 10 Spring Gardens, London SW1A 2BN (**www.britishcouncil.org**). The Council is well represented in Portugal. Apart from its school in central Lisbon, there are several centres throughout the metropolitan area, in Almada, Alverca, Cascais, Miraflores and Parede as well as in Coimbra and Oporto. TEFL jobs are also published in the TES (*Times Educational Supplement*) on Fridays and in the *Guardian's* EFL pages on Tuesdays. Otherwise, look in the Yellow Pages in any Portuguese city, where you will find many private language schools.

Schoolteaching

The existence of large ex-pat communities means there are a good many private schools where English is the language of instruction. Many of these offer their alumni an education based on the national curriculum, others follow the American system. This creates a demand for teachers. *The News* (Portugal's main English-language newspaper) has a classified advertising section where jobs may appear.

Tourist Industry

Approximately 250 tour operators worldwide have Portugal on their list of destinations, which generates a lot of work both for locals and outsiders. The type of jobs that come up include working with children, doing administration work at resorts, or working as a tour representative. There may also be jobs for sports instructors, teaching scuba diving and horse riding or coaching tennis or golf. In the main tourist areas there are often jobs available for bar staff, waiters and cooks. Nightclubs, bars and discotheques also need people to distribute promotional flyers or work behind the bar (good DJs may even get hired!). For all such jobs it is best to approach major tour operators directly, and you can find work just by turning up and asking. The work is seasonal but does at least give you a chance to experience living and working in Portugal.

Translating and Interpreting

Clearly this is not an option unless you are practically bilingual in Portuguese and English. As a trading and sea-faring nation, Portugal has many economic ties with the rest of the world and there is a strong demand for business documents and correspondence to be translated into English. Companies often require staff to interpret conference proceedings.

It is possible to work for yourself, although you need to build up a lot of contacts before you can be certain of reasonable and regular earnings. Another possibility is to contact translation agencies who often farm out the work to self-employed translators. A full-time post as a translator is hard to come by. Look for agencies in the Yellow Pages or contact either of the following, which are well-established and reputable firms: Traducta Serviços de Tradução e Interpretação, Rua Rodrigo da Fonseca 127 - 1° Dto 1070-240 Lisboa (**t** 00351 213 883 384, **f** 00351 213 857 886, **info@traducta.pt**, **www.traducta.pt**) or AIP-Assistentes Intérpretes de Portugal, Avenida da República 41–3, 1050-187 Lisboa (**t** 00351 217 994 360, **f** 00351 217 994 369).

Working Conditions

Wages in Portugal are low. Average earnings in countries such as Germany or the UK are in the region of two and a half times higher and, while the cost of living is lower, it is not *that* much lower. Consequently, unless you find a well-paid job in a large international company your spending power will be significantly lower than that of a German or British worker. If you are dependent on local wages you will have to live modestly and cannot expect to save very much.

On the other hand, employment brings a number of benefits. All full-time employed persons are entitled to 22 weekdays of paid holiday. The annual salary is customarily divided into 14 payments, the 'extra' salary being paid at Christmas and in summer. There are also 13 statutory national holidays (*see* 'Portuguese Holidays and Celebrations', p.303) and, in most places, one more local holiday, offering considerable scope for long weekends! The working week is still longer in Portugal than in most other EU countries and is now fixed at 40 hours (eight hours a day as a rule). There is also a guaranteed minimum wage of around €356 a month.

Trade union membership is relatively high in Portugal, especially in industry and manufacturing and also in the public sector. Under Salazar, unions (*sindicatos*) were tightly controlled and strikes were not permitted but since the 1974

Revolution union pressure has resulted in considerable improvements in labour conditions. EU membership and inward investment have also helped to improve working conditions. While equal pay for women is enshrined in law, women on average earn less than men. Their level of participation in the workplace is, however, comparatively high in relation to other EU countries.

Self-employment

Many people opt for self-employment or running a business. Both have advantages and disadvantages. When operating as a self-employed worker (*trabalhador por conta própria*) or as a sole trader (*empresário em nome individual*) you do not have the security of a work contract, paid holidays or compensation if you lose your job. The work can be irregular and you may be loathe to turn down an unattractive job or commission simply because you do not know what the next week or month will bring.

It is relatively easy to deal with the formalities of being self-employed or a sole trader. For the steps required to get a residency permit *see* **First Steps and Reasons for Buying**, but you must also register with the tax authorities and have a tax card, or fiscal card (*cartão de contribuinte*). On registering as self-employed you will also be given a receipts book (*caderneta de recibos*) in which you record payments received and which must be presented when you make your tax declarations. Many of the expenses incurred in self-employment, such as entertaining clients, travelling, purchasing of equipment, etc., are tax deductible. In general, the deductible limit may not exceed 32.5 per cent of gross income from self-employment. You must also make your own social security contributions (*Segurança Social*), the equivalent of NI payments in the UK.

Both tax and social security are very complex issues, however, and if you plan to be self-employed you are advised to seek the advice of a good accountant since you could end up paying too much or, unwittingly, not enough – only to be penalized later if the tax authorities carry out an inspection.

Certain professions are regulated in some EU member states (though not in all) and recognition of qualifications may be necessary before you undertake any work. Before starting to work, check that your qualifications are valid and, if not, begin the validation process. This will involve producing originals of qualifications, sworn translations of these, a breakdown of courses taken leading to the degree or diploma, and proof that you have practised for a required number of years. Some useful addresses in Portugal are:

- **Ministério da Educação, Departamento do Ensino Superior,** Núcleo Pedagógico, Avenida Duque d'Avila 137 - 4°, 1050 Lisboa (**t** 00351 213 546 070/ 213 547 270, **f** 00351 213 579 617).
- **Ministério da Educação, Departamento do Ensino Secundário,** Avenida da Boavista 1311, 5°, P-4100 Porto (**t** 00351 226 002 610, **f** 00351 226 094 339).

- **CENOR, Centro Nacional de Recursos para a Orientação,** Departamento do Ensino Secundário, Avenida da Boavista 1311, 5°, P-4100 Porto (**t** 00351 226 002 610/21/25, **f** 00351 226 094 339).
- **Instituto de Emprego e Formação Profissional,** Direcção de Serviços de Avaliação e Certificação, Rua de Xabregas 56, P-1900 Lisboa (**t** 00351 218 682 967, **f** 00351 218 862 117).

More information can be found on the EU websites:

http://europa.eu.int/comm/internal_market/en/qualifications/02-52.htm
http://europa.eu.int/scadplus/citizens/en/pt/1079834.htm

Generally speaking, the higher the qualification, the more likely it is to be related to a regulated profession. If you belong to a professional body by virtue of your qualifications, you should be able to get help and advice from them. If you have a university degree, as opposed to a professional qualification, and wish to get it legalized and recognized in Portugal, you should contact the Legalization Office of the Foreign and Commonwealth Office at Old Admiralty Building, Whitehall, London SW1A 2LG (**t** (020) 7008 1111, **f** (020) 7008 1010) and ask for information on legalization by Apostille in accordance with the Hague Convention of 5 October 1961.

Starting Your Own Business

In terms of business start-ups, foreigners have had had their full share of failures, as well as some success stories. So many people for instance think that running a shop, a bar or a restaurant in a pleasant, sunny place represents a guaranteed income and a relaxed way of earning it. Wrong – think again! This kind of self-delusion is generally a recipe for disaster. Again, many people hoping to set up in business have been in paid employment most of their working lives and may have no experience of running their own business. Worse still, they are unlikely to be familiar with Portugal, speak Portuguese, understand market conditions or cope with the fearsome bureaucracy that can be expected.

Setting up or taking over a business is only a realistic proposition if:

- **You have some experience of running a company, preferably in the same line of business as the one you want to set up.**
- **You can honestly say to yourself that you have a nose for business (after much self-examination).**
- **You have capital, enough to get you through those difficult early years when the business is still getting established.**
- **You have done sufficient market research, and have strong evidence that there really is a niche in the market and that your proposed business has more than a fighting chance.**

- **You have looked thoroughly into all the bureaucratic, legal and tax issues involved.**
- **You have spoken to those who have gone before you and succeeded (and those who have failed – their story can be just as illuminating).**
- **You are patient and can deal stoically with mountains of red tape.**
- **You are prepared to work long hours.**
- **You have got a good, straight, clear-minded lawyer and financial adviser. Both should be recommended by people you know who have used their services and are satisfied.**
- **You speak Portuguese well.**
- **You are doubly sure of all preceding points!**

If you meet all of these conditions then you may be in with a chance. You must then consider the following:

- **Where are you going to establish your business?** This is even more important than when buying a property to live in – location is all for a business. A brief glance at the difference between rental or purchase price of premises in a prime tourist location and another in a back street should make this obvious.
- **What type of business do you want to establish?** Bars, cafés, restaurants and other catering establishments are classic choices – and many ex-pats do run them. It is worth remembering, however, that they are essentially seasonal businesses, so you may have to survive for a year on the takings from the high season. There is also no shortage of such places and competition between them is very fierce. Though it may be many people's first choice when it comes to running their own business, ironically it is the one that offers fewest guarantees of success. Beyond catering, foreigners tend to look at running businesses that are also connected to tourism and leisure, such as campsites, accommodation, riding schools, language academies, rural hotels or B&Bs.
- **Are you going to buy a business that is already established?** This may be a good idea, as it may involve less of an adventure than setting up a new one. The business may already have a client-base and many of the formalities should have been dealt with already. But, if it really is a going concern, why is the current owner selling it? Is the business going downhill and he wants to offload it at your expense? Has the business lost out to new competition in the area? Are the accounts straight or are there lots of hidden debts? Above all, does the owner know something that you do not? Is there for instance some development about to happen up the road that will negatively affect trade?

Remember, not everybody in business is straight. There are plenty of people out there who would sell their grandmother and who would have no qualms about offloading a lame duck business onto the first unsuspecting newcomer. Do not let that person be you. This is where your financial adviser has a vital role to play. It may turn out, after an exhaustive study of the accounts, the competition and local market prospects, that you are being offered the opportunity of a lifetime. But be wary and be sure.

• **Are you going to start a business from scratch?** Starting from nothing is a far more risky affair. If you are planning to set up a business to compete with similar, already-existing companies, remember they have a head start on you. This is not to say that you cannot offer a better product or service to secure a market share, or destroy the competition completely. You can, if you do it the right way. But there may not be enough of a market for two, three or four businesses of the same type in one small town. Enter into competition without knowing the size of the potential market and you could be wasting time and money.

• **Are you going to employ staff to work in your business?** If so, there are a host of issues to consider. Employing staff can be expensive and, as legislation tends to protect workers' rights it is not easy to dismiss employees when the going gets tough. Employers must pay workers' social security contributions, including 22 days' paid holidays each year. If you employ more than five members of staff, 90 per cent of the work force must be from Portugal or the EU.

There are two basic types of employment contract: fixed-term and uncertain duration. Both are for a minimum of six months but a fixed-term contract must state the date of termination, up to a period of three years. A contract of uncertain duration, typically to cover someone who is temporarily absent, can be terminated by giving notice, which varies according to the length of time the person is employed for. Failure to terminate without sufficient notice can lead to employees staying on in their jobs. It is also possible to contract workers using a temporary employment agency.

Employing people can be a difficult issue. It is as well to know the legal position and understand your obligations towards your workers. Again, seek the advice of both your lawyer and financial adviser.

Setting up a business is a challenge – not least from the bureaucratic point of view. The administration has tried to make life easier for would-be entrepreneurs and there are now channels through which help and advice may be sought. One is the ICEP, the Portuguese Investment, Trade and Tourism Institute, which is the nearest thing possible to a one-stop shop for people wanting to do business. The ICEP has several offices throughout Portugal and in many countries throughout the world, among them the UK and Ireland. Its role is to promote Portuguese businesses abroad and provide information for potential investors in the country. You are likely to find English-speakers in their offices in Portugal, as well as those abroad. The *Centros de Formalidades das Empresas* (Business Formalities Centres) can also be helpful. Known as CFEs, they are also one-stop shops for the setting-up of a company (*sociedade*). Here they will explain the setting up process from A to Z, tell you exactly what documents are needed and where to get them, provide information and advice on the most appropriate type of corporate structure, inform you about legal and financial aspects (i.e. the minimum capital legally required) and put you into contact with relevant government bodies.

There are also government agencies that may give incentives (tax breaks) and grants for certain types of business. These are especially aimed at businesses that encourage the use of new technologies and raise product quality, those that help to bring production methods into line with EU requirements and those that encourage the improvement of productivity, hygiene and are environmentally sound. Funds may also be available to enterprises that are likely to stimulate employment in depressed areas. The body that channels incentives, in close collaboration with the CFEs, is the *Instituto de Apoio às Pequenas e Médias e ao Investimento* (IAPMEI), the Institute for Small and Medium-Sized Enterprises and Investment.

Useful addresses are:

- ICEP's main office at Avenida 5° de Outubro 101, 1050-051 Lisboa (**t** 00351 217 950 500, **f** 00351 217 937 521, **www.icep.pt**).
- In the UK, the ICEP premises with the Portuguese–UK Chamber of Commerce at 22–25ª Sackville Street, London W1X 1DE (**t** (020) 7494 1844, **f** (020) 7494 1822, **www.portuguese-chamber.org.uk**).
- In the Irish Republic the ICEP is at 54 Dawson Street, Dublin 2 (**t** 00353 1670 9133/4, **f** 00353 1670 9141, **info@icep.ie**).
- The main office of the Centros de Formalidades das Empresas at Avenida Columbano Bordalo Pinheiro 86, 1070-065 Lisboa (**t** 00351 217 232 300, **f** 00351 217 232 323, **www.cfe.iapmei.pt**).
- The IAPMEI in Rua Rodrigo Fonseca 73/73ª, 1269-158 Lisboa (**t** 00351 213 836 000, **f** 00351 213836 283, **www.iapmei.pt**).

Money and Banking

The Euro

Portugal was among the first wave of countries to introduce the euro on 1 January 2002. In use for large international transactions since January 1999, the euro is now the official currency of Austria, Belgium, Finland, France, Germany, Greece, Ireland, Italy, Luxembourg, the Netherlands, Portugal and Spain. A euro consists of 100 cents or 'eurocents'. All euro coins are legal tender in every member state irrespective of their national origin. Portuguese prices are generally expressed with the € symbol after the amount (unlike those in this book). A full stop is usually used between millions, thousands and hundreds and a comma separates euros from cents. In this book the standard British way of expressing numbers is used, so what in Portugal might read 99.999,99€ is expressed here as €99,999.99.

Pound–Euro Conversion Chart

Exchange rates change constantly; these should be taken only as a guideline.

£1	€1.43	€1	£0.70
£5	€7.15	€5	£3.50
£10	€14.30	€10	£7
£50	€71.50	€50	£35
£100	€143	€100	£70
£500	€715	€500	£350
£1,000	€1,430	€1,000	£700
£5,000	€7,150	€5,000	£3,500
£10,000	€14,300	€10,000	£7,000
£50,000	€71,500	€50,000	£35,000
£100,000	€143,000	€100,000	£70,000
£500,000	€715,000	€500,000	£350,000
£1,000,000	€1,430,000	€1,000,000	£700,000

Portuguese banks used to be mainly state-run dinosaurs whose inefficient, old-fashioned way of operating was legendary. Things have changed a lot in the last decade and banks have been privatized (with the exception of the Caixa Geral de Depósitos), modernized and have also introduced new technologies. Electronic and internet banking in the country now compares favourably with that of other countries and cash machines are to be found just about everywhere, including in supermarkets. The 'Multibanco' system allows card-holders with accounts held at many different banks, both from Portugal and abroad, to make use of cash points all over Portugal. The main banks are the Banco Comercial Portugues (BCP) (which bought out the Banco Portugues do Atlántico (BPA) in 1995), the Champalimaud Group, which owns Banco Totta e Açores and Banco Pinto e Sotto Mayor, the Espírito Santo Group and the Caixa Geral de Depósitos. Foreign banks are also represented, among them familiar names such as Barclays and Citibank and powerful Spanish banking groups, such as Banco Santander Central Hispano (BSCH) and Banco Bilbao Vizcaya y Argentária (BBVA).

As a rule, banks are open 8.30am–3pm, although some branches in commercial and tourist areas may stay open as late as 6pm. Banks close at weekends and on public holidays.

Bank Accounts

Residents and non-residents can open bank accounts in Portugal. While not strictly necessary, non-resident property owners are advised to open a Portuguese account for reasons of convenience. Paying utilities bills on time (by standing order) is the most powerful argument in favour of opening an account, since doing it by transfer from abroad is slower and may prove expensive. Failure to pay the bill on time may result in your electricity or water being cut off and paying bank charges for the privilege.

Which Bank?

Residents clearly have a lot to gain by having a local account, especially if they are receiving a pension or other income from abroad. Banking needs vary from person to person. If you are retiring to Portugal or running a business, you may need a full and fairly sophisticated banking service. If, however, you are a tourist with a holiday home, your banking needs are likely to be very simple and your choice of bank will largely be governed by the convenience factor – whether the bank is near your property and also whether the staff at the bank speak English. If you do not speak Portuguese, you may prefer to deal with a bank where the staff speak your own language.

There are advantages to banking locally. It will make you feel part of the local community and, more importantly, will make the local community feel that you want to be part of them. If you have the luxury of a choice between various convenient banks that speak English, perhaps the most significant factor to take into account would be the bank's charging structure for receiving money. Portuguese banks charge for absolutely everything – and some charge a lot more than others for the simple task of receiving money sent from the UK. Many Portuguese banks also offer excellent internet banking facilities.

Which Type of Account?

Most people will operate a simple current account (*conta corrente*). There are no cheque guarantee cards in Portugal, yet cheques are still widely accepted (if reluctantly) because of the severe penalties that result from abuse of a cheque (see below). Portuguese banks generally pay very little interest on current accounts – about 0.1 per cent. They do not usually pay interest on current accounts held by non-residents. It is also sensible to have a deposit account (*depósito a prazo*). Most banks will arrange for the balance on the current account over a certain sum to be transferred automatically into an interest-bearing account. Interest rates in Euroland are low.

If your needs are more sophisticated than this, study carefully the various types of account available to you. These and their terms of conditions of use differ substantially from the accounts you may be familiar with in the UK.

Opening an Account

Once you have made your choice, go to the branch and open an account. To do so you must be over 18 years of age. Take along some form of ID – which may be either your passport or residency card. Provide proof of an address in Portugal and take along your tax card. If you are not a resident but own a property you will have the tax card anyway. If you have not yet bought a property, you can still obtain the fiscal card, which is required by anybody with financial dealings in Portugal.

It is much easier to open an account on the spot in Portugal than to do it from abroad. If you wish to open an account from abroad you have to look for a branch of the bank in question in your own country, ask for an application form and stipulate at which branch in Portugal you wish the account to be held. If you are not in Portugal most of the time this is not important as the bank will send all correspondence to the address in the country where you are resident.

Your Existing UK Account

If you become a full-time resident in Portugal, it is still a good idea to maintain at least one account open at home. Similarly, if you go back to live in your home country but keep on your Portuguese property, it is sensible to keep an account open there. If you are regularly moving large sums of money between countries then you are best advised to maintain an account in Portugal as well. As a rule it is useful to maintain a couple of accounts, one for everyday spending and another for larger transactions.

'Bad' Cheques

Do not even think about writing a cheque on your Portuguese bank account if there are not sufficient funds in that account to cover the value of the cheque. Bounced cheques lead to substantial bank charges and later problems with your bank and others. If you bounce three cheques, your bank can ban you from writing cheques on any Portuguese bank for up to two years.

'Offshore' Accounts

These are the subject of considerable mystique. Many people resident in Portugal think that by having an offshore bank account they do not have to pay tax in Portugal. This is not true. They only do not pay the tax if they illegally hide the existence of the bank account from the Portuguese taxman. *See* 'Taxation', pp.168–83.

There is no reason why you should not have an offshore bank account but you should only do so for a good reason. If you are thinking of taking up residence in Portugal, you should take careful financial advice.

Cars and Other Private Transport

Importing a car from the UK may only add difficulties to your life. UK cars are generally right-hand-drive models and in Portugal they drive on the right side of the road – an additional hazard. Getting hold of spare parts may also be difficult. Right-hand-drive cars are easily spotted as being 'foreign' (whether imported or not), making them more of a target for car thieves. For all these reasons, you may well decide that it makes more sense to acquire a car in Portugal. Prices vary depending on the model of car. Some are cheaper in Portugal than elsewhere in Europe, others are more expensive.

Buying Vehicles in Portugal

If you buy a Portuguese car from a dealer, the dealer will often register it for you. Otherwise, unless you live in a main tourist area and know someone who has already done it, get someone to do it for you.

Importing Vehicles to Portugal

Temporary Import

You may bring any EU-registered motor vehicle into Portugal for a continuous period of up to 180 days within a given calendar year. This applies to ordinary saloon cars and also to light goods vehicles, trailers, caravans, motorhomes and motorcycles. These rules are applicable in the follwing circumstances:

- **The vehicle is registered in the name of a person who is not resident in Portugal.**
- **The vehicle is brought into Portugal by its registered owner or the person designated to look after it, (the 'keeper' – written authorization is needed).**
- **The vehicle is only for private use.**
- **The vehicle is driven only by its registered owners, or designated keepers, who themselves may not be established, resident or employed in Portugal.**
- **The owner or designated keeper is in possession of the vehicle's registration documents at all times and can produce them on demand to the competent authority.**

Permanent Import

If you intend to become a resident in Portugal, you may import a vehicle tax-free provided you meet the following conditions:

- **The vehicle is only for your private use.**

- **You are in the process of transferring your residency from another EU member state in which you have resided legally for at least 185 days.**
- **You bought the vehicle and paid full tax on the transaction in your former country of residence.**
- **You, as the registered owner, have used the vehicle in that former country of residence for at least six months prior to importing it.**

How to Import a Vehicle

To import a vehicle you must make an application within 12 months of arrival at your local customs office. The application should be submitted along with:

- **The vehicle's logbook.**
- **A certificate of compliance or form 1402, which is issued by the Direcção Geral de Viação (the Portuguese vehicle licensing authority), confirming that the vehicle has undergone an inspection similar to the MOT.**
- **Your driving licence .**
- **Proof that you have applied for a residency permit.**
- **Your tax card (*cartão de contribuinte*) and the last three years' tax declarations or a document from the tax office attesting to income earned in Portugal over the past three years (it may be less if you have not been there for so long).**
- **A certificate of cancellation of residence from your former country of residence (in the case of the UK, such a document is not issued; the consulate will provide you with one to this effect if you can show that you have applied for a residency permit in Portugal).**

You may be asked for additional documents, so contact the customs authorities before making the application to avoid having to make a second trip after applying. Once your application has been submitted and is in process, you may be issued with a limited-validity authorization (*guia de circulação*) permitting you to drive the vehicle while the application is being handled. Once the importation procedure is complete, you cannot sell, loan, pledge or hire the vehicle for the next 12 months and it may only be driven by the registered owners or 'keepers' and immediate family members. You can only import one vehicle tax-free every five years.

Motor Vehicle Documentation

If you run a vehicle in Portugal, you must carry the following documents: **ownership registration document** (*título de registo de propriedade*), obtained at the Vehicle Registration Office (*Conservatória do Registo Automóvel*); **vehicle registration document** (*livrete*), issued by the Vehicle Licensing Authority

(*Direcção Geral de Viação*); **road tax document**, which you purchase annually in June from the local tax office or selected newsagents – the cost varies according to the vehicle's age and size, and it is displayed in the top right-hand corner of the windscreen; **insurance** – third-party is the minimum, and an insurance stamp must be displayed in the bottom right-hand corner of the windscreen; your **ID and driving licence**.

MOT – *Inspecção Periódica Obrigatória* (IPO)

This is compulsory for all vehicles over four years old, is biannual between four and seven years and annual from then on. The IPO must be carried out at an authorized garage where you must produce proof of ownership, the logbook and your tax card before the test is carried out. Once the test is passed, a stamp confirming this is issued and should be placed below the insurance stamp in the bottom right-hand corner of the windscreen.

Car Rental

Car rental is cheaper in Portugal than practically anywhere else in Europe and, apart from the large international companies such as Avis, Europcar, Hertz and Budget, there are many small, local rental companies which are inexpensive. You can find them in all major towns and many smaller places, too; just look in the Yellow Pages. Many have offices at international airports too.

To rent a car you must show proof of identity (ID card or passport for EU citizens and passport for other nationals) and a valid driving licence. A green card is essential and it's wise to take out insurance coverage and collision insurance. Cars are not usually hired out to anyone under 21 though some companies may insist on 23 as the lower age limit. It is also common for rental companies to ask for proof that you have held your licence for a minimum period of 12 months.

Driving Licences

If you have a national driver's licence, you need to exchange it for a Portuguese-issued licence within 12 months of taking up residence in Portugal. You can use a community model driver's licence until it expires but it is still a good idea to exchange this licence for one issued by the Portuguese authority (*Direcção Geral de Viação*) for the following reasons:

- **In Portugal, the address on the licence must reflect the holder's address. If you are resident with a foreign licence then this will not be the case.**
- **The licence can only be renewed or replaced by the original issuing authority, but the *Direcção Geral de Viação* will not renew or replace a licence on which an overseas address figures.**

- **When your licence expires, the Portuguese authorities will not renew it unless you take (and pass) a new driving test.**

Insurance

This is not a matter to be taken lightly. It is essential to insure your home, your car, your family and yourself against all eventualities. It is beyond the scope of this book to go into the finer points of insurance companies and the products they offer but some pointers as to which type of policies might be the best and what they cover follow.

The growth in overseas home ownership has spawned a corresponding growth in tailor-made products to suit the needs of individuals and families who buy property abroad, whether to live in or as an investment. As with all other aspects of property purchasing, it is advisable to look at as many options as possible, go over the fine print and get advice both from experts and from those who have gone before you in order to be able to make an informed decision. Do not sign anything or pay any money until you are absolutely sure that you have chosen the best possible policy. As a general comment, it is probably safer to take out insurance with a large, well-established company, preferably one with experience internationally (and in Portugal). Remember – not being insured or having insufficient insurance cover could cost you dearly.

Insuring Your Home

Whether you use a Portuguese or an international company to insure your home, you are best off with a policy that covers the house (i.e. the building, contents and third-party liability).

It is advisable to find a policy that will cover you for damages that may occur to the building. There are possible causes of damage that are beyond your worst nightmare, so is always best to expect the worst. Obvious things to insure for are damage caused as a result of fire, flooding, burglary, storms, gas explosions, heavy rain, high winds, freezing weather and acts of vandalism. Less likely but still worth including in the policy are natural catastrophes such as lightning or even earthquakes, though you may have to insist on this risk being added to the policy; remember that Portugal suffered a severe tremor in 1755. Items to insure include outbuildings, such as the garage, the garden and any garden furniture, satellite dishes, the swimming pool and/or tennis court, fences, gates and driveways. Beware that no insurance company is likely to pay on a claim if it can be shown that your property had structural faults – all the more reason to have a thorough inspection done before buying.

As for the contents, they should be covered against the same risks. Usually, insurance companies will pay for clothing, bedding and furniture to be replaced, though they may not pay the full replacement value if items lost or damaged are old and therefore partially worn out. A good insurance policy should provide cover for accidental damage to plumbing and electrical installations, damage caused by burglars on entering, replacement of locks after a burglary, loss of keys, alternative accommodation if your house is rendered uninhabitable and the value of food in a deep freeze if the electrical installations give out or you suffer a power cut. Some of these things may not be covered within the terms of a standard policy, so you must look into issues such as the likelihood of power failure and insist on its risks being added to the policy.

If you have any valuable items in the house such as cameras, camcorders, computer equipment, jewellery or antiques, you should document them photographically or on video and keep receipts in a safe place, preferably off the premises. No claim will be considered without them. For a company to insure villas and ground- or first-floor apartments, you will have to install iron bars over the windows and a reinforced door and the company may insist on an alarm system or other security devices.

If you buy an apartment, as opposed to a villa, the community will most likely have insured the whole building, and annual renewal of the policy will be a percentage of your community charges. Find this out before buying. If the building is not insured, or if the insurance is not comprehensive enough, think about buying elsewhere. You must, however, take out a policy covering you for third-party damage to other properties in the block which happens as a result of burst pipes or a fire in your apartment.

It may be harder to get insurance for a holiday home, or at least you must expect to pay a higher premium. Insurance companies view holiday homes as being more at risk owing to the fact that this type of property is likely to stand unoccupied for lengthy periods. It is wise to tell the company that you want a policy specifically for a holiday home, since taking out a general policy may result in claims being dismissed if the truth emerges. The premium charged is likely to be calculated on the number of days' occupancy and certain coverage may be temporarily suspended if the property is left empty for lengthy periods. Check the small print very carefully indeed. It will almost certainly include exclusion clauses, for example limiting cover for theft or storm damage in your absence.

The premium will be calculated by taking various factors into account, among them the building's size, date of construction, value, location (high burglary rates in a given area push the price up) and value of contents. If something happens and you have to make a claim, inform the insurance company as soon as possible after the event and never more than a week after it occurs. If you have been the victim of a burglary you must report this to the police and include the report (*denúncia*) with your claim. This is more difficult if you are away when the robbery occurs, so check with the insurance company to see if any provision is made for such situations. Finally, if you take out the policy in a country other than Portugal, make sure that the policy is valid under Portuguese law.

Insuring Your Car

Most aspects of car insurance are now standardized within EU regulations, which require that all vehicles within the Union be fully insured for third-party damage. This means that you can insure your vehicle with a company in the UK or Portugal or any other member state and are covered for accidents that occur in any EU country. Note that the following stipulations are made concerning insurance companies:

- **The company must be a member of the national motor vehicle insurers' bureau and the guarantee fund of the member state in which your vehicle is registered.**
- **If the company does not have an establishment in the member state in which your vehicle is registered, it must have designated a representative authorized to settle claims in that member state.**

If you cause a road accident, your green card or your insurance certificate is proof that you have compulsory third party insurance, which means the victims can claim compensation. Notify your insurance company of the accident and supply any necessary documents (such as the police report of the accident). The injured party will contact his own insurer, who will in turn contact the National Motor Vehicle Insurance Bureau. This bureau will look after the formalities between the two insurance companies and the injured party.

In the event of an accident for which you are not liable, you are entitled to compensation in accordance with the rules in force either in that member state where the accident occurred or in your country of residence (if the level of compensation is higher there). These rules still differ from one member state to another but you have minimum cover of €350,000 for any personal injuries sustained and €100,000 for material damage. However, the total amount of cover may be limited in some member states when there are several victims involved in a single claim. If the accident is caused by an uninsured or unidentifiable car, you are entitled under EU law to compensation from the motor vehicle guarantee fund of the member state in which the accident occurred, in accordance with the rules in force in that member state.

For more information, look at:

http://europa.eu.int/scadplus/citizens/en/pt/01080002.htm

Insuring Your Family and Yourself

If you are not entitled to health coverage within the Portuguese state system (and even if you are), private health insurance is recommended. This is for several reasons. If you are not covered by the state system and do not have insurance, you may end up spending huge sums of money in the event of an accident or illness. If you are entitled to state coverage, you may find the inadequacies of the Portuguese system off-putting (*see* 'Health and Emergencies', pp.229–31).

Other sound reasons for taking out private cover are: a greater choice of specialists, access to treatment without a long wait, and more chance of being attended to in your own language. For many people this last factor is just as important as the others, since trying to explain an ailment or injury in Portuguese may test your linguistic ability to the limits. Just as with home or car insurance, you are advised to look around and check out what different companies offer. Pay special attention to the small print. You may find that some services are not available for six months and that only basic treatment is covered in the period immediately after taking out the insurance. There are many companies that specialize in policies for foreign residents.

The following UK companies provide health cover for those living abroad:

- The **Exeter Friendly Society**, Lakeside House, Emperor Way, Exeter EX1 3FD (**t** 0808 055 65 75, **www.exeterfriendly.co.uk**). This company has a policy called Interplan Euro which is tailor-made for the expatriate living in Spain or Portugal for a minimum of 180 days a year.
- **BUPA International**, BUPA House, 15–19 Bloomsbury Way, London WC1A 2BA (**t** (01273) 208 181, **www.bupa-intl.com**).
- **PPP Healthcare** (allied with the AXA group) Phillips House, Crescent Road Tunbridge Wells, Kent TN1 2PL (**t** (01892) 503 856, **f** (01892) 503189; **www.ppp healthcare.com**).

Home Utilities and Services

Electricity

Electricity is not cheap in Portugal when compared with the rest of the EU. Not all houses are connected to the grid, especially remote rural properties where it might be necessary to run a generator, although in more popular tourist areas practically everyone has it. On buying or renting a property, one of the first things you should do is get the electricity contract put in your name or make a new one if the property is new. This is done at the local office of *Electricidade de Portugal* (EDP), **t** 800 505 505. EDP is responsible for the distribution of electricity. Do not confuse this company with REN, the *Rede Eléctrica*

Nacional, responsible for the transmission of electricity. You will need to provide proof of identity and of occupancy of the property. It is important to make sure that the last occupant is up to date with their bills on leaving the property – otherwise you might have to pay them.

Voltage is 220AC at 50MHz in Portugal and all plugs are of the two-pin type found all over Europe. UK three-pin appliances will need the plug changing or an adaptor, so take a supply with you if you are going to use various appliances brought from home. Electrical devices brought over from the USA (running at 110v) will need a converter or a transformer to work. Some come with a 110/220 switch. Check this and switch to 220 before plugging in. Appliances that run on 240v (including some TVs) might be a little slow or not work at all. Check this before you go; you might find it is better to buy locally, as electrical devices are not expensive and may be better designed to fit into a Portuguese house. Washing machines and fridges, for example, come in certain, standard dimensions and fitted kitchens are built to take them. Imported appliances simply may not fit.

Modern properties are generally well wired and safe. Older properties may need rewiring or at least an inspection from an EDP-authorized electrician, who will issue a safety certificate or recommend a new installation. Electricity is metered and the company will not authorize connection of the meter or installation of a new one if the wiring is not up to scratch. Check the wiring well before moving in as it may take some time to get reconnected if it has to be replaced. A rural property with no electricity supply can require either an expensive connection from the nearest point of the grid or the installation of a generator. Many people who live in rural properties do, in fact, choose to install a generator anyway, and a small one is useful to cover your needs during power cuts, which are not infrequent in some areas.

Bills are monthly and not always based on actual consumption but an estimate, as is the case with water. It pays to learn to read your electricity meter so that you can see whether the amount you are paying roughly corresponds to the electricity consumed. The estimate should generally be lower, though this is not always the case and you might be paying over the odds. If this is the case, contact EDP and they will do a reading and adjust your bill accordingly. Direct debit is the best way of paying, especially if you are absent (or absent-minded), as non-payment will result in the service being suspended. It is possible to pay a fixed sum every month, calculated on the basis of the previous year's average monthly consumption, in which case the meter is read at the end of the year and you or the EDP pay the difference.

Gas

Apart from in Lisbon and the surrounding area, most Portuguese people do not have piped gas. Elsewhere bottled butane (*butano*) and propane (*propano*) is used for cooking, heating and hot water. Bottled gas is a cheap option, far more economical than electricity, and if installations are regularly inspected it is quite safe. Many Portuguese cookers have two or three gas burners and one electrical ring. An inspection is necessary before you can contract bottled gas from a local supplier. If all installations are in good condition the property will be awarded a safety certificate.

Bottles (*garrafas*) may be picked up at stores or delivered to your home – the service is quite efficient. On buying the first bottle you pay a deposit, and from then on, every time you need gas you swap an empty bottle for a full one. As they are heavy, it is worth having bottles of gas delivered (give the delivery man a tip, especially if you live on an upper-floor apartment without a lift). Prices fluctuate. Currently the 11 kilo bottle for domestic use costs just over €12. Larger bottles of 45 kilos are also available. These are especially useful if you live a long way from the nearest supply point or let your property.

Water

Water is a major issue in the southern half of the Iberian peninsula. In general, the greener, wetter north of both Portugal and Spain get more than enough rainfall, while the drier southern half does not get enough. Water shortages there are a fairly common occurrence; so too are restrictions in summer when supplies are low. Vast numbers of people visit the Algarve every summer, the country's driest region (along with the Alentejo), and it is here that there is most demand. Swimming pools, showering tourists, golf courses and English-style lawns all take their toll on an already insufficient supply. Restrictions or low reserves can mean that the supply is cut off for several hours a day or that pressure is too low to enjoy a decent shower.

These problems may or may not be solved by the massive £1.2 billion megadam project at Alqueva in the Alentejo. This highly controversial project has been hailed by politicians as marking the end to the region's perennial water problems. Environmentalists have taken a different view.

Before buying a property – especially a rural one – it is essential to find out what the likelihood is of water supplies being cut off or restricted. If your neighbours-to-be tell you that this is commonplace, either buy somewhere else or make sure an alternative supply is available to cover your needs during shortages. In rural areas, many people have a well (*poço*) or a borehole (*furo*) to bring water up from below ground; an electric pump is often used for this purpose. In some areas you may have to register a borehole at the local town hall and get a licence to use it. Even then you have no guarantee of water all the time; wells sometimes dry up in summer too. It is therefore advisable to have a water storage tank (*depósito*) installed either on the roof to capture rainwater, or underground. Tanks can also be filled by tanker lorries or from a borehole when supplies are abundant.

If you buy a property that is already connected to the water supply you have to get the contract put in your own name (as in the case of electricity) by presenting your identification and proof of occupancy at the town hall. Make sure that the previous owner or occupier has paid all bills, otherwise you will have to pay them. If you are non-resident, give the authorities your foreign address or that of your representative in Portugal.

Water is metered in Portugal and the cost can vary considerably from one area or even municipality to another, since in some places it is the responsibility of the local council, while in others it is in the hands of private contractors. Prices have generally increased recently, which has encouraged people not to waste water. Bills are usually bi-monthly. You can pay them at the town hall or by direct debit from your bank account. Since meter-reading can be infrequent, the company often sends an estimate of water used. This is fine unless the estimate is far in excess of real consumption over a period of time. Be careful if the estimate is low. When the water company does eventually get around to reading the meter you could suddenly be charged a lot of money. Keep an eye on your bills as there have been many cases of overcharging. Charges are normally in three price bands; the more you use, the more you pay per cubic metre.

Try to economize on water use as much as possible. If you own a villa you can easily get through fantastic amounts unless you find ways of saving. Water used on pools and gardens can represent up to 80 per cent of your water consumption.

- **Make sure your irrigation system is properly installed and working – check that the sprinklers are correctly sited and their 'aim' is right.**
- **Do not irrigate during the heat of the day, as almost half of the water evaporates before it even gets to the plants.**
- **Get any leaks repaired promptly, especially in the case of pools; a lot of water is lost underground without being noticed. It is cheaper to repair the pool than to pay for water loss.**
- **Try to keep usage down below 100 cubic metres; after that the highest rates begin to apply. For villas on plots of up to 800 sq m this should be feasible except perhaps in July and August.**
- **Urge pool and garden maintenance contractors to save as much as possible, vacuuming through the filter rather than 'to waste'.**
- **Consider an alternative garden design to a large lawn, which is costly to maintain (Moorish-style gardens are beautiful, cool and shady). If you want a large grassy area, sow a resilient grass strain such as Bermuda grass.**

Hot Water, Heating and Air-conditioning

Apartments, especially those built for holiday use, often come with a small electric water heater. This is fine for a couple on holiday but is not adequate for a family. A couple of showers and one load of dishes generally uses up all the hot water and you have to wait more than an hour for it to heat up again. For more permanent use you should think of installing either a larger heater (of about 75 litres capacity) or a gas water heater. Electric water boilers are cheaper, cost less to install and, if you take advantage of the cheaper night tariff, can be economical. Gas heaters are costlier to buy and plumb in, but they can provide unlimited hot water, heated from the butane bottle, and may be cheaper in the long run.

Surprisingly, a good central heating system is recommended even in the south of Portugal. In the north it is essential. There is a range of options available using gas, electricity or solid fuel. Some people invest in solar energy, which is expensive to install but, given the amount of sunlight, can prove cheaper in the long run. The technology employed is still not up to providing all electrical needs and heating throughout the whole year, so solar systems are usually used to complement another form of heating.

Many properties, even newly built ones, are advertised with a wood-burning stove. This is the most popular choice, especially since you may also use a stove or fireplace to provide hot water. Firewood is inexpensive, especially in summer when it is a good idea to lay in supplies for the winter.

Electrical heating systems are less used owing to the high cost of electricity and are only really viable if you install storage heaters to take advantage of lower night-time rates. Gas is a reasonably cheap option. Individual heaters with rollers and a space for a butane bottle are very common as a localized form of heating. Do not use them in enclosed areas for too long and always make sure you have good ventilation. Remember, too, that they also dry out the air. Central heating systems that run off bottled gas are common and not overly expensive to install for a small to medium-sized property. Gas-fired under-floor heating is also popular, especially in older, renovated properties.

Old properties are generally poorly insulated, so whatever system you use will not be economical unless you invest in good insulation, otherwise more than half of your heat might just disappear through the roof or the windows. Roof insulation and double-glazing are always money well spent, particularly if you buy a property in central or northern Portugal, but you should consider getting the work done even in the Algarve. Newly built properties should, if regulations are respected, come with proper insulation and damp-proofing, though some builders conveniently forget the rules.

In southern Portugal it can get very hot in summer, so you may consider air-conditioning an essential item rather than a luxury. Some modern properties are built with air-conditioning already installed but you cannot rely on that.

There is a wide choice of air-conditioning systems available, ranging from small units on wheels (for cooling down one room) to large systems covering the whole house. The downside of air-conditioning is that if the system is not well maintained and kept clean it can become a health hazard and may bring on breathing problems.

Communications

Portugal's communications systems have improved greatly in recent years. The postal service is more efficient, the phone system quite modern, mobile users span the generations and the small e-mail- and internet-using community is growing.

Postal Services

Portugal does not have the best postal service in the world but it has been modernized in recent years. There are offices of the **CTT** (*Correios e Telecomunicações*, **www.ctt.pt**) in practically every town and many small shops sell stamps (*selos*). In both cases look for the sign of the red horse carrying a rider blowing the post-horn against a white background. In large towns and cities, post offices are usually open from either 8.30 or 9am to 7pm Mon–Fri, and Sat until 12.30pm. In smaller towns they often close at lunchtime, 12.30–2pm, and may only stay open until 6pm. The main central post office in Praça dos Restauradores in Lisbon has extended hours, until 10pm Mon–Fri and until 6pm Sat; Lisbon Airport has a 24-hour branch.

Portuguese **postcodes** have recently changed format. Previously they comprised four digits, now they are seven, made up of a group of four digits (the original number) followed by a dash and then another group of three, which narrows down the location for sorting purposes. New codes still respect the old ones, so 1070-065, Lisboa would have been simply 1070 before. This is reassuring, as many people still do not use the full version.

When sending a letter abroad you have three choices of service whose delivery time does not differ greatly. First class mail is known as *correio azul*, ('blue post') and mail sent to European destinations from continental Portugal and the Azores takes three days, according to the CTT's website. From Madeira it can take up to five days.

Recently added to CTT's range of services is *azul prime*, a more expensive service, with rates approximately double those of the normal *correio azul* with delivery times of three days to Europe (the same) and five days (one more!) to the rest of the world. Why pay double for a similar service? Possibly the only advantage is the 'track and trace' service by which you can monitor your mail. If you post a letter in a rural area, expect it to take a little longer to be delivered.

Fast, efficient communications are provided by courier services (*mensageiros*). *Correios* has its own messenger service, EMS, which is quick, inexpensive and reliable. Otherwise, most larger international couriers have offices in Portugal.

Telephones

The Portuguese telephone service has recently undergone a profound transformation. The network has been modernized and state-of-the-art technology has been employed. The monopoly formerly operated by **Telecom Portugal** has also been broken up and, with new providers allowed to compete for market-share, the price of calls has come down. Telecom Portugal remains the largest provider, but subscribers can now use the services of **Novis** and **Oni** for provision of fixed telephone services. At first sight it may appear that they are all much the same, but different providers charge different rates for different types of call and there will generally be various special offers and deals available. As in the UK, the best thing to do is get all the information from all of the providers, then highlight the tariffs for the types of call that you are most likely to need.

Whichever provider you choose, you are not completely restricted to using only their services, as there is now the system of 'selection and pre-selection of operator'. This is a form of indirect access that allows you to choose a different provider for certain calls (e.g. national and/or international). Find out the different rates for different types of call and choose the operator accordingly.

Telecom Portugal's own cheap rate is 9pm–9am on weekdays, all day at weekends and on public holidays. Other providers may have cheap rates at slightly different times. If you are unhappy with the service provided by your own operator you can change to another without having to change the number of your line. This is called 'porting' your number. There are some very informative pages on these matters (in English) on the website of ANACOM (*Autoridade Nacional de Comunicações*), **www.icp.pt**, the body responsible for fair competition. Other websites worth visiting are Portugal Telecom, **www.telecom.pt**; Novis, **www.ip.pt**; and Oni, **www.onisolutions.pt**.

If your new house in Portugal already has a telephone line installed then you must get it put into your name. If the line is still 'live' it is useful to arrange ahead of time with the previous occupants to have it transferred to your name on the moving-in date. This will save any confusion over bills. If the line is 'dead' (i.e. because the house has not been occupied for some time), or there is no line at all and you want to be connected, you must apply to Telecom Portugal, who still handle the network itself, regardless of which provider you choose to access the network. You will need the usual documents: proof of identity (passport or residency) and proof of occupancy, which may be either the deeds or a rental contract. Expect connection to take between a few days and a few weeks, depending on where you are. It used to take forever, so do not despair!

Portuguese **telephone numbers** were changed in 2000 and since then there are no longer any area codes. All numbers now begin with a 2 and are made up of nine digits, wherever you are calling. Lisbon numbers all begin with 21 (plus seven more digits), Oporto numbers with 22, Algarve numbers with 28, etc. If you have a number from before 2000 with its area code beginning with a zero (by no means impossible) you could try replacing the zero with a 2 and you may be lucky. However, some smaller places needed an extra digit to make the number up to nine digits, so the trick may not work. From outside the country the code is +351 then the nine-digit subscriber number.

For **emergencies** of all types call **112**.

For **directory enquiries** (which are charged) call **118**. Most post offices have telephone directories for all regions of Portugal or check the directory enquiries website, **www.118.pt**.

Payphones work with 5, 10, 20 and 50 cent coins as well as with the euro and two euro pieces. They are often out of order and impractical for international calls. To avoid this problem, you can buy a phonecard, *cartão telefónico*, available at post offices, press kiosks, tobacconists and other points.

Mobile Phones/Cellphones

Portuguese of all generations are in love with their mobile telephones and it is not unusual to spot a little old lady dressed in black happily chatting away on her Nokia while riding the clattering 28 tram in Lisbon. Call costs are still high compared with other countries but that does not seem to stop people.

There are currently three domestic operators: Optimus, TMN, and Telecel, which is Vodafone in its Portuguese incarnation. When entering Portugal with a mobile phone from another country, be sure to activate the roaming service. Depending on the operator used by the person at the other end, your calls will be handled by one of the Portuguese networks. As with fixed lines, it is possible to use different operators for certain calls, and if you decide to change the operator with whom you have contracted the service this is also possible – as is 'porting' your number.

Mobile numbers in Portugal all begin with either 91, 93 or 96. As always, it pays to shop around and see what the different operators have to offer. All three operators have websites, but only Telecel-Vodafone has pages in English, which only contain business information. If you want to know where to find a phone, look for *pontos de venda* at the bottom of the Optimus home page (**www.optimus.pt**), to the *contactos* link and then *lojas* on the TMN page (**www.tmn.pt**).

Fax Machines

Though overshadowed by e-mail these days, the fax is still a reliable and quick way of staying in touch. If you take your own fax machine to Portugal make sure it is compatible and that repairs and spare parts are available there – otherwise buy locally. Faxes may be sent from and received at post offices; charges are by the page and by distance. If you find the service a little slow and cumbersome, alternative points for sending and receiving are travel agencies and stationers, who will provide the service for varying charges.

Internet and E-mail

If you and your family or friends are connected up, e-mail is rapid and cheap. If you do not have a computer or a telephone line at home there are now cyber cafés in most cities and towns of any size. Hotmail and Yahoo-type addresses are accessible from anywhere in the world, as are many other providers these days. If you want to contract service with a local provider, Telepac is one of the most popular in Portugal and offers the Netpac package for a reasonable rate. Contact them on **www.telepac.pt** or freephone **t** 800 200 079.

Education

For an overview of the educational options (state and private) that are available in Portugal, *see* 'Educating and Raising Children', pp.24–7. Here is some more information on schools and enrolment procedures.

The State System

Infant Education

Education is compulsory in Portugal. Pre-school is optional but it is a good idea to send your children to a state-run *jardim de infância*, as it is free and will give them a good start in Portuguese. Places may be limited depending on demand in the area where you live. Alternatively, there are many privately run pre-school establishments where the facilities may be better.

Primary Education

Compulsory basic education (*ensino básico*), starting from age six, consists of three stages and lasts until age 15. Children aged six on or before 15 September must be enrolled for their first year at school during that calendar year. Those reaching six between 16 September and 31 December may also be authorized to attend if parents request this during the annual enrolment period. The school year lasts from mid-September to the end of June.

Pupils are taught by the same teacher for all subjects in the first stage and have different teachers for each subject in the second and third stages. The core subjects in the first stage include the environment, Portuguese, mathematics, and personal and social development or religious education. These same areas are continued in the second stage in wider multidisciplinary areas that also include languages, social studies, science, art and technology, PE and extra-curricular activities. In addition to the same core subjects, the third stage introduces an optional second foreign language, music or technology courses.

Assessment is a complex area and is regulated nationally. It combines continual assessment and written exams. Poor performance in more than three subjects (particularly if two are Portuguese and mathematics) may mean repeating the year. At the end of the third stage (the last year of compulsory schooling), students must pass tests on all third-stage curricular subjects (*provas escritas globais*). At the end of the third stage, satisfactory attendance and passing the exams earns a basic education certificate (*diploma de ensino básico*).

Upper Secondary and Post-secondary Education

Education at this level, really the second stage of secondary education, can take the form of general education (*ensino secundário/cursos gerais*), technological courses (*cursos tecnológicos*), vocational studies in vocational schools (*escolas profissionais*) or art courses. Entry is determined by successful completion of the nine years of compulsory education. Students wishing to enter vocational schools (*escolas profissionais*) must have completed compulsory education or obtained an equivalent qualification. The national curriculum core subjects in general and technological education are Portuguese, a foreign language, introduction to philosophy, PE, personal and social education or religion. Courses are organized into four branches of study, namely scientific and natural, arts, economic and social, and humanities. Within each of these groups, separate courses are designed for both general and technological students.

Assessment is carried out by teachers in accordance with ministerial guidelines. National final examinations are taken at the end of the three years of general education and successful students receive a *diploma de estudos secundários*; students completing the technological courses also receive a vocational certificate. In vocational schools, successful students receive a *diploma de estudos secundários* and a vocational certificate.

Private Schools

Many foreign residents choose to put their children through private schooling not only because of deficiencies in the Portuguese state system but because they simply feel happier that their children are getting an education more in tune with their cultural background. Many become residents in Portugal after their children have become accustomed to the English or American system and feel that it would be unfair to disrupt their children's progress. English-language private schools are not found everywhere in Portugal, but tend to be concentrated in the areas favoured by ex-pats, e.g.

Greater Lisbon, Oporto, the Algarve and Madeira. If you choose to go and live in the Alentejo or Trás-os-Montes, boarding school or the local system will be your only choices.

There is range of foreign schools that provide education for all ages, from toddlers to pre-university level. Some even have nursery facilities, while other exclusively nursery schools act as feeders to a nearby infants' school. Some are excellent, most are quite good, but others are barely adequate. Watch out for those run on a shoestring – the educational equivalent of the 'bucket-shop'. None is free. If you are planning to send your child to a private school it is essential to visit or at least seek advice and recommendations from other parents.

British schools in Portugal teach the national curriculum syllabus leading to GCSE and A-levels or, in the case of American schools, the equivalent high school qualifications. Many also prepare students for the International Baccalaureate which is especially useful for those planning to go on to university; the title is recognized in many countries other than the UK, Ireland or the USA. While most British schools claim to achieve academic excellence, emphasis is also placed on other aspects of the child's overall development and these schools provide a well-rounded education that gives the student a broad outlook and a well-trained, flexible mind. This is further enhanced by the presence of children from a variety of backgrounds, since foreign diplomats and business people often send their children to such schools. A high percentage of students from the better private schools in Portugal (some schools claim as high as 90 per cent) go on to university studies in many other countries.

Fees are not cheap. Pre-school fees may be more than €2,000 a year, infant school fees €4,000–5,000, junior school fees €5,000–6,500 and fees for the final years over €8,000. Add to this the cost of uniforms (often compulsory), extra-curricular activities, the bus to and from school, trips and a few extras – and get out your calculator!

Health and Emergencies

Portugal is not a country that presents any particular health risks to foreigners other than perhaps the risk of sunburn or sunstroke in summer. Asthmatic and other respiratory complaints are also fairly common owing to pollen in country areas, or pollution in the larger cities. The Portuguese themselves are a healthy nation. Statistics relating to longevity and coronary complaints are encouraging. This is largely due to a Mediterranean-style diet that makes much use of olive oil and garlic and in which fish, rice and salad are staples. Where the Portuguese let themselves down is through smoking, alcohol consumption and road accidents. AIDS statistics, especially in prisons and amongst the 15–24 age group, are alarmingly high – the second highest in Europe. The Portuguese also take less exercise on average than people in other European countries.

State Health Care

State-run health care, despite improvements in recent years, is still deficient in many areas of Portugal. The Minister of Health recently called the system a 'national shame' and it is going through a difficult period. Waiting lists for operations are long and thousands of patients do not have a doctor in their local health centre (*centro de saúde*). Worrying stories in the press concerning medical blunders are common, as are complaints about disregard for the most basic rules of doctor–patient care. Another problem is that away from the big cities there is no choice but the public hospital. Private hospitals only exist where there is demand and the money to support them, while there is also a shortage of specialists in certain important fields. However, the system is uneven. The greater Lisbon area, for example, has five hospital beds for every 1,000 inhabitants, a figure that is on a par with other areas of Europe. Lisbon and Oporto, actually, probably have a surfeit of doctors. Plans are now under way to tackle these issues. An ambitious scheme for public–private partnerships has been launched, allowing the private sector to take part in the management and financing of hospital units. Government plans include the construction of 10 new hospitals and the renovation and replacement of several others. This programme will cost somewhere in the region of €1.6 billion. Public- and private-sector partnership is to be extended to other aspects of health service. A new Hospital Bill, presented in autumn 2002, provided for state hospitals to be managed by private entities while remaining under state ownership. Increased hospital services are also to be contracted out to the private sector, while further reforms include reduction in waiting lists and reform of prescription procedures.

Despite its defects, the system is not entirely bad;, if you are an EU or EEA citizen you are entitled to use it mostly free of charge, whether you are a working in Portugal or are retired. If you are working, you will be issued with a *livrete de assistência médica* either by your local health centre, the regional centre (*Administracões Regionais de Saúde*) or directly by your employer. If you are living on a pension or your own means and have paid insurance contributions into your own country's system, you have the same rights as a Portuguese person.

Private Health Care

Many foreign residents prefer to use private health facilities, which are numerous enough in ex-pat areas. It is not difficult to find doctors and dentists who speak English, and there are many practices, clinics and small hospitals catering for the resident and temporary foreign population. There are also plenty of specialists in other areas such as physiotherapy, psychotherapy, aromatherapy, homeopathic medicine and even Reiki, many of whom advertise in English-language newspapers and magazines. There are clinics for alcohol and drug-abusers and the Algarve has several health farms for those wanting to lose weight, clean out the system and generally rejuvenate themselves.

Emergencies

The best way of dealing with emergencies is to be ready for them. Depending on where you are, emergency services may be better or worse-equipped, faster or slower to respond, although in major cities and tourist areas they tend to be better.

One telephone number you must learn is **112,** which serves for the fire brigade (*bombeiros*), the ambulance service (*ambulância*) or the police (*polícia*). Ask for the appropriate service. English is often spoken but you cannot guarantee this, so learn at least those three words and enough Portuguese to describe your location, say your address and explain your problem.

Take the trouble to learn the basic words and phrases relative to any condition you might be suffering, particularly if this is likely to worsen at any given moment. For some useful expressions, *see* **References**. The more remote your house, the more important this is. If you have friends and good neighbours that you know you can count on in an emergency, keep their telephone numbers visible, close to your own phone. Most private health schemes have a number you can call in emergencies; learn it or keep it equally visible.

Welfare Benefits

People can qualify for welfare benefits in one of three ways – by enforced reciprocal EU–EEA rules, under the rules of the country where they pay social security contributions or under the rules of the country where they are living.

The General EU Rules

The basic idea behind the EU–EEA rules is that persons exercising their right to move from one EU–EEA state to another should not lose out on their welfare benefit rights by doing so. The people covered by the EU–EEA rules are:

- **Employed and self-employed nationals of EU–EEA states.**
- **Pensioners who are nationals of EU–EEA states.**
- **Subject to certain restrictions, members of the families of the above, whatever their nationality.**
- **Civil servants of EU–EEA states and members of their families, provided they are not covered by an enhanced scheme for civil servants in their own country. This is generally not a problem for UK civil servants.**

Note that the EU–EEA rules do not cover the economically inactive (people retired early, students, etc.). The rules cover:

- **Sickness and maternity benefits.**
- **Accidents at work.**
- **Occupational diseases.**
- **Invalidity benefits.**
- **Old-age pensions.**
- **Widows and other survivors benefits.**
- **Death grants.**
- **Unemployment benefits.**
- **Family benefits.**

The rules do not replace the national benefits to which you might be entitled. They coordinate the national schemes. They decide in which of several possible countries a person should make a claim and which country should pay the cost.

Apart from the basic principle that you should not lose out by moving within the EU, the other principle is that you should only be subject to the rules of one country at a time. The law of a member state cannot – except in the case of unemployment benefit – take away or reduce your entitlement to benefit just because you live in another member state. If you remain entitled to, say, a UK benefit whilst living in Portugal, payment of benefit to which your were entitled in your original member state can be paid in a number of different ways, depending on the state and benefit concerned:

- **It can be paid by the benefit authorities in the member state in which you now live acting on behalf of the benefit authorities in your original country.**
- **It can be paid to you directly in your new country by the benefit authorities in your old country.**

There are two main factors in deciding which rules apply to you:

- **Which country insures you?** You are insured in the country where you carry out your work. If you work regularly in more than one member state you are insured in the country where you live. Short-term posting (less than one year) to another country is ignored. Retired people who have only worked in one member state will remain 'attached' to that state for pension and other purposes for the rest of their lives. People who have worked in several states will have built up pension entitlements in each member state in which they worked for more than one year.
- **In which country do you live?** Some benefits flow from your presence in a country. Each potential benefit, both in the UK and in Portugal, has associated rules stipulating which categories of people are entitled to benefit from it.

What Portuguese Benefits Can You Claim?

The law is complex, so if you think you may have an entitlement to benefit, seek specialist advice. If you need to claim benefits in Portugal then your entitlement will be determined by the social security payments you have made in Portugal and any relevant contributions made in the UK.

• **Accidents at work**: Unless you have worked in Portugal at some time, you are not likely to benefit from this. It is outside the scope of this book.

• **Occupational diseases**: Unless you have worked in Portugal at some time, you are not likely to benefit. These benefits are outside the scope of this book. You should continue to receive any benefits you are entitled to in your former country – e.g. the UK. Unless you have been insured in several member states, the amount of the benefit you will receive will be calculated solely in accordance with your former country's (normally the UK's) rules. You will still have to comply with directions received from the UK authorities in respect of medical examinations, etc.

• **Old-age pensions**: Unless you have worked in Portugal at some time you are not likely to benefit from a Portuguese pension. You will, of course, continue to receive your UK pension – *see* 'Retirement', pp.198–9.

• **Unemployment benefits**: If you lose your job, the Portuguese unemployment benefit authority must take into account any periods of employment or NI contributions paid in another EU country when calculating your entitlement to benefits in Portugal. You must, however, have made at least some insurance payments in Portugal prior to claiming unemployment benefit in Portugal. That means you cannot go to Portugal for the purpose of claiming benefit. You should obtain form E301 from the UK benefit authorities (or from your home state if it is not the UK) before going to Portugal. If you travel to Portugal to seek employment there are restrictions on your entitlement to benefit:

- **You must have been unemployed and available for work in your home country for at least four weeks before going to Portugal.**
- **You must contact your 'home' unemployment benefit authority and obtain form E303 from them before leaving for Portugal. If you do not have this, payment of benefit in Portugal can be delayed substantially.**
- **You must register for work in Portugal within seven days of your arrival.**
- **You must comply with all the Portuguese procedural requirements.**
- **You will be entitled to benefit for a maximum of three months.**
- **If you cannot find a job during that period you will only be entitled to continuing unemployment benefit in your home country if you return within the three-month period. If you do not, you can lose all entitlement to benefits.**

- **You are only entitled to one three-month payment between two periods of employment.**

- **Family benefits**: If the members of your family live in the same country you are insured in, then that country pays the benefits. You are entitled to the same benefits as nationals of that state. If your family does not live in the same country as you are insured in, then, if you are entitled to benefits under the rules of more than one country, they will receive the highest amount to which they would have been entitled in any of the relevant states.

If you work in one state and your spouse works in another state the benefit is paid by the state in which the children live, with, if necessary, a top-up from the state in which the other parent works. Pensioners normally receive family benefits from the state that pays their pension.

In practical terms these cases are complex and you should seek advice.

What UK Benefits Can You Claim?

Welfare benefits in the UK are divided into 'contributory' and 'non-contributory' benefits.

The former are benefits to which you only become entitled if you have paid (or been credited with) sufficient National Insurance contributions to qualify you for payment. The latter do not depend on your having paid any National Insurance contributions.

In the UK there are various classes of National Insurance contributions. Not all rank equally for benefits purposes, and some types of National Insurance contributions cannot be used as qualifying payments for certain benefits.

Class 1: Paid by employees and their employers and consisting of a percentage of income up to a certain maximum.

Class 2: A flat-rate payment paid by self-employed people.

Class 3: Voluntary payments made by people no longer paying Class 1 or Class 2 contributions. These protect their right to a limited range of benefits.

Class 4: Compulsory 'profit-related' additional contributions that are paid by self-employed people.

The differing types of NI payments qualify you for these various benefits.

As well as being categorized as 'contributory' and 'non-contributory' benefits, benefits are also categorized into 'means-tested' and 'non-means-tested' benefits. The former are paid only if you qualify under the eligibility criteria for the benefit in question and are also poor enough to qualify on financial grounds – generally including income and savings. The latter are paid to anyone who meets the eligibility criteria, irrespective of their wealth. (Means-tested UK benefits are likely to be of little interest to the resident in Portugal.)

NI Contributions and Entitlement to UK Benefits

	Class 1	Classes 2 and 4	Class 3
Maternity Allowances	Yes	Yes	No
Unemployment Benefit	Yes	No	No
Incapacity Benefit	Yes	Yes	No
Widow's Benefit	Yes	Yes	Yes
Basic Retirement Pension	Yes	Yes	Yes
Additional Retirement Pension	Yes	No	No

• **Accidents at work**: Any benefits you presently receive from the UK benefits system as a result of an accident at work should remain payable to you despite the fact you have moved to Portugal.

• **Occupational diseases**: Any benefits you receive from the UK benefits system as a result of an occupational disease should remain payable to you despite the fact you have moved to Portugal.

• **Invalidity benefits**: Any National Insurance benefits you receive from the UK benefits system as a result of invalidity should remain payable to you despite the fact you have moved to Portugal. Attendance Allowance, SDA and DLA are not usually payable if you go to live abroad permanently.

• **Old-age pensions**: If you are already retired and you only ever paid National Insurance contributions in the UK you will receive your UK retirement pension wherever you choose to live within the EU–EEA. You will be paid without deduction (except remittance charges) and your pension will be updated whenever the pensions in the UK are updated. If you have established an entitlement to a retirement pension in several EU countries by virtue of working in them, all of the pensions will be payable to you in Portugal. Once again they will be paid without deduction (except remittance charges) and your pension will be updated whenever the pensions in those countries are updated. If you have not yet retired and you move to Portugal (whether you intend to work in Portugal or not) your entitlement to your UK pension will be frozen and the pension to which you are entitled will be paid to you at UK retirement age.

This freezing of your pension can be a disadvantage, especially if you are still relatively young when you move to Portugal. This is because you need to have made a minimum number of NI contributions in order to qualify for a full UK state pension. If you have not yet done this but are close, it may be worth making additional payments while you are resident overseas. You may choose to pay either by continuing Class 2 or Class 3 contributions.

You may pay Class 2 contributions if:

- **you are working abroad.**
- **you have lived in the UK for a continuous period of at least three years during which you paid NI contributions and you have already paid a set minimum amount of NI contributions.**

- **you were normally employed or self-employed in the UK before going abroad.**

You may pay Class 3 contributions if:

- **you have at any time lived in the UK for a continuous period of at least three years.**
- **you have already paid a minimum amount of NI contributions in the UK.**

Class 2 contributions are more expensive but, potentially, cover you for maternity allowance and incapacity benefits. Class 3 contributions do not. In both cases you apply in the UK on form CF83. The decision as to whether to continue to make UK payments is an important one.

- **Widow's and other survivors benefits**: Any benefits you receive from the UK benefits system as a result of your being a widow should remain payable to you despite the fact that you have moved to Portugal.
- **Unemployment benefits**: You may be able to get contribution-based Jobseeker's Allowance in the EU–EEA for up to 13 weeks if you:
  - **are entitled to contribution-based Jobseeker's Allowance on the day you go abroad.**
  - **have registered as a jobseeker for at least four weeks before you leave (this can be less in special circumstances).**
  - **are available for work and actively seeking work in the UK up to the day you leave.**
  - **are going abroad to look for work.**
  - **register for work at the equivalent of a job centre in the country you are going to within seven days of last claiming Jobseeker's Allowance in the UK (if you do not, you may lose benefit).**
  - **follow the other country's system for claiming benefit.**
  - **follow the other country's benefit rules, such as being available for and actively seeking work, that would have applied if you had stayed in the UK.**

Crime and the Police

Despite a recent rise in crime (often blamed on immigration), Portugal still remains a relatively tranquil, crime-free society. Violent crime is not really a problem suffered by foreign residents, since it is mostly restricted to drug-related incidents in the slum areas on the outskirts of Lisbon and other larger cities. A UN survey in 2000 on violent crime worldwide cited Portugal as one of the safest countries in which to live.

Burglaries are a problem in areas where there are large numbers of foreign residents, and again these are often drug-related. Villas left empty for long periods of time, especially those rented to tourists, are the main targets. Changeover days are notorious for burglaries. This is when visitors are at their most vulnerable – recently arrived, relaxed and forgetful of basic security precautions. Burglars tend not to be sophisticated – they go for anything that is easy to sell (cameras, jewellery, cash).

Muggings (though statistically low) are becoming a problem in cities like Lisbon and Oporto. Pick-pockets and bag-snatchers operating in shopping areas and on public transport are more of a problem. In tourist areas it pays to be vigilant. Car crime is also fairly common and foreign-registered cars are frequently targets for break-ins and robberies. Nothing valuable should ever be left in an unattended car, either in full view or hidden. In smaller towns and cities, street crime is not much of a problem at all.

How to Avoid Being Robbed

Avoiding crime is really a question of being practical, alert and showing common sense.

On the Beach and in the Streets

- **When travelling by air, train or coach, especially on arrival at the airport or station, always keep your luggage in full view. Your money, credit cards and important documents should be spread around as many different pockets, handbags, money belts, etc. as possible. This reduces the risk of *losing everything* in one go.**
- **If you are sitting outside at a café, do not drape coats or jackets over the back of a chair, or leave them out of sight under the table. Keep them on your lap or in an empty chair next to you.**
- **Carry shoulder bags, handbags or small rucksacks across your chest or at the front of your body. If you are walking along a narrow street keep them on the pavement side, away from the road. Keep a hand placed over your bag, which should be fastened.**
- **Take as few valuables and as little money as possible to the beach. If you are in a group, one person should stay behind while the others swim. If you are alone, choose a spot next to a respectable-looking family and ask them to watch over your things when you go into the water.**
- **Do not carry large amounts of cash; take just enough for your needs such as shopping, a meal or an evening out. Use a money belt or if it is not too hot wear a jacket with an inside pocket that can be fastened.**
- **When changing money or withdrawing from a bank, ask for small denomination notes. If you have larger denominations, do not wave them around; try to get to a bank or shop where you can change them for smaller notes.**

- Do not wear expensive jewellery or watches when out in unknown areas.
- Body language can make you a target or dissuade thieves. Even if you do not know your way around, try not to look lost. Walk in a confident manner, looking straight ahead. Avoid standing on a street corner looking at a map. Plan where you are going before setting off and try to memorize the route.
- Watch out for thieves who work in pairs or teams, one at either end of a street. They often use mobile telephones to communicate the presence of their next victim. Be careful of strangers who ask for directions or who 'politely' let you get on to the bus or tram first.
- If you turn into a street where there is obviously drug-pushing (and consuming) going on, turn around and walk away briskly.
- If you are held up at knife or gunpoint, hand over your goods. *Do not argue or try to be a hero.* If you only have a small amount of money on you the loss is minor compared with what may otherwise happen.

Car Crime

- Never leave anything valuable in the car, not even in the boot, when it is unattended, especially overnight. Foreign-registered cars are frequent targets for break-ins.
- Where possible, leave your car in an attended car park. This is no guarantee as robberies do happen and owners do not usually accept responsibility, but it is still a safer option than leaving the car on the street.
- Keep your windows closed when stopped at traffic lights and be careful of people selling paper handkerchiefs or offering to clean the windscreen.

Burglary and Break-ins

This is a problem in larger towns and cities and in tourist areas such as the Algarve where properties (especially villas) are left unoccupied for long periods or rented out. Guests at rental villas are frequently victims.

- Insure your home before moving in.
- Be alert when moving house; do not leave jackets, coats or bags with wallets and purses in them unattended.
- If you are moving into a newly built property, change all external locks on arrival. Many different people will have been involved in the building, fitting and finishing off. You never know how many copies are going around. Double locks are recommended and the insurance company may insist on them.
- If you let your property out, change the external locks annually.
- If you are having a property built, order a wall-safe to be built in.

• **Have an armoured door (*porta blindada*) fitted if there is not one already. Many modern houses and apartments come with this pre-fitted. The door should have a spy-hole so that you can see who arrives.**

• **Villas and apartments on the ground, first and second floors should have metal security bars (*gradas de segurança*) fitted on windows. The insurance company will almost certainly insist on this. This also applies to windows and doors that give on to an internal patio.**

• **Have a burglar alarm installed – there is a huge range available.**

• **Install random time light switches to give the impression that the property is occupied even when it is not.**

• **If you have a holiday home that is not used frequently, do not leave anything of value there.**

• **If you rent your property out, include warnings to guests in the information pack provided. Recently arrived holidaymakers are often over-relaxed and burglaries frequently happen on changeover days. Burglars are observant and know when to strike.**

• **In case of burglary, report it to the police immediately. You cannot make an insurance claim if you do not present a copy of the report (*denúncia*).**

Police Forces

As in many other European countries, Portugal has more than one police force, who often go armed. Certain areas of responsibility are assigned to each, though they may overlap in their functions. It has taken a long time for Portuguese people to overcome the mistrust felt towards law enforcement bodies for their role in the Salazar dictatorship. The police have worked hard to improve their image but sometimes old authoritarian attitudes manifest themselves.

• ***Policia de Segurança Pública* – Public Security Police**: The grey-uniformed PSP are the city police. Foreign residents will have dealings with them as they are responsible for residents' cards, handling traffic offences in cities, directing traffic and patrolling the streets, and are the force to which most crime is reported.

• ***Brigada de Trânsito* – Traffic Police**: The traffic police, or highway patrol, are to be seen on the main roads and are responsible for controlling speeding, dangerous driving, non-use of seat belts, etc. for which they may fine you on the spot. They are normally responsible for dealing with accidents.

• ***Guarda Fiscal* – Coastguard**: As Portugal is now on the drug importation route from South America, the 'Fiscal Guard' have their work cut out. Their remit also includes towns and villages that are a little way inland.

• ***Guarda Nacional Repúblicana* – National Republican Guard**: Not to be messed with, the GNR is a paramilitary organization that is generally called in when there is a threat to public order.

Taking Your Pet to Portugal

If you keep a pet in Portugal and wish to take it with you on trips home, or if you are moving to Portugal and taking your pet, you should be aware of the current regulations. Portugal and the UK both belong to the PETS 'animal passports' scheme, by which animals may be moved freely between those EU (and other) countries which are signatories. The Azores and Madeira are excluded. The Republic of Ireland does not at present have a PETS scheme, so if you take your animal back from Portugal it will have to go into quarantine unless you are entering from the UK. (Other signatories are: Andorra, Austria, Belgium, Denmark, Finland, France, Germany, Gibraltar, Iceland, Italy, Liechtenstein, Luxembourg, Monaco, the Netherlands, Norway, San Marino, Spain, Sweden, Switzerland and Vatican City.)

The scheme applies only to dogs and cats (including guide dogs) that are resident in either the UK or one of the PETS qualifying countries. Animals that meet the scheme's rules can enter (or re-enter) the UK without having to undergo six months' quarantine. The same applies in reverse. Animals that do not meet all the rules must go into quarantine, though you might be able to obtain early release if they can be shown to comply with the necessary PETS requirements. To bring your animal into the UK under PETS from one of the qualifying countries you must carry out the following procedures:

- **Have your pet fitted with a microchip. This is for identification purposes and can be done in any country.**
- **Get your pet vaccinated against rabies. This must be done in a country that is a signatory of the scheme.**
- **Once vaccinated, your animal must be blood-tested to make sure that the vaccine has provided a satisfactory level of protection against rabies. This test must also be done in a participating country.**
- **Once the blood test has shown nothing nasty, then you will be given the PETS certificate. This is effectively the animal's 'passport'.**
- **If you have this done outside the UK and intend to take the animal back with you there is a six-month waiting period before the PETS certificate is valid, because an animal that is infected before vaccination would not be protected against rabies. Six months (equivalent to the length of quarantine) is the time needed for most infected animals to display any clinical signs of rabies. This applies even in cases of countries where 'virtually no rabies' has been reported.**
- **If you wish to keep your pet ready to travel under the Pet Travel Scheme you must ensure that it is given an anti-rabies booster jab on or before the 'Valid until' date on the PETS certificate. You should then apply to your government-approved vet (a local veterinary inspector in the UK) for a new PETS certificate.**

• If you lose the certificate you will need to obtain a new one from a government-authorized vet in a qualifying country. The vet will need to be satisfied that your pet meets the necessary requirements of the scheme i.e. it has first been microchipped, then vaccinated and has then had a blood test showing satisfactory protection against rabies.

• When taking your pet back to the UK, it must be treated against ticks and a tapeworm 24–48 hours before it is checked in for the journey to the UK. Any qualified vet can carry out the treatment. The vet must also issue an official certificate of treatment to show that this treatment has been carried out. You will have to sign a declaration (PETS 3) that your animal has not been outside any of the PETS qualifying countries (listed in the accompanying form PETS 3A) in the six months before it enters the UK. Your animal must enter England from a PETS country travelling on an approved route with an approved transport company.

Contact the **Veterinary Laboratory Agency**, New Haw, Addlestone, Surrey KT15 3NB (**t** (01932) 357 345; **f** (01932) 357 856).

Portuguese Food and Drink

Eating out in Portugal is a delight. Food is generally of excellent quality and eating well is not expensive. Visitors and residents must get used to eating a little later than in northern Europe, though eating times are by no means as exaggeratedly late as in neighbouring Spain. Lunch is served 1–3pm and dinner 8pm to midnight, though do not expect to be served much later than 10pm in out-of-the-way places.

Throughout the day it is possible to drop into any one of a thousand bars for a restorative drink or snack – quick snacks are still very much a part of the culture in Portugal.

Restaurants and Main Meals

There are a wide variety of restaurants available, from modest to top-class. At the lowest end of the range are *tascas*, small and usually family-run taverns where the tablecloths are made of paper and the crockery might have seen better days, but where service is friendly and the food simple but always wholesome. At the other end, there are designer restaurants that would not be out of place in London, New York or Milan. Most come somewhere between these extremes. International cuisine is increasingly a part of the restaurant scene both in the main cities and in tourist areas, so getting pasta, pizza, curry, hamburgers, Tex-Mex, etc. is not a problem.

On arrival in a typical Portuguese restaurant several snacks are placed before you, without being ordered. This may be some bread rolls (*pão*), a pat of butter (*manteiga*), and a combination of some little cheeses (*queijinhos*), slices of spicy sausage (*chouriço*) or olives (*azeitonas*). You end up paying for these whether you wanted them or not, but since service can be quite slow they do make a welcome entrée. Main courses tend to be served in very generous portions and come accompanied by rice or potatoes, greens and a salad. Strictly traditional restaurants still offer a starter, then a fish dish followed by a meat dish and a pudding. The concept of *nouvelle cuisine* does not work well in the Portuguese context – portions are rarely minimalist. If you have a smaller appetite and find you cannot eat everything, you could just ask for a half portion (*uma meia dose*), a legitimate request that is usually respected.

Service is not generally charged in simpler cafés and restaurants though by paying for the starters you have effectively paid a form of cover charge. Tipping is at the discretion of the diner but 10 per cent is generally acceptable. Tip generously, however, in the place that you plan to make your 'regular'. This can pay off later in terms of friendly service and, maybe, the odd drink on the house.

Fish and seafood, as you might expect for a coastal nation, figure largely in Portuguese cuisine (*cozinha portuguesa*). For fish eaters, in fact, Portugal is not far short of paradise and the range on offer is astounding. Probably the most typical of all fish served is cod (*bacalhau*), for which, they say, there are 365 different recipes! One of the most common ways of preparing fish is to salt it and grill it. This is often the way with cod but also with sardines (*sardinhas*) and *dourada*, a type of bream. Also found frequently on the menu, battered, fried or cooked in the oven as appropriate, are red mullet (*salmonetes*), tuna steaks (*atum*), swordfish (*espadarte*), sole (*linguado*), grouper (*garoupa* – not unlike bream but better) and scabbard (*peixe de espada*). Look out also for crabs (*caranguejos*), shrimps (*camarões*), cuttlefish (*chocos*), clams (*ameijoas*), barnacles (*perceves*), squid (*lulas*), prawns (*gambas*) and, of course, lobsters (*lagostas*).

There is no lack of choice for meat-eaters either. Steaks – veal, beef or pork – often come simply grilled or done on a hot plate with little or no spices. They can be livened up with some *piri-piri*, a chilli sauce that originates from the former colony of Timor and which can pack quite a punch. It goes especially well with chicken (*frango*), which figures on just about every menu in almost every restaurant. Chicken is best when barbecued (*no churrasco*) or grilled (*na grelha*). Beef can be a little tough and not especially tasty but pork is almost always good. Highly recommended is pork cooked with clams (*porco à alentejana*) from the Alentejo region. Another delicious regional variety is roast suckling pig (*leitão assado*) from the Bairrada region but found on menus throughout the country. Lamb is generally very good indeed. Plain, grilled ribs, *costoletas*, are the most common way of serving up lamb but look out for it in the hearty *ensopado* stew. Roasted kid (*cabrito*) is considered a great delicacy but the animal must be slaughtered very young to be savoured at its best.

Look out also for soups (*sopas*) and stews (*ensopados*), which in Portugal are cheap, wholesome and extremely filling. *Caldo verde* is a standard, a broth made from cabbage and potato and sometimes with ham in chunks or slices. A classic that is found on many menus is *sopa à alentejana*, a garlic (lots of garlic!) and bread soup served with a poached egg in it; this soup should not be taken on a romantic dinner date. *Cozido à portuguesa* is a stew with various meats, sausages and cabbage, and *feijoada* is a bean stew that comes with either meat, seafood or snails.

The sweet-toothed are in luck in Portugal as desserts, *sobremesas*, are very good and there is an unbelievable range of sticky, gooey, high calorie puddings and cakes. On a typical restaurant menu you are likely to find rice pudding (*arroz doce*), custard (*leite crème*), caramel pudding (*pudim*) and chocolate mousse (*mousse de chocolate*), which can be excellent. For those who are not so sweet-toothed there is always the option of cheese, of which there are many varieties. Try *queijo de ovelha*, ewe's cheese; *queijo fresco*, cottage cheese; or *requeijão*, a cheese not unlike ricotta.

Vegetarians may have a rough time in Portugal, except in tourist areas where restaurants have begun to appreciate that not everybody eats meat or fish. However, waiters in traditional restaurants may still look at you with puzzled amusement if you ask for vegetarian food. As a vegetarian you are likely to do a lot better in an Indian, Chinese or Italian restaurant if there is no specifically 'veggie' establishment to be found.

Breakfast (*O Pequeño Almoço*)

The Portuguese are not overly concerned about breakfast. The name '*pequeño almoço*' means, as in French, 'little lunch'. For many Portuguese, breakfast means getting charged up on caffeine before beginning the (long) working day. If you want to take breakfast outside your home your best bet is to make for a café or pastry shop (*pastelaria*). There you will find a basic continental-style breakfast on offer: coffee with a croissant or similar type of pastry.

Coffee comes in many sizes and forms but at breakfast time a *galão*, a large, milky coffee, is often preferred, or, failing that a simple *café com leite*, white coffee. For an early-morning pick-me-up caffeine hit, a *bica*, small, strong and generally with a pile of sugar stirred in, is recommended. There are more pointers to Portugal's complex coffee-drinking culture below in 'Coffee, Tea and Soft Drinks', p.251. For those who cannot do without a solid, English-style breakfast, there are cafeterias in the main tourist areas that will do the full fried 'works', and these days it is not uncommon to find places that cater to foreign breakfasting habits and provide cereals, fruit juice and toast with marmalade or jam.

Lunch (*O Almoço*)

Many Portuguese people have lunch out rather than going home and in any town or city there is no shortage of establishments offering *almoços* or *comidas*. Many do not qualify as restaurants as such but are taverns (*tascas*), cafés (*cafetarias*), beer houses (*cervejarias*), specialized fish and seafood establishments known as *marisquerias* or *casas de pasto*, cheap dining rooms offering a set-menu three-course meal served only at lunch time.

Lunch is usually served from 1pm onwards – though in tourist areas it is possible to be served earlier.

Always worth looking at if you are on a budget is the *ementa turística*, which does not mean 'tourist menu' but the set meal of the day. It usually consists of two courses with a couple of choices for each plus beer or wine. Going *à lista* (à la carte) can be much more expensive.

Dinner (*O Jantar*)

Served from about 7.30 or 8pm. Dinner may be as small or large as your system can take. Generally speaking the *ementa turística* is not served at dinner time and it is more common to go *à lista*.

Snacks

Bars, cafés, cafeterias and *pastelarias* offer a wide range of options for snacking either between or as an alternative to meals, especially if you are not feeling up to a full meal. The classic Portuguese snack is the *prego no pão*, a steak sandwich, which may also come with a fried egg. If this seems a little bland, you can ask for some *piri-piri* to give it a bit of zing. In Madeira the steak is marinated in this sauce and garlic too.

There are also many deep-fried snacks, such as *rissóis*, a kind of meat patty or rissole, *pastéis de bacalhau*, cod fish cakes. In some places you will see some familiar-looking triangular things. Ask the name and you will be told that they are called *somousas* (samosas), a legacy from Portugal's colonial past in the Indian sub-continent. Sandwiches (*sandes*) of every type are available on demand, commonly filled with cheese, which is often of the bland, processed variety, ham (*fiambre*) or cured ham (*presunto*), which is much tastier. A *sande mista* is a toasted sandwich with ham and cheese.

Regional Cuisine

Portugal's geographic and cultural diversity is also expressed through its food; just about anywhere you go you will find something special that is unique to the region.

Alentejo

The Alentejo region is famous for its cuisine. *Lisboetas* often drive out at weekends to eat lunch. The most famous dishes are the *porco à alentejana*, pork cooked with clams, and the garlic-rich soup *sopa à alentejana*, but it does not end there. Try *ensopado de cabrito*, kid stew, and *coelho frito*, rabbit fried in local olive oil. Bread and cheese never makes for a disappointing meal, so try goat's cheese from Alandroal or the ewe's cheese from Serpa, Nisa or Évora. Cakes and pastries from here take some beating; especially good are the cakes baked with eggs and almonds from the convents in Portalegre and Beja.

The Algarve

Be sure to try some seafood soups, *sopas de marisco*; Lagos-style octopus on the grill, *polvo na grelha*; and grilled squid or cuttlefish, *lulas grelhadas* or *chocos grelhados*. There are also lots of fig and marzipan pastries, shaped like little animals or fruits.

Lisbon Region

The range of fresh fish and seafood in Lisbon is just unbeatable – and meat-eaters also do well. It being the capital, it is possible to find dishes from all over the country, although *Lisboeta* cuisine is fairly simple, honest fare. From the region itself there are lots of local specialities, such as goat and sheep cheeses from Sobral de Monte Agraço and from Azeitão, the latter especially tangy and best eaten while still runny. Also the excellent pastries from Malveira and Loures; nut and egg dainties from Cascais; *zimbros*, gin cakes from Sesimbra; and *queijadas*, little cheese cakes, from Síntra. Best of all are the custard tarts, *pasteis de nata*, from Belém.

Costa de Prata

Fresh fish and seafood enrich all regional dishes from here, like the popular fish stew (*caldeirada*) and the eel (*caldeirada de enguias*) from Aveiro. Meat dishes are good, too, like the grilled pork kebab (*espetada de porco*) made in Barraida and the kid casserole (*chanfana*) from Coimbra. Just about every town has its own pastries and cakes such as the *pão de ló*, a fluffy cake with a hole in the middle, from Alfeízerão and Ovar, the *arrufadas* from Coimbra and Aveiro and the dry cookies, *cavacas*. An interesting savoury option is the bean-paste cakes (*pastéis de feijão*) from Torres Vedras.

Costa Verde

Things get pretty hearty the further north you go in the Costa Verde region. Here you will find the classic cabbage and potato broth (*caldo verde*), cod prepared many different ways, pork fillets (*rojões*), duck (*pato*), with rice or octopus (*à Margarida da Praça*). Also try roasted kid (*cabrito assado*) in Monção and, not to be missed, the famous Oporto-style tripe (*tripas à moda do Porto*).

Montanhas

Heartier still is the inland northern cuisine of Montanhas. Try the *alheirãs*, sausages made of veal meat and bread from Bragança, particularly popular in the winter, and the *feijoada à transmontana* stew from Vila Real. Probably the most famous of all is the *bola de carne*, meatloaf, from Lamego. Also not to be missed is the excellent smoked ham (*presunto*) and the young partridges (*perdizes*) from Pinhel. Roasted kid (*cabrito assado*) is done over rice soaked in the meat's juice. For the adventurous there is the *maranhos*, lamb and chicken giblets with rice, and the *morcelas*, blood sausages, a bit like black pudding. It is unforgivable not to try the famous ewe's cheese (*queijo da Serra*) from the demarcated cheese region of Serra da Estrela.

Madeira

Among Madeira's many specialities are the *espetadas* (veal kebabs), tuna fish steaks (*atum*) and the excellent swordfish (*espada*), often served with banana. The *bolo de mel*, honey cake, is a Madeira classic and the tropical fruits, bananas, papayas, avocados, passion fruits and mangoes are all excellent. And, of course, there are the Madeira wines.

The Azores

Specialities here are the many types of grilled fish and original dishes like the 'Holy Ghost' soup, made of beef and vegetables; the *robalo*, bass, roasted over an *alambique*; octopus stew with wine sauce; yam with pork sausages (*linguiças*); and the famous *cozido das furnas*, a stew from São Miguel that is left simmering in a pot for five or six hours in the hot burning lava of the Furnas Valley. A good cheese, like a tangy cheddar, is São Jorge, from the island of the same name.

Drinks

Wine

Portugal produces a great deal of wine but exports relatively little. Everybody has heard of the fortified Port and Madeira wines; the light *vinho verde* (green wine) also enjoys a certain fame and Mateus rosé is not an unfamiliar label, but Portuguese wine remains a subject for those in the know or who live there.

It is difficult to find any noticeably poor wines in Portugal. Table wines as served in most medium-priced restaurants are generally pleasant and at times very good. In cheaper restaurants, red wine may come chilled, which may be a way of disguising its mediocrity (or else lack of respect for a decent wine!). Like other wine-producing countries, Portugal has recognized that presentation is probably as important as content, so you need to be careful not to pay too much for what may be perfectly ordinary wine. Most meat dishes are accompanied by red wine (*vinho tinto*), while white wine (*vinho branco*) goes with fish. However, the Portuguese do recommend red wine when eating cod as this fish has a strong flavour that can spoil the taste of a delicate white. Rosé wine (*vinho rosado*) has defenders and detractors but, if quite dry, can make for a very refreshing accompaniment for either meat of fish dishes.

There are over 20 recognized wine-producing regions in Portugal, resulting in great variety in terms of both characteristics and quality. Thanks to the efforts of a handful of top producers, one region that enjoys certain international fame is Dão. This small area between Coimbra, Viseu and Guarda produces reds that tend to be on the strong side, deep in colour and full-bodied, and which have been likened to Burgundy wines. There are also some notable aromatic and fruity whites from the same area.

To the west of Dão is Bairrada, between Coimbra and Aveiro, one of the chief wine-producing regions. Bairrada red wines are notably smooth, deep-coloured and full-bodied. The whites tend to be quite robust but fruity, holding their own when drunk with stronger-tasting food, and the rosés are fresh and fruity. There are also sparkling wines from here, going from medium-dry to Brut. Further north, inland and east of Porto, is the Douro region, famed of course for port, but many producers there are now making good table reds that are full of character, as well as some lovely, fresh, fruity whites.

To the south of Porto is the Minho region where *vinho verde* is made. '*Verde*' refers not to the colour but to the fact that these are very young wines. There are in fact *vinhos verdes tintos*, *brancos* and *rosados*. Somewhat lower in alcohol content, these wines are light and refreshing, especially the slightly sparkling whites.

Inland from the coastal strip running from Leiria towads Lisbon is the Estremadura region which produces light, easy-to-drink wines at the cheaper end of the scale, though it has recently yielded some top quality produce. Inland from Estremadura, to the north and east of the capital and touching on the Alentejo, is the region of Ribatejo, which produces some very good reds that are tannic while still young but which become full-bodied and slightly spicy after five years. The Alentejo itself, occupying almost a third of all of Portugal's wine-producing area, has had some difficult years recently owing to drought, but there are many small producers who are currently making some of the country's most palatable fruity reds. South of the Alentejo is the Algarve, where the range of red wines is much wider than that of the whites. Wines from here tend to be robust, richly fruity in flavour and high in alcohol content.

Wine Glossary

adega	a cellar or winery
agardente	brandy (you can also ask for *um brandy* and will be under stood); it literally means 'firewater'
bagaceira	a strong drink, not unlike Grappa, made by distilling *bagaço*, the grape skins and pips that are left over after fermentation
branco	white
carvalho	oak wood used for making casks
cepa	a vine
claro	new wine
CVR	regional wines that are produced in a specific region using a minimum of 85 per cent of locally grown grapes
DOC	Denominação de Origim Controlada, the equivalent of the French Appellation Controlée; DOC wines come from a limited geographical area
doce	sweet
engarrafado	bottled
espumante	sparkling
garrafa	a bottle
garrafeira	this word refers in Portugal to either a wine or a blend of wines from more than one region with no restriction on the varieties of grape unless indicated as a 'Garrafeira RD'; the wine must be of good quality – red wine is aged in wood for two years, white wine is aged for six months
IPR	Regulated Origin of Wines that have displayed specific characteristics for a minimum of five years, and therefore a superior wine to that of a DOC
licoroso	wine that is high in alcohol content
maduro	mature table wine
pipe	a cask for shipping or maturing wines
reserva	old wine from a good year
rosado	rosé
seco	dry
Selo de Origem	the seal of origin guaranteeing the authenticity of a demarcated wine
tinto	red
uva	grape
velho	old wine
VEQPRD	sparkling wine from a denominated region
VLQPRD	quality liquor wine from a denominated region
vinha	vine
vinho	wine
vinho de mesa	table wine
vinho verde	a young wine, NOT green in colour!
VQPRD	quality wine from a denominated region

Madeira

There are some excellent wines produced in offshore Portugal, one of the best-known being the fortified Madeira wine. Vines were introduced to the island as long ago as the 15th century when the island was still almost completely forested over. When the trees were burnt to clear land for cultivation (a process that apparently took seven years to complete), the resulting mixture of volcanic soil and potash proved especially favourable for vine cultivation. Madeira wine as it is known today is achieved by subjecting it to temperatures of between 40° and 50°C either before or after fermentation. There are basically four types of Madeira wine, each named after the grape used. Sercial, aged for eight years, is the driest and is served as an apéritif or to accompany fish. Verdelho is medium-dry and is served with cake. Bual is medium-sweet and often replaces port at the table. Malmsey, the sweetest and heaviest of the four, is best as a digestive after a heavy meal.

Port

Port wine became popular in England in the late 17th century when the importation of French wines was banned from 1679 to 1685 and again from 1702 to 1714. The 1703 Methuen Treaty reduced duty on Portuguese wine in return for reductions on duties paid by British wool exporters. It was discovered then that by adding small amounts of brandy the wine travelled better, although another century would pass before port became the refined, fortified wine product that is so well known today. For a while in the mid-18th century port had a bad reputation as unscrupulous exporters took advantage of the booming business to pass off adulterated, ersatz port as the genuine thing. The Marquês de Pombal put a stop to this by founding the *Companhia Geral de Agricultura dos Vinhos do Alto Douro* and establishing the world's first demarcated wine region in 1756. The two measures ensured quality by regulating the quantities produced, fixing the minimum and maximum prices, and putting an end to all disputes concerning quality.

The demarcated region stretches almost 100km along the upper Douro valley and its tributaries. Vineyards (*quintas*) are on terraced slopes, some of them up to 500m above sea level. More than 40 varieties of grapes, harvested in September, are used for making port, but they are not crushed by foot these days, whatever the tourist brochures will have you believe. The semi-fermented '*must*' is then mixed with a controlled quantity of brandy. This prevents the fermentation continuing, leaving the wine free from the natural grape sugar. The wine is then kept in casks until the following March when it is transported by boat down the Douro to Vila Nova de Gaia where it is left to mature, still in the cask (though vintage ports are an exception to this), inside the lodges (*armazéns*) prior to bottling. The lodges, despite retaining their English names, are mostly in the hands of multinationals these days.

Pass the Port

Drinking port in company is not just a question of sitting down, cracking open a bottle and drinking it. There is far more to it than that and there is a right way, or rather, a left way, to serve port. Traditional etiquette has it that port is always passed clockwise, from right to left around the table. The bottle or decanter starts with the host who serves the person to his right, then himself and then passes the port to the person on his left. This person in turn serves himself and passes it on again and so it continues until the port arrives back in front of the host. The origins of this ritual are unknown but, according to one legend, it is to avoid angering the devil that always lurks behind your left shoulder. Another story says that by using your right hand to pass the bottle, you cannot stab your neighbour with your sword, unless you are left-handed! Some British port drinkers consider it bad manners to ask for the port for a refill. If a forgetful guest does not pass the port on, the host traditionally asks, 'Do you know the Bishop of Winchester?' A guest well versed in port etiquette will, abashed, pass the port along. If the guest answers, 'No,' he is told, 'He is an excellent chap, but he never passes the port.'

There are four basic types of port, although there are several sub-types too: white port (*branco*), red (*tinto*), ruby (*tinto aloirado*) and tawny (*aloirado*). Vintage ports are not made every year but when the wine from a particular *quinta* is judged to be of sufficient quality. These wines are only left for a couple of years in the cask and are then bottled and left to mature there. Vintage ports need to spend 10–15 years in the bottle and must be decanted to separate out the sediment. As these ports are highly expensive, an alternative is to buy late-bottled vintage ports (LBV), usually transferred to the bottle after five or six years, which are almost as good and a lot cheaper.

For more information on port take a look at the following websites:

- **www.the-port-man.fsbusiness.co.uk**
- **www.portugal-info.net/wines/port**
- **www.ivp.pt** (the site of the Instituto do Vinho do Porto)

Beer

Beer (*cerveja*) is also widely drunk in Portugal. *Sagres* and *Super Bock* are brands found just about everywhere, but there are also quite a few local brews. The town of Silves, in the Algarve, puts on a week-long beer festival every summer and many lesser-known labels can be tried there. If you want a draught beer ask for *um imperial*. If you prefer it in the bottle, ask for *uma garrafa*. In tourist areas there are many English-style 'pubs' serving household names like Guinness, Bass, Newcastle Brown, Bud, Coronita and more.

Coffee, Tea and Soft Drinks

There are probably few countries in the world where the simple act of asking for a cup of coffee can involve making so many decisions. To ask for just *um café, por favor,* is to miss out on a world of possibilities. At breakfast time *um galão* is often favourite, a large, milky coffee that fills a gap. Do make sure to ask for it *da máquina* as it is guaranteed to be fresh and not from an urn. If you want something more approaching a cappuccino ask for a *meia da leite* (a half of milk) or if it's a caffeine hit you are after ask for a *bica*, a small, strong black coffee or even a *duplo* (double) when you are really desperate. If this is too strong you can temper it with a drop of milk, *um pingo*, making a *café pingado*. Decaf drinkers should ask for *um descafeinado*.

Tea (*chá*) is usually served straight. If you want it with milk ask for *um chá com leite* or *um chá com limão* if you prefer it with a slice of lemon. Do not confuse this with a *chá de limão* as that means a glass of hot water with lemon rind. Just about all standard soft drinks are available in Portugal; ask for them by brand name and you will be understood.

Water

In Portugal, tap water varies in quality depending on where you are. Although it is usually safe to drink, it can sometimes taste unpleasant since so many chemicals are needed to purify it. When asking for tap water to drink you will be asked if you want it *fresca* or *natural*, which can be confusing, but the first is cold, the second means at room temperature. Bottled water (*água mineral*) comes like everywhere else, still (*sem gás*) or fizzy (*com gás*).

Shopping

Many people in Portugal, nationals and ex-pats alike, have taken retail therapy to heart – happily subscribing to 'shopping-mall chic'. Many large, gleaming malls have sprung up in Lisbon and in other cities and the young and newly affluent proudly see them as signs of Portugal's progress.

In Lisbon, Spanish names like Zara, the boutique chain, and the Corte Inglés department store are now well established, and international chains such as FNAC have set up shop too. Within a few years it is likely that high street names familiar in Britain and the rest of Europe will be dotted all over Lisbon and other large cities. Large food retail chains, familiar names elsewhere in Europe, have also penetrated the Portuguese market. Lidl, Auchan, Carrefour and Continente are among them, taking advantage of the rise in car ownership to establish out-of-town hypermarkets. As a result, shopping habits have changed, damaging town centres, where smaller traders have felt the pinch. Nowadays many people do a big weekly or fortnightly shop and bring their purchases home in the car. In areas where there are large ex-pat communities there are an increasing number of shops either run by foreigners or enterprising locals that cater to their needs and tastes. It is easier these days to find Marmite, proper tea bags, books in English and good jam.

Despite this, well over half of all retail trading in Portugal goes on in small, **family-run businesses**. In many towns there is usually a fascinating range of shops selling the same specialized goods and services that they have for generations, among them cobblers, salt-cod vendors, haberdashers, herbalists, bespoke tailors, *charcuteries*, *pâtisseries*, numismatists, ceramics and tile dealers, and liquor shops. When shopping in such places your language skills will be put to the test, but traditional shopkeepers are usually patient with foreigners and appreciate even the most fumbled attempts at speaking their language. The fun of shopping away from the big stores is that you will find items that are simply unobtainable elsewhere and get a glimpse of the real Portugal.

Another way of savouring the real Portugal, is *o mercado*, at the **market**. Colourful, boisterous and fun, the market is a fundamental part of Portuguese life and always worth a visit whether you end up buying anything or not. Covered markets are to be found in most towns and cities, open on all shopping days and selling fresh produce that is often better-priced and more appetizing than the packaged goods on offer in supermarkets, even though much of Portugal's best fruit and vegetables are exported. Apart from food you will find a range of other products including clothing, footwear, kitchenware, textiles, ceramics, music on CD or tape, fresh flowers and house plants, and pottery. Books, antiques (and plenty of junk), old postcards, furniture, live animals and fake designer-label clothes may also be found in markets. In some regions there are markets on only one or two days of the week, though you may find the same traders and goods in the next town on another day. Local tourist offices usually provide information about market days.

Portugal is not generally considered as one of Europe's better countries for shopping, although how important that is probably depends on how much you enjoy shopping. If you live in the south or in a rural area and find shopping limited, you can always go to Lisbon or to Sevilla in Spain, where the choice of shops is far wider. Consumer goods such as cameras, TVs, videos, DVDs, stereos and electrical appliances are cheaper than they were but are still more expensive than in many other EU countries.

While the purchasing power of the Portuguese has risen in recent years, it is still not high enough to attract the range of goods ex-pats might expect in their own countries. But it is still possible to get the electrical goods and gadgets necessary for the average home locally, especially since they are guaranteed not to be incompatible.

Probably the best buys in Portugal are locally made **craft products**, and every region, town and village has something unique. Ceramics, tiles, porcelain, wickerwork, embroidery, glasswork, wrought-iron, hand-woven fabrics, leather goods and a large variety of artisan-made products are available just about anywhere. They are ideal as gifts, or to add a local touch to your home.

Shopping hours vary. Traditional shops and supermarkets in urban areas tend to open 9am–1pm and again 3–7pm. Small, family-run businesses often do not open on Saturday afternoons. Larger shops, hypermarkets and shopping malls often stay open throughout the lunch hour and until much later in the evening, perhaps until 10pm. Many also open on Sundays. Designer boutiques and club-wear shops, on the other hand, often do not open in the morning at all, preferring an afternoon start and trading until as late as midnight. Markets are usually a morning affair, particularly the one-day travelling village markets, but some also open in the afternoons much like normal shops.

Credit and debit cards are widely accepted in larger stores, hypermarkets and shops that do a lot of tourist trade. In smaller shops and markets expect to pay in **cash** and try to have the right amount of change or at least only small denomination notes. Anything bigger than €50 may be difficult for a small trader to handle.

Media

Newspapers and Magazines

There is a wide range of national and regional daily newspapers available in Portuguese. This might seem surprising considering Portugal's small population and relatively high illiteracy rate. Among the most important are the *Correio da Manhã*, a serious general news daily; *Público*, a quality paper with good coverage of national and international news plus a good arts supplement on Fridays; the sister papers *Diário de Notícias* and *Jornal de Notícias*, with a slightly old-fashioned format but with good regional sections; and the *Diário Económico* which, as its name suggests, focuses on finance and economy. There is also the weekly *Expresso*, a bulky publication with countless supplements.

The more serious newspapers often have extensive classified sections, which can be useful if you are searching for a job, accommodation or a bargain. Sports or, to be more exact, football fans are catered for by *A Bola*, *Record* and *O Jogo*, three dailies with about 10 per cent of their space given over to other sports. They are biased towards Benfica, Sporting and FC Porto respectively. Together they are Portugal's most read press.

Fado

Dealing usually with themes such as lost and unrequited loves, betrayal, past glories and despair, *fado* (from the Latin *fatum*, fate) is to the Portuguese what flamenco is to the Spanish and the blues to Afro-Americans. Emerging in the early 19th century in Lisbon's old Moorish quarter, the genre is still best heard in the smoky *fado* houses in that area, Mouraria, nearby Alfama and the Bairro Alto across town. Generally, the *fadista* sings solo, accompanied by a 12-stringed *guitarra portuguesa* and a four-stringed *viola* (Spanish guitar). The guitar at times highlights the singer's melody and at others plays solo, the viola accompanies both, providing rhythm. *Fado*'s origins are the subject of heated discussion, some arguing that it was a legacy of the Moors, others that it was introduced from Brazil but most agree that there is an element of the medieval Provençal troubadour tradition in there somewhere. Few also dispute its origins in working-class poverty, and by the mid-19th century *fado* was firmly associated with Lisbon lowlife. It did, though, become popular with the upper classes too, and eventually intellectuals and poets would get involved, writing lyrics that helped the genre to become more sophisticated.

During the 20th century, with the spread of radio and the gramophone record, *fado* grew to become the country's national music form, and Salazar and his regime elevated it to a mythical status. This association of *fado* and Salazarism caused the genre to lose popularity and many young people nowadays prefer pop, rock and other imported forms, although *fado* is enjoying a revival of late and is reaching audiences outside Portugal. There is a new generation of *fadistas*, among them Mariza, Mozambique-born, Mouraria-raised, who won a BBC radio award in March of this year. Other names to look out for are Mísia, who fuses *fado* with other styles (to the chagrin of the purists), the more classical Camané, Mafalda Arnuth and Argentina Santos, a legend, who may come out of the kitchen of her Alfama restaurant to sing to diners. Amália Rodrigues, formerly a fruit-seller (so the legend goes), became *fado*'s most internationally known exponent, singing at the Olympia in Paris and on Broadway. When she died in 1999 the country was in the run-up to general elections and Prime Minister António Guterres suspended campaigning for three days, declaring that the country had 'lost its voice and part of its soul'.

English-language and Other Foreign Press

In areas popular with ex-pats, there are news stands that sell practically the whole range of English-language dailies (UK and international), as well as the leading French, German, Dutch, Scandinavian and Italian newspapers. In the Algarve there are even publications in Ukrainian and Russian. As a rule, the international editions of the *Guardian*, *The Times*, the *Independent* and the *Daily Telegraph* are available from late midday onwards, although delivery can become a little erratic the further you go off the beaten track. The main British tabloids are printed in Spain and arrive earlier.

Mainland Portugal has two regular English-language newspapers; the weekly *The News*, and *The Anglo-Portuguese News* (APN) while Madeira has the monthly *Madeira News Magazine*. *The News* offers mainly Algarve-centred news and also has listings and classifieds, making it useful both for jobs and property. The online edition **www.the-news.net** has Lisbon and Oporto sections as well as others dedicated to business and sport. There are also regular downloadable PDF files dealing with property and travel and occasional supplements covering subjects such as education. *The Anglo-Portuguese News*, published in Estoril, is more amateur in its presentation and has no online version but provides information, both local and foreign, of interest to the ex-pat community as well as useful classifieds.

There are not many **magazines** specifically for the foreign community although Algarve residents have the glossy *Essential Algarve*, published in English and German, with articles covering fashion, lifestyle, music, travel, wine and motoring, plus regular features, listings and restaurant and nightlife guides. Competing with this is *Algarve Good Life*, a glossy monthly with news, features, a pull-out financial supplement and events listings that go far beyond the region to include Lisbon, Oporto and Andalusia.

Television

Research shows that the Portuguese spend a lot of time watching TV. Like most countries these days, programmes include game shows, soaps, reality shows, *Big Brother* and popular 'docudramas'. But there are also the more serious and highbrow – well-researched documentaries, news programmes with extensive foreign coverage, classical music and good movies (which are not dubbed). Quality TV caters to a small minority, while (not surprisingly) the less serious end of the range attracts higher ratings!

Until the mid-1990s there were only two **public channels**, *RTP1* and *RTP2*, which broadcast for a limited number of hours a day. Since then two private channels, *SIC* and *TVI*, have been operating. With capital from the Brazilian Globo group, *SIC* quickly began to attract audiences with a diet of Brazilian soap operas and other undemanding content. Realizing that news was important, it launched *SIC Notícias*, a cable channel, in 2001. *TVI* was set up by the Catholic Church, but failed to attract audiences; foreign investment was needed to help it survive. As a result, the content changed as it tried to compete with *SIC* by offering the same mixture of popular soaps, game shows and football. Faced with mounting competition, *RTP1* has downgraded its programme content to appeal to a wider audience, while *RTP2* continues to offer subtitled films, programmes of regional interest, sport (other than football) and gives minority religions exposure too. **Cable television** is now widely available in the major cities, with about 30 channels on offer, among them CNN, MTV, BBC Prime plus the 24-hour *SIC Noticias* news channel.

Watching Portuguese TV can be enlightening, not least for the insight it gives into Portuguese culture and for its usefulness as a language-learning tool.

If you are thinking of taking a TV and/or video to Portugal, check out first whether they are compatible – most likely they will not be. Portuguese television sets and videos function on the PAL/BG system, as does most of continental Europe, whereas British models use the PAL/I system. If they are not compatible, check to see if the equipment can be modified or else buy locally.

TV licences in Portugal were abolished in 1991, but the government is currently thinking of reintroducing a licence scheme.

Satellite Television

Clearly more interesting for many resident foreigners, satellite television offers a huge range of content in many languages, with ever-more possibilities in prospect. English-language viewers with the right equipment can watch CNN, Sky (Premium, Cinema, News, Sports), Eurosport, the Disney Channel, the Discovery Channel, TNT and plenty more besides.

For most of these you need a satellite dish of minimum 80cm diameter (though one of 120cm or greater guarantees better reception in Portugal and allows for more programmes from around the world) and a decoder as the images are scrambled. To receive programmes, you generally have to pay a monthly subscription. One of the most popular is Sky (**www.sky.com**) which offers a bewildering array of packages, 96 of them, ranging from £12.50 to £38 per month. The latter gets you the whole range of films, sports and other entertainment. Once you have signed up and paid, Sky send you a smart card which is inserted into the decoder. The problem is that this must be done via a UK or Irish address, but most people get a friend or family to send it to them. Cards are available in Portugal, but they are expensive. Installing the equipment, if you are not technically minded, can be tricky. Some very useful notes on getting Sky while abroad are available at **www.satcomm20.co.uk**.

The BBC also has worldwide TV services nowadays. The *BBC Prime* service offers international viewers a mixed bag of the best from the BBC and is available throughout Europe, the Middle East and Africa through cable and satellite operators. Look at **www.bbcprime.com** for more information.

Radio

There is a very wide range of radio stations in Portugal, many of them local – and localized – and people listen to a lot of radio. Local stations often broadcast just to one region or even one town and its surrounding area and the content is highly localized and often good-quality.

On a national level there are three state-run stations: *Antena 1*, *Antena 2*, and *Antena 3*. The first broadcasts on both FM and MW, the other two on FM only.

Antena 1 is good for news and football, *Antena 2* (94.4 FM) for classical music and *Antena 3* (100.3 FM) plays a wider range of music. *Rádio Renascença*, owned by the Church, is also national and has several stations, all of them somewhat staid in content. Other stations worth tuning into are *TSF* (89.5 FM) for news and current affairs interspersed with pop music and live football commentary, and *Nostalgia* (104.3 FM) for 'oldies' from the 60s to the 80s.

The BBC World Service is widely available on several wavelengths, but you will need a good short-wave radio. Look in *The Anglo-Portuguese News* for the wavelengths (which may change) and programme details. In Lisbon and the Algarve you are likely to come across an English-language station (or slot on a Portuguese station) with news, views, chat and music aimed principally at the ex-pat population. One is the *BIG FM* (92.4FM), a mixture music spanning four decades and a talk show.

Listening to Portuguese radio will help your Portuguese greatly. What at first seems like a stream of sound will after a time break down into more meaningful chunks and, eventually, into fairly comprehensive understanding.

Learning and Speaking Portuguese

Whether you choose to live in a ex-pat community or in a more integrated way, learning some Portuguese is still important as emergencies may occur in which you have no option but to understand, or be understood, in the local language. If you are planning to work or run a business, proficiency in the language is vital. Learning any language is also fun, need not be a chore, and can give you a great sense of achievement when you begin to feel that you are making headway.

Courses

If you decide to learn Portuguese, it is best to start immediately, preferably before you go house-hunting and definitely before you settle in Portugal. There are many options (in the UK and Ireland) although Portuguese is not as popular as its neighbour, Castilian Spanish, so you may have to look harder to find tuition locally. Many universities have Spanish departments in which Portuguese and the other languages of the Iberian peninsula are taught. They may or may not offer courses for non-faculty students, but they will usually be able to offer advice on where to look for classes. Most universities with a Portuguese department have some connection with the Instituto Camões, a state-run institution whose mission is the promotion of Portuguese language and culture worldwide. The Instituto's website, in Portuguese only, is **www.instituto-camoes.pt** and the address in Lisbon is Rua Rodrigues Sampaio 113, 1150-279 Lisboa (**t** 00351 213 109 100, **f** 00351 213143 987).

Another good place to start is Canning House, in London, where the Hispanic and Luso-Brazilian Council, a non-political, non-profit making organization, is based. The Council can provide you with an extensive list of places where Portuguese is taught, as well as the names of private tutors. The majority are in London, but there are others nation-wide. Canning Houseis at 2 Belgrave Square, London SW1X 8PJ (**t** (020) 7235 2303, **f** (020) 7235 3587, **www.canninghouse.com**),

Private Academies and Private Tutors

Berlitz is a long-established language-teaching institution with academies worldwide. At their centre in London they offer courses in European and Brazilian Portuguese and if there is demand they will provide courses in their other UK centres. Contact Berlitz Language Centre, 9–13 Grosvenor Street, London W1A 3BZ (**t** (020) 7915 0909, **f** (020) 7915 0222).

Another well-established language-teaching company is Inlingua, with centres throughout the UK and Europe. Offering courses in many languages at all levels, it is based at Rodney Lodge, Rodney Road, Cheltenham, GL50 1HX (**t** (01242) 250 493, **f** (01242) 250 495, **www.inlingua-cheltenham.co.uk**). Cactus Languages offers tailormade one-to-one and group courses at all levels – Suite 4, Clarence House, 30–31 North St, Brighton BN1 1EB (**t** (01273) 775 868 or **t** 0845 130 4775, **www.cactuslanguage.com**).

Private tuition is another, if costlier, option. Expect to pay £20–30 per hour. If the whole family takes classes with the same teacher it may work out cheaper per hour. The list provided by Canning House has many private tutors based in the London area. The London-based Institute of Linguists also has a database with private Portuguese tutors all over the UK. Contact them at Saxon House, 48 Southwark Street, London SE1 1UN (**t** (020) 7940 3100, **f** (020) 7940 3101, **info @iol.org.uk**, **www.iol.org.uk**).

Self-study

The BBC has several online language courses that you can follow if you have Real Audio Player. Look at **www.bbc.co.uk** and follow the links to education. The main options are French, Spanish and German but if you click on 'Other languages' you will access Portuguese.

- ***Discovering Portuguese* an introduction to the language and culture of Portugal. There is a course book and cassette pack, both sold separately but designed to be used together.**
- ***Talk Portuguese*, a short course for absolute beginners. As above, there is a course book and cassette pack, both sold separately, but designed to be used to be used together.**

O Prémio Nobel

To date Portugal's only winner of the Nobel Prize for Literature, José Saramago, is referred to by his compatriots as that, *O prémio Nobel*, since the language does not distinguish between the award and the winner. Of humble origins, Saramago, now 80, did not finish school as he had to go out and earn a living, training as a mechanic, doing various manual jobs and then becoming a journalist, translator and writer. A long-serving, though critical, member of the Portuguese Communist Party, Saramago is given to holding forth on all manner of issues such as globalization, the lack of values in this materialistic age or the Israel–Palestine conflict. His books have often upset conservatives in Portugal being, they say, mere vehicles for his left-wing views, which may be true but does not detract from them. But the apparently sweeping, simplistic nature of some of his judgements made in public is in marked contrast to the complex interplay of ideas in his novels in which he employs fantasy, the supernatural and symbols to explore his favourite theme, the conflict between the individual and authority.

As a novelist, he gained an international recognition quite late, with *Baltazar and Blimunda* (1982). A playful, if blasphemous fantasy, this novel was set in Portugal in the 1700s against the background of the Inquisition and deals with a priest who wanted to build a flying machine. His *The Year of the Death of Ricardo Reis*, in which the protagonist engages in a dialogue with the ghost of the poet, Fernando Pessoa, is widely regarded as one of his best novels, as is *The History of the Siege of Lisbon*, in which a proofreader inserts a simple 'no' to completely change the interpretation of history. In the early 1990s he really upset the Catholic establishment and Portuguese conservatives with his bitterly sarcastic *The Gospel According to Jesus Christ* in which he interprets the Gospels from an ironic view, inventing new miracles and prophesies. Maybe that is why he decided to go and live in Lanzarote in 1992. Not necessarily that accessible, his refusal to use punctuation is an obstacle for some readers. It is worth persevering as Saramago's books (available in excellent English translations thanks to the late Giovanni Pontiero) contain, in his own words 'the possibility of the impossible, dreams and illusions, [these] are the subject of my novels'.

- *Get By in Portuguese* (book and cassette pack). This is aimed at the post-beginner who now wants to travel and use the language more widely.

There are many other self-study courses available and it is worthwhile paying a visit to Grant & Cutler, 55–57 Great Marlborough Street, London W1F 7AY, the UK's largest bookshop specializing in foreign language books including language-learning material, technical dictionaries, foreign films, academic literature and popular fiction.

Learning in Portugal

There are many options ranging from beginner's level to improving on language skills acquired before you arrive. The Instituto Camões (*see* p.257) is a good place to start. If they do not have courses running near where you live, they will be able to advise you on where to go. Many of the larger, internationally established language-teaching organizations such as International House (**www.ihworld.com**) and Inlingua (**www.inlingua-cheltenham.co.uk**) have branches or franchises in Portugal. Consult their websites for information on their centres and courses in Portugal. Cactus Languages (*see* p.258) also organizes courses in Portugal as well as in the UK.

Language Exchange

The cheapest option (at home or in Portugal) is to find a native Portuguese speaker who is looking to improve his or her English. You get together for an hour or two, as often as you can, and spend half of the time speaking in one language, half in the other. This can be very productive once you are past the early stages, as there is no particular pressure or deadlines, such as pushing ahead to complete a course book. It may also be the beginning of a friendship, as well as enabling you to learn about Portuguese culture.

Portuguese Politics

Two historical events have helped to shape Portugal over the last 30 years. The first was the overthrow in 1974 of the regime that Salazar had established, though he himself had died four years previously. Cracks in the regime had begun to show during the early 1960s, when pro-independence ideas began to take root in the colonies and the country became involved in deeply unpopular military campaigns in Angola, Guinea Bissau and Mozambique.

The military was divided between those who wanted to hold on to the colonies at any price and those who favoured a more autonomous federation of Portuguese-speaking countries. The split was between ranks and generations. Younger, lower-ranking officers adopted increasingly radical positions and supported the progressive General Antonio Spínola, and later Major Otelo Saraiva de Carvalho who became leader of the Movimento das Forças Armadas and masterminded a (relatively) bloodless coup against the regime. As a result of the 'Carnation Revolution', elections were held two years later in 1976, leading to the first constitutional parliament.

Since then, the country has been run by a parliamentary system, the *Assambleia da República*, elected every four years and a president who is elected every five years. The colonies were given independence, a huge number of

Portuguese colonials returned home, followed by thousands of former colonial subjects, which left the economy in tatters. Following the revolution, the constitution was worded in very left-wing terms, calling for the creation of a 'classless' state based on public ownership of land, natural resources, and the principal means of production. Two later revisions have since modified such ambitions.

There are numerous political parties but only a handful have any influence with the electorate. The longest-established is the PCP (Communist Party of Portugal), which had to go underground during the Salazar years. Despite the collapse of the Soviet Union and Eastern Bloc the party continues to be 'Stalinist' in outlook and maintains a certain influence among the industrial working class and in rural Alentejo. With the passing of the older generation, it has already lost much of its influence on the left to Bloco da Esquerda (Left Block) coalition, a relative newcomer to the scene. The PP (Popular Party), heir to the conservative CDS, is conservative in the classic sense of the word and has its power-base in the north among the professional classes, the propertied upper-middle classes and right-leaning Catholics. The PS (Socialist Party) is a much younger grouping, founded by Mário Soares in 1974, and is characterized by its moderate, anticommunist, social democratic ideology. The PSD (Social Democratic Party) leans more to the centre-right, despite its name.

The 2002 elections were won by a coalition of the PSD and the PP, who won 48.9 per cent of the overall vote and control 119 out of 203 seats in the *Assambleia*. The PS is now the chief opposition party, with 96 seats (having received 37.9 per cent of all votes). There is also a coalition between the Communists and the Greens, with 12 seats, and Bloco da Esquerda with three seats. Among the many challenges faced by the coalition government are the current economic recession, problems with employment, education, health and the judicial system. The country also needs to attract more inward investment, to compensate for any future loss of EU funding.

Religion

Over 95 per cent of Portuguese people are Roman Catholics. Though people may be less ardent and congregations smaller than they used to be, the Church still wields a lot of power in Portuguese society. Many people, despite adopting more liberal lifestyles and sexual attitudes, are deeply influenced by their Catholic upbringing. For the faithful, a church is never far away; attending mass and confession is easy. For those interested in ecclesiastical architecture and popular forms of religious expression, Portugal is a feast.

The most celebrated place of devotion is Fátima, where some believe the Virgin made several appearances to three shepherd children in 1917. She apparently made three prophecies concerning the end of the Second World War, the fall of communism and one other – which the Vatican keeps under lock and key and only reveals to incoming Popes. All year round, in every village town and city, there are thousands of *festas* celebrating an array of saints, many of whom are not recognized as such in Rome. In many places, especially the mountainous areas of the north, Catholic rituals are combined with much older, pre-Christian pagan rituals.

The Portuguese constitution, however, guarantees freedom of religion, and Church and State were separated in 1911. Many Protestant churches of differing denominations have been established, especially in areas popular with ex-pats. In Lisbon there is a mosque and a synagogue, as well as active Buddhist and Hindu communities.

In the Algarve, Anglican worshippers have three congregations to choose from within the Chaplaincy of Saint Vincent. St Luke's is an Anglican Church situated between Loulé and São Bras, and the other two have their services in local Roman Catholic churches courtesy of the Bishop of the Algarve.

Sport

One of Portugal's great attractions is the opportunity to take part in some form of outdoor sporting or recreational activity throughout most of the year. Spectator sport is mostly focused on football but it is also possible to watch tennis, golf, motor-racing, roller hockey, dressage, yachting events and surfing.

Participative Sport

Portugal's climate and extensive coastline mean the range of sports and recreational activities available is very wide indeed, including golf, archery, horse-riding, lawn bowls, hill-walking, sailing, tennis, water-skiing, scuba-diving, surfing and windsurfing. In the Serra da Estrela, in the Montanhas region, winter sports are available, though many Portuguese skiers also go to Spain.

Golf is one reason why so many people choose to holiday or live in Portugal. The Algarve alone has over 25 courses, though some of them are for beginners and are attached to larger, more prestigious courses. Many of the courses are superbly landscaped and set in outstandingly beautiful locations. Fees can vary widely, depending on the course and the time of year, with discounts for low season – spring and autumn tending to be more expensive than winter and the height of summer. Rates at the more exclusive courses such as Pinheiros Altos or Quinta do Lago can be in the region of €150 a round, while at places such as Penina there are resort and academy courses where the top price is €42. Discount rates apply at different times of the year and out of season can be as low as 60 per cent of the full rate. Information about all of the Algarve's courses, including contact details, fees and instructions on how to find them, can be accessed at **www.algarvegolf.net**.

Golf is by no means confined to the Algarve. The Lisbon area has several excellent courses – some offering championship standard – so too the Costas de Prata and Verde, Beiras and Minho, in the far north and at inland locations such as Vidago, in Montanhas. Madeira and the Azores provide offshore alternatives. For more information about courses throughout the country, take a look at **www.golfeurope.com** and click on Portugal. A list of clubs by area appears and from there it is just one further click to access course details. A little less informative but useful nonetheless is **www.worldgolf.com**.

Portugal is a haven for sailors with no fewer than 19 marinas listed at **www.marina-info.com** and several more ports with anchorage facilities. Some are very exclusive, as at Vilamoura. Others are brand new, as is the case of the Lagos marina, but there are sailing or yacht clubs in practically all main coastal towns. Surfers and windsurfers fare well in Portugal with over 600km of west-facing Atlantic coast. There are any number of practically undiscovered small bays, as well as notable surf beaches. The best time of the year is late winter and early spring, and those who know say that Nazaré has the best swell along the whole coast. There are also international surfing and bodyboarding events held throughout the year. For more information, take a look at **www.offitsface.com** and **www. wannasurf.com** – both sites have information on beaches, waves and events. For those who enjoy scuba-diving and snorkelling, there are many opportunities – especially in the Algarve.

Spectator Sport

For most people in Portugal, the equation is quite simple: *Sport = Football*, full stop. There is no doubt about it, *o futebol* is an important part of many Portuguese people's lives, especially (but not exclusively) for men. It also gives rise to the country's most frequently read press, as well as being one of the most frequent (impassioned) topics of conversation.

Football is almost the only sport in which Portuguese players, clubs – and the national squad – have achieved international success, but Portugal's national squad has often failed to live up to expectations, despite producing many great talents over the years and a reputation for being 'Europe's Brazil' – owing to its characteristically attractive, skilful style of play. For a long time Portugal relied heavily on the talents of black players recruited from former African colonies. It was an 'Afro–Portugal' team that finished third in the 1966 World Cup, beating the then champions, Brazil, en route. Since then the furthest the *selecção* has got in big-time competition was third place in Euro 2000. The Japan–Korea World Cup was disastrous for Portugal. Led by Real Madrid star Figo, the team fell at the first hurdle (including defeat by the USA) and came home early.

Portugal's great footballing hope is the Euro 2004 tournament, for which several stadia are being completely rebuilt. These are to be complemented by several new ones – including one in Faro. It is doubtful if the excitement and revenue generated by the competition will help those in charge of the domestic game to address its deep-seated problems – but a good time should be had by all. Information is available in various languages at **www.uefa.com**.

Football is not the only spectator sport in Portugal. At the Fernanda Pires da Silva racing circuit, near Estoril, motor-racing enthusiasts can see car- and bike-racing. The management there is still trying to upgrade the facilities to bring Formula 1 back to Portugal. Tennis fans can take in the Estoril Open tournament, held around Easter, which often attracts top names. Portugal also has a long tradition of dressage and the Hipódromo do Campo Grande in Lisbon hosts the Internacional Concurso Oficial de Saltos. Golf fans should look out for the Algarve Open, held every year in April at the prestigious Vale do Lobo course, with many top names participating.

Bullfighting (*A Tourada*)

As in Spain, bullfighting is not thought of as a sport but rather as an art form – an expression of aesthetics. Unlike in Spain, however, the bull is not put to the sword in the arena (with the exception of certain places). What many do not know is that it is later slaughtered out of sight. In Spain the *matador* is the protagonist. In Portugal it is the *cavaleiro*, decked out in splendid 18th-century attire, who rides a magnificent Lusitano horse and goads the bull by sticking small spears in it. The horsemanship of the *cavaleiro* is greatly appreciated by the crowd and an important part of the spectacle. Another difference between the *tourada* and the Spanish *corrida* is that this phase is not the prelude to the entrance of the *matador* but is followed by the dramatic struggle between the half-dozen *forcados* and the bull. The lead *forcado* awaits the charge of the bull and then hangs on for dear life, often to the horns, which are usually capped. Then, with the aid of the remaining *forcados*, the object is to wrestle the bull to a standstill.

The *tourada* no longer has a mass following, but neither is there much of an anti-bullfighting lobby either. The law banning the killing of bulls in the ring has been challenged recently. In Barranco, a town near the Spanish border in the Alentejo, bulls have in fact been killed in the arena for years, but no action was taken against the *matadores*, who were usually touring Spanish or Mexican bullfighters. Animal rights campaigners went to court to see the law enforced. Parliament responded by maintaining the ban, but reducing the sentence from a lengthy jail sentence to a small fine in those places where there was actually a tradition of killing bulls. Barrancos thus enjoys special status. It remains to be seen whether this will serve as a precedent and if more towns adopt the 'Spanish-type' bullfight.

Letting Your Property

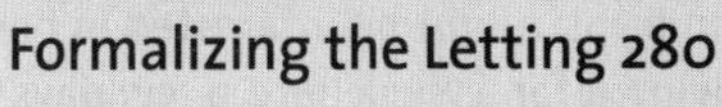

08

A growing number of foreign property-buyers are beginning to see Portugal as a country it is possible to own not only a second home that increases in value, but also one where there is rental income to be made. Traditionally this has not been the case, as the Portuguese property market was not geared up for making either substantial capital gains or money from letting. This is changing, the market – *in certain areas and for certain types of property* – is now beginning to yield good returns both in terms of capital appreciation and rental income.

This trend looks likely to continue so long as interest rates remain low throughout the EU. This will encourage more foreign buyers to Portugal, where there are still properties at reasonable prices – while the Portuguese tourist industry continues to bring in substantial numbers of visitors looking for self-catering accommodation. A good property does not have to stand empty. If you buy in the right place it can generate 10 per cent (or more) of its value in rental income annually. *This, it should be stated, is not the case all over the country, nor can everybody who buys a second home expect to make a profit.* However, it would be most unwise to assume that you will be able to pay off a hefty mortgage by means of rental income. Nevertheless, rental income, even if it does not make you rich can (at least) help you to recoup a part of your investment, cover maintenance and upkeep costs and pay for your own holidays there.

You could be buying for one of two main reasons. First, you might approach the whole question purely as a business venture and expect to make profits from letting. On the other hand, you might be interested in having a place to use as often as you can, enjoying it for a week here, a few days there, a proper holiday maybe once a year. In addition, while you are not there you may like to let it out to holidaymakers and earn 'a little on the side'. Both are perfectly valid options but you have to be clear about what you want and can realistically expect. Which brings us back to the eternal cry 'location, location, location'!

If you are interested in making some money – or profits – from rentals, your choice of location is absolutely crucial. You have to think first who your potential clients might be and then put yourself in their shoes. You have to figure out what they are most likely to want from their week or fortnight in your home and then mould the 'product' to suit their tastes. Location, décor, facilities provided – all should be designed with a certain customer profile in mind.

If you fit into the other category, what might be called the 'sometime' or 'casual' lessor, then your choice of location, décor and facilities will be determined more by your own tastes and needs, since the property is primarily for your own use. Doing this will inevitably reduce its rental potential but increase your own enjoyment of the property. You should, though, be

prepared to compromise in order to make the place appealing enough to attract people willing to rent.

This chapter deals with the various issues involved with property letting such as where to buy to increase rental potential, how to equip your property, how to advertise it and management agencies.

Location, Choice of Property and Rental Potential

No decision will be more important than your choice of location. There are certain areas of Portugal where it is easy to let and it does not take a genius to figure out why. Other areas are much less likely to attract people willing to rent – for reasons that are just as obvious. A beach property (apartment or villa) on the Algarve is always going to get more takers than a farmhouse in the Alentejo, however beautifully furnished the latter may be. A property in an area with a higher flow of tourist traffic is, quite simply, better placed to tap into that flow. If you do buy in a bit of a backwater you will probably have done so for reasons other than pure commercial return.

But even the backwater *can* attract takers, if you market your property well and 'target' it at particular clients. There are plenty of people who positively loathe the idea of a resort holiday surrounded by thousands of other golf-playing ex-pats, and actually prefer something different – in an altogether more secluded spot. There are success stories in quiet backwaters, where the attractions include bird-watching, country hikes – and silence. Their customers go home, rave about them to their friends and set off a spiral of recommendations that serve better than any advertising or top location.

Attractions

In the Algarve, the weather is the chief reason why the tourist season lasts virtually the whole year round. It is the region's principal (but by no means only) attraction. There are high, mid and low seasons but there is also a steady flow of visitors throughout the winter months. This means that a well-located property has letting potential outside the main season, as well as during the busiest summer months. Madeira, too, has potential for letting all year round, as winter is practically non-existent there. This would not apply so much to a property north of Oporto or in the inland mountain regions. Clearly weather is a major factor to be considered.

Attractions can mean different things to different people. Beaches are clearly 'attractive', especially clean, well-kept ones. Good nightlife, dining facilities and access to shopping for those on a self-catering holiday are all aspects that can make a property more attractive for letting. Marinas, facilities for water sports, riding or golf courses are others. In non-beach locations there are any number of features that count as 'attractions' depending on the type of visitor. Market towns attract tourists, as do museums, castles, monasteries, Roman ruins, Romance churches and Gothic cathedrals. Still others prefer spectacular scenery and the attractions of hill-walking, rock-climbing or mountain-biking. There are plenty of people who go for these things, rather than for the more obvious coastal attractions.

Ultimately, the appeal of a rental property lies in the eye of the tenant/ beholder. So it is a question of emphasising those features.

Access

Convenience and accessibility are also important factors that affect a property's rental potential. For most visitors, 'conveniently located' means a relatively short distance (not much more than an hour and a half) from the airport – at both ends of the trip. This is another reason why the Algarve is so successful at attracting tourists. Not only is Faro airport well situated in the middle of the region – with the new motorway, most points along the whole coast are not much more than an hour away – but it can also be reached from many UK regional airports, bringing in visitors who might otherwise not come if forced to travel to London in order to fly.

It also helps tremendously if your property is easy to locate. A villa that is not far from a main road and is well signposted is far easier to let than one that is 'up a country lane, behind a hill, past the olive groves, then ask João the goatherd'. This is not to say that a property in a more remote location cannot ever be let, either. Some people may positively fancy the idea of asking João the goatherd for directions. Nevertheless, it does help to prepare an 'information pack' that includes a clear, well-marked map and to put up some signposts in the lane. Whatever your particular client profile, it pays to take the question of accessibility seriously.

Letting and Management Agencies

If you do not want to do your own marketing – and many owners cannot be bothered – then it may be a good idea to try to let your property through a letting or management agency. Many of these have grown up in the main tourist areas, precisely because so many owners are absent or do not have either the time or expertise to attract clients. If this is the case for you, then it may be a good idea to talk to some agencies before buying. The advice they give you as to what can be let (and what cannot), and for what price may help you to make your decision on which property to buy in the first place. They know the market and the clients and are aware of their needs – things that may be unfamiliar to you. Moreover, if the agency believes that you are a potential customer, it is very much in their interests to advise you on a suitable property for letting.

For more information on this, *see* 'Management Agencies', pp.276–9.

The Right Property

Even though 'location' is apparently all, within choice locations there are properties that attract guests and others that do not. Many apartment blocks, for example, have some apartments with sea views and others looking inland or at another block. The sea view adds rental potential, while the sight of just more balconies and windows reduces it. A property with a pool is much easier to let than one without. Villas, even small ones, are more attractive than apartments so can usually be let for more. An ugly apartment block (no matter how nice inside) will not attract rentals as much as a pretty villa or townhouse even if it is bigger, more comfortable, in better condition and better-equipped. It helps if your property is photogenic!

If you buy a property in an urban location, it is easier to rent a small apartment than a large house. Those most typically attracted by a city holiday are individuals and childless couples who come to see the sights. Conversely, a larger apartment or house is better in a resort location as families and groups are more likely to be interested in that type of holiday. It is important to find out a property's real rental potential before you buy. A simple way of finding this out is to contact several property agencies, say that you are looking to rent a property of the same characteristics as the one you have in mind and ask how much it costs for a week or a fortnight and during the high and low seasons. What they tell you should give a good indication of how much you might expect to make.

The Right Price

As with any other business, the profit margin (when letting a property) is the gap between your costs and your income. If you have bought with the expectation of making capital gains on a later resale, then rental income is incidental, though not unwelcome. If you have bought with the aim of using the property a lot yourself, then rental income is something that will help cover costs. It is not impossible for either to be profitable, though. If you buy a property at the cheaper end of the market in an area where there is more or less a year-round flow of tourists your investment might pay off as high and mid season rentals may yield between 3 and 6 per cent and you enjoy the property during low season. A more expensive property in an area with a shorter season may bring in more money per week but over a shorter period. Then again, you have more time to enjoy it.

Legal Restrictions and Obligations

Like any other business activity in Portugal, having a property for short-term lets is subject to several layers of bureaucracy. The local tourist office should be informed of your intention to let and local authorities should in theory inspect the premises to check that safety regulations are complied with. These affect gas appliances, heating systems and electrical installations and may oblige owners to install fire extinguishers and blankets, first aid kits, as well as taking out insurance for public liability (*responsabilidade civil*). A management agency, if you use one, should take care of all these aspects – as well as paying taxes and utilities bills on your behalf – but if you're doing it on your own then expect some detailed paperwork and prepare to be patient. In reality, not all local councils are that strict, but be aware that if they suddenly decide to enforce long-ignored regulations, fines can be stiff.

Bear in mind also that not all communal properties allow unrestricted letting, or may oblige the owner to do it through an offshore company (though, importantly, the legal and tax situation of these companies is in flux at the moment). Check before buying that you can let your apartment when and to whom you want.

You are also obliged to declare rental income, whether you are resident in Portugal or not. If you let as an individual this will be part of your personal income tax, IRS (*Imposto sobre o Rendimento das Pessoas Singulares*) and if you let through an offshore company then you pay corporate income tax, IRC (*Imposto sobre o Rendimento das Companhias/Corporações*). The latter option is, in any case, less of an advantage than it used to be. This is in addition to other taxes you will have paid on purchasing the property. A good management agency will take care of this for you, or at least offer you assessment. However, only you are responsible for meeting your tax obligations. Failure to pay tax on rental income constitutes fraud. Many have got away with it for years but the Portuguese government is making efforts to improve the efficiency of its tax system and are giving increased powers to its tax inspectors. *See* **Financial Implications**, pp.168–83.

Equipping the Property

Having been through the process of selecting and buying a property, now comes the fun bit – fitting it out and making it pretty. First impressions count for a lot, so the outside should look well kept. This includes gardens, swimming pools, driveways and paintwork, as well as fences or hedges. The interior is no less important and here you have to be careful. There is no accounting for taste and what you like is not necessarily what others will find appealing. Rather than trying to fulfil your own decorative fantasies, you should be practical and go for a fairly neutral décor that will not put people off. You should also make sure that fittings are appropriate to the likely needs of your target clients. For example, if your clients are likely to make use of nearby water-sports facilities (such as water-skiing) make sure there is adequate space for storing the skis and a drying area for wetsuits.

Much of what follows may be provided by a management agency if you put your property on their books. Check very carefully what the agency will commit itself to providing and what not. Whatever the agency undertakes to do, there are some personal touches that only you can add and that will leave a positive impression on guests – enough to make them return and/or recommend your property to their friends.

- **Documents**: People who take a villa or apartment feel reassured when they are given plenty of information to read. It is a good idea therefore to have an 'information pack' ready to send to all potential guests. The local tourist office will almost certainly provide free copies of most things you need, which should include a local map and leaflets about attractions in the area. You should also include detailed directions to your house, a list of emergency telephone numbers, possibly the address and telephone number of a trustworthy neighbour (preferably English-speaking – if your guests are) who can be contacted if anything goes wrong, as well as your own contact details. If your property is managed, the agency might well provide all of this as part of their service and they will most likely have their own problem-solvers just a phone call away.

  There is no harm in leaving copies of the same information inside the property, since guests may easily forget to bring the pre-visit pack with them. It is also a good idea to leave up-to-date local listings magazines – with information about upcoming events in the area and a page or two of your own personal recommendations on places to eat and drink, shops, special haunts that your guests might not stumble across by themselves – and rainy-day suggestions. A Portuguese phrase book might not go amiss either, and some properties come with a few guide books on the shelves and other reading matter too. A supply of undemanding novels may well be appreciated! Many people also leave a guest book which visitors fill in with (hopefully) positive comments. This is always a good source of feedback.

- **Welcome**: Another important aspect, that puts your guests at ease, is to make sure there is someone on hand to welcome them. This might be part of the management agency's services but, if not, how about that same trustworthy neighbour mentioned above?

• **Cleanliness**: Your property should be left at least as clean and tidy as you would expect yourself when taking an apartment for a holiday. Bathrooms and kitchens should shine and have that recently cleaned smell, beds should be made and the sheets should be crisp. Again, a management agency should make sure that this happens but if you let independently be sure to find a reliable cleaner from the local area.

• **Kitchen**: Providing state-of-the-art kitchen cutlery or gadgets is not necessary but the kitchen should be fully equipped with good quality, hard-wearing cutlery, crockery, grater, chopping board, ovenware, pots and pans, teacloths and oven gloves. A modern fitted kitchen is recommended, with a large fridge, a microwave, a food mixer or juicer and electric kettle. All equipment should work reliably and user's instructions should be provided. Do not forget the corkscrew either!

• **Laundry facilities**: A good, solid, easy-to-programme washing machine and tumble dryer should be provided. Guests may also appreciate detergent as they are unlikely to bring it with them.

• **Bedrooms**: Nothing can ruin a guest's stay more than a horrible, saggy mattress. It is not a good idea to skimp on these. Look for good quality, sprung mattresses and expect to replace them every so often. Protect them with inexpensive mattress coverings which should be replaced frequently. Sheets should be provided and also replaced with a certain frequency. Guests do not like threadbare, patched bedlinen. Plastic undersheets should also be provided if you are going to let to families with small children. Make sure enough blankets are kept in wardrobes in case of a cold spell. The wardrobes themselves (preferably fitted) should be spacious, with plenty of hangers, and aired frequently to stop them from smelling musty.

• **Living areas**: Avoid the temptation to 'do it on the cheap' but do not buy top-range or designer furniture either. Be practical. Go for sturdy, hard-wearing chairs, tables and sofas with easily washable covers. You may want to add some personal touches too, such as pictures or flower vases, but be careful not to impose your own taste too much, and put them out of the reach of small children. A TV is much appreciated, especially if tuned to satellite channels – but leave instructions not to mess around with the settings other wise you will need a technician to re-set them! A simple video machine is not a bad idea either. Provide basic cleaning materials, a broom, a dustpan, a mop and bucket and possibly a vacuum cleaner, especially recommended for beach properties as sand gets everywhere.

• **Heating and air-conditioning**: The vagaries of weather, even in the sunnier parts of Portugal, can make an effective heating system advisable. Air-conditioning is also recommended in a top property but can be expensive to run. If you buy a modern holiday home on an *urbanização*, the chances are both will be already fitted; otherwise expect to invest a fair amount of money on this.

• **Swimming pool**: Having one is a great advantage as far as rental potential goes, even if your property is close to a beach. Make sure the pool is well-maintained and clean. This will not be your personal responsibility if the pool is communal though it will form part of your communal expenses. Properties with private pools attract more people willing to rent and at a higher price than those with communal ones.

• **Little details**: A few tea bags, some coffee, a litre of milk, sugar, salt and pepper, a loaf of bread and a bowl of fruit all make guests feel at home immediately. Some owners also leave a small supply of useful things like stock cubes and packet soups in the kitchen cupboard. If you really want to impress them, how about a bunch of flowers and a bottle of wine?

Marketing

You could have bought the most desirable holiday home in Portugal and have great expectations as to the money it is going to earn you. But now comes the hard part – marketing it.

Not everybody who owns a second home can be expected to be a marketing genius but you can learn quickly what works and what doesn't – and you will, especially after you've made an expensive mistake or two. In the long term, it is to be expected that a good property will have a client base that has been built up on the basis of satisfied holidaymakers who not only return themselves but also recommend you to their friends. Those friends in turn recommend you to other friends, and so it continues. At the beginning, though, you may need to do a lot of work and make choices between various media. Advertising can be a very hit-and-miss affair (despite what experts say) with no guarantee that money spent will necessarily yield results. However, one thing is sure. People these days are becoming more discriminating and sensitive as to how well, or badly, you respond to their enquiries. Do not delay in getting back to people, follow up on enquiries, keep them on file for the future.

If you are planning to do your own advertising, there are several channels to use, but you have to choose the most appropriate and effective. Whichever you use, you should be equipped to cope with enquiries swiftly and efficiently. Having a telephone goes without saying, but you need an answering system too, and listen to your messages regularly. Have a supply of information packs ready to send at short notice. A fax machine is useful, though fewer people use them these days. An e-mail address is also very handy. *See* 'Personal Website and E-mail', p.275, for suggestions on how to use your computer as a marketing tool.

Directories and Web Directories

Directories and joint information booking services can be a useful way of getting your property seen by lots of potential customers. Traditionally such information has been produced in brochure or magazine format but it is now becoming increasingly web-based. Generally, the arrangement is that you pay for exposure, but then deal with enquiries and bookings yourself. One very well-known and widely distributed directory is *Private Villas*, where an ad occupying a sixth of a page with a colour photo and blurb will cost you £750 for 12 issues – or a third of a page for £1,420. This might seem expensive but the fact that 80 per cent of advertisers renew each year would indicate that this directory is helping them to move their properties. It might represent around a month's income or no more than a week's income if your home is a luxury villa. The directory also has a website, **www.privatevillas.co.uk**, where magazine advertisers are automatically given free space, though this is set to change as the web services will be combined with *Dalton's Weekly*. The new site, **www.daltonsholidays.com**, operational from October 2003, will offer free web advertising for *Private Villas* and *Dalton's Weekly* advertisers for the remainder of the 2003 season and cut-price exposure from then on. If you prefer to advertise just through web directories, these are getting quite cheap these days. For example, if you post your property on **www.villasandrentals.co**, a standard listing, including four photos and an availability calendar, costs as little as £12.42 per month or £149 for a whole year. Another website, **www.holiday lets.net**, offers a similar service for £99 and lets you create, edit and manage your own ads. Another site, **www.algarve-rentals.com**, bills itself as an 'arm' for property owners in return for a commission on successful rentals; the fee is negotiable. Quite how effective internet advertising really is depends on the number of hits, how well the site works, how well the information is presented and many other factors.

Press Advertising

Box advertisements in newspapers can be quite expensive – possibly in the region of £200 – and may not produce many enquiries unless they are repeated many times, which multiplies the cost. Classifieds are seen by many people and cost much less, meaning you can keep the ad running almost permanently. On the other hand, they do not really give your property the chance to 'shine', as your advertisement will just sit in the middle of hundreds of others. Many people, though, continue to use newspapers as their main window on to the world. Major UK dailies all have international property pages and advertising space in their travel supplements. Magazines with substantial travel sections are also good places to advertise and you might try more specific publications if you are aiming at a particular type of client. Surfing, scuba-diving, equestrian and sailing magazines could all bring in enquiries from those looking to go to Portugal to indulge their favourite hobby or sport. In Portugal, there are two local English-language newspapers, *The News* and *The Anglo-Portuguese News*. *The News* has a website and is read not just by residents in Portugal.

Personal Website and E-mail

You could always prepare your own web page, or pay to have one done. Keep it simple and effective, avoid flashy presentations, let the user get to the useful information – prices, photos, booking details and form – in no more than three clicks. Make sure the web address does not already exist and is one that is likely to come up in the 'sites found' using normal search criteria. **www.fredsmith-sportuguesevilla.co.uk** is probably not much use! Beware, internet promotion is a big business and it can work out quite expensive to get your site to the forefront on leading search engines. Unless you are a professional web designer and programmer, do not attempt to bill via the internet; a bank transfer or cheque is probably a more reliable means.

Even if you do not want to go as far as setting up a website, you can still use a computer as an effective advertising aid. If you have your information pack on your computer you can e-mail it to possible customers, saving on paper, printing and photocopying. Be sure to have the information in several versions which can be opened by all users.

Doing Deals

Once you have become acquainted with other property-owners in your area, you might choose to form an alliance with them. If you all have similar properties for similar rental prices then you can pass on excess custom to your neighbours and, hopefully, they will do the same for you. This is especially useful when you get enquiries from three families all wanting to rent in the same week.

Your Own Contacts

In the end, you may find that the cheapest and most effective form of advertising is word of mouth. If your property is genuinely attractive, friends, friends of friends and work colleagues could turn out to be your most regular customers. This is especially the case if you are looking to fill the property part-time. News spreads fast, satisfied renters tell their friends and so it goes on. If you work for a large organization you can advertise internally, via the intranet, on workplace notice-boards or through sector-based magazines aimed at the employees.

Be careful when renting to friends, though, as the issue of payment might be quite delicate. They are not likely to abscond without paying (unless they never were your friends really) but do offer them a reasonable price and let them know that they are paying less than a 'commercial' tenant. Reducing your price to your own contacts need not mean making a dent in your income as you will have saved on advertising costs.

Management Agencies

You may find that you do not have the time, the imagination or the energy to go about marketing your property or to keep tabs on it. Supervising cleaners, caretakers and other maintenance staff can be difficult, especially if you are not even based in Portugal yourself. This is where the management agency steps in as a far simpler solution. The rentals market has generated a booming trade in management agencies in recent years. Agencies come in all shapes and sizes. Some are actually a department of an estate agent's and their services may be offered at a good price if you buy through them. They cater, usually, to different market segments, some specializing in exclusive villa properties, others in apartments, others in a mixture of both. The services they offer, apart from marketing your property, can range from highly comprehensive maintenance to fairly basic cleaning and overseeing of changeover days. They charge correspondingly higher or lower commission fees, which can oscillate between 10 and 30 per cent of your gross rental income. This may seem a lot, but if you consider the potential income lost through not marketing the property properly yourself, you may find that you end up making more over a period of time.

You do have to choose carefully and keep tabs on the agency yourself as service quality varies. The worst-case scenario is the agent who rents your property out, does not inform you and keeps the money for himself. Others may be simply inefficient and not good at drumming up custom. Still others are highly professional, straight and provide an excellent service.

Among the services provided by a reliable agency you may expect the following, usually as part of an overall package but sometimes as an extra:

- **Making regular (weekly or fortnightly) checks on your property when it is not occupied and airing it.**
- **Reporting promptly if there has been a problem such as storm damage, flooding, vandalism or a break-in.**
- **Cleaning and maid service during and between occupancy.**
- **Supervising laundry arrangements.**
- **Supervising other support staff such as gardeners, pool-cleaning services, window cleaners, etc.**

- Providing a welcome service for guests, including giving instructions for use of electrical equipment, gas fittings, etc.
- Reporting breakages and damages to you. They should warn guests that broken items must be paid for and oblige them to leave a deposit before occupancy.
- Preparing full reports on more serious damage, in case there is a lawsuit.
- Checking the inventory of all equipment and gadgets, before and after occupancy. Guests should not have their deposit returned if items have gone missing.
- Prompt payment of utilities bills on your behalf and provision of statements that bills have been paid.
- Calling in plumbers, electricians, glaziers, etc. for emergency repairs, without consultation, and informing you afterwards.
- Supervising general repairs, with prior consultation and your approval. Obviously you will be charged separately for these.
- Paying your rental income, minus their commission, into the bank account of your choice. Informing you of payments made.

Note that 'reasonable' wear and tear is to be expected and is difficult to insure against, as is the case with accidental damage. Breakages are usually only minor, and wanton acts of vandalism are rare, but legal action may be taken if and only if a report is made.

Among owners' duties and obligations in a typical management agreement are the following:

- Leaving a float of money in an account so that the agency staff can make payments on your behalf and charge their monthly or quarterly fee.
- Keeping the account in the black. Few agencies will pay your bills if your account with them is in the red. A balance of about €500 should be sufficient.
- Paying reasonable amounts of interest when the account goes into the red and telephone and mailing costs if the agency has to track you down to sort out the situation.
- Paying reconnection charges if you have not left sufficient funds to pay bills and been cut off. (A good agency will warn you of impending suspension of service.)
- Leaving three sets of keys to the property with the agency.
- Leaving sufficient supplies of bed linen, blankets, etc.
- Preparing a full inventory of all items in the house (both the agency and the owner keep a copy).

- **Complying with all legal requirements made on rental properties. The agency will do liaison work on your behalf but you are ultimately responsible for fire protection, etc.**
- **Giving sufficient notice (most commonly three months) of your intention to dispense with the agency's services.**

Selecting an Agency

Before committing yourself to signing a contract with a management agency, there are several things you should check thoroughly:

- **Are you dealing with an officially registered company and what references (i.e. from other customers) are available?**
- **What is the atmosphere like in their office? How do they receive you when you walk in off the street? Is there any sign that they are actually busy letting properties?**
- **How frequently do they check on properties while they are unoccupied?**
- **Can you see examples of their marketing? Is it just local or do they advertise internationally? Do they advertise in the glossy property magazines?**
- **Can they provide you with a typical example of an information pack that is sent to prospective clients? If so, do you like the image they project? (If they cannot do this, look elsewhere!)**
- **Will they allow you to look at some of the properties they manage? (If not, look elsewhere.) If they can, how clean and well maintained do the properties look? It may be useful here to pose as a prospective tenant rather than property owner or get a friend to do it for you.**
- **Which maintenance and repair companies do they use? Do you have any guarantee of the expertise and workmanship of these companies?**
- **In cases of emergency, can they be contacted around the clock? If so, is this for an additional fee or is it part of the package?**
- **Which services are included as part of the package and which as 'extras'?**
- **Do they offer a standard-type contract or are there various types available with different levels of services?**
- **If you have not actually bought a property yet, ask them what rental income you can expect to generate from one similar to the one you have in mind. This could prove to be very illustrative. They might actually advise you against buying the property in this or that location. If they are right then they could have saved you a lot of disappointment.**
- **Finally, and most important of all, how much do you have to pay for their services?**

Contracts and Controlling the Agency

Once you have agreed to use an agency's services, you will be asked to sign a contract with them. Contracts can contain all manner of clauses. Many clauses are standard in almost every contract but others may not appear to be in your interests. If the more onerous clauses are not negotiable then you are advised to look for another agency that is more flexible. It is always a good idea to have the contract checked over by a Portuguese lawyer to make sure it is legal:

- **How frequently do they provide statements of rental income and outgoings? Are these statements broken down by weeks, months or quarterly? Are they prepared to be flexible and provide statements on demand or with the frequency you require?**
- **What control do you have over annual or monthly payments for items such as taxes, electricity water and telephone?**
- **Are you allowed to use the property yourself during the peak season? Some agencies include a clause that does not allow you to!**
- **What notice must you give if you wish to stop using their services? Many insist on three months.**
- **If you want to let family or friends use your property, how much notice do you have to give the agency?**
- **Can they arrange long-term rentals if the possibility comes up?**

Ways of Controlling the Agency

- **If your property has a telephone installed, call every week – a good time would be the day after changeover day – and check whether there are guests. If there are, on receipt of your statement, make sure that there is income for that specific week.**

- **Get a friend to pose as a potential client from time to time. Does the company follow up the enquiry as stated in the contract?**

- **If you are in the area, drop in at your property. Is it clean and in good condition as promised in the contract? If there are guests, are they happy with the property, the welcome, the back-up service?**

- **If the agency undertakes repair work on your behalf (a good one should consult you before doing any job other than an emergency call-out), check that the work done is of a standard that justifies the cost as reflected in your statement.**

- **Do not be afraid to let the agency know that you are going to monitor their services. If they are good, this should not worry them.**

Formalizing the Letting

If you use the services of a management agency, most have a standard-format rental agreement ready for customers to sign. If you are dealing with bookings by yourself you will need to have a document drawn up ready. This is usually quite a simple document in which customers, by signing, agree to abide by the rules of the community (if your property is on an estate), to respect your property and pay for any damages, to be out by a certain time on the changeover day, etc.

You as the owner guarantee in the contract that the property is in a habitable condition and that the services provided match with those advertised. As well as this, the contract should inform customers of your insurance coverage and let them know that you are not liable for their personal possessions.

References

09

Dictionary of Useful and Technical Terms

Adega	Wine cellar or vat room
Administador	Administrator, e.g. of a community of property owners
Advogado	Lawyer or solicitor
Agrimensor	Surveyor
Água	Water
Água da rede	Mains waters
Aldeia	Village
Alfândega	Customs
Alpendre	Porch
Alta qualidade	Top quality
Alugar-se	For rent or to let
Aluguel	Rental
Aluguel de carro	Car rental
Amortizar/amortização	Instalments. The gradual reduction of a debt in equal payments (as in a mortgage)
Andar	Floor, storey
Anexo	Annexe or outbuilding
Antena parabólica	Satellite dish
Apartamento	Apartment, flat
Apartamento conjugado	Studio apartment
Apartamento com cozinha	Self-catering apartment
Apartamento separado	Separate apartment, such as one that comes with a villa
Aquecedor de água	Water heater
Aquecimento central/ de água a gas	Central/gas water heating
Aquecimento eléctrico	Electric heating/radiator
Ar condicionado	Air-conditioning
Arco	Arch
Área coberta	Covered area
Área de construção	Constructed area
Área de habitação	Built/internal area
Área de lote	Plot size
Arrendamento	Lease
Armário	Cupboard, wardrobe
Armário embutido	Built-in-wardrobe
Arquitecto	Architect
Arrecadação	Storeroom
Arrecadação na cave	Basement store cage
Arrumo	Storage
Ascensor/elevator	Lift, elevator
Aspirador	Vacuum cleaner
Assoalho	Floor
Associaçao dos Mediadores do Algarve (AMA)	Algarve Estate Agents Association
Associaçao de Mediadores Inmobiliários (AMI)	Estate Agents Association
Associaçao de proprietários ou condóminos	Community of owners in a community development

Avenida	Avenue, usually abbreviated *Av* or *Av*ª
Azulejos	Tiles, often blue and white, used to decorate buildings
Banho	Bath
Bairro	Town district, quarter (*alto* is upper and *baixo* lower)
Balcão	Balcony
Balde do lixo	Dustbin or trash can
(em) Boas condições	(in) Good condition
Boletim/certidão oficial	Official bulletin or certificate
(em) Bom estado	(in) Good condition
Caderneta predial (rustica)	Property registration document (rural)
Caderneta predial (urbana)	Property registration document (urban)
Caixa d-água	Water tank
Câmara municipal	Town hall
Câmbio	Exchange. Also the currency exchange rate
Campestre	Rural, rustic
Campo	Countryside, ground, field, stadium
Canalização	Plumbing, sewage system
Carpete	Fitted carpet
Carpintaria	Woodwork, carpentry
Cartão de contribuinte	Tax card
Cartão de residência	Residence card/permit
Casa	House
Casa de aldeia	Village house
Casa antiga	Old house
Casa de banho (completo)	(Full) bathroom
Casa de banho com chuveiro	Bathroom with shower
Casa de banho privativa	En-suite bathroom
Casa de campo/ casa campestre	Country house or chalet
Casa de fazenda	Farmhouse or house on a farm
Casa de férias	Holiday or second home
Casa de hóspedes ou visitas	Guest house
Casa independente/separada	Detached villa
Casa modelo	Show house
Casa renovada	Renovated house, e.g. old village house or cottaqe
Casa rústica	Rustic or simple country house
Casa senhorial	Manor house
Castelo	Castle
Cave	Wine cellar, basement
Centro de saúde	State-run health centre
Centro de jardinagem	Garden centre
Cerâmica	Ceramic (e.g. tiles)
Cercado	Fenced
Certidão de registro	Property certificate of registration
Chão de madeira	Wooden floor
Chão de mármore	Marble floor
Chalé	Detached villa
Chaminé	Chimney

Chave no mão	Ready to occupy, i.e. a fully built and decorated property
Cheque de viagem	Traveller's cheque
Churrasco	Barbecue
Cidade	Town or city
Cisterna	Water tank/cistern
Citação	Quotation
Cláusula de anulação	Annulling or conditional clause (e.g. in a promissory contract)
Código postal	Postal code
Cofre	Safe
Compra	Purchase
Comprador/a	Purchaser, buyer
Compropriedade	Co-ownership
Comunidade	Community
Comunidade de proprietários	Community of owners in a community development such as an apartment block or townhouse development
Condomínio	Condominium
Condominio fechado	Condominium in secure building
Congelador	Freezer
Conserto	Repair
Conservatória do registro predial	Land registry
Conservatório	Conservatory
Constructor	Builder
Consultor financeiro	Financial or tax consultant
Conta	Bill
Conta bancária	Bank account
Contabilista	Accountant
Contador (electricidade, gás, água)	Meter (electricity, gas, water)
Contentor de lixo	Dustbin/trash can
Contrato/acordo	Contract
Contrato de arrendamento	Rental contract, lease
Contrato de mediação	An exclusive contract between a vendor and an estate agent to sell a property
Contrato de promessa de compra e venda	Promissory contract
Contrato de venda	Sales contract
Contribuição autárquica	Property tax, rates
Cópia certificada/legalizada	Authorized or certified copy
Correio	Post office
Costa	Coast
Cozinha	Kitchen; is also cuisine
Cozinha aberta	Open plan kitchen
Cozinha (embutida) americana	American (fitted) kitchen
Cozinha cantina	Kitchen-diner
Custos/gastos	Costs or charges
Débito directo	Direct debit
Departamento de estrangeiros	Foreign residents' department, e.g. at a town hall

Dependência/anexo	Outbuilding, annexe
Depósito	Deposit (down payment)
Depósito de água	Water tank
Depósito de garantía/segurança	Guarantee or security deposit
Desmobiliado	Unfurnished
Despachante	An official agent licensed by the government to act as a middleman between members of the public and the bureaucracy
Despensa	Pantry, larder
Dinheiro na mão/ pronto pagamento	Cash
Direito de passagem	Right of way
Direitos reais de propriedade	Real property rights
Domiciliação de pagos	Standing order, e.g. for payment of utility bills
Domicílio	Home, residence
Domicílio fiscal	Main residence for tax purposes
Ducha	Shower
Dúplex	Duplex, maisonette, two-storey building
Duplo	Double
Edifício	Building
Electricidade	Electricity
Elevator	Elevator/lift; also a funicular railway
Emolumento	Arrangement fee
Empréstito	Loan
Empreteiro	Builder, contractor
Endereço	Address
Energia	Energy, electricity supply
Entrada	Hallway
Equipado/a	Equipped
Escada/escadaria	Stairway, staircase
Escritório	Office, study
Escritório imobiliário/ de mediador	Estate agent's office
Escritório de vendas e de Aluguer	Sales and rental office
Escritura pública de compra e venda	Notarized deed of sale
Esgoto	Drain, sewer
Espaço para a piscina	Room for a pool
Espaçoso/a	Spacious
Esquentador	Water heater
Estábulo	Stable
Estacionamento (privativo)	Parking (private)
Estado	State, condition
Estalagem	Inn
Estatutos/regras	Statutes, rules or by-laws, e.g. of a community development
Estimativa	Estimate
Estores	Blinds, shutters

Estrada	Road
Estrada nacional	Main road designated EN on maps
Estragado	Dilapidated, run-down
Estúdio	Studio apartment
Estudo	Study
Factura	Bill
Feira	Outdoor market on fair
Fiança	Security deposit, surety
Fogareiro	Cooker, stove
Fonte	Spring
Forno	Oven
Fossa séptica	Septic tank
Fosso	Ditch or water channel
Freguesia	Parish
Frigorífico	Refrigerator
Furo	Borehole
Garagem (dupla)	Garage (double)
Garantia	Guarantee, warranty
Garrafa de gás	Gas bottle
Gastos/despesas	Fees or expenses
Gastos de comunidade	Community fees
Geminada	Semi-detached (usually refers to terraced townhouses)
Gerador	Generator (for electricity)
Gradeado	Fenced, e.g. garden
Grades de segurança em ferro	Iron security bars/grilles (fitted over a window)
Guarda	Keeper or guard
Habitação	Dwelling, residence
Hall de entrada	Entrance hall
Hectar	Hectare, 10,000 square metres (2.471 acres)
Herdade	Large farm
Hipermercado	Hypermarket
Hipoteca	Mortgage
Honorários	Fees
Imposto	Tax
Imposto de automóveis	Car tax
Imposto comercial	Company or corporation tax
Imposto de mais valias	Capital gains tax
Imposto de selo	Stamp tax
Imposto sobre o Rendimiento das Pessoas Singulares (IRS)	Personal income tax
Imposto sobre as Sucessões e Doações	Inheritance and gift tax
Imposto sobre o Valor Acrescentado (IVA)	Value added tax
Imposto sucessório	Inheritance tax
Inquilino	Tenant

Inspeção/vistoria/revista	Property inspection or survey
Interior	Hinterland, the inside of a house
Inventário	Inventory
Invernadero	Conservatory or greenhouse
IRS	Personal income tax
IVA	VAT
Janela	Window
Janela com batente	French window
Jardim (comunal)	Garden (communal)
Ladrilho	Tiles, tiled floor
Lago	Lake
Lar	Home
Lareira	Fireplace
Largo	Small square, plaza
Lavabo	Toilet
Lavadora	Washing machine
Lavanderia	Laundry or utility room
Lei	Law
Lei de arrendamentos urbanos	Law governing property rentals
Lei de propriedade horizontal	Law of horizontal division of a community development defining the legal rights and obligations of owners
Leilão	Auction
Licença	Licence
Licença de abertura	Opening licence (for a business)
Licença fiscal/alvarã	Business licence or permit
Licença de habitabilidade	A certificate certifying that a property can be lived in, which is issued when a building conforms with the building standards and codes
Licença de obras	Building licence
Licença de primera ocupação/ licença de habitação	Licence required for the occupation of a building, necessary to have an electronic meter installed
Licença de utilização	A licence issued by a town hall defining the use to which a property or land can be put (residential, commercial, agricultural etc.)
Ligação (de electricidade ou água)	Connection (of electricity or water)
Lista de habitantes	List of inhabitants, e.g. of a town
Lixo	Rubbish, garbage
Localidade	Locality
Localização	Location
Loja	Shop or store
Loja de ferragens	Ironmonger's
Lote (de terreno)	Plot (of land)
Lote para construção	Building plot
Luxo/luxuoso	Luxury/luxurious
Manutenção/sustento	Maintenance
Máquina de lavar (roupa)	Washing machine

Mármore	Marble
(em) Mau estado	(in) Poor condition, dilapidated
Mediador autorizado/ imobiliário	Estate agent
Memória descritiva	List of building materials and specifications for a new property
Mercado	Market
Metros (quadrados)	(Square) metres
Mobilado/mobiliado	Furnished
(Sem mobília)	(Unfurnished)
Modernizado	Modernized
Moradia	Dwelling, home
Móveis/com móveis	Furniture/furnished
Mudança	Move house
Multipropriedades	Timeshare
Município	Municipality, local authority
Muro	Wall
Muro refratário	Heat-reflecting wall for a fireplace
Notário	Notary public, the legal professional who handles the conveyancing for all property sales in Portugal (UK = solicitor)
Nova(o)/recente	New
Número de identificação fiscal (NIF)	Fiscal/tax number
Obra	Building job/work
Oferta	Offer
Oferta especial/de ocasião	Special offer
Ordem de despejo	Eviction order
Paço	Palace or large country house
P*agamento mensal*	Monthly payment
Palácio	Palace
Parabólica	Satellite dish.
Parcela para construão	Building plot
Parcialmente construída	Partially constructed or completed
Parecer camarário	A certificate from the town hall stating what can be built on a plot of land
Parede	Wall
Parede divisória/medianero	Partition/party wall
Parque	Park
Parque de estacionamento	Parking
Pátio de fazenda	Farmyard
Pedreiro	Bricklayer or stonemason
Pensão	Boarding house/bed and breakfast
Perigo	Danger
Permuta	A contract whereby two parties agree to exchange properties; usually one party pays the other a sum to compensate for the difference in value

Persianas	Blinds, shutters
Piscina	Swimming pool
Piscina aquecida	Heated swimming pool
Piscina com aquecimento solar	Solar-heated swimming pool
Piscina comunitária	Communal (shared) swimming pool
Piso	Floor (of a multistorey building)
Plano da Ordem Costeira (POC)	Coastal building law
Plano Regional de Ordenamento do Território Algarve (PROTAL)	Planning law in the Algarve curbing uncontrolled development
Planta de construção	Plan of building plots
Poço	Well
Poder limitado na procuração	Power of attorney
Polícia municipal/local	Municipal or local police
Pomar	Orchard
Porta	Door, gate or portal
Porta blindada	Armoured/security door
Porta corrediça	Sliding door
Porta janela	French window
Portão	Gate
Porteiro	Caretaker/concierge/doorman in an apartment block or *urbanização*
Potência (électrica)	Power rating of a property's electricity supply
Pousada	Lodging or inn. Also the name of Portugal's luxury chain of state-run hotels, many of which are located in former castles, monasteries, palaces, convents and manor houses, and/or in outstanding settings
Praça	Main square
Praia	Beach
Preço	Price
Prédio	Building
Prédio de apartamentos	Block of flats/apartments
Prédios rustica	Rural or rustic property
Prédios urbanos	Urban property
Presidente	President or chairman, e.g. of a community development
Presidente da Câmara	Mayor
Primeira linha junto ao mar	Front line sea position e.g. on the beach
Processo/acção judicial	Lawsuit
Procuração	Power of attorney or proxy
Procurador	Attorney, proxy or holder of a power of attorney
Promotor/promovedor	Developer, e.g. of an *urbanização*
Propriedade	Property
Propriedade agrícola	Agricultural property
Propriedade rural	County property
Propriedade urbana	Town property
Província	Province, e.g. Algarve
Qualidade	Quality
Quarteirão/bairro	Neighbourhood or city quarter

Quarto	Room, bedroom
Quarto de casal	Room with a double bed
Quarto duplo (com dois camas)	Double bedroom (with two beds)
Quarto de empregada	Maid's room
Quarto grande	Large room
Quarto individual/simple	Single room
Quarto principal	Master room
Quinta	Farmhouse or house on a farm
Quota/acção (de proprietário)	An owner's share of a community development, used to calculate the percentage of community fees to be payed
(em) Razoável estado	(in) Reasonable condition
Recente	Recent, new
Recibo	Receipt
Recolha de lixo	Rubbish collection
Reformado	Renovated, reformed, modernised.
Registro de propriedade	Property registry
Relatório	Report
Renda	Income
Renovação	Renovation
Renovado	Renovated
Reparação	Repair
Repartião de finanças	Tax office
Reposição bancária	Bank repossession
Representante fiscal	Fiscal representative
Rés-do-chão (R/C)	Ground floor
Residência	Residence, address
Residência fiscal	Main residence for tax purposes
Residência habitual/principal	Main or primary residence
Residente	Resident
Restauração	Restoration
Ribeiro	Stream
Rio	River
Roupeiro	Fitted (built-in) wardrobe
Rua	Street
(em) Ruínas	In ruins
Sala	Room
Sala comun	Living–dining room
Sala de estar/visitas	Living room, lounge
Sala de inverno	Conservatory (literally, 'winter room')
Sala de jantar	Dining room
Sala de jogos	Entertainment room
Salão	Large room, salon
Sanitários	Public toilets
Segunda casa/residência	Second or holiday home
Segurança social	Social security
Seguro	Insurance
Seguro de bens domésticos	Household insurance
Seguro civil contra terceiros	Third party or public liability insurance

Seguro de viagem	Travel insurance
Seguro-saúde	Health insurance
Selo fiscal	Official stamp (on a document)
Serviço de Estrangeiros e Fronteiras (SEF)	Government department dealing with foreigners
Sinal	Deposit, also means 'sign' as in '*sinais de tráfico*'
SISA	Property transfer tax
Sistema de esgotos	Sewage system
Sistema de segurança	Security system (e.g. an alarm)
Situado/a	Situated
Soalho (de madeira)	Floor (wooden)
Sobrecarga/sobretaxa	Surcharge
Sociedade de Mediação Imobiliária	Society of Estate Agents
Solar	Manor house or important town mansion
Solário	Solarium, sun roof
Solicitador	Solicitor
Solo	Land, ground
Soma	Amount
Sossegado/a/sossego/a	Peaceful, quiet
Sotão	Attic, loft
Sotão de luxo	Penthouse
Taxa	Tax
Taxa de juro	Interest rate
Taxa rodoviária	Road tax
Taxas comunitárias	Community fees
Telhado	Roof
Telhado plano/açoteia	Flat roof
Temporário/a	Temporary or short term
Tênis	Tennis
Terra/terreno	Land, plot
Terraço	Terrace
Terraço coberto	Covered terrace
Terraço fechado	Terrace with windows
Terreno	Plot of land
Terreno agrícola	Agricultural land
Terreno para construção	Building land
Terreno rural	Rural land
Terreno urbanizável	Agricultural land that can be changed to building land
Testamento	Will
Tijoleira	Floor tiles
Tijolo	Brick, brickwork
Todos os gastos/despensas	All fees or charges/expenses
Torre	Tower
Tranqüilo	Quiet, peaceful
Transferência	Banker's order
Transferência de propriedade	Transfer of property, conveyancing
Traspasse/trespasse	Lease or transfer of property
Trave de madeira	Wooden beam

Tribunal de expropriações	Special court for disputes over property expropriation
Turismo	Tourist office
Último piso	Top floor
Urbanização	Purpose-built housing estate development
Urbano	Urban
Urgente	Urgent
Usufruto/interesse vitalício	A life interest, e.g. in a property
Valor tributável	The fiscal or rateable value of a property fixed by the local council, on which property taxes are calculated
Varanda	Veranda, balcony
Varanda envidraçada	Conservatory
Velho	Old
Vende-se/à venda	For sale
Vendedor/a	Vendor or seller
Vestiário	Changing room
Vestíbulo	Entrance hall
Vidrado duplamente	Doubled glazed
Vidro/cristal	Glass
Viga	Beams
Vigas de madeira	Wooden beams, beamed ceiling
Vila	Town, villa
Vista	View
Vista da costa	Coastal views
Vista do campo	Country views
Vista do mar	Sea views
Vista panorâmica	Panoramic views
Vivenda	Residence, dwelling
Vizinhança	Neighbourhood

Portuguese for Survival

Pronunciation

While structurally not dissimilar to Castilian Spanish, and readable if you are familiar with that language, Portuguese is likely to cause you problems when it comes to pronunciation and comprehension. Spoken Portuguese is often said to sound more like an eastern European language owing to the proliferation of shushing consonants that are sometimes slurred together and the closed and nasal vowels, some of which are ignored at the end of words.

Consonants

The underlined capitals represent the stressed syllable, or should we say 'The **CA**-pitals repres**ENT** the **STRESS**ed Syllable.'

• **C** is hard (as in 'k') before all letters except 'e' and 'i'. Before these letters it has the sound of a liquid 's'. Thus *'conceder'* (to concede or grant) is pronounced 'kon-say-**DARE**'.

• **Ç** (cedilla) is a soft 'c' that comes before other vowels and is pronounced like an 's' sound as in '*açucar*' (sugar). Pronounce it 'a-**SSOO**-kar'.

• **Ch** is a bit softer than in English, coming out more like a 'sh', so '*chá*' (tea) is more like 'sha'.

• **J** is like the 's' sound in 'treasure' or 'measure'.

• **Lh** together make a 'lyuh' sound, a bit like the 'lli' in 'million'. '*Filho/filha*', (son/daughter) are thus '**FEEL**-yo' and '**FEEL**-ya'.

• **M** on the end of words like 'sim' is nasal and either hardly heard or more like a half-pronounced 'n'. So '*sim*' is more like the Spanish '*sí*'.

• **Nh** together make a 'nyuh' sound (similar to the 'ñ' in Castilian) so '*vinho*' is rendered '**VEEN**-yo'.

• **Q** is always hard like 'k', as in '*quente*' (hot), rendered '**KEN**-tay'.

• **S** before a consonant or at the end of the word is more of a 'sh' sound; try 'Cascais', rendered 'kash**KAISH**'. Otherwise it is a liquid 's' as in English. 'Sagres', a town in the Algarve and a popular make of beer, is '**SAH**gresh'.

• **X** is also a 'sh' as in '*baixo*' (low) which is pronounced '**BY**-show'.

Vowels

More of a problem than consonants for English speakers, they can be flat and truncated or sometimes long and open but are easy to miss when listening to a Portuguese person speaking quickly. English people really should not complain, as 'standard southern' English has more than 20 vowel sounds!

Certain accents make Portuguese vowels longer, more nasal, easier to hear and more familiar to the English ear.

These are the tilde (squiggle) '˜', the circumflex '**^**' and the acute '´'.

• Thus in '*alemã*' (German woman, or something German and feminine) the 'ã' at the end is more like the French '-an' ending and is rendered 'a-lay-**MAH**' or even 'a-lay-**MAIN**' (if you know your French pronunciation!). In '*português*' (Portuguese, the language or something masculine and Portuguese) the last syllable is a little more elongated and nasal and is rendered 'por-too-**GAISH**'. '*Café*', (coffee or café) is easy; say it 'ka-**FAY**'.

• Very common at the end of many words is the '-ão' sound as in '*galão*' (a large milky coffee). The '-ã' is like a little yelp 'Ow!' but cut off before it is finished so you would ask for 'um ga-**LAOW**'. Words ending in '-ão' in the plural become '-ões' so two large milky coffees would be '*dois galões*', 'doysh ga-**LOYSH**'.

• Vowels when they come together are usually pronounced separately as in '*adeus*' (goodbye) which is 'a-**DAY**-oos'. Some vowels together, though, make a sound of their own. This is the case with 'ei', as in '*leite*' (milk), which is like a long 'a' and pronounced '**LAY**-tay' or 'ou', as in '*doutor*' (doctor) which is said 'dow-**TOUR**'.

• Vowels with no accent over them at the end of words are sometimes not pronounced at all. Thus '*carne*' (meat) sounds like 'karn'.

• An 'a' with a grave accent, 'à', is usually an abbreviation of 'a+a' meaning 'at the' (something feminine) so '*à uma da tarde*' is 'at one o'clock in the afternoon' (literally 'at the one of the afternoon').

Survival Vocabulary

Numbers

1	*um/uma**	30	*trinta*
2	*dois/duas**	40	*quarenta*
3	*três*	50	*cinquenta*
4	*quatro*	60	*sessenta*
5	*cinco*	70	*setenta*
6	*seis*	80	*oitenta*
7	*sete*	90	*noventa*
8	*oito*	100	*cem*
9	*nove*	101	*cento e um/uma**
10	*dez*	200	*duzentos-as*
11	*onze*	300	*trezentos-as*
12	*doze*	400	*quatrocentos-as*
13	*treze*	500	*quinhentos-as*
14	*catorze*	600	*seiscentos-as*
15	*quinze*	700	*setecentos-as*
16	*dezasseis*	800	*oitocentos-as*
17	*dezassete*	900	*novecentos-as*
18	*dezoito*	1,000	*mil*
19	*dezanove*	1,001	*mil e um/um**
20	*vinte*	1,100	*mil e cem*
21	*vinte e um/uma**	2,000	*dois/duas mil*
22	*vinte e dois/duas**	100,000	*cem mil*
		1,000,000	*um milhão*
		2,000,000	*dois milhões*

* One and two may be masculine or feminine in Portuguese, depending on what they refer to. Thus '*um homem, dois homens*' is 'one man, two men', '*uma mulher, duas mulheres*' is 'one woman, two women'. The same applies when speaking of 21 or 22, 31 or 32 (and so on) things or people, plus hundreds and thousands of masculine or feminine things are rendered differently. 200 men would be '*duzentos homens*' but 200 women would '*duzentas mulheres*'.

Days and Months

Sunday	*domingo*
Monday	*segunda-feira*
Tuesday	*terça-feira*
Wednesday	*quarta-feira*
Thursday	*quinta-feira*
Friday	*sexta-feira*
Saturday	*sábado*
January	*janeiro*
February	*fevereiro*
March	*março*
April	*abril*
May	*maio*
June	*junho*

July	*julho*
August	*agosto*
September	*setembro*
October	*outubro*
November	*novembro*
December	*dezembro*

First Contacts

Yes	*Sim*
No	*Não*
Please	*Por favor*
Thank you	*Obrigado/a* (if it is a man/woman speaking)
You are welcome	*De nada*
No, thank you	*Não, obrigado/a*
Excuse me	*Queira desculpar*
What is your name?	*Como se chama?*
Which country do you come from?	*De que país é que vem?*
Do you speak English/French?	*Fala inglês/francês?*

Greetings

Hello	*Olá*
Good morning	*Bom dia*
Good afternoon	*Boa tarde*
Good night	*Boa noite*
Goodbye	*Adeus/ciao* (formal/informal)
How are you?	*Como está?*
Fine, thank you	*Bem, obrigado/a*
See you tomorrow	*Até amanhã*
Have a good journey	*Boa viagem*
Have fun	*Divirta-se*
Good luck	*Boa sorte*
Feeling good?	*Bem disposto/a?*

Signs, Notices and Public Information

Attention	*Atenção*
Bank	*Banco*
Closed	*Fechado*
Fire Brigade	*Bombeiros*
Free entry	*Entrada livre*
Full up	*Esgotado*
Guide	*Guia*
Information	*Informações*
Lift	*Elevador*
No entry	*Entrada proibida*
Open	*Aberto*
Open from... to...	*Aberto da... às...*
Please do not...	*É favor não...*

Post	*Correio*
Push	*Empurre*
In the road	*Achei isto na rua*

Shops, Services and Communications

Bakery	*Padaria*
Bar	*Bar*
Beer hall	*Cervejaria*
Butcher	*Talho*
Café	*Café*
Cake shop	*Pastelaria*
Cobbler	*Sapateiro*
Florist	*Florista*
Grocer's	*Mercearia*
Hairdresser	*Cabeleireiro*
Hypermarket	*Hipermercado*
Laundry	*Lavandaria*
Market	*Mercado/praça*
Optician	*Oculista*
Restaurant	*Restaurante*
Shoe-shop	*Sapataria*
Shop	*Loja*
Stationer's	*Papelaria*
Supermarket	*Supermercado*
Tobacconist	*Tabacaria*
E-mail	*Correio electrónico*
Envelope	*Envelope*
Express mail	*Correio expresso*
Letter	*Carta*
Mail	*Correio*
Mobile telephone	*Telemóvel*
Post box	*Marco do correio*
Post office	*Correios/estação dos correios*
Postal order	*Vale postal*
Stamp	*Selo*
Telegram	*Telegrama*
Telephone	*Telefone*
Telephone box	*Cabina telefónica*
Telephone call	*Chamada telefónica*
Telephone number-	*Número de telefone*
Can you repair...?	*Pode consertar...?*

Travel

Aeroplane	*Avião*
Airport	*Aeroporto*
Arrivals	*Chegadas*
Boat	*Barco*
Bus	*Autocarro*

Car/automobile	***Automóvel***
Connections	***Ligações***
Departures	***Partidas***
Diesel	***Gasóleo***
Distance	***Distância***
Driver	***Condutor***
Garage	***Garagem***
Gas	***Gás***
Information	***Informações***
Kilometres	***Quilómetros***
Lost and found	***Objectos perdidos***
Passengers	***Passageiros***
Petrol	***Gasolina***
Reservations	***Reservas***
Road	***Estrada***
Station	***Estação***
Taxi	***Táxi***
Ticket	***Bilhete***
Ticket office	***Bilheteira***
Train	***Comboio***
Tram	***Eléctrico***
Underground	***Metro***
Van	***Camioneta***

Some Phrases

How do I get to Lisbon/Coimbra...?	***Para ir a Lisboa/Coimbra...?***
Which is the road to Lisbon/Coimbra?	***Qual é a estrada para Lisboa/Coimbra?***
Is this the bus/train for...?	***É este o camboio/autocarro para...?***
Where is...?	***Onde é...?***
the train/coach station?	***a estação de comboios/autocarros?***
the bus/tram stop for...?	***a paragem de autocarro/eléctrico para...?***
What time does it leave/arrive?	***A que horas parte/chega?***
Where are you going?	***Para onde vai?***
I'm going to...	***Vou a/para...***
A single/return ticket to...	***Um bilhete de ida/de ida e volta para...***
Two tickets to...	***Dois bilhetes para...***
Can you tell me where to get off?	***Pode-me dizer onde é que desço?***

Accommodation

Guest house (B&B)	***Pensão***, may also be a ***residência/residencial***
Hotel(s)	***Hotel (hotéis)***
Inn (quality hotel)	***Estalegem***
State-run hotels in historic locations (castles, etc.)	***Pousada***
Youth hostel	***Pousada de juventude***
Room(s)	***Quarto(s)***
Single/double	***Simple/duplo***
...(with) en-suite bathroom	***... com quarto de banho***
Key	***Chave***

Shower	***Chuveiro***
Blanket	***Cobertor***

Some Phrases

Have you got any rooms free?	***Há/Tem quartos vagos?***
For how many people/nights?	***Para quantas pessoas/noites?***
For two/four/six...	***Para duas/quatro/seis...***
I would like a single/double room.	***Queria um quarto simple/duplo.***
... with en-suite bathroom.	***... com quarto de banho.***
I've got a room reserved in the name of...	***Tenho un quarto reservado em nome de...***
What time is breakfast?	***A que horas é o pequeño almoço?***

One final reminder: in Portuguese, '*no*' does not mean 'no'. To say 'no' (the opposite of 'yes') you have to say '*não*' (remember the little cut-off yelp). '*No*' is the contracted form of 'em + o', 'in the (masculine thing/place)...'. So, '*no hotel*' does not mean there isn't a hotel, it means 'in the hotel'.

Internet Vocabulary

Arroba	@
Barra	/ (forward slash)
Barra barra	//
Base de dados	Database
Buscar	To browse
Decifrar	Decode
Dois pontos	: (colon)
Eliminar	Delete
(endereço de) email/correio electróncio	E-mail (address)
Encerrar	Shut down
Online	Online
Ponto	. (dot)
Rede ('***net***' for internet – both are feminine)	Network
Reiniciar	Re-start
Seleccionar	To select
Traço	- (hyphen)
Traço em baixo/sublinhado	_ (underline)
Utente	User
www	'double u', (as in English)

Directory of Contacts

Major Resources in the UK and Ireland

Portuguese Embassy, London
11 Belgrave Square, London SWIX 8PP
t (020) 7235 5331
f (020) 7245 1287/7235 0739
www.portembassy.gla.ac.uk

Portuguese Consulate General, London
Silver City House, 62 Brompton Road, London SW3 1BJ
t (020) 7581 8722

Portuguese Consulate, Manchester
Alexandra Court, 93 Princess Street, Manchester M1 4HT
t (0161) 834 1821

Portuguese Consulate, Edinburgh
25 Bernard Street, Edinburgh EH6 6SH
t (0131) 555 2080

Honorary Portuguese Consul, Belfast
Hurst House, 15–19 Corporation Street, Belfast BT1 3HA

Honorary Portuguese Consul, Bristol
4 Knoll Court, Sneyd Park, Bristol BS9 1QX
t (01272) 658 042

Portuguese Consulate, Jersey
14 Conway Street, Saint Helier, Jersey
t (01534) 877 188

Portuguese Embassy, Dublin
Knocksinna House, Knocksinna, Dublin 8
t (00353) 289 4416

British Resources in Portugal

British Consulate, Lisbon
Rua São Bernardo 33, Lisbon 1249-082
t (00351) 213 924 000
f (00351) 213 924 185
ppa@lisbon.mail.fco.gov.uk

British Consulate, Oporto
Avenida da Boavista 3072, Oporto 4100-120
t (00351) 226 184 789
f (00351) 226 100 438
consular@oporto.mail.fco.gov.uk

British Consulate, Portimão
Largo Francisco A Mauricio 7-1°, Portimão 8500-535
t (00351) 282 417 800
f (00351) 282 417 806

Foreign Embassies in Portugal

Australia
Rua do Marquês de Sá da Bandeira 8, Lisbon 1300
t (00351) 213 530 750

Canada
Edificio Vitória, Avenida da Liberdade 196–200, Lisbon 1269
t (00351) 213 164 600
f (00351) 213 164 695

Great Britain
Rua de São Marçal 174, Lisbon 1200
t (00351) 213 929 440
f (00351) 213 924 186
www.uk-embassy.pt
Open 9–11.30am, 2–4pm, Mon–Fri, closed Sat.

Ireland
Rua da Imprensa à Estrela 1–4, Lisbon 1200-684
t (00351) 213 929 440
f (00351) 213 977 363

South Africa
Avenida Luís Bivar 10, Lisbon 1050
t (00351) 213 535 041

United States of America
Avenida das Forças Armadas, Lisbon 1600-081
t (00351) 217 273 300
f (00351) 217 268 914
www.american-embassy.pt

Business and Tourism Organizations in the UK and Ireland

Portuguese–UK Chamber of Commerce
22–25ª Sackville Street, London W1X 1DE
t (020) 7494 1844
f (020) 7494 1822
www.portuguese-chamber.org.uk

ICEP (Portuguese Trade and Tourism Office)
22–25ª Sackville Street, London W1X 1DE
t (020) 7494 1844
f (020) 7494 1822
www.icep.pt
You can get hold of a useful publication here, 'Guide for Investors in Portugal'.

Trade Partners UK
International Group, Kingsgate House, 66–74 Victoria Street, London SW1E 6SW
t (020) 7215 4776
f (020) 7215 8405
www.tradepartners.gov.uk

ICEP – Ireland
54 Dawson Street, Dublin 2
t (00353) 1 670 9133/4
f (00353) 1 670 9141

Removal Companies

All of the companies listed here are affiliated either to FIDI or OMNI.

Davies Turner Worldwide Movers
49 Wates Way, Mitcham CR4 4HR
t (020) 7622 4393
f (020) 7720 3897
Removals@daviesturner.co.uk, www.daviesturner.co.uk/movers

Robinsons International Removals
The Gateway, Priestly Way, Staples Corner, London NW2 7AJ
t (020) 8208 8484
f (020) 8208 8488
london@robinsons-intl.com, www.robinsons-intl.com

John Morgan & Sons
30 Island Street, Belfast BT4 1DH
t 028 9073 2333
f 028 9045 7402
info@morganremovals.com, www.morganremovals.com

Sterling Corporate Relocation
Hallmark House, Rowdell Road, Middlesex UB5 6AG
t (020) 8841 7000
f (020) 8841 3500
mail@sterlingmovers.com, www.sterlingmovers.com

Stewart, Harvey & Woodbridge
129–169 Whalebone Lane South, Dagenham RM8 1AU
t (020) 8517 0011
f (020) 8592 0827
shw@shwlondon.co.uk, www.shwlondon.co.uk

Michael Gerson
Downland Close, London N20 9LB
t (020) 8446 1300
f (020) 8446 5088
moving@michaelgerson.com, www.michaelgerson.com

White & Co
Hillsons Road, Botley, Southampton SO30 2DY
t (01489) 774 900
f (01489) 774 977
www.whiteandcompany.co.uk

Internet Sites

Property

A simple search such as 'portugal+property' on any search engine such as Google throws up, literally, hundreds of results. Here is a list of some of the better sites; it is by no means definitive:

www.algarve-key.com
www.algarvemanor.com
www.algarve-properties.info
www.algarve-resorts.com
www.casalgarve.com
www.cerronovo.com
www.coelho-correia.com
www.colinaverde.com
www.dsialgarve.com
www.east-algarve.com
www.filneto.pt
www.garveigh.com
www.headland.pt
www.homesoverseas.co.uk
www.homes-unique.com
www.imobitabua.com
www.imoregioes.com
www.international-homes.com
www.kgvillas-algarve.com
www.manor-park.com
www.oceanicodevelopments.com
www.premierpropertiesonline.net
www.property-in-the-algarve.com
www.quintadomar.com
www.quintaproperty.com
www.remax.pt
www.rusticportugal.com
www.sunnyhomesportugal.com
www.sunshinevillas.com
www.vernon-algarve.com
www.vigiasa.com
www.vilamarque.com

Tourism

www.algarve.net
www.algarve.org
www.algarve-web.com
www.alltravelportugal.com
www.portugal-info.net
www.portugal-insite.pt
www.portugal-live.net

www.portugal.org
www.portugal-web.com
www.portugalvirtual.pt
www.travel-portugal.com

Golf

www.algarve-golf.com
www.golfeurope.com
www.worldgolf.com

Wine and Gastronomy

http://www.ivp.pt/
http://www.vinologia.com/

Portuguese Holidays and Celebrations

1 January	New Year's Day
4 March	Carnival
18 April	Good Friday (variable)
25 April	Freedom Day
1 May	Labour Day
10 June	Portugal Day
19 June	Corpus Christi
15 August	Assumption
5 October	Republic Day
1 November	All Saints' Day
1 December	Restoration of Independence Day
8 December	Immaculate Conception
25 December	Christmas Day

Further Reading

General Portugal Tourist Guides

Cadogan: Portugal, David J.J. Evans (Cadogan Guides)
AA Baedeker's Portugal, Mark Turner (AA Publishing)
Blue Guide: Portugal, Ian Robertson (A&C Black)
Exploring Rural Portugal, Joe Staines & Lia Duarte (Christopher Helm)
Fodor's Portugal, Eugene Fodor (Fodor's Travel Publications)
Frommer's Portugal, Porter John Wiley & Sons Inc (18th ed available from February 2004)
Insight Guides: Portugal (APA Publications)
Lonely Planet: Portugal, Julia Wilkinson, John King (Lonely Planet)
Michelin Red Guide: España and Portugal 2003 (Michelin Red Guides)
Portugal (DK Eyewitness Travel Guides), Martin Symington (Dorling Kindersley Publishing)

Rough Guide to Portugal, Mark Ellingham et al (Rough Guides)
Top 10 Travel Guide: Algarve (DK Eyewitness Top 10 Travel Guides)

Food and Wine

Cuisines of Portuguese Encounters, Cherie Hamilton (Hippocrene Books)
Port and the Douro (Classic Wine Library), Richard Mayson (Mitchell Beazley)
Portugal's Wines and Winemakers, Richard Mayson (Mitchell Beazley)
Portuguese Cooking: The Authentic & Robust Cuisine of Portugal, Carol Robertson (North Atlantic Books)
Portuguese Homestyle Cooking, Ana Patuleia Ortins (Roundhouse Publishing)
The Food of Portugal, Jean Anderson, William Morrow (Hearst)
The Taste of Portugal: A Voyage of Gastronomic Discovery Combined with Recipes, History and Folklore, Edite Viera (Grub Street Publishing)
The Wines and Vineyards of Portugal (Classic Wine Library), Richard Mayson
Uma Casa Portuguesa: Portuguese Home Cooking, C. Azevedo (Summerhill Press)

Phrase Books, Portuguese Courses and Dictionaries

AA Essential Portuguese Phrase Book, W Bennett (AA Essential Phrase Books)
An Essential Course in Modern Portuguese, Clive Willis (Harrap)
Collins Pocket Portuguese Dictionary (Collins)
Discovering Portuguese, Book and Cassettes (BBC)
Get By in Portuguese, Book and Cassettes (BBC)
Portuguese Made Nice & Easy! (Research and Education Association)
Portuguese Verbs and Essentials of Grammar, Sue Tyson-Ward (NTC)
Teach Yourself Beginner's Portuguese, Sue Tyson-Ward (Hodder & Stoughton)
Teach Yourself Portuguese Language, Life and Culture, Sue Tyson-Ward (Hodder & Stoughton)
The Rough Guide to Portuguese (A Dictionary Phrasebook) (Rough Guides)
Traveller's Portuguese (Collins)

History and Contemporary Politics

A Concise History of Portugal, David Birmingham (Cambridge University Press)
Muslim Spain and Portugal: A Political History of Al-Andalus, Hugh Kennedy (Longman)
Journey to Portugal: A Pursuit of Portugal's History and Culture (Panther), Jose Saramago, et al. (Harvill Press)
Portugal, The Land and Its People, M. Kaplan (Penguin)
Portuguese Seaborne Empire, C.R. Boxer (Carcanet Press)
Prince Henry 'the Navigator': A Life, Peter Russell (Yale University Press)
The Developing Place of Portugal in the European Union, Jose M. Magone (Transaction Publishers). Available from December 2003
The Portuguese Empire, 1415-1808: A World on the Move, A.J.R. Russell-Wood (The Johns Hopkins University Press)

Special Interest, Sport, Architecture, etc.

Birdwatching Guide to the Algarve, Kevin Carlson (Arlequin Publications)
Globetrotter Golfer's Guide: Portugal: Over 50 Courses and Facilities, Michael Gedye (New Holland Publishers)

Oceansurf Guidebooks: Portugal, Stuart John Butler, Tim Nunn (Watersports Books)
Portuguese Gardens, Helder Carita, Homem Cardoso (Antique Collector's Club)
Portuguese Needlework Rugs, Patricia Stone (EPM Publications)
The Fires of Excellence: Spanish and Portuguese Oriental Architecture, Miles Danby, Matthew Weinreb (Garnet Publishing)
Walking in Portugal, Bethan Davies, Ben Cole (Pili Pala Press)

Literature

Portuguese writers to look out for are Luis Vaz de Camões, Fernando Pessoa, José Maria Eça de Queiroz, the contemporary novelists Antonio Lobo Antunes (often tipped for the Nobel prize), José Cardoso Pires and José Saramago (winner of the 1998 Nobel Prize for Literature).

Climate Charts

Average Monthly Temperatures °C (daily maximum and minimum) and Rainfall (monthly mm)

	Jan	Feb	Mar	April	May	June	July	Aug	Sept	Oct	Nov	Dec
Bragança												
Max	8	11	13	16	19	24	28	28	24	18	12	8
Min	0	1	3	5	7	11	13	13	10	7	3	1
Rainfall	149	104	133	73	69	42	15	16	39	79	110	144
Faro												
Max	15	16	18	20	22	25	28	28	26	22	19	16
Min	9	10	11	13	14	18	20	20	19	16	13	10
Rainfall	70	52	72	31	21	5	1	1	17	51	65	67
Funchal												
Max	19	18	19	19	21	22	24	24	24	23	22	19
Min	13	13	13	14	16	17	19	19	19	18	16	14
Rainfall	64	74	79	33	18	5	0	0	25	76	89	84
Lisbon												
Max	14	15	17	20	21	25	27	28	26	22	17	15
Min	8	8	10	12	13	15	17	17	17	14	11	9
Rainfall	111	76	109	54	44	16	3	4	33	62	89	103
Oporto												
Max	13	14	16	18	20	23	25	25	24	21	17	14
Min	5	5	8	9	11	13	15	15	14	11	8	5
Rainfall	159	112	147	86	87	41	20	26	51	105	148	168

Weights and Measures

Weight

Imperial	Metric	Metric	Imperial
1 oz	28.35 g	100 g	3.5 oz
1 pound*	454 g	250 g	9 oz
1 cwt	50.8 kg	500 g	18 oz
1 ton	1,016 kg	1 kg	2.2 pounds

* A metric 'pound' is 500g, g = gramme, kg = kilogramme

Capacity

Imperial	Metric	Metric	Imperial
1 pint	0.57 litre	1 litre	1.76 pints
1 gallon	4.54 litre	5 litres	8.80 pints

Length

Imperial	Metric	Metric	Imperial
1 inch	2.54 cm	1 cm	0.39 inch
1 foot	30.48 cm	1 m	3.25 feet
1 yard	91.44 cm	1 km	0.62 mile
1 mile	1.6 km	8 km	5 miles

Note: cm = centimetre, m = metre, km = kilometre

Temperature

°Celsius	°Fahrenheit	
0	32	(freezing point of water)
5	41	
10	50	
15	59	
20	68	
25	77	
30	86	
35	95	
40	104	

Celsius to Fahrenheit: multiply by 9, divide by 5 and add 32.
Fahrenheit to Celsius: subtract 32, multiply by 5 and divide by 9.

Appendices

Appendix 1

Checklist – Do-it-yourself Inspection of Property

Task ✓

Title – check that the property corresponds with its description in the title:

Number of rooms

Plot size

Plot

Identify the physical boundaries of the plot

Is there any dispute with anyone over these boundaries?

Are there any obvious foreign elements on your plot such as pipes, cables, drainage ditches, water tanks, etc?

Are there any signs of anyone else having rights over the property – footpaths, access ways, cartridges from hunting, etc?

Are any parts of what you are buying physically separated from the rest of the property – e.g. a storage area or parking area in a basement several floors below an apartment or a garage on a plot on the other side of the road from the house which it serves?

Garden/Terrace

Are any plants, ornaments, etc. on site not being sold with the property?

Pool – is there a pool? If so:

What size is it?

Is it clean and algae-free?

Do the pumps work?

How old is the machinery?

Who maintains it?

What is the annual cost of maintenance?

Does it appear to be in good condition?

Walls – stand back from property and inspect from outside:

Any signs of subsidence?

Walls vertical?

Any obvious cracks in the walls?

Are the walls well pointed?

Any obvious damp patches?

Any new repairs to walls or signs of re-pointing?

Roof – inspect from outside property:

Does the roof sag?

Are there any missing/slipped tiles?

Do all faces of the roof join squarely?

If there is lead flashing, is the lead present and in good order?

Task	✓
Guttering and Downpipes – inspect from outside property:	
All present?	
Do they seem to be in good order?	
Securely attached?	
Fall of the guttering constant?	
Any obvious leaks?	
Any signs of recent repairs?	
Enter Property	
Does it smell of damp?	
Does it smell 'musty'?	
Does it smell of dry rot?	
Any other strange smells?	
Doors	
Any signs of rot?	
Close properly – without catching?	
Provide a proper seal?	
All locks work?	
Windows	
Any signs of rot?	
Open and close properly – without catching?	
Provide a proper seal?	
Window catches work?	
Any security locks? Do they work?	
Any sign of excessive condensation?	
Floor	
Can you see it all?	
If you can't see it all, will a surveyor be able to get access to the invisible parts easily?	
Does it appear in good condition?	
Is there any sign of cracked or rotten boards, tiles or concrete?	
Under Floor	
Can you get access under the floor?	
If so, is it ventilated?	
Any sign of rot?	
What are the joists made of?	
What is the size (section) of the joists?	
How close are joists?	
Are joist ends in good condition where they go into walls?	
What is maximum unsupported length of joist run?	
Any sign of damp or standing water?	

Task ✓

Roof Void

- Is it accessible?
- Is there sign of water entry?
- Can you see daylight through the roof?
- Is there an underlining between the tiles and the void?
- Any sign of rot in timbers?
- Horizontal distance between roof timbers?
- Size of roof timbers (section)?
- Maximum unsupported length of roof timbers?
- Is roof insulated – if so, what is the depth and type of insulation?

General Woodwork

- Any signs of rot?
- Any signs of wood-boring insects?
- Is it dry?

Interior Walls

- Any significant cracks?
- Any obvious damp problems?
- Any signs of recent repair/redecoration?

Electricity

- Is the property connected to mains electricity?
- If not, how far away is the nearest mains electricity?
- Check electricity meter:
  - How old is it?
  - What is its rated capacity?
- Check all visible wiring:
  - What type is it?
  - Does it appear to be in good physical condition?
- Check all plugs:
  - Is there power to the plug?
  - Does a plug tester show good earth and show 'OK'?
  - Are there enough plugs?
- Lighting:
  - Do all lights work?
  - Which light fittings are included in sale?

Water

- Is the property connected to mains water?
- If not, what is the size of the storage tank?
- If not connected to the water supply, how near is the nearest mains water supply?
- Do all hot and cold taps work?

Task ✓

Water (*cont.*)

- Is flow adequate?
- Do taps drip?
- Is there a security cut-off on all taps between the mains and tap?
- Do they seem in good condition?
- Are pipes insulated?

Hot Water

- Is hot water 'on'? If so, does it work at all taps, showers, etc?
- What type of hot water system is fitted?
- Age?

Gas – is the property fitted with city (piped) gas? If so:

- Age of meter?
- Does installation appear in good order?
- Is there any smell of gas?

If the property is not fitted with city gas, is it in an area covered by city gas?

If it is in an area covered by city gas, how far away is the nearest gas supply?

Is the property fitted with bottled gas? If so:

- Who is the supplier?
- If there is a safety certificate, when does it expire?
- Where are bottles stored?
- Is the storage area ventilated to outside of premises?

Central Heating – is the property fitted with central heating? If so:

- Is it 'on'?
- Will it turn on?
- What type is it?
- Is there heat at all radiators/outlets?
- Do any thermostats appear to work?
- Are there any signs of leaks?
- How old is the system?
- When was it last serviced?
- If it is oil-fired, what capacity is the storage tank?

Fireplaces

Is property fitted with any solid fuel heaters? If so:

- Is there any sign of blow-back from the chimneys?
- Do the chimneys (outside) show stains from leakage?
- Do the chimneys seem in good order?

Task ✓

Air-Conditioning

Which rooms are air-conditioned?
Are the units included in the sale?
Do the units work (deliver cold air)?
If the units are intended also to deliver heat, do they?
What type of air-conditioning is it?
How old is it?
When was it last serviced?

Phone

Is there a phone?
What type of line is it?
How many lines are there?
Is there an ADSL line?
Does it all work?
Number?

Satellite TV

Is there satellite TV?
If not, is the property within the footprint of satellite TV?
Who is the local supplier?
Does it work?
Is it included in the sale?

Drainage

What type of drainage does the property have?
If septic tank, how old is it?
Who maintains it?
When was it last maintained?
Is there any smell of drainage problems in bathrooms and toilets?
Does water drain away rapidly from all sinks, showers and toilets?
Is there any inspection access through which you can see drainage taking place?
Is there any sign of plant ingress to drains?
Do drains appear to be in good condition and well pointed?

Kitchen

Do all cupboards open/close properly?
Any sign of rot?
Tiling secure and in good order?
Enough plugs?
What appliances are included in sale?
Do they work?
Age of appliances included?

Task ✓

Bathroom

Security and condition of tiling?
Is there a bath?
Is there a shower?
Is there a bidet?
Age and condition of fittings?
Adequate ventilation?

Appliances

What appliances generally are included in sale?
What is not included in the sale?

Furniture

What furniture is included in sale?
What is not included in the sale?

Repairs/Improvements/Additions

What repairs have been carried out in the last two years?
What improvements have been carried out in last two/10 years?
What additions have been made to the property in last two/10 years?
Do they have builders' receipts/guarantees?
Do they have building consent/planning permission for any additions or alterations?
Are any repairs needed? If so, what, and at what projected cost?

Lifts

Are there any lifts forming part of your own property?
How old are they?
When were they last maintained?
Do they appear to be in good condition?

Common Areas

What are the common areas belonging jointly to you and other people on the complex?
Are any repairs needed to those areas?
Have any repairs already been approved by the community?
If so, what and at what cost?

Disputes and Defects

Is the seller aware of any disputes in relation to the property?
Is the seller aware of any defects in the property?

Appendix 2

Checklist – What Are You Worth?

Asset	**Value Local Currency**	**Value £s**
Current assets		
Main home		
Holiday home		
Contents of main home		
Contents of holiday home		
Car		
Boat		
Bank accounts		
Other cash-type investments		
Bonds, etc		
Stocks and shares		
PEPs		
Tessas		
ISAs		
SIPS		
Other		
Value of your business		
Value of share options		
Future Assets		
Value of share options		
Personal/company pension – likely lump sum		
Potential inheritances or other accretions		
Value of endowment mortgages on maturity		
Other		

Index

Portugal touring atlas

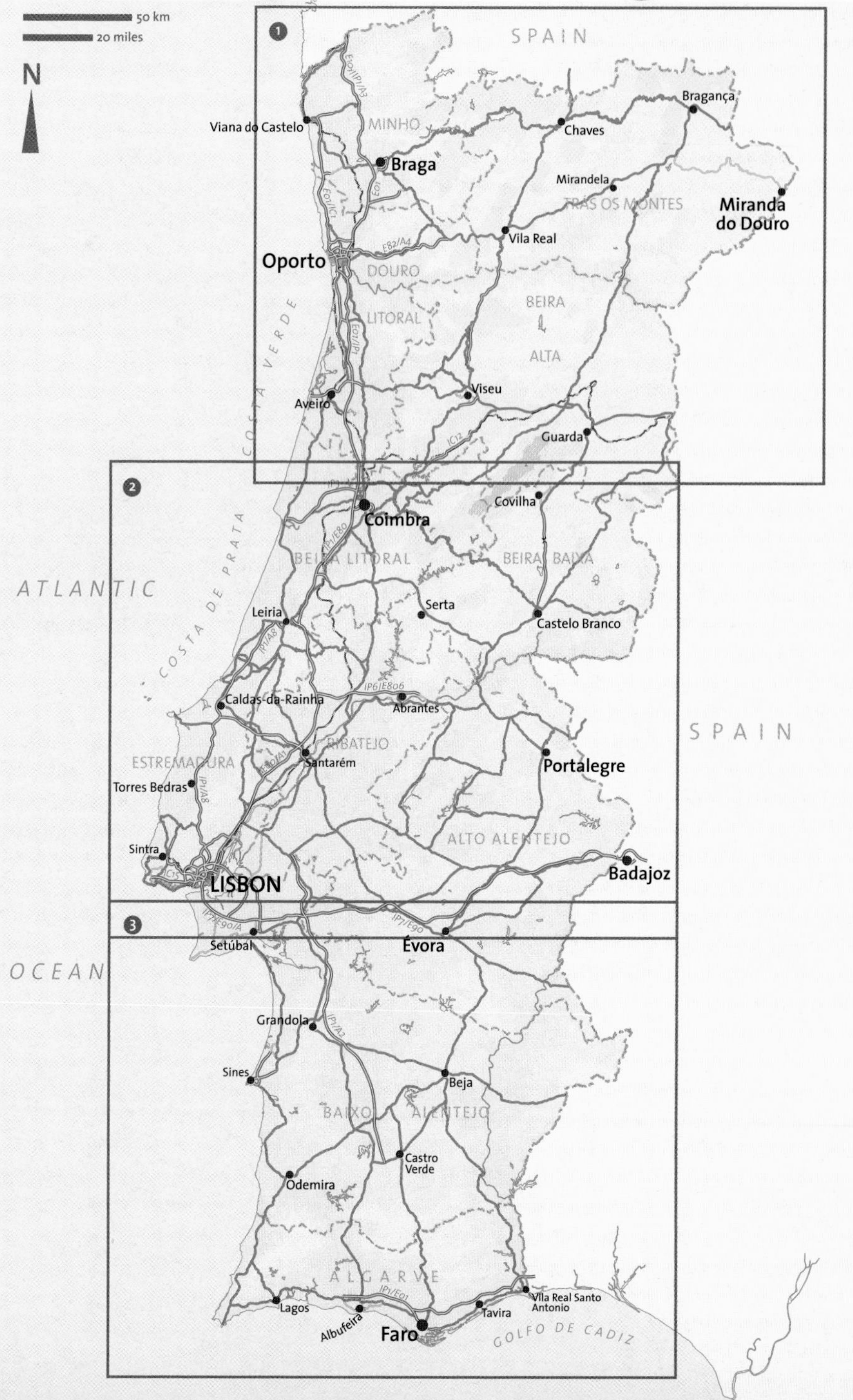

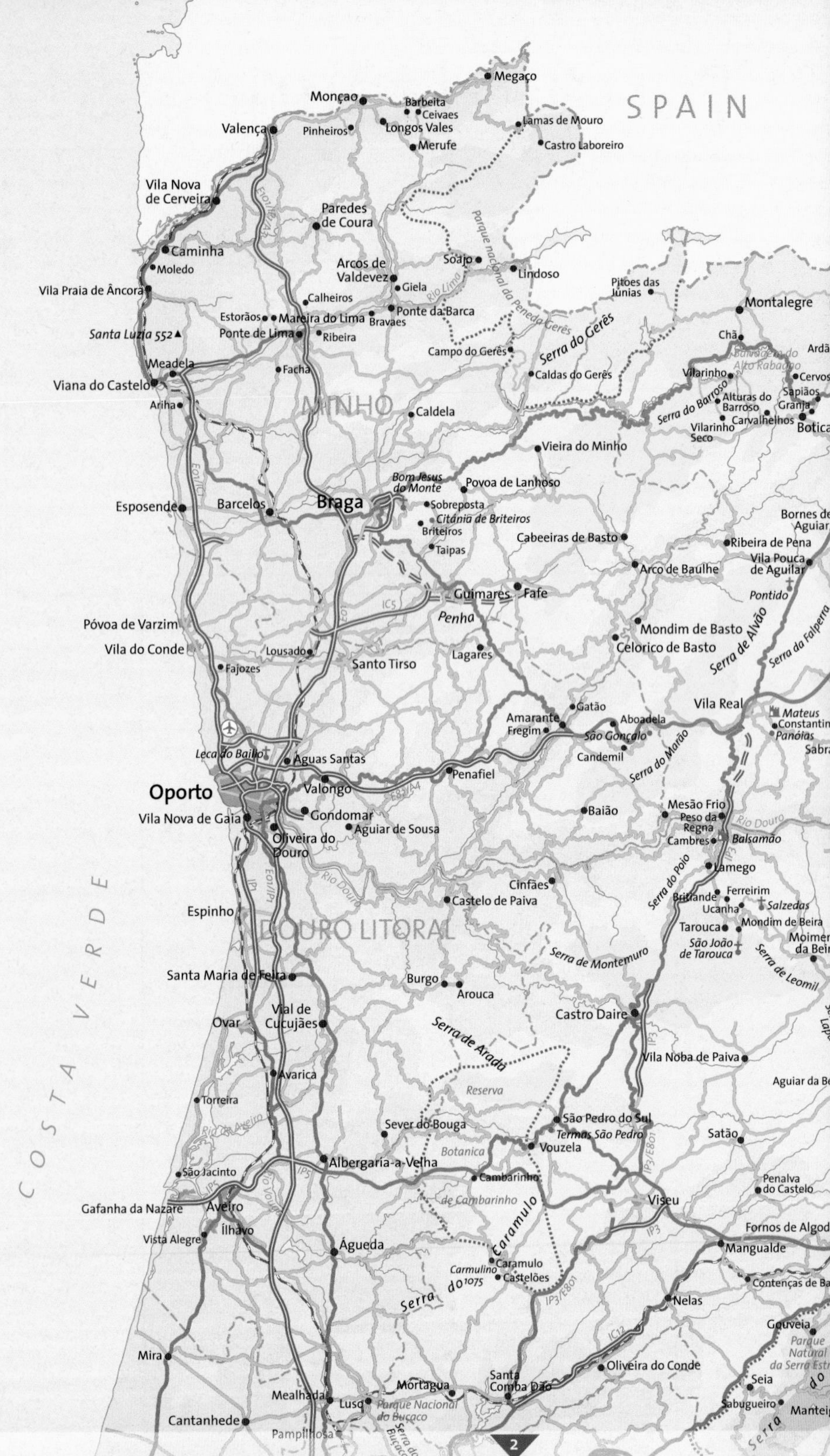
SPAIN
COSTA VERDE
MINHO
DOURO LITORAL
Megaço
Monçao
Barbeita
Ceivaes
Valença
Pinheiros
Longos Vales
Merufe
Lamas de Mouro
Castro Laboreiro
Vila Nova de Cerveira
Paredes de Coura
Parque nacional da Peneda Gerês
Caminha
Moledo
Vila Praia de Âncora
Arcos de Valdevez
Giela
Soajo
Lindoso
Rio Lima
Calheiros
Estorãos
Mareira do Lima
Ponte da Barca
Bravaes
Pitoes das Junias
Montalegre
Santa Luzia 552
Ponte de Lima
Ribeira
Serra do Gerês
Chã
Campo do Gerês
Meadela
Facha
Caldas do Gerês
Vilarinho
Barragem do Alto Rabagão
Ardãc
Cervos
Viana do Castelo
Ariha
Caldela
Serra do Barroso
Alturas do Barroso
Sapiãos
Granja
Vilarinho Seco
Carvalhelhos
Boticas
Vieira do Minho
Bom Jesus do Monte
Povoa de Lanhoso
Esposende
Barcelos
Braga
Sobreposta
Citânia de Briteiros
Briteiros
Bornes de Aguiar
Cabeeiras de Basto
Ribeira de Pena
Taipas
Arco de Baulhe
Vila Pouca de Aguilar
Guimares
Fafe
Pontido
IC5
Póvoa de Varzim
Penha
Mondim de Basto
Serra de Alvão
Serra da Falperra
Vila do Conde
Lousado
Lagares
Celorico de Basto
Santo Tirso
Fajozes
Vila Real
Gatão
Mateus
Amarante
Aboadela
Constantim
Fregim
São Gonçalo
Panóias
Leca do Bailio
Candemil
Sabras
Águas Santas
Serra do Marão
Penafiel
Oporto
Valongo
E82/A4
Gondomar
Baião
Mesão Frio
Peso da Regna
Rio Douro
Vila Nova de Gaia
Aguiar de Sousa
Cambres
Balsamão
Oliveira do Douro
IP3
Serra do Poio
Lamego
E01/IP1
Rio Douro
Cinfães
Ferreirim
Britiande
Castelo de Paiva
Salzedas
Espinho
Ucanha
Tarouca
Mondim de Beira
São João de Tarouca
Moimen da Beira
Serra de Montemuro
Serra de Leomil
Santa Maria de Feira
Burgo
Arouca
Castro Daire
Vial de Cucujães
Ovar
Serra de Arada
Vila Noba de Paiva
Avarica
Reserva
Aguiar da Bei
Torreira
São Pedro do Sul
Rio de Aveiro
Sever do Bouga
Termas São Pedro
Satão
Vouzela
IP3/E801
Botanica
Albergaria-a-Velha
São Jacinto
Cambarinho
Penalva do Castelo
de Cambarinho
Caramulo
Viseu
Gafanha da Nazare
Aveiro
Fornos de Algodr
Ílhavo
Vista Alegre
Águeda
Mangualde
Carmulino 1075
Caramulo
Castelões
Serra do
Contenças de Bai
Nelas
IC12
Gouveia
Parque Natural da Serra Estre
Mira
Oliveira do Conde
Santa Comba Dão
Mortagua
Seia
Mealhada
Luso
Parque Nacional do Buçaco
Sabugueiro
Manteig
Cantanhede
Pampilhosa
Serra do Buçaco

25 km
10 miles
N
Verin
Serra da Coroa
Serra de Montezinho
Rio de Onor
Franca
Rio Sabor
Parque Natural de Montezinho
Varge
Vinhais
Senjurge
Aguas Frias
Pedra Bulideira
Castro de Avelãs
Bragança
Gimonde
Seara Velha
Santo Estêvão
Chaves
São Julião de Montenegro
Rebordelo
Outeiro
Vidogo
Vilarandelo
Torre de Dona Chama
Valpaços
Lamas de Podence
Vimioso
Macedo de Cavaleiros
Tresminas
Mirandela
Algoso
Miranda do Douro
TRÁS OS MONTES
Murça
Sendim
Mogadouro
Serra do Mogadouro
Vila Flor
Sampaio
Alijo
Castelo Branco
Carrazeda de Ansiães
Rio Sabor
Pinhão
Lagoaça
Torre de Moncorvo
Mata Nacional do Reboredo
Serra do Reboredo
Quintana do Vale do Meão
São João da Pesqueira
Rio Douro
Pocinho
Vila Nova de Foz Coa
Freixo de Espada a Cinta
Rio Douro
Freixo de Numão
SPAIN
Barca de Alva
Penedono
Rio Coa
Barregem Vilar
Marialva
Sernancelhe
Figueira de Castelo Rodrigo
Castelo Rodrigo
Ponte de Abade
Serra da Marofa
Trancoso
Pinhel
Vila Franca das Naves
Freches
Almeida
Celorico da Beira
Ratoeira
Vilar Formoso
Cavadoude
Faia
Linhares
Estrela
Guarda
Rio Mondego
Valhelhas
2
Belmonte
Sabugal

25 km
10 miles
N
Cantanhede
1
Luso
Serra do Buçaco
Pampilhosa
IP3
Quiaios
São Marcos
São João do Campo
São Martinho de Árvore
Coimbra
Buarcos
Figueira da Foz
Montemor-o-Velho
Rio Mondego
Lavos
Condeixa-a-Nova
Condeixa-a-Velha
Conimbriga
Penela
IP1/E80
BEIRA LITORAL
COSTA DE PRATA
Pombal
Viera de Leira
Figueiro dos Vinh
Marinha Grande
São Pedro de Muel
Pinhal de Leiria
Marrazes
Leiria
Dornes
Aguas Belas
Ferreira do Zêzere
Batalha
Vila Nova de Ourem
Ourem
São Jorge
São Mamede
Porto de Mós
Nazaré
Fátima
Convento de Cristo
Tomar
Aljubarrota
Alcobaca
Albados
Mira d'Aire
São Pedro de Tomar
São Martinho do Porto
Parque Natural dos Serras de Aire e Candeeiros
Serre de Santo Antonio
Estacion Lamarosa
Olaia
Farilhoes
Estelas
Berlenga (Reserva Natural)
Serra dos Candeeiros
Torres Novas
IP6/E80
Entroncamento
Constânci
Almourol
Caldas-da-Rainha
Cabo Carvoeiro
Peniche
Obidos
Casével
Golegã
Atouginia da Baleia
Rio Maior
Chamusca
ESTREMADURA
Rio Tejo
Lourinhã
Alpiarça
Santarém
RIBATEJO
Porto Novo
Almeirim
Cartaxo
São Pedro da Cadeira
Torres Bedras
Estacion Setil
IP1/A8
E80/A1
Alenquer
Salvaterra de Magos
Ericeira
Sobreiro
Benavente
Convento
Mafra
Vila Franca de Xira
Coruche
Póvoa da Galega
Bucelas
Rio Sorraia
Loures
Colares
Palacio Nacional
Cabo da Roca
Sintra
Convento dos Capuchos
Castelo dos Mouros
Serra de Sintra
Odivelas
Cacem
Queluz
Lavre
Cabo Raso
Cascais
Torre
LISBON
Ajuda
Estoril
Oeiras
IC15
Boca do Inferno
Carcavelos
Belem
Ponte do 25 Abril
Montijo
Santo Isidro de Pegões
Costa do Estoril
Almada
Barreiro
Costa da Caparica
Vendas Novas
BAIXO ALENTEJO
IC32
IC21
Costa do Sol
Pinhal Novo
IP1/A12
Montemor-o-Novo
IP7/E90/A2
Marateca
Palmela
Vila Fresca do Azeitão
Castelo São Filipe
Setúbal
3
Vila Nogueira de Azeitão

2

1

Sabugueiro
Manteigas
Valhelhas
Parque Natural da Serra Estrela
Estrela
Torre 1993
Loriga
Penhasda Saúde
Belmonte
Sortelha
Sabugal
Unhais da Serra
Covilha
Boidobra
Serra de Acor
Penamacor
Fundão
Serra da Gardunha
Alpedrinha
Castelo Novo
Serra do Ramiro
Casal da Serra
São Vicente da Beira
Soalheiro
Medelim
Relva
Monsanto
Penha Garcia
Proença-a-Velha
São Miguel de Acha
Idanha-a-Velha
Castanheira de Pera
Monte dos Lomeiras
Serra do Muradal
BEIRA BAIXA
Oleiros
Alcafozes
Idanha-a-Nova
Senhora da Graça
Troviscal
Serra do Cabeço da Rainha
ernache do Bomjardim
Serta
Castelo Branco
Ladoeira
Zebreira
Nossa Senhora de Nércoles
ale de Serrâc
Proenca-a-Nova
Represa
Castrum São Martinho
Monforte da Beira
Rosmaninhal
astanheira
Vila de Reí
Vila Velha de Rodão
Marlpico do Tejo
arrage do astello do Bode
Mação
ardoal
Rio Tajo
SPAIN
Abrantes
Gavião
Rossio ão Sul do Tejo
Alpalhão
Castelo de Vide
Senhora da Penha
Valencja da Alcantara
Marvão
Bemposta
São Mamede
Parque Natural da Serra de São Mamede
Crato
Portalegre
Ponte de Sor
Alegrete
Alter do Chão
Arronches
Montargil
Nossa Senhora da Grace dos Degolados
Avis
Fronteira
Monforte
Santa Eulália
Campo Major
Mora
Sousel
Veiros
São Vicente e Ventosa
Pavia
ALTO ALENTEJO
Elvas
Aqueducto da Amoleira
Estremoz
Vimiero
Badajoz
Borba
Vila Viçosa
Quinta dos Lóios
Évora Monte
Arraidlos
IP7/E90
Redondo
São Bente de Castris
São Miguel de Machede
Evora

3

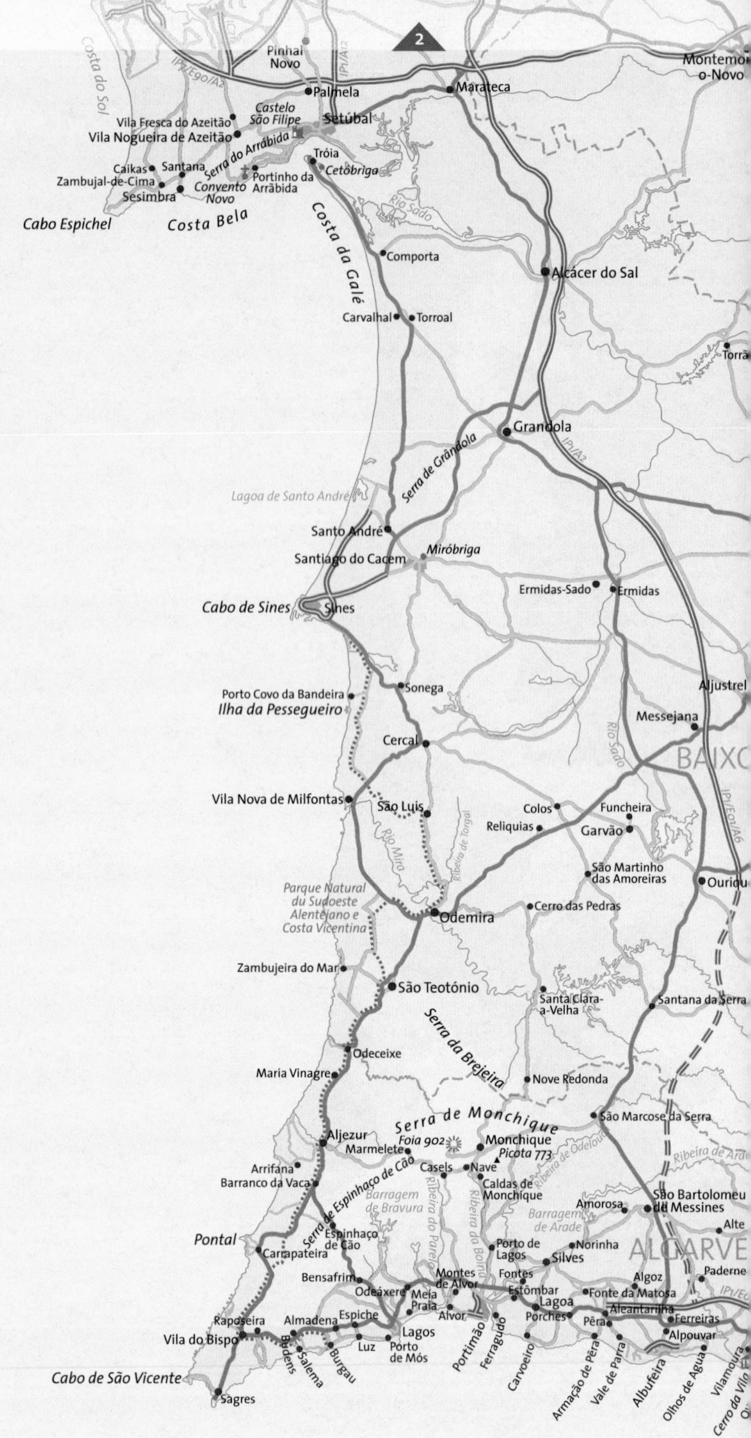
2
Pinhal Novo
Palmela
Marateca
Montemor-o-Novo
Castelo São Filipe
Setúbal
Vila Fresca do Azeitão
Vila Nogueira de Azeitão
Serra do Arrábida
Tróia
Cetóbriga
Caikas
Santana
Zambujal-de-Cima
Sesimbra
Convento Novo
Portinho da Arrábida
Cabo Espichel
Costa Bela
Costa da Galé
Costa do Sol
Rio Sado
Comporta
Alcácer do Sal
Carvalhal
Torroal
Grandola
Serra de Grândola
Lagoa de Santo André
Santo André
Santiago do Cacem
Miróbriga
Ermidas-Sado
Ermidas
Cabo de Sines
Sines
Sonega
Porto Covo da Bandeira
Ilha da Pessegueiro
Aljustrel
Messejana
Cercal
Vila Nova de Milfontas
São Luis
Rio Mira
Ribeira de Torgal
Colos
Reliquias
Funcheira
Garvão
São Martinho das Amoreiras
Parque Natural du Sudoeste Alentejano e Costa Vicentina
Odemira
Cerro das Pedras
Zambujeira do Mar
São Teotónio
Santa Clara-a-Velha
Santana da Serra
Serra da Brejeira
Odeceixe
Maria Vinagre
Nove Redonda
Serra de Monchique
São Marcos da Serra
Aljezur
Foia 902
Monchique
Picota 773
Marmelete
Arrifana
Barranco da Vaca
Casels
Nave
Caldas de Monchique
Serra de Espinhaço de Cão
Barragem de Bravura
Barragem de Arade
Amorosa
São Bartolomeu de Messines
Pontal
Carrapateira
Espinhaço de Cão
Porto de Lagos
Norinha
Silves
ALGARVE
Bensafrim
Montes de Alvor
Fontes
Estômbar
Algoz
Paderne
Odeáxere
Meia Praia
Alvor
Lagoa
Fonte da Matosa
Alcantarilha
Raposeira
Almadena
Espiche
Porches
Pêra
Ferreiras
Vila do Bispo
Lagos
Luz
Porto de Mós
Alpouvar
Budens
Salema
Burgau
Portimão
Ferragudo
Carvoeiro
Armação de Pêra
Vale de Parra
Albufeira
Olhos de Agua
Cabo de São Vicente
Sagres
ATLANTIC OCEAN

3
2 ALTO ALENTEJO
ÉVORA
São Bente de Castris
São Miguel de Machede
Redondo
Santiago do Escoural
Monte das Flores
Casa Branca
Quinta de Valverde
Montoito
Aldeia do Outeiro
Corval
Telheiro
Monsarraz
Reguengos de Monsarraz
Xerez de Baixo
Mourão
Alcáçovas
Viana do Alentejo
Alvito
Serra de Mendro
Vidigueira
Odivelas
Cuba
Rio Guadiana
Moura
Barrancos
Safara
Santo Aleixo da Restauração
Ferreira do Alentejo
Beringel
Beja
Ervidel
Pisoes
Santa Clara de Louredo
Serpa
Vila Verde de Ficalho
São Brás
Aldeia Nova de São Bento
SPAIN
Trindade
ALENTEJO
Ribeira de Terges
Pule do Lobo
Serra de Serpa
Amendeoira
Algodor
São Marcos da Ataboeira
Corte Gafo de Cima
Serra de Mertola
Castro Verde
Mina de São Domingues
Ribeira de Alvaca
Moreanes
Mertola
Ribeira de Oeiras
São Sebastião dos Carros
São Miguel do Pinheiro
Almodôvar
Ribeira do Vascão
Alcoutim
Sanlucar de Guadiana
Martim Longo
Pereiro
Barrada
Ribeira da Foupana
Serra do Caldeirão
Corte João Marques
Vaqueiros
Parque Mineiro Cova das Mouros
Maeixial
Corte Serranos
Vermelhos
Ribeira de Odeleite
Cachopo
Odeleite
Portela
Serra de Alcaria do Cume
Montes Novos
Azinhal
Salir
Barranco do Velho
Junqueira
Monte Francisco
Estorninhos
Castro Marim
Sapal de Castro Marim
Ayamonte
Querença
Malhada de Peres
Palheirinhos
Vila Nova de Cacela
Attura
Vila Real Santo Antonio
Clarianes
Eira da Palma
São Brás de Alportel
Loulé
Santa Catarina da Fonte do Bispo
Conceição
Cacela Velha
Monte Gordo
Santa Bárbara de Nexe
Milreu
Serra de Monte Figo
Santo Estêvão
Cabanas
Almancil
Estoi
Tavira
Ferrarias
Moncarapacho
Luz de Tavira
Santa Luzia
Vale do Lobo
Pechão
Ilha de Tavira
Quinta do Lago
FARO
Olhão
Parque Natural da Ria Formosa
Ilha da Armona
Ilha do Ancão
Ilha da Barreta
Cabo de Santa Marie
Ilha da Culatra
GOLFO DE CADIZ
N
25 km
10 miles